MW01470073

REPRODUCING ATHENS

REPRODUCING ATHENS

MENANDER'S COMEDY, DEMOCRATIC CULTURE, AND THE HELLENISTIC CITY

Susan Lape

PRINCETON UNIVERSITY PRESS
PRINCETON AND OXFORD

Published by Princeton University Press, 41 William Street,
Princeton, New Jersey 08540
In the United Kingdom: Princeton University Press, 3 Market Place,
Woodstock, Oxfordshire OX20 1SY

Library of Congress Cataloging-in-Publication Data

Lape, Susan, 1965–
Reproducing Athens: Menander's comedy, democratic culture, and the Hellenistic city/Susan Lape.
p. cm.
Includes bibliographical references and index.
ISBN 0-691-11583-4
1. Menander, of Athens—Knowledge—Athens (Greece).
2. Politics and literature—Greece—Athens—History—To 500.
3. Menander, of Athens—Political and social views. 4. Political plays, Greek—History and criticism. 5. Athens (Greece)—Politics and government. 6. Athens (Greece)—In literature.
7. Democracy in literature. 8. Comedy. I. Title.
PA4247.L37 2004
882′.01—dc21 2003040451

British Library Cataloging-in-Publication Data is available

This book has been composed in Janson

Printed on acid-free paper. ∞

www.pupress.princeton.edu

Printed in the United States of America

10 9 8 7 6 5 4 3 2 1

Contents

Abbreviations

Editions, Journals, and Reference Works

A&A	*Antike und Abendland*
ABSA	*Annual of the British School at Athens*
AC	*L'Antiquité Classique*
AClass	*Acta Classica*
Acme	*Acme: annali della Facoltà di lettere e filosofia dell'Università degli statale di Milano*
AHB	*Ancient History Bulletin*
AJA	*American Journal of Archaeology*
AJP	*American Journal of Philology*
AncSoc	*Ancient Society*
AncW	*Ancient World*
A&R	*Atene e Roma*
Arnott	W. G. Arnott, ed. and trans., *Menander*, 3 vols. (Cambridge, Mass., 1979–2000)
Austin	M. M. Austin, ed., *The Hellenistic World from Alexander to the Roman Conquest* (Cambridge, 1981)
BICS	*Bulletin of the Institute of Classical Studies of the University of London*
Burtt	J. O. Burtt, trans., *Minor Attic Orators*, vol. 2 (Cambridge, Mass., 1954)
CA	*Classical Antiquity*
CE	*Chronique d'Égypte*
CJ	*Classical Journal*
C&M	*Classica et Mediaevalia*
CP	*Classical Philology*
CQ	*Classical Quarterly*
Dion.	*Dioniso*
EMC	*Échos du Monde Classique*
ESJ	*European Studies Journal*
FGrH	F. Jacoby, ed., *Die Fragmente der griechischen Historiker* (Berlin, 1923–58)
F.-S.	W. W. Fortenbaugh and E. Schütrumpf, eds., *Demetrius of Phaleron: Text, Translation, and Discussion* (New Brunswick, N.J., 2000)
Gow	A.S.F. Gow, ed., *The Fragments*, by Machon (Cambridge, 1965)

G&R	*Greece and Rome*
GRBS	*Greek, Roman, and Byzantine Studies*
Hesp.	*Hesperia*
HSCP	*Harvard Studies in Classical Philology*
IG II^2	*Inscriptiones Atticae*, ed. J. Kirchner, Inscriptiones Graecae, editio minor, 2–3 (Berlin, 1923–40)
ISE	L. Moretti, ed., *Inscrizioni storiche ellenistiche*, 2 vols. (Florence, 1967–75)
JHS	*Journal of Hellenic Studies*
K.-A	R. Kassel and C. Austin, eds., *Poetae Comici Graeci* (Berlin, 1983–)
Kock	T. Kock, *Comicorum Atticorum fragmenta*, 3 vols. (Leipzig, 1880–88)
K.-T.	A. Körte and A. Thierfelder, eds., *Menandri quae supersunt*, 2 vols. (Leipzig, 1957)
LCM	*Liverpool Classical Monthly*
Lex. Rhet. Cant.	E. O. Houtsma, ed., *Lexicon Rhetoricum Cantabrigiense* (Leiden, 1870)
LSJ	H. G. Liddell, R. Scott, and H. S. Jones, eds., *Greek-English Lexicon*, 9th ed., with suppl. (Oxford, 1968)
MH	*Museum Helveticum*
Mnem.	*Mnemosyne*
PCPhS	*Proceedings of the Cambridge Philological Society*
Philol.	*Philologus*
P&P	*Past and Present*
Prom.	*Prometheus*
QS	*Quaderni di Storia*
QUCC	*Quaderni Urbinati di Cultura Classica*
RAAN	*Rendiconti dell'Accademia di Archeologia, Lettere e Belle Arti di Napoli*
RC	C. B. Welles, ed., *Royal Correspondence in the Hellenistic Period* (London, 1934)
RD	*Revue Historique de Droit Français et Étranger*
REG	*Revue des Études Grecques*
RhM	*Rheinisches Museum für Philologie*
RIDA	*Revue Internationale des Droits de l'Antiquité*
Sandbach	F. H. Sandbach, ed., *Menandri reliquiae selectae*, rev. ed. (Oxford, 1990)
SCO	*Studi Classici e Orientali*
SIFC	*Studi Italiani di Filologia Classica*
Sisti	F. Sisti, ed., *Misumenos*, by Menander (Genoa, 1986)
TAPA	*Transactions of the American Philological Association*

Wehrli	F. Wehrli, ed., *Die Schule des Aristoteles*, vol. 4, *Demetrios von Phaleron* (Basel, 1968)
WS	*Weiner Studien*
ZPE	*Zeitschrift für Papyrologie und Epigraphik*
ZRG	*Zeitschrift der Savigny-Stiftung für Rechtsgeschichte, romanistische Abteilung*

Authors and Works

Aes.	Aeschines
And.	Andocides
Ar.	Aristophanes
Ach.	*Archarnians*
Lys.	*Lysistrata*
Nub.	*Clouds*
Thesm.	*Thesmophoriazusae*
Arist.	Aristotle
E.N.	*Nichomachean Ethics*
M.M.	*Magna Moralia*
Pol.	*Politics*
Rhet.	*Rhetoric*
[Arist.]	[Aristotle]
A.P.	*Constitution of Athens*
S.E.	*Sophistic Refutations*
Athen.	Athenaeus
Cic.	Cicero
Leg.	*On the Laws*
Dem.	Demosthenes
Din.	Dinarchus
Diod.	Diodorus Siculus
D.L.	Diogenes Laertius
Gell.	Aulus Gellius
Hes.	Hesiod
Erg.	*Works and Days*
Hyp.	Hyperides
Epit.	*Epitaphios Logos*
Is.	Isaeus
Isoc.	Isocrates
Paneg.	*Panegyricus*
Lucian	
Dem. Enc.	*Encomium of Demosthenes*
Lycur.	Lycurgus

Mel.	Meleager
A.P.	*Palatine Anthology*
Men.	Menander
Asp.	*Aspis*
Dis Ex.	*Dis Exapaton*
Dys.	*Dyskolos*
Epit.	*Epitrepontes*
Geōr.	*Geōrgos*
Kol.	*Kolax*
Mis.	*Misoumenos*
Pk.	*Perikeiromenê*
Sam.	*Samia*
Sik.	*Sikyônioi*
Paus.	Pausanias
Philoch.	Philochorus
Pl.	Plato
Mx.	*Menexenus*
Prot.	*Protagoras*
Rep.	*Republic*
Plb.	Polybius
Plautus	
M.G.	*Miles Gloriosus*
Truc.	*Truculentus*
Plut.	Plutarch
Alex.	*Alexander*
Dem.	*Demosthenes*
Demetr.	*Demetrius*
Mor.	*Moralia*
Per.	*Pericles*
Phoc.	*Phocion*
Sol.	*Solon*
Them.	*Themistocles*
[Plut.]	[Plutarch]
Vit. X Orat.	*Lives of Ten Orators*
Polyaenus	
Strateg.	*Strategemata*
Ter.	Terence
Ad.	*Adelphoe*
An.	*Andria*
Eun.	*Eunuch*
Theoc.	Theocritus
Theophr.	Theophrastus
Char.	*Characters*

Thuc.	Thucydides
Xen.	Xenophon
Oec.	*Oeconomicus*
Hell.	*Hellenica*
Symp.	*Symposium*

REPRODUCING ATHENS

1

Narratives of Resistance and Romance

DEMOCRACY AND COMEDY IN THE EARLY HELLENISTIC PERIOD

Resilient Democracy and the Rise of Romantic Comedy

Athenian history between the battle of Chaeronea in 338 B.C. and the end of the Chremonidean War in 260 is punctuated by one military disaster after another. At Chaeronea, Philip of Macedon won a decisive victory over Athens and its allies, enabling him to gain effective control of Athenian foreign policy. In 322 Athens suffered a much more catastrophic defeat in the Lamian War, the Greek-led rebellion against Macedonian rule. In the ensuing peace settlement, Antipater, the de facto ruler of Macedon, installed Macedonian troops in the city, replaced the democratic government with an oligarchy, executed leading democratic politicians, and relocated many disfranchised democrats to Thrace. These measures, despite their severity and scope, did little to disturb the Athenian commitment to democracy. Following Antipater's death in 319 the Athenians restored the democracy, apparently in the hope of regaining the pre–Lamian War status quo. The problems that erupted with Alexander's unforeseen death, however, had not really been solved. Alexander's would-be successors were still in the process of attempting to seize and define their own spheres of control. Accordingly, without the military power to defend themselves against the emergent military kingdoms, the Athenians were soon forced to capitulate yet again, this time to Antipater's son Cassander. Like his father before him, Cassander continued to employ highly coercive measures to control the Greek cities, including the imposition of oligarchic constitutions and the installation of military garrisons. While the wealth requirement for citizenship under this second oligarchic regime was fairly low, Cassander took an additional, more invasive, step of installing a manager of domestic affairs within the city itself. For the next ten years, Demetrius of Phaleron ruled Athens as a virtual regent on Cassander's behalf.[1]

[1] For the Greek loss at Chaeronea as leading to the enslavement of the Greeks, see Diod. 16.88.2. For Athens and the Lamian War, see Diod. 18.8.9–13.6, 15.1–9, 16.4–17.8; Paus. 1.25.3–5; Hyp. 6 (*Epit.*); Plut. *Phoc.* 23–26, *Dem.* 27–28. For the oligarchy imposed on Athens in 322, see Plut. *Phoc.* 27.3–28.1, 28.4–29.1; Diod. 18.18.4–6. And for Antipater's

Although Demetrius of Phaleron is generally credited with ruling well—even hostile sources acknowledge the material prosperity his regime brought to the city—the Athenians were only too eager to restore the democracy.[2] They seized the first opportunity to oust him from power, even though doing so meant dealing with autocrats. When Demetrius Poliorcetes, one of Cassander's chief rivals in the struggle for the empire and the Greek cities, made an unexpected appearance in the Athenian harbor in 307, the Athenians readily accepted his assistance and reestablished the democracy.[3] While fifteen years of oligarchic domination seems not to have diminished the Athenian preference for democracy, it did give the Athenians time to come to terms with the new realities of international politics and their city's diminished place within them. By 307 the Athenians were ready to compromise with external autocratic rulers for the sake of maintaining democracy in the city. In fact, the policy of liberating the Greek cities from oligarchic rule adopted by Demetrius Poliorcetes and his father, Antigonus Monophthalmus, made it seem like the Athenians were not compromising at all.

But the reality of Athens's subordinate position became clear when Demetrius Poliorcetes took up residence in the city and, according to some reports, actually moved into the Parthenon. Whatever the truth of the situation, his continued presence in Athens revealed the incompatibility between democracy and dependence on autocratic rule. Athenian relations with Demetrius deteriorated to such an extent that in 301 they refused him entrance to the city. Although Athens declared its neutrality in the affairs of the *diadochoi* (successors), in 295 Demetrius was able to regain control of the city. This time there seems to have been little or no attempt to make even a pretense of maintaining democratic proprieties; the period is explicitly described in later Athenian sources as an oligarchy.[4] Once again, however, the familiar pattern recurs: in 287 the Athenians restored the democracy and, more significantly, managed to retain it for another twenty-five years or so in a period that was both intensely democratic and nationalistic. But in 260, Demetrius's son, Antigonus Go-

general policy of installing oligarchies in the Greek cities after the Lamian War, see Diod. 18.18.8, 55.2, 57.1, 69.3. For Polyperchon's policy of freeing the Greeks from Antipater's oligarchies, see Diod. 18.55.2, 56. For Cassander's settlement with Athens, see Diod. 18.74.3; Paus. 1.25.6. For the monarchical nature of Demetrius of Phalerum's regime, see Plut. *Demetr.* 10.2.

[2] See Demochares' scathing description of Demetrius's regime, *FGrH* 75 F 4 = Plb. 12.13.8–11 = 89 F.-S. = 132 Wehrli. Lehmann (1997, 80–82) argues that since Demetrius of Phaleron's regime had proven to be a successful alternative to democracy, the restoration of the democracy in 307 attests to a remarkably strong democratic commitment on the part of the Athenians.

[3] Plut. *Demetr.* 8.3–10; Polyaen. *Strateg.* 4, 7, 6; Philoch. *FGrH* 328 F 66.

[4] Habicht 1997, 90 with n. 85.

natas, recaptured the city and imposed measures that seem to have finally and effectively curtailed the possibility of effective political resistance.[5]

The history of this period—roughly the transition to the Hellenistic age—might be told as a story of decline, the downfall of the polis and democracy in the face of the more powerful emergent military kingdoms. While this narrative characterizes Athens militarily, it does not capture the complexities of the domestic political scene. Although the constitutional seesawing of the period brought nearly 150 years of democratic stability to an end, Athens's insistent if ultimately ill-fated democratic rebellions speak to the continuity of democratic ideology—the set of beliefs and practices that sustained the identity of Athenian citizens as specifically democratic citizens.[6] The more vigorously the Macedonians attempted to eliminate the democracy, the more passionately committed to it the Athenians became. The indelibility of democracy in the Athenian imagination is attested by a decree honoring the mercenary Kallias of Sphettos for (inter alia) abiding by democratic law during a period of oligarchic rule.[7] By attributing an existence to the democracy during a period of oligarchic rule, the decree invests the democracy with an ontological permanence, declaring it impervious to the ephemeral Macedonian interventions.

The resiliency and intensity of Athens's democratic ethos during this period is remarkable and indeed puzzling because the conditions that made democracy possible were either interrupted, altered, or no longer in existence at all. Under the classical democracy, political institutions were the primary arena in which democratic ideals were instantiated and enacted.[8] In addition, they provided the key site in which social and political tensions were mediated and negotiated.[9] During the transition to the Hellenistic age, however, these institutions for many years ceased to

[5] See Ferguson 1911, 184–85.

[6] This study employs an Althusserian conception of ideology as a representation of "the imaginary relationship of individuals to the real conditions of their existence" that "always exists in an apparatus, and its practice, or practices" (Althusser 1971, 162, 166). In speaking of the continuity of democratic ideology, I am referring to the tenacity of democratic identity, i.e., the fact that individual Athenian men continued to see themselves first and foremost as democratic citizens, as well as to the continuity of the values and beliefs associated with the democratic political regime. I do not follow Althusser's conception of the subject-constituting power of ideology (see further below).

[7] The relevant sentence runs as follows (the beginning is damaged): "he allowed his property to be confiscated in the oligarchy so as to act [in no way] against the laws or against the democracy of all the Athenians" (Shear 1978, lines 80–83). See also the honorary decrees for Euphron of Sicyon, the New Comic poet Philippides, and Demosthenes, for similarly powerful declarations of democratic sentiment; IG II^2 448, IG II^2 657, Plut. *Mor.* 851c.

[8] For the importance of institutions to the practice and ideology of democratic citizenship, see Ober 1989; R. Osborne 1990; Hansen 1991; Wolin 1996; Johnstone 1998.

[9] See Ober 1989 and Johnstone 1998.

operate according to democratic principles. At the same time, the emergence of Macedonian military kingdoms undermined the ideal of the citizen-soldier, a crucial pillar of the democracy's ideological foundation. The ability and duty of every citizen to fight for the state, whether as a hoplite or thete, underwrote the egalitarian logic of the democratic political order.[10] Every citizen could claim an equal stake and standing within the democracy, no matter what his place in the social hierarchy, because in the end he was willing to fight and give his body in service to the state. Although the Macedonians took away this power, drastically attenuating the citizen-soldier ideal, all available evidence demonstrates that Athens's commitment to democracy remained strong, becoming perhaps even more deeply ingrained than before.

The persistence of the Athenian democratic ethos during a period in which the democracy had lost its institutional and military mooring raises a number of important questions. How was democratic culture produced and reproduced in the absence of democratic political institutions? How did individuals continue to identify as democratic citizens? What sources of democratic identity emerged to fill the gulf left by the loss of the citizen-soldier ideal and the suspension of democratic institutions? Lycurgus's prosecution of Leocrates contains an important clue. In the aftermath of the battle of Chaeronea, the Athenians passed a number of emergency measures, including one stipulating that every able-bodied man could be called on to defend the city against the Macedonian invasion that, at the time, seemed imminent (Lycur. 1.16–17, 1.41). Leocrates, however, fled the city, allegedly in violation of this decree. When he returned to the city eight years later, Lycurgus, architect of democratic renewal after Chaeronea and avid public prosecutor, sought to make an example of him by prosecuting him for treason. To emphasize the egregiousness of Leocrates' disloyalty and default on his civic obligation, and in effect to depict him as the sort of citizen who was really responsible for the defeat at Chaeronea, Lycurgus describes the atmosphere of desperation and panic in the city immediately after the battle:

> When the defeat and disaster had been reported to the people and the city was tense with alarm at the news, the people's hope of safety had come to rest with the men over fifty. Free women could be seen crouching at the doors in terror inquiring for the safety of their husbands, fathers, or brothers, offering a spectacle degrading to themselves and to the city. The men who were far past their prime, advanced in life, exempt by law from service in the field, could be seen throughout the city, debilitated with age wretchedly scurrying with cloaks pinned double about them. Many sufferings were being visited upon the city; every citizen had felt misfortune at its worst; but the sight which would have

[10] See further Ridley 1979; Loraux 1986; Winkler 1990a; and chapter 7 below.

most surely stirred the onlooker and moved him to tears over the sorrows of Athens was to see the people vote that slaves should be released, that aliens should become Athenians, and the disfranchised regain their rights: the nation that had once prided itself on being autochthonous and free. (Lycur. 1.40–41)[11]

Remarkably, Lycurgus does not claim that the most devastating consequence of Chaeronea was the catastrophic loss of citizen lives or even the city's desperate dependence on the elderly. Rather, it was the fact that the Athenians approved a proposal to free the slaves and to enfranchise foreigners and those who had been disfranchised. According to Lycurgus, this measure—proposed but never actually implemented—was the real tragedy of Chaeronea. The implementation of the emergency decree would have destroyed the city more completely than any mere battle, Lycurgus suggests, because it would have contaminated the autochthonous ancestry or "racial purity" that made the Athenians who they were and underwrote the city's democratic identity.[12]

The myth of autochthony was fundamental to the cultural imaginary of the Athenian democracy.[13] To emphasize this point is not to make any claim about whether the Athenians literally believed their ancestor or ancestors were "sprung from the earth."[14] Rather, the political significance of the myth arises from the kind of story it enabled the Athenians to tell about themselves. It supplied a narrative about the shared origins and ultimate relatedness of a people of diverse origins and statuses. In so doing, it provided a crucial theoretical justification for democratic egalitarianism and exclusivity.[15] Supposed common kinship furnished a basis for commonality and hence equality between citizens and, at the same

[11] Trans. adapted from Burtt.

[12] For the translation of *autkhthōn* in Lycur. 1.41–42 as "racial purity," see Harris 2001, 172.

[13] For the connections between democracy and autochthony, see further Loraux 1986, 192–93, and 1993, 3–22, 37–71; Walsh 1978; Montanari 1981; Saxonhouse 1986; Connor 1994; Ogden 1996; Dougherty 1996. E. E. Cohen (2000, 80–103) argues to the contrary that autochthony was not central to the Athenian conception of civic identity because there was a contradiction between the doctrine itself and cultural practices. However, contradictions between official ideologies and social practices are a frequently attested feature of culture systems (e.g., Giddens 1979; Bourdieu 1977). Moreover, even if no one literally believed that the doctrine was true, this has no necessary bearing on its importance as a narrative of national culture; see further Connor 1994, 38.

[14] Rosivach (1987) argues that in Athenian literature autochthony designates a people who have always inhabited the same land, rather than being "born from the earth," as defined by LSJ and numerous recent commentators. But for evidence of the latter sense, see, e.g., Euripides' *Ion*, passim, and artistic representations of Erichthonios being delivered from and by the earth (allegorically represented as a woman) discussed in Shapiro 1998.

[15] See Loraux 1986, 1993; Rosivach 1987, 303; Ogden 1996, 167–69; Dougherty 1996, 254–56; J. Hall 1997. Autochthony is also often linked to freedom; see Pl. *Mx.* 239a–b; Dem. 19.261; Lycur. 1.41.

time, a reason for differentiating citizens from all noncitizens. But paradoxically, though the myth provides a model of generation that justifies the exclusion of foreigners and women from the political order, the Athenian discourse of autochthony is "inextricably tied to sexual reproduction,"[16] and hence to the very realm of women it seems to exclude. This slippage was perhaps inevitable since in practice the autochthonous purity of the citizen body was maintained and secured through the polis's rules of sexual reproduction.

In 451/0, on Pericles' proposal, the Athenians passed a law limiting citizenship to those born from two native Athenians.[17] Although the law as we have it does not mention marriage per se, it effectively redefined what counted as a legitimate marriage.[18] Previously, the state had allowed a citizen to marry and father children with either an Athenian or a foreign-born woman. After the passage of the Periclean law, however, children born from foreign women were no longer eligible for citizenship, and correspondingly, foreign women were no longer eligible for Athenian marriage.[19] Thus, the practical effect of the law's requirement was to

[16] Loraux 1993, 57.

[17] [Arist.] *A.P.* 26.4; Plut. *Per.* 37.2–4. Although the law may have been relaxed during the Peloponnesian War, it was reinstated as part of the democratic restoration of 403; see Athen. 577b for the decree of Aristophon, and Eumelus *FGrH* 77 F2 = Scholiast Aes. 1.39 for the decree of Nicomenes. The principles of the Periclean law were reinforced by subsequent legislation banning marriage between *astoi* and *xenoi* ([Dem.] 59.16). For the possible aims and purposes animating the passage of the Periclean citizenship law, see Rhodes 1981, 331–35; Patterson 1981; Walters 1983; Humphreys 1974; Connor 1994; Boegehold 1994; Ogden 1996.

[18] The fact that the law—as attested in [Arist.] *A.P.*—does not mention "legitimacy" has led some commentators to question whether marital status was relevant for the transmission of citizen status; see MacDowell 1976; Sealey 1984. The majority of scholars agree, however, that there was a direct correlation between the state's marriage rules (which in effect were rules defining legitimate sexual reproduction) and citizen status; see Humphreys 1974; Rhodes 1981, 331–33; Patterson 1991a, 1998, 110; Ogden 1996; Lape 2001, 97 with n. 64. Many scholars have argued that the link between legitimacy and citizen status goes back to Solon; see Humphreys 1974, 90; Davies 1977–78, 114–15; Ogden 1996, 43; Wolff 1944, 77–79 (despite the fact that he dates the transformation of marriage into an institution of citizenship to Kleisthenes). If there was a link between legitimacy and citizenship, there was of necessity also a link between marriage and citizen status in Solonian Athens; see Lape 2002–03. Thus, what changed with the Periclean law of citizenship was what counted as a marriage for purposes of citizen status. For the role of Solon's laws in creating citizenship as an institution and an ethos, see Manville 1990.

[19] E. E. Cohen (2000, 71), however, argues that citizenship was based on territorial residence for more than one generation rather than on Athenian nativity. This argument hinges on defining *astoi* (the term employed in the laws pertaining to citizenship to designate those eligible for citizen status and those eligible to bear citizens) as a purely territorial designation meaning "local residents." Although Cohen is right to emphasize that *astos* is not a synonym for *politēs* (citizen), the conclusion that *astos* refers exclusively to territorial residence does not follow. On the meaning of *astos/astē*, see also Lévy 1985. In fact, there is

invoke rules of sexual reproduction—that is, to delineate who could bear legitimate children with whom—in order to produce the democratic citizen body and to separate citizens from noncitizens.[20] It has recently been argued that the passage of this law was a symbolic statement of autochthonous pride.[21] Whether or not the Athenians were thinking in such terms when they passed the law, the operation of the law did, over time, foster the perception that Athenian citizens were racially distinct from other Greeks and from all noncitizens.[22] The very requirement of bilateral native parentage for citizen status promoted the belief that both parents transmitted "Athenianness" to their children, and hence that the

---

evidence associating *astos* with bloodline, nativity, and descent. For instance, *astos* must refer to nativity in Aristotle's discussion of the evolution of citizenship laws in democracies (*Pol.* 1278a28–35). If it referred to local residence, there would be no distinction between the various types of democratic membership rules he discusses. In critiquing Cohen's position, Roy (1999, 15 n. 25) points out that he has not countered Whitehead's arguments (1977) against the view that metics were *astoi*.

[20] I stress that I am offering an account of the official ideology based on Athenian law and legal discourse rather than attempting to describe the historical reality. Connor (1994, 35–38) argues that there was a considerable blurring of the essentialist status boundaries in practice. He suggests that children of mixed unions—between citizens and metics, slaves, and *hetairai*—frequently found their way onto the citizen rolls. Attic lawsuits provide evidence that such violations happened or at least were believed to happen (e.g., Dem. 57, 59; Is. 3, 6). At the same time, however, a core commitment to the state's rules of sexual reproduction is attested by the crackdown on infractions that occurred in 346 when the Athenians held a statewide scrutiny of the citizen body to weed out imposters; see Dem. 57, with Libanius's hypothesis; Aes. 1.77–78, 86, 114, 2.182; the scholiast on Aes. 1.77; Dilts 1992, 33; Isaeus (12 *For Euphiletus*); Harpocration, s.v. *diapsēphisis* (= Androtion *FGrH* 324 F 52); Diller 1937, 98–100; Whitehead 1986, 106–9; Scafuro 1994, 183 n. 12.

[21] Ogden 1996, 166–73.

[22] The role of the law in fostering the belief that adherence to the state's rules of sexual reproduction produced citizens with the requisite "Athenianness" is attested by the topos (found in Old Comedy and oratory) of undermining a citizen's perceived political credentials and patriotism by impugning his bloodline or the status of his parents. After the implementation of the Periclean law of citizenship, putatively bad citizens were stigmatized as noncitizens, as men whose foreign blood or spurious birth rendered them innately hostile to the state; see Aes. 2.78, 2.173–74, 177, 3.171–72; Dem. 21.149–50; Din. 1.15, with Connor 1992, 168–70; Ober 1989, 268–70; Harding 1987, see further on maternal inheritance, ch. 3 n. 5. Despite this stigmatization of citizens with putatively bad blood, the Periclean law of citizenship primarily fostered processes of auto-referential racism, an emphasis on the (imagined) positive qualities and characteristic thought to inhere in the citizen group and to be transmitted and conserved through the processes of sexual reproduction. For auto-referential vs. altero-referential racialization, see Guillaumin 1995, 29–60. I use the concept of race ideology to designate the processes of identification encouraged by the citizenship law because the law anchored civic identity in an idea of common descent and in the biophysical schema of sexual reproduction. The hallmark of race ideology is a belief in the heritability of supposedly morally salient physical, intellectual, spiritual, or moral characteristics; see Balibar 1991; Frederickson 2002, 170. For the racialization of democratic citizen identity, see Lape forthcoming. For ethnic processes and democratic citizenship, see B. Cohen 2001.

rules of sexual reproduction preserved the racial purity of the citizen body.[23] While fidelity to the rules of sexual reproduction enshrined in the Periclean law was correlated to the generation of good Athenian and good democratic citizens, deviation from the state's reproductive rules was believed to produce "citizens" characterized by an innate hostility to the city and its democracy. To cite an extreme example, among the many abominations attributed to Alcibiades, the bad boy of the fifth-century democracy, was his having produced a son with a Melian slave woman, effectively breeding an enemy of the democratic state (And. 4.22–23).

The state's rules of sexual reproduction composed and maintained the internal and external boundaries of the citizen body. At the same time, they preserved and transmitted the Athenianness and autochthonous ancestry that underwrote democratic national ideology. It is thus not surprising that Lycurgus identifies these status distinctions as the one thing that the Athenian polis could not survive without. The Athenians could lose everything, Lycurgus suggests—men, military power, and their foreign policy—so long they retained the status distinctions (created and iterated by the rules of sexual reproduction) that effectively made them who they were. These long-standing associations indicate that it is quite possible (if indeed not probable) that the state's matrimonial citizenship system—and all practices, ideologies, and identifications that went with it—compensated for the attenuation of the traditional sources and practices of democratic identity in the period between Chaeronea and the Chremonidean War. Macedonian military supremacy and interventions in domestic democratic politics did nothing to interfere with the production of democratic citizens and civic ideology from below in the seemingly mundane practices of marriage and sexual reproduction. Unfortunately, lack of evidence makes it impossible to investigate whether and how actual marriage and gender practices assisted in reproducing democratic ideology during the period of Macedonian takeovers. Nevertheless,

[23] A conceptual slippage between autochthony and sexual reproduction is attested by the orators' frequent claim that the Athenians' autochthonous origins made them "legitimate" citizens. See Dem. 60.4, and especially Lycur. 1.100, citing a lengthy fragment from Euripides' *Erechtheus*. For the associations between autochthony and sexual reproduction, see Ogden 1996, 168; Loraux 1993, 57. Accordingly, the Periclean law of citizenship is also linked with the myth of autochthony; see Loraux 1986, 150; Rosivach 1987, 303 n. 34; Connor 1994, 37; Ogden 1996, 166–73; R. Osborne 1997, 11; Diller 1937. There were gaps between the ideology of autochthonous racial purity, guaranteed by the state's citizenship law and its official foundation story, and actual citizenship practices. For instance, although the naturalization of foreigners was infrequent, its very possibility demonstrates that the state could bypass its own rules of sexual reproduction to confer Athenianness; on naturalization, see M. J. Osborne 1981–83; Hansen 1991, 130. In addition, the operation of the Periclean citizenship law led to an emphasis on Athenianness issuing from biological reproduction that, over time, may have offered an alternative to the doctrine of autochthony.

although we cannot evaluate the role of marriage and gender practices in compensating for the recurrent loss of democratic institutions and manhood practices, we can consider their depiction on the comic stage. By a remarkable coincidence, New Comedy, a genre whose plots obsessively adhere to and enact the Athenian state's matrimonial and reproductive norms, emerged in Athens at about the same time the Macedonians began their efforts to undermine and eradicate the democracy. In fact, New Comedy's productive period (the last "new" Athenian cultural form) exactly coincides with the tumultuous period of the successor wars (roughly 323–260 B.C.), out of which the settled pattern of Hellenistic kingdoms finally emerged.[24]

So far, out of the sixty-four known poets of New Comedy, only the works of Menander have been recovered to any extent.[25] We have one complete play, the *Dyskolos*; one nearly complete play, the *Samia*; and substantial portions of five other plays, as well as scenes and fragments from many of Menander's works.[26] In addition, there are seven certain Roman adaptations of Menander's plays that can be used to supplement the evidence. Although Menander's extant plays and fragments do not represent New Comedy in its entirety, they do constitute a considerable subtype of the genre.[27] Moreover, Menander was not only a prolific exponent of the genre, writing more than one hundred plays in a career of about thirty years, but he was also, according to ancient authors, its star.[28] And, in contrast to many New Comic playwrights, Menander was a native Athenian, the son of a flamboyant anti-Macedonian general, with an insider's knowledge of Athenian law and democratic culture.[29]

Yet, on the face of it, Menander's comedy seems to offer little insight into contemporary Athenian affairs. The extant plays and fragments not only generally eschew politics but also tell the same basic story of how a

[24] N. J. Lowe (2000, 221) argues that New Comedy did not simply die out with the death of Philemon (and the Athenian defeat in the Chremonidean War) but rather that the canon closed.

[25] According to the anonymous *On Comedy*, there were sixty-four poets of the New Comedy, only six of whom were worthy of note (Men. *vita* 3 K.-A.).

[26] Arnott (1970; 1979–2000, vol. 1; 2000a), Handley (1979), and Blume (1998, 16–45) review the recovery of Menander's works in this century. Sisti (1987) and Arnott (1996b) offer general introductions to Menander and his comedy. For a bibliography of Menandrian scholarship, see Katsouris 1995.

[27] On the generic classification of Menander's comedy, see Henrichs 1993; on generic change in ancient comedy more generally, see Csapo 2000, and Nesselrath 1990 on middle comedy.

[28] Ancient assessments of Menander's work are assembled in Men. 83–170 test. K.-A. For the survival of Menander's works in antiquity, see Easterling 1995. On the "elite" reception of Menander by Plutarch, see R. L. Hunter 2000.

[29] For the dates of Menander's life and career, see *vita* 1–4 K.-A.; de Marcellus 1996. Menander was the son of Diopeithes, the general whose tactics were defended by Demosthenes (Men. *vita* 2 K.-A.; Dem. 8).

young citizen in love overcomes various obstacles to win the young woman of his choosing. In most cases, the plays culminate with the marriage of the citizen hero and heroine, or with the reconciliation of a marriage after an estrangement.[30] Although the emergence of this cultural narrative—with its unprecedented focus on ordinary citizens who marry for love—has traditionally been thought to have nothing to do with democracy, the rise of Menander's family romances, I will argue, is inextricably tied to the continuity of Athenian democratic and transnational polis culture during the initial and most fraught period in the transition to the Hellenistic era. My central claim is that Menandrian comedy not only depicts and champions fundamental precepts of Athenian democratic ideology but that it also, in certain cases, offers reactions to and commentaries on immediate political events. Comic narratives defend polis life against the impinging Hellenistic kingdoms, often by transforming their representatives into proper inhabitants of the polis, and by breaking down internal divisions between citizens based on status and economic class.[31] With such representations, the performance of Menander's comedies filled the void left by the suspension of democratic institutions and the attenuation of democratic manhood practices.[32]

Like several recent studies, this book attempts to resituate Menander's comedy in its contemporary political contexts.[33] It gives an account of the role of Menander's comedy in the political struggles between the Hellenistic kingdoms and the Greek cities and in the reproduction and subver-

[30] See Wiles 1991, 29; cf. 2001.

[31] For the political and cultural survival of the Greeks cities (other than Athens) in the Hellenistic period, see Gauthier 1993; Giovannini 1993; Gruen 1993; Ma 1999.

[32] Thanks to the recent studies by Rosivach and Wilson, the idea that theatrical audiences in Menander's day were drawn primarily from the middle and upper classes has been effectively discredited. Previous commentators had assumed that Demetrius of Phaleron abolished the *theorikon*, the state distribution to citizens for attending the City Dionysia and Panathenaia, thereby preventing the poor from attending the theater. Even if Demetrius did abolish the *theorikon* (an act for which there is no evidence), the overall composition of theatrical audiences would probably have been little affected. The cost of admission to the Dionysia was modest, probably two obols, and required only on five days per year. (The sole explicit evidence for the cost of a seat at the theater is Dem. 18.28.) Furthermore, Rosivach (2000) points out that there is no evidence that a fee was ever charged for the Lenaia. Finally, Wilson (1997: 100) argues that the primary purpose of the *theorikon* was never one of "poor relief." He proposes instead that the distributions to citizens in a context in which everyone else—metics, foreigners, etc.—had to pay served to highlight civic membership in heterogeneous festival contexts. There is a vast literature on the civic context of dramatic festivals in Athens; see Goldhill 1990, 2000. For the performance contexts of Menander's comedy and the material conditions of theatrical production and festival sponsorship, see further chapter 2.

[33] See P. G. Brown 1992b; Giglioni 1982, 1984; Hofmeister 1997; Konstan 1995; Major 1997; Mossé 1992a; Patterson 1998, 180–229; Rosivach 2001; Scafuro 1997; Treu 1981; von Reden 1998; Omitowoju 2002.

sion of democratic status boundaries. To these ends, it draws on the New Historicist insight that literary representations do not reflect or mirror political and cultural histories taking place elsewhere—that is, outside the text—but rather are active participants in the cultural and political negotiations of their times.[34] Comedy, I maintain, made things happen in the world by offering narratives that enabled civic audiences to make sense of the manifold changes taking place in the early Hellenistic period within a traditional polis-based conceptual framework, and at the same time crucially reinforced democratic matrimonial and gender practices. Thus, although like David Konstan and Vincent Rosivach, I attend to the ideology of comic texts, I focus primarily on comedy's role as a producer rather than as a product of ideology.[35] If ideology is not natural but rather a distortion of the way "things really are," to paraphrase Althusser, then it follows that ideology must be constantly constructed and replenished to maintain its imaginary appearance as natural or real. Menander's family romances were just such producers of democratic orthodoxy: they make the democratic cultural order seem natural and thus the only one imaginable in spite of the manifold conditions challenging its dominance.

Comedy's constituting or ideological work can be conceptualized by likening the comic narrative to a performative speech act, an utterance that does what it says. Although comic narratives are fictional and consequently do not literally bring about citizen marriages, the marriages they enact promise the birth of new citizens and hence the perpetuation of the democratic polis. Thus, the performative efficacy of a comedy is not identical with the play itself, but rather arises from the narratives it offers audience members to think about and identify with.[36] With its recurrent tales of citizen making, comedy scripts or performs the survival of democratic culture before the fact. By deploying certain conventions of per-

[34] For New Historicism or "cultural poetics," see Greenblatt 1988; Montrose 1989; Newton 1989.

[35] Konstan's readings of comedy (1995, 5) are symptomatic: they explicate the contradictions on the level of plot and character that reveal the inevitably incomplete ideological labor of the text in reassembling cultural givens into unified compositions. Although this approach is associated with a tradition of criticism that treats texts as expressing already-existing ideologies (P. Smith 1988, 24–40), Konstan also emphasizes that contradictions in comic texts open space for ideological change.

[36] J. L. Austin (1962) initially distinguished constative utterances, descriptive statements that are either true or false, from performatives, utterances that do not refer to an already existing state of affairs but rather produce new effects. What I am claiming is that a play is a performative speech act that produces certain consequences rather than a species of constative utterance that merely describes or refers to a social reality. Austin also distinguishes illocutionary speech acts, utterances that produce effects in the saying (e.g., as when a judge declares, "I sentence you"), from perlocutionary acts, acts that produce certain consequences by their utterance; see further Felman 1983 and Petrey 1988 on speech acts in literature. My study elaborates the perlocutionary effects of comic narratives.

spective, plot pattern, character, and theme, comic narratives or speech acts interpellate theatergoers as citizens and acculturated polis inhabitants—which is just to say, they provide stories that enable audience members to identify as democratic citizens without reference to the political regime actually in power.[37]

Although I argue that the comic marriage plot operates as a vehicle for political and cultural reproduction, I am not claiming that these processes were either seamless or totalizing. My central thesis is that Menander's comedy is constituted by countervailing narrative trajectories to reproduce and resist the civic social order. When considered from the perspective of the contest between the Greek polis and the Hellenistic kingdom, comedy's propensity to preserve and reproduce democratic culture against encroachment from the Hellenistic kings and kingdoms appears paramount. In other words, the historical circumstances threatening the culture of the polis and democracy transform what under ordinary circumstances would be processes of cultural and political reproduction into vehicles of implicit political resistance. At the same time, however, comedy's family romances are often subversive of the democratic cultural order they instantiate. In part, this is because comedy's reproduction of democratic culture against various Hellenistic outsiders allows for a relaxation of the internal status boundaries that traditionally secured the citizen's place in the intra-polis hierarchy (i.e., the boundaries between free persons and slaves, men and women, and citizens and foreigners). In addition, the reproduction of democratic civic ideologies in the comic marriage plot makes all too clear what the official ideology normally elides: the contradictions and arbitrary exclusions of women, foreigners, and slaves on which the democratic political order was based. Finally, comedy's subversive emphasis also arises from its generic convention of empowering women to plot and promote the interests of the democratic polis and to serve as moral exemplars for men. By enabling women to act with more agency and moral authority than democratic culture traditionally allowed or recognized, comedy clears the terrain for a remodeling of conventional gender and status categories.

[37] I am not using "interpellation" in the strong Althusserian sense that supposes a seamless link between ideology and subjectivity. Rather, I am following Judith Butler in conceptualizing interpellation as a kind of performative (perlocutionary) speech act that may succeed or fail in constituting the subject in ideology, or may work in ways other than those that were intended (Butler 1997, 24–28, 31). This modification is in keeping with Althusser's theory, since his own examples of the interpellative function of ideology depend on linguistic acts (e.g., the voice that names, the policeman's hailing). Thus, to claim that comedy interpellates theatergoers as citizens by encouraging civic identifications is not to claim that this process always worked or that its effects were necessarily final when it did work.

The Politics of Marriage and the Comic Marriage Plot

Menander's comedy has traditionally been judged nonpolitical on two grounds: because of what the comedies say and what they do not. To take the former point first, Menander's comedy is considered nonpolitical, or as representing an "escape" from politics, because its subject matter—stories of love, marriage, and romantic intrigue—has seemed to many commentators to be by its very nature nonpolitical.[38] This position, however, tells us more about the culturally conditioned assumptions of modern critics than about the historically specific meanings of Menander's marriage plays. Marilyn Katz's recent work on the history of the study of ancient Greek women is helpful here. Katz convincingly argues that the categories through which ancient women have been studied—domesticity, education, marriage, and social life—are the legacy of the nineteenth-century cult of bourgeois domesticity and the naturalized conception of neatly demarcated public and private spheres on which it was based.[39] In other words, according to Katz, classical scholars have not thought it relevant to investigate the political importance of women, including the theoretical and practical significance of their exclusion from political rights in Athens, because of unexamined assumptions about what properly constitutes the parameters of women's lives.

Although Katz is primarily concerned with the study of women in ancient Greece, her conclusions are equally applicable to the study of Menander's comedy. The preconceptions of modern critics concerning what can be construed as political have inhibited inquiry into the political and ideological significance of Menander's romantic comedies. Yet matters of marriage and the family are today highly political, as ongoing debates concerning polygamy and same-sex marriage well attest, and in ancient Athens they were no less so. In the United States, state governments define and so construct marriage by requiring that a person be married only to one person at a time and that marriage partners be of opposite sexes.[40] Similarly, though ancient Greek has no precise word for marriage

[38] For Menander's comedy as an escape from politics, see Tarn 1952, 273; Green 1990, 73; Davies 1977–78, 114. For the emphasis on the "family" in Menander's comedy as by definition "nonpolitical," see Barigazzi 1965a, 18; Major 1997.

[39] Katz 1995, 1999. Katz traces the nineteenth-century triumph of a separate spheres ideology to eighteenth-century political debates in which theorists appealed to an idealized construction of ancient Greek women as secluded and domestic to legitimate the position of women in their own visions of the sociopolitical order. For the asymmetry between the liberal conception of the public and private as distinct spheres and Athenian configurations, see D. Cohen 1991a; Humphreys 1993: 1–32.

[40] There is a vast literature on the role and interest of modern nation-states in defining

or the conjugal family, the democratic polis nevertheless defined marriage and the legitimate form of the citizen family by stipulating who could bear legitimate children with whom.[41] Furthermore, in democratic Athens the link between marriage and the state was more pronounced and transparent than it is in modern Western nation-states. For the polis both defined what counted as a legitimate marriage and it also employed marriage to constitute, reproduce, and maintain the integrity of the citizen group.

Because the Periclean citizenship law evoked marriage, or rules of legitimate sexual reproduction, to define the democratic citizen group, these rules and their attendant practices and processes came to be thought of not only as constituting and transmitting "Athenianness" but also, over time, as ensuring the production of citizens endowed with the values and aims of the citizen group itself. There is, of course, nothing intrinsically democratic about norms of sexual reproduction and marriage or the forms of social identity attached to them. But the very fact that the Periclean law of citizenship invokes these processes to delineate membership in a democratic citizen group created the conditions whereby they could be inflected with democratic significance. Accordingly, abiding by the state's rules of sexual reproduction was thought to produce not just noble, patriotic, and loyal citizens—that is, citizens with the right "racial" credentials—but also citizens endowed with an innate democratic disposition. According to the Athenian orator Aeschines, democratic citizens must have free birth on both their mother's and father's sides (which is another way of saying that they must be born according to the laws) to ensure their support for democratic law and to prevent antidemocratic behavior (Aes. 3.169). There is, to be sure, some slippage between the idea that having the right birth credentials made the citizen "Athenian" and hence naturally loyal to the Athenian state and the idea that the possession of these prerequisites made the citizen innately democratic.[42] To render this overlap, which ultimately stems from the state's tethering of political reproduction to state-authorized rules of sexual reproduction, I employ the concepts of democratic nationalism and democratic culture.[43]

---

marriage, and, in turn, on role of marriage laws in shaping national identities and characters; see Cott 1995; Stevens 1999.

[41] On marriage and the family in Solonian and classical Athens, see also Leduc 1992; Patterson 1998; Cox 1998; Pomeroy 1997; Vérilhac and Vial 1998; Lape 2002–03; on marriage in the Hellenistic period, see Vatin 1970.

[42] A similar overlap between the racial and political occurs in the correlation between autochthony and democracy found in Athenian funeral orations.

[43] I employ the concept of "democratic nationalism" to emphasize that democratic political identity is inextricably linked with Athenian national identity. It is now widely accepted that national formations are not distinctive products of modernity; see, e.g., Stevens 1999, 48 and passim; E. E. Cohen 2000: 3–4, 79–80. The existence of a political society is regarded as necessary for the emergence of the nation/national identity; see A. D. Smith

I use these concepts to underscore that the identity of democratic citizens (and hence democratic political ideology) was constituted through processes of gender, kinship, race or Athenianness, and sexual identity—in other words, through processes related to sexual reproduction that we today associate with national and or cultural processes rather than with democratic politics.[44]

Menander's comedy stages the national culture of Athens's democracy or, more simply put, democratic culture. According to one recent commentator, New Comedy was "the most rule bound and programmed of all classical narrative genres."[45] For present purposes, what is significant about comedy's standardized conventions and rules is that they are precisely the legal and social norms underpinning the national culture of Athens's democracy. If genre is defined "as a discursive form capable of constructing a coherent model of the world in its own image,"[46] then the model that comedy constructs is the democratic cultural order. Menander's plays never allow a violation of the laws or ideology pertaining to Athenian citizen membership.[47] For instance, although female citizens in comedy sometimes bear children outside the marriage context, in every case the status of these children is eventually normalized by the belated marriage of their parents. More significantly, Menander's comedies often conclude by enacting the laws of citizen marriage (or the closest equivalent to such laws that Athenian culture possessed). The romantic plot

1991, 9; Stevens 1999. Rather than opposing the Athenian democracy and the "Athenian nation" as distinct models for analyzing Athenian culture, I maintain that the democratic political order was dependent on and constituted through invocations of birth, kinship, gender, race, foundational stories, and common culture—in other words, through processes of nationalism. My understanding of the formation of national identities is indebted to Balibar (1991), A. D. Smith (1991), and Stevens (1999). Finally, my conception of "democratic nationalism" finds direct support in the Athenian myth linking democracy and egalitarian principles (*isonomia*) to autochthony—equality of birth (*isogonia*); see Lys. 2.17–19; Pl. *Mx.* 239a3–4; and further references cited in note 15 above.

[44] For the interimplication of gender and democratic identity produced by the operation of the Periclean citizenship law, see further chapter 3.

[45] N. J. Lowe 2000, 190. Although New Comic poets could manipulate these generic rules or "models of writing," they could not discount or dispense with them (Todorov 1990, 18). Thus, although the extant comedies and fragments are exceptionally rich and varied, comedy's originality consists in its creative deployment of certain standardized conventions (Goldberg 1980; Zagagi 1994).

[46] For this definition of genre, see Conte 1994, 132.

[47] New Comedy never violates the Athenian law restricting marriage to native Athenians (Fredershausen 1912, 208; Ogden 1996, 174–80; Lape 2001). On Menandrian comedy's fidelity to Athenian law, see also Gomme and Sandbach 1973; Fantham 1975, 44–45; MacDowell 1982, 42–52; P. G. Brown 1983; and on pretrial disputing tactics, see Scafuro 1997. Préaux (1960, 232) remarks that Athenian law in Menandrian comedy has the force that a decree of fate or a religious curse has in tragedy. On the use of Roman comedy as a source for Athenian law and judicial practice, see Paoli 1962; Fantham 1975; Scafuro 1997.

regularly culminates with a performance of the *enguē*, the speech act that was adduced to establish the existence of a marriage in Athenian legal discourse.[48] In this ceremony, one citizen pledged his daughter or ward to another citizen for the explicit purpose of producing (or "plowing," in the agricultural metaphor of the formula), *gnēsioi* (legitimate children). Consequently, comic performances both create the conditions for reproducing the polis and perform the state's laws of familial and political reproduction. By enacting the *enguē* ceremony, comedy promises the generation of new citizens—that is, young men who possess the requisite birth requirement for civic and familial membership. In this way, comedy produces and reinforces the overlapping pattern of familial and political membership at the heart of democratic national culture.

By using citizen marriage and its promise of the civic fertility as its privileged narrative outcome, Menander's plays stage the culture of democratic citizenship. Even those plays that deviate from the marriage plot pattern uphold the norms and laws of citizenship. Although the correspondence between the laws of genre and the laws of citizenship invests Menander's comedy with a deeply nationalistic perspective, the plays never promote the citizenship system in a heavy-handed way: Menander's protagonists marry for considerations of love rather than law. Yet the passions of Menander's protagonists always—in the end—happily dovetail with the norms of civic law and ideology. The marriage of hero and heroine often initially seems to be impossible, usually for reasons of the heroine's presumed noncitizen status, but in the end all barriers are removed by last-minute recognitions, amazing coincidences, twists of fate, and the elimination of obstacles that seemed insurmountable. Thus, comedy stages the citizenship law by deploying the characteristic devices of the narrative mode of literary naturalism.[49] Although these devices often lead to situations improbable in the extreme, they nevertheless have the effect of lending the norms of civic matrimony an air of inevitability. According to Kathleen McCarthy, the naturalistic mode in comedy "perform[s] the function of hegemonic discourse" by making "the world

[48] In the *Dyskolos* (842–44), Kallippides pledges his daughter to Gorgias: "I entrust my daughter to you, young man, for the procreation (plowing) of legitimate children and I give three talents along her as dowry" (ἀλλ᾿ ἐγγυῶ παίδων ἐπ᾿ ἀρότῳ γνησίων / τὴν θυγατέρ᾿ ἤδη μειράκιόν σοι προῖκά τε / δίδωμ᾿ ἐπ᾿ αὐτῆι τρία τάλαντα). In Men. *Pk*. 1013–14 and *Sam*. 726–27, the formula appears in a slightly different form: the verb used in these plays is *didōmi*, "give." See further on the *enguē* Wyse 1904, 289–93; Wolff 1944, 51–53; Harrison 1968–71, 1:3–9; Patterson 1990, 56 n. 64; Vérilhac and Vial 1998, 232–47. For the wedding in Athens, see Oakley and Sinos 1993. For metaphors of the female body and sexual reproduction, see duBois 1988.

[49] On the mode of naturalism in New Comedy, see McCarthy 2000, 11–14; Konstan 1983, 24–25, and 1995, 4; Wiles 1991, 63–65, 71.

around us seem to be the one that is destined."[50] In the case of Menander's plays of citizen marriage, what seems to be destined are precisely the familial and romantic arrangements necessary to reproduce the democratic state. In Menander's comedy, the devices of literary naturalism operate to naturalize (i.e., to make essential and impervious to change) the correlation between sexual and political reproduction enshrined in Athenian law. In so doing, the formulaic marriage plot offers a powerful affirmation of citizen identity as well as a myth of the democratic polis as natural and self-generating.[51]

Comedy's Constitutive Political Silence

The political import of comedy's stories of citizen marriage must be taken together with what comedy excludes from representation. Although Menander wrote in what was arguably among the most tumultuous and eventful periods in Athenian history, the chaos of the times barely surfaces in his extant plays and fragments. Critics and historians have often taken this silence at face value, as a reflection of political decline and apathy engendered by the emergence of the Hellenistic kingdoms. According to this view, comedy eschewed contemporary affairs because they were too desperate and depressing for a citizen audience longing for retreat into escapist fantasies.[52] Certainly, contemporary events may have

[50] McCarthy 2000, 14.

[51] Although the repetitiveness of comic plot patterns has often provided a justification for devaluing the genre (e.g., Green 1990, 77–78), repetition itself provides important evidence for what was most culturally important. Why, after all, did audiences need the same stories, over and over? The argument that comedy's repetitive and naturalistic marriage plots stage a myth of citizen identity is related to E. Hall's thesis (1997) that tragedy employs recurrent plot patterns to affirm a citizen's place in the social world. For the repetition of familial themes in Roman declamation and the formation of Roman elite identity, see Beard 1993. G. Murray (1943, 43) links comedy's repetitive plots to fertility myth.

[52] For the apparent absence of politics in Menander's comedy as escapism from grim contemporary realities, see Gomme and Sandbach 1973, 23–24; Green 1990, 73–74. Although Davies draws attention to Menandrian comedy's obsessive concern with the political issue of citizen status, he also interprets it as escapism (1977–78, 113–14). Recent studies have challenged the conventional and completely untheorized assumption that the absence of direct references to contemporary events is equivalent to a generalized political apathy. For instance, Major argues (1997) that the seemingly apolitical domestic orientation of Menandrian comedy is a pro-Macedonian political gesture. This argument, however, assumes that the domestic is by definition nonpolitical. Von Reden (1998) argues that New Comic characters embody political behavior and attitudes—but where she posits elite political philosophy as the reference point that defines what counts as appropriate behavior, I argue that the dominant reference point is the democratic polis that supplies the rule system of the genre; see also Patterson 1998, 188.

been at times too grim to contemplate; one need only think of the report that the Macedonians cut out Hyperides' tongue.[53]

In contrast to previous commentators, however, I maintain that rather than mirroring the political apathy of the citizenry, comedy's political silences tell us something about the ideological work of comedy. Although Macedonian-backed oligarchies held power in Athens for more than half of Menander's career, Menander's extant plays and fragments never acknowledge this fact.[54] Comedy's elision of this state of affairs is, I would argue, performative rather than descriptive: that is, comedy creates a reality rather than simply reflecting the status quo. By eliding or ignoring contemporary politics, comedy denies Athenian subordination to Macedonian rule, effectively misrecognizing the polis's "real" conditions of existence.[55] Viewed from this perspective, comedy's political silence can, at least in some cases, be understood as a form of resistance in its own right.[56]

Although Menander's plays never depict Macedonian power in Athens, they do acknowledge the Hellenistic kingdoms and the manifold threats that they posed for the Greek cities. But comedy redefines polis–kingdom relations from its own civic perspective and, in so doing, prioritizes and disseminates its own civic moral norms.[57] It developed conventions for representing the Hellenistic threats that allowed the polis to contain and control them. For instance, female citizens are often dislocated from

[53] While one tradition reports that the Macedonians cut out Hyperides' tongue, according to an alternative version Hyperides bit off his own tongue ([Plut.] *Vit. X Orat.* 849a–b).

[54] In most cases, Menander's plays cannot be precisely dated to determine whether they were first performed during periods of oligarchy. *Dyskolos* is an exception: it won first prize at the Lenaia in 316, right at the onset of Demetrius of Phaleron's oligarchic political regime. The play as we have it, however, contains no allusion to Demetrius's regime or its Macedonian sponsorship (see further chapter 4). Perhaps Menander's play *Nomothetēs* was a piece of transparent political propaganda intended to garner support for the oligarchic regime and *nomothesia* of Demetrius of Phaleron. Conversely, it is equally easy to imagine that the play was a vicious parody of Demetrius performed after his expulsion from the city. For the *Nomothetēs*, see K.-A. 251–54. For the reference to the *gynaikonomoi* in Menander's *Kekruphalos* (208 K.-A.) as a parodic and perhaps subversive reference to Demetrius's regime, see chapter 2.

[55] During the transition to the Hellenistic era, comic theater—once an ideological state apparatus in Althusser's sense—becomes a vehicle of resistance to Macedonian power.

[56] It should be emphasized that political commentary does not completely disappear in New Comedy. See Webster 1970, 100–110, on Greek New Comedy generally; Burstein 1980, on Menander's *Halieis*; Major 1997, reviewing political allusions in Menander and Greek New Comedy; Wiles 1984, on the *Dyskolos*; Habicht 1993, on Archedikos; Philipp 1973, on Philippides; Garzya 1969, on *Sikyōnioi*; and LeGuen 1995, on the political and cultural importance of the institution of theater in the Hellenistic polis.

[57] In this respect, comedy is analogous to public decrees, which also supplied a civic language for structuring relations between the Greek cities and the Hellenistic rulers, for Athens, see Kralli 2000; on the decrees of the Greek cities in Asia Minor, see Ma 1999.

family and community because of the disorder caused by conditions of chronic warfare. Women are abducted by pirates, sold as slaves, captured in warfare, and so on. Yet in every case, lost female citizens are "found," or restored to their true social statuses, enabling them to fulfill their civic destiny of becoming lawful wives and bearers of legitimate children.[58] Plays following this plot pattern offered audiences a transnational political myth allegorically coded in stories of threatened female fertility, equating the fulfillment of female reproductive destiny with the reproductive fate of the polis itself.[59]

Constituting Citizens: The Laws of Genre and State

Menander's flexible but formulaic plot patterns establish a correspondence between the processes of biological and political reproduction that is the cornerstone of comedy's work both in and out of Athens. At the same time, however, the fact that the marriage plays naturalize the legal and social conventions of the classical democracy provides important information about law and cultural practice in democratic Athens.[60] In Menander's time the very survival and reproductive future of the democratic polis were at stake. For the most part, comedy denies or refuses to countenance the undeniable dangers facing the city. Instead, it deals with threats to the democratic polis by making it immune to real change through strategies of naturalistic nationalism. That is to say, comedy employs the devices of literary naturalism to naturalize exactly the conditions needed to perpetuate the national culture of Athens's democracy. For this reason, comedy provides us with an important window on the norm-producing (i.e., the "norming") power of Athenian democratic culture, despite its being largely a product of the early Hellenistic era. To be more specific: by repeatedly dramatizing the citizenship system in action, comedy also dramatizes the role of Athenian law in shaping sexual, gen-

[58] Konstan remarks: "In an epoch of social stress and change, new comedy represented on stage a world where tensions evanesce through the mechanisms of plot" (1983, 24). See also Konstan 1995, 166.

[59] Given that the citizen identity of Athenian women issued solely from their role in producing citizens, it might be more accurate to say that the plight of female citizens in comedy expresses in microcosm rather than allegorizes the plight of the polis. In any case, the convention of using female characters as allegories for political principles has a long tradition in Athenian comedy (e.g., Ar. *Lys.* 1114).

[60] Historians and literary critics alike have begun to use Menander's comedy to supplement the study of Athenian social history and social values. See Arnott 1981; Préaux 1957, 1960; V. Hunter 1994, 6; Konstan 1995, 141–52; Scafuro 1997, 7–8. On comedy as a source for Hellenistic social history, see Patterson 1998, 195; Mossé 1989, 1992b; Salmenkivi 1997.

der, racial, and kinship identities—and, by implication, the role of these identities in structuring and sustaining democratic political identity.[61]

It seems useful to clarify the most contentious element of this claim, namely that Athenian law had a hand in fashioning the sexual identity of democratic citizens, since questions of sexuality, and indeed whether there is a "history of sexuality," remain tremendously fraught in recent scholarship.[62] A central area of contention centers on whether "sexuality" is constructed or essential. Rather than reducing the investigation of sexual practices and attitudes to what are ultimately ontological questions, one can consider the range of meanings and associations that a given culture attaches to sexual activity and attitudes.[63] In the Athenian case, it is clear that the Periclean law of citizenship attached a heterosexual imperative to democratic citizen identity. Although the citizenship law does not compel any specific behaviors, by stipulating the conditions for citizen status it also informs the bearers of that status of how they are supposed to behave.[64] Because the law constructs citizen status with reference to the sex act between two married or subsequently married natives, it enjoins the good democratic citizen to live up to his identity by pro-

[61] For the role of the Periclean citizenship law in reshaping traditional gender arrangements, see R. Osborne 1997; Stears 1995; Leader 1997. My argument that the state played a role through the citizenship law in forming the gender, kinship, racial, and sexual identities of Athenian citizens is related to Stevens's argument that the modern state reproduces gender inequalities by regulating marriage: "Rather than pre-existing sex differences being reflected in and exacerbated by laws, the very definition of matrimony suggests the institution is constitutive of inequity in roles related to reproduction. . . . Gender is what occurs through very specific rules a political society develops as it reproduces itself" (1999, 210).

[62] For the question of whether the categories of sexuality and sexual orientation can be legitimately applied to ancient Greek and Roman culture, see Halperin 1990, 2002; Larmour, Allen, and Platter 1998, 28ff. For the existence of homosexuality in classical antiquity, see Richlin 1993; Sissa 1999; Hubbard 1998; for a critique of constructivism, see Thorton 1991. For the homosexual as a modern construct that does not correspond to the ancient figure of the *kinaidos*, see Winkler 1990a; Gleason 1990; Halperin 1990, 2002. According to these scholars, gender rather than sexuality was the principal axis through which the *kinaidos* was defined; i.e., the *kinaidos* was presumed to jettison his masculine role for a feminine one. On the *kinaidos*, see also Davidson 1997, 167–82, who views insatiable desire as his defining feature, and chapter 7 below.

[63] To ask this question is not to assume the constructionist position in advance: it allows for the possibility of conclusions with essentialist implications, should the evidence warrant them.

[64] In Bourdieu's terms, the Periclean law is an act of institution: it imposes an identity by imposing the name "citizen." "To institute, to assign an essence, a competence, is to impose a right to be that is also an obligation of being so (or to be so). It is to *signify* to someone what he is and how he should conduct himself as a consequence. In this case, the indicative is an imperative" (Bourdieu 1991, 120). On the role of Athenian constitutional laws in conferring rights, obligations, and statuses, and thus in shaping social practice, see Carey 1998; Ober 2000; Lape 2002–03.

creating in the politically sanctioned format. Consequently, the law implicitly urges heterosexual practice, not as a fundamental source of human identity but rather as an input into democratic citizen identity.

Menander's comedy sheds light on the historically specific intermingling of "sexual" and political identity in democratic Athens. As it uses the laws of democratic citizenship and marriage as its own generic conventions, comedy dramatizes how juridical norms inform what seem to be freely chosen social practices by (inter alia) establishing the prior conditions that define what counts as legitimate sexual reproduction. In contrast to previous and perhaps contemporary Athenian comedy, Menander's extant works do not depict love between men. In fact, Plutarch famously identifies the absence of pederasty from Menander's plays as a source of their ethical utility (*Mor.* 712c).[65] This interpretation obviously tells us more about Plutarch's cultural milieu and his own preconceptions than about the originary conditions accounting for the elision of love between men in Menander's plays. Unlike Plutarch, I see this absence as the result of political norming rather than ethical considerations. Comedy portrays the laws of Athenian citizenship in action, laws that tacitly enjoined the citizen to marry and father legitimate citizens. By naturalizing these laws, comedy forecloses the possibilities and contexts for non-reproductive sexualities.[66] Thus, although comedy does not depict how citizens actually complied with the law, it does expose the law's implicit power to channel the erotic energies of Athenian citizens, and in that way to employ a form of "heterosexual" identification to buttress the identity of democratic citizens.

Comedy's Poetics of Political Membership

By using the laws of citizen marriage to structure its romantic plots, comedy illuminates the processes of democratic nationalism as well as mechanisms of political survival in the transition to the Hellenistic age.

[65] For a discussion of this passage and Plutarch as a reader of Menander, see P. G. Brown 1990b; Gilula 1987. The eschewal of male homosexuality may be a peculiarity of Menander's comedy. Diphilus, a New Comic poet, wrote a play titled *Paiderastai* (57 K.-A.), and Antiphanes, a poet who straddles both Middle and New Comedy, wrote a *Paiderastēs* (179 K.-A.); see Dover 1989, 149; R. L. Hunter 1985, 154.

[66] R. L. Hunter states that "the almost total absence of homosexuality from Menander's surviving plays is probably determined more by the plots than by changes in public habits" (1985, 13; cf. the similar comments by Dover 1989, 151). The absence of male homosexuality from Menander's comedy and from the state constructed in Plato's *Laws* seems to be tied to a similar reproductive imperative. When the primary aim of political theory and practical politics became ensuring the reproduction of the state through strict rules of marriage and reproduction, same-sex love may have begun to appear positively subversive.

Nevertheless, the plays cannot be pillaged as a direct source of information for "the way things were" in either the classical or the Hellenistic periods, for comedy dramatizes the citizenship law in action using its own conventions, themes, plot devices, and formulaic narrative patterns. In so doing, it adds to and transforms the raw materials of democratic matrimonial practices. Comic plots convey important political information, set up patterns of audience identification, and participate in broad politico-cultural processes because they obsessively iterate the norms of citizenship, and more specifically, because of the literary and generic strategies that they use in those iterations.

The standard Menandrian play begins with a problem.[67] The young citizen protagonist is always already hopelessly in love; something or someone, however, stands in the way of his romantic happiness. The narrative trajectory focuses on how the romantic difficulty is resolved. The ideological meanings and messages conveyed by a given play issue from what has to change in order to bring about the formulaic happy ending. What is the barrier to the protagonist's desire and how is it removed? In Menander's seven best-preserved plays, the problem is an ethical flaw, either internal to the protagonist or externalized in a blocking character or romantic rival.[68] For instance, in the *Aspis*, Smikrines, an obsessively greedy old man, tries to marry an heiress to get his hands on her newfound fortune. The staging of his romantic defeat becomes the subject of the comedy itself when the characters put on a play within the play, dangling another, even wealthier, heiress before Smikrines' eyes. That the greedy character loses out in the romantic contest offers a strong negative commentary on his overvaluation of economic forms of wealth. At the same time, that he acts so outrageously and shows himself to be the wrong man for the heroine increases the sense that the romantic hero is the right man. Accordingly, the nature of the obstacle or blocking character implicitly articulates the sociopolitical values promoted in the comedies by calling attention to the kinds of people who are, and are not, fit to inhabit and to propagate in the new comic society.

But in many plays and fragments, the emphasis is less on bringing about the defeat of hyperbolically villainous rivals and blocking characters than on how the young citizen protagonist eventually obtains the woman he "loves" in marriage. In the *Dyskolos*, *Perikeiromenē*, *Misoumenos*, *Sikyōnioi*, and to some extent the *Samia*, the hero gets the girl not only because he is less offensive than his perceived rival (if there is one) but

[67] In the following paragraphs, I am borrowing from and historicizing Frye's seminal analysis of comic plot structure (1957, 163–85). For a historicization of Frye's mythos of romance, see F. Jameson 1981, 103–35. For the applicability of Frye's conception of comedy to New Comedy, see Konstan 1983; McCarthy 2000, 13.

[68] Cf. Konstan 1983, 29; Lape 2000.

also and more centrally because of his own character as he discloses it in his efforts to win the heroine.[69] In most cases (excepting the *Perikeiromenē* and *Misoumenos*), the hero does not have to please the heroine or win her consent to the marriage. Rather, in these comedies it is the man or men who control access to the heroine whose expectations the protagonist must meet. Accordingly, Menander's romantic comedies are thoroughly homosocial: that is, the citizen's love for a woman operates to produce and strengthen bonds between men rather than between men and women.[70] For example, in the fragmentary *Sikyōnioi* the hero's eventual romantic success hinges on his ability to convince a democratic assembly that he is eligible and worthy of winning the girl. The assembly scene (discussed in chapter 7) offers a particularly good illustration of the homosocial plot pattern: male deliberation about the heroine's romantic and social fate creates and cements specifically political bonds between men. In this play, the marriage contest serves less as a surrogate for democratic institutions (as often in other plays) than as the stuff of democratic politics itself.

By fitting the Periclean law to the agonistic comic plot form in which the protagonist must somehow win the heroine, Menander's comedies often add new sociopolitical significance to the civic marriage system. In comedy, citizens are those characters with "connubial rights," as David Konstan puts it.[71] The right to marry signifies civic membership, a right that was in theory ascribed at birth: you were either born with the requirements for citizenship or not. In comic plots, however, this status is a necessary but not a sufficient condition for citizen marriage. The mere fact that a young man is a citizen often carries little or no weight with the heroine's guardian. Instead, the protagonist has to live up to the guardian's standards of what makes a man worthy. In the *Dyskolos*, Sostratos wins the heroine because, according to her brother, he was willing "to treat a poor man as his equal" (767–69). In other words, he gets the girl specifically because his actions demonstrate an egalitarian attitude. The insistence that economic status does not make the man, so to speak, is a central tenet of the Athenian democracy.[72] Thus, by linking the protagonist's romantic success to his egalitarian commitments, the *Dyskolos* promotes a kind of democratic natural selection. Sostratos gets

[69] For the idea that Menander's characters represent or embody political positions, see von Reden 1998, 277; Préaux 1957, 99–100. See Garyza 1969, with reference to the *Sikyōnioi*, and P. G. Brown 1992b, on flatterers and parasites.

[70] According to Sedgwick (1985), homosocial desire is a social force that operates within the structural context of heterosexuality but aims at forging social bonds between members of the same sex.

[71] Konstan 1983, 18.

[72] Ober 1989; Ober and Strauss 1990; Morris 1996, 2000; Raaflaub 1996.

the girl and affirms his citizenship neither because he is a citizen by birth nor because he is young and rich. Rather, what makes him eligible for marriage in this play is his display of the beliefs and values that made democracy possible. In the *Dyskolos*, then, Sostratos's entry into the citizen marriage system hinges on his ability to meet specifically democratic entrance criteria.

Opposites Attract: Rape, Romance, and Democratic Selection

The culmination of Menander's plays usually engenders a social transformation. Simply put, the plays begin and end in very different places. The resolution of the comic problem, whether it involves removing obstacles or winning over initially intractable blocking characters, brings with it the foundation of a new society free from whatever injustices and illusions initially held sway.[73] The narrative emphasis on making the new community generally means that the comedies do not depict the new community in action. In many cases, however, the matrimonial union itself encapsulates in microcosm the principles and norms of the resultant society.

Many Menandrian plots bring about the marriage of a wealthy citizen to the daughter of a seemingly poor, or at any rate less wealthy, citizen.[74] This is striking because economically mixed marriages were the exception rather than the norm in Athenian society. In theory, all that a man or woman needed to be eligible for citizen marriage was citizen birth. The marriage system operated to constitute and delimit the Athenianness of the democratic population. Yet as the marriage system produced and protected the external boundary between citizen and noncitizen, and Athenian and non-Athenian, it also produced and reproduced stratifications within the democratic citizenry. The norms of marriage were crucially responsible for the reproduction of economic inequalities in Athens. The social convention of dowering daughters to husbands who stood to inherit roughly proportional patrimonies ensured that the wealthy and the less wealthy would marry their respective economic

[73] According to Frye, "The society emerging at the conclusion of comedy represents . . . a kind of moral norm, or paradigmatically free society. Its ideals are seldom defined or formulated: definition and formulation belong to the humors, who want predictable activity" (1957, 169–70). I adapt this point, arguing that the ideals of the new society are symbolized by what is expunged or reformed in the process of making the new community or by the structure of the matrimonial union itself.

[74] For the rape plot, see further chapter 3, note 76. The analysis in the following paragraphs summarizes Lape 2001.

KLP

peers rather than each other.[75] Consequently, the marriage system reproduced an intergenerational pattern of economic stratification within the polis along with the democratic family form.[76]

Although Menandrian comedy is scrupulously faithful to Athenian laws of citizenship and marriage, the same cannot be said for its depiction of the dowry system. Comedy frequently uses literary strategies and tropes that work to dismantle or evade the dowry system, thus enabling the formation of economically mixed marriages. To this end, it privileges passion rather than traditional economic considerations as the most important element in the making of citizen marriages.[77] In many cases, however, passion is not sufficient to bypass the social convention emphasizing the importance of economic status in the making of marriages. To circumvent this deeply entrenched system, comedy frequently deploys a "rape plot" in which a wealthy citizen rapes the daughter of a less wealthy citizen.[78] While the fact of premarital rape probably had no formal implications for the dowry, in practice it had a leveling effect.[79] It enabled the victim's family to provide a dowry commensurate with their own socioeconomic status rather than proportional to the husband's expected inheritance. In this way, rape takes economics out of the matrimonial equation. Accordingly, comedy deploys rape, at least in part, to make a fresh start. With one violent act, it dismantles deep-seated social stratifications, reassembling the social order according to more egalitarian norms.

This productive power issues from the specifically civic harm that rape engenders; in the world of Menander's comedy, rape is an injury not to the "individual" but rather to citizen status. It is precisely because women possessed citizen status—a specifically sexual and reproductive status—that this form of injury cannot be repaired by the courts or recompensed in economic terms; no amount of money can restore the victim's civic chastity.[80] Rape entailed sexual experience, and that fact alone called a

[75] See Is. 3.49, 51; Foxhall 1989, 34; Schaps 1979, 74–75. Although the dowry is analogous to the patrimony, Cox (1998, 117–19) shows that the size of a woman's dowry was considerably smaller than the inheritance her brother(s) received.

[76] For the conjugal family as the democratic family form, see Lape 2002–03.

[77] For eros in comedy, see further chapter 3.

[78] For the rape motif in New Comedy, see Fantham 1975; Doblhofer 1994, 57–63; Konstan 1995, 141–52; Pierce 1997, 163–84; Scafuro 1997, 238–78; Rosivach 1998, 113–50; Sommerstein 1998: 100–114; Lape 2001, 79–120. For the rape plot motif in the *Dyskolos*, see chapter 4.

[79] The oblique references in Roman New Comedy to laws that compelled the rapist to marry his victim are not considered to be reliable evidence for Attic law; see Harrison 1968–71, 1:19; Scafuro 1997, 241–43.

[80] This "chastity" is not a matter of morality in the modern sense; see Konstan 1995, 148–49.

woman's perceived ability to bear legitimate children into question, thus undermining her civic status.[81] Similarly, monetary compensation cannot normalize the status of the bastard child inevitability born in cases of rape. The only civic solution to these status injuries is the marriage of rapist and victim. In this way, the rape creates a civic matrimonial imperative that transcends and renders irrelevant traditional matrimonial considerations based on class, status, and kinship. It provides a means of rebuilding the social order in accordance with principles antithetical to its own already operative and deeply entrenched conventions. To be sure, in some cases the impoverished heroine unexpectedly turns out to be wealthy or comes upon a considerable dowry.[82] But by that time, the ideological damage has been done: the plays always send the message that the protagonist's desire to marry the heroine overrides economic considerations.

Thus, although comedy represents wealth as a good thing and poverty as something to endure and to hide, it escapes the elitist associations of this position by creating new societies in which everyone is wealthy or well-off. Accordingly, this emphasis represents not a concession to an elitist ideology but rather an adaptation or bourgeoisification of the Old Comic fantasy of a return to a golden age of abundance.[83]

In two of the plays, the *Dyskolos* and the fragmentary *Geōrgos*, intermarriage between the rich and the poor is prompted by the apparent moral exemplarity of the heroine's brother as well as by the heroine's desirability. In the *Geōrgos*, a wealthy young man has raped and impregnated a poor neighbor woman. He professes to be in love with her and has promised her mother, Myrrhine, that he will marry her. When the play begins, however, the heroine is on the verge of delivering the baby and the young man is about to be married off to his own (homopatric) half-sister (*Geōr.* 10). Although Athenian law allows this type of marriage, it is always presented as the wrong marriage in the extant plays and frag-

[81] The matrimonial imperative also arises because rape in comedy always leads to the birth of a child whose status must be normalized by the belated marriage of its parents.

[82] There is a general consensus, based largely on the size of dowries, that Menandrian comedy portrays upper-class families from the leisure class (Gomme 1937) or perhaps from the upper-echelon "liturgical" class (Casson 1976). On the size of dowries in comedy, see also Golden 1990, 174–79. On the socioeconomic status of comic characters, see also Préaux 1957, arguing that comedy encodes the concerns of the elite, and Hoffmann 1998. Although comedy depicts the possession of wealth in a positive light, it does not follow that the genre supports or endorses an elitist ideology, or a status quo based on the inequitable distribution of wealth; for this view, see, on the *Dyskolos*, Rosivach 2001; Hoffmann 1986; on the *Samia*, Hofmeister 1997. Comic fantasies do away with the status quo characterized by inequities in wealth distribution by making everyone "wealthy," or less poor. See further Lape 2001, 105–12, and below.

[83] Carrière 1979; Auger 1979; Zeitlin 1999.

ments.[84] In some cases, comedy depicts and celebrates close kin marriages. In the *Aspis*, Kleostratos probably marries the daughter of his paternal uncle, and his sister certainly marries his paternal uncle's stepson. The reason that comedy discriminates against homopatric half-sibling marriage in particular, rather than against close kin marriages generally, is probably the underlying class bias associated with the former marriage strategy. Aristocrats and elites anxious to preserve bloodlines, status, and wealth are associated with half-sibling marriage.[85] In this type of marriage, the dowry and patrimony remained in the same family, ensuring the reproduction of economic and social status. Although many details of the *Geōrgos* are unknown, it is certain that the youth managed to evade the planned half-sister marriage in order to marry his impoverished rape victim.

Given the pattern found in other Menandrian plays, it is likely that the *Geōrgos* concluded with the formation of two marriages and possibly with the restoration of a third. It is a general rule of comedy's reproductive economy that no fertile female citizen remains unattached in a play's conclusion.[86] It is therefore highly likely that the protagonist's wealthy half-sister, like the heroine rape victim, was also given in marriage in the end. Since the only other young available citizen (known) in the play is Gorgias, the heroine's brother, he is the most likely candidate for the role of groom. Like the *Dyskolos*, then, the *Geōrgos* probably contained two interclass marriages, with one structured by the unusual pattern of the male "marrying up"—that is, marrying a woman more wealthy than himself.[87] In both plays, what makes such a marriage possible is the characterization of "Gorgias" (in each case, the name of the male character who marries a more wealthy woman) as the play's moral exemplar. In both works, Gorgias's selfless concern for the well-being of others wins him and his family a (potential) way out of poverty.[88] In the *Geōrgos*, however, the underlying (civic) solidarity of rich and the poor is emphasized by the correlated contrasts between free persons and slaves and between Greeks

[84] Keyes 1940; Ogden 1996, 180.

[85] See Humphreys 1993, 25.

[86] Plautus's *Epidicus* is an exception; see Ogden 1996, 179–80.

[87] Based on the slave's comment that Gorgias treated his wealthy employer, Kleainetos, like a father, many commentators plausibly suggest that Gorgias was discovered to be Kleainetos's long-lost son later in the play, and thus not really "poor" after all. The difficulty with this reconstruction is that we do not know how Myrrhine (Gorgias's mother) managed to pass the children off as legitimate without a father in attendance; see Gomme and Sandbach 1973, 105–7.

[88] Because Gorgias nursed him back to health after a near-fatal injury, Kleainetos decides to marry Gorgias's sister; according to the slave Daos, the marriage will mean the end of poverty for the entire family (77–79). On Gorgias's heroic rescue of Knemon in the *Dyskolos*, see chapter 4.

and barbarians. The play sets Gorgias's willingness to minister to his wounded wealthy employer "like a father" against the callous neglect of the barbarian slaves. In this way, comedy subordinates the economic distance between the rich and poor by emphasizing the common structure of feeling existing among citizens arising from kinship, status, and, in this case, ethnicity.

When the social dynamics of comedy's matrimonial unions are considered, Menander's place in the tradition of Greek political thought emerges more clearly. The modification of the family and the use of marriage strategies to abolish economic inequalities and the attendant social ills of greed and self-interest have a long history in political philosophy and Old Comic political commentary. For instance, to solve the social and political problems arising from economic inequality, Praxagora in Aristophanes' *Ecclesiazusai* and Socrates in Plato's *Republic* each propose to abolish individual "nuclear" families. Both protagonists argue that the elimination of conjugal kinship will end private acquisitiveness and ownership as well as the intergenerational transmission and accumulation of wealth. In each case, however, the disappearance of individual families leaves the new society vulnerable to certain reproductive difficulties, including incest, a failed or sterile form of reproduction. Rather than doing away with the matrimonial family, Menander's comedy uses literary, ethical, and gender strategies to adapt the existing family structure to produce new egalitarian ends. Comedy's attempt to work within existing social conventions rather than to do away with them recalls the theory of one ancient lawgiver. According to Aristotle (*Pol.* 1266a40–b5), the Chalcedonian Phaleas argued that the institution of economic egalitarianism (specifically through the equalization of land allotments) was possible only when cities were first being founded. In cases of already existing cities, he believed that a redistribution of the land along more equitable lines would provoke rather than ameliorate social tensions. Thus, to remodel existing societies Phaleas proposed that the rich should give but not receive dowries; likewise, the poor should receive but not give dowries to their daughters.

In Menander's comedy, the union of sexual opposites in marriage provides a context for bringing together social opposites, and hence for building a community free (or at least more free) from stratifications of class and social status.[89] But the power of marriage to unify diverse social constituencies relies on a pattern of gender differentiation. Although

[89] In Plato's *Laws*, marriage is also presented as an institution capable of remodeling the state to either productive or detrimental effect. The Athenian Stranger recommends that the state use marriage not only to maintain the economic status quo but also for the eugenic purpose of producing emotionally well-balanced citizens (773).

comedy allows wealthy men to marry the daughters of the poor—and, in so doing, to reinstitute the social order along more homogeneous lines—the same is not true in reverse. When male characters actively seek to marry women more wealthy than themselves—or contemplate doing so—the motivation for the marriage is always presented in terms of economics rather than passion and sentiment.[90] In every case, the privileging of financial considerations proves disastrous for the men in question. These characters either lose out in the matrimonial contest or end up being dominated by too powerful wealthy wives. Simply put, marriages based on money invert the traditional gender hierarchy. As a speaker in a fragment from an unidentified Menandrian play puts it:

ὅταν πένης ὢν καὶ γαμεῖν τις ἑλόμενος
τὰ μετὰ γυναικὸς ἐπιδέχηται χρήματα,
αὑτὸν δίδωσιν, οὐκ ἐκείνην λαμβάνει.

(802 K.-A.)

When a poor man marries and
accepts property with the wife
he gives himself rather than taking her.

The speaker here adapts the conventional betrothal formula according to which active men "give" and "take" passive female reproductive objects. He suggests that when poor men marry wealthier women, they become like women—objects—ceding their gender power to their wives' economic power. According to the speaker in a fragment from a comedy by Anaxandrides, a woman's economic superiority in marriage transforms marriage into slavery, rendering the dowered wife a despot and the poor husband a slave (53.4–7 K.-A.). A speaker in Menander's *Misogunēs* describes the gender inversions elicited by the overwealthy wife in explicitly antidemocratic terms:

γυνὴ πολυτελής ἐστ' ὀχληρόν οὐδ' ἐᾶι
ζῆν τὸν λαβόνθ' ὡς βούλετ'· ἀλλ' ἕν ἐστί τι
ἀγαθὸν ἀπ' αὐτῆς, παῖδες·

(K.-A. 236. 6–8)

A rich wife is a burden. She doesn't allow her
husband to live as he pleases. Nevertheless, there is
one good to be gained from her: children.

[90] The only certain instance in which the plot brings about the marriage of a male character and a more wealthy woman occurs in the *Dyskolos* (although it probably also occurs in the *Geōrgos*). Gorgias can marry above his class precisely because he does not seek to do so and because friendship and ethics work to subordinate the stratifying effects of economic difference. See further chapter 4.

According to the speaker, there are two sides to every coin, even to a rich wife. On the positive side, a rich wife can give a man children. The speaker's sentiment reflects the prevailing ideology, which defined female identity by (and confined it to) attributes of gender. In theory, if not in practice, female social identity was supposed to be limited to functions of gender—most especially, to the sexual significance attached to the female body. The problem with the rich wife, according to the speaker, is that her wealth gives her a power above and beyond her gender identity. More specifically, it is a power to curtail a man's distinctively democratic freedom to "live as he pleases."[91] This marked reference to a key democratic catchphrase makes vividly clear the antidemocratic political consequences of marrying up, for men at any rate.[92] In every case, men who marry for money end up being dominated by overly powerful wives; the net result is not greater economic equality but rather the loss of democratic freedom. In these matrimonial unions, the antitype to comedy's right happily-ever-after wedding, marriage becomes a figure for oligarchic and tyrannical oppression. Moreover, as so often in Athenian tragedy, the antidemocratic household is ruled by a woman.[93] By emphasizing what can go wrong when women are on top, so to speak, these marriages also tacitly adumbrate what the normative gender hierarchy secures for the male citizen: democratic freedom and equality.

The Power of Love: Female Selection and Male Education

In Menander's egalitarian marriage plays, marriage guarantees the reproduction of democratic citizens and the production of a more egalitarian social order. In plays of this type, political processes and negotiations are played out in a homosocial context. Romantic protagonists win their heroines by winning the approval of other men. Generally speaking, this approval requires only that the protagonists be who they already are. They must demonstrate egalitarian ethical competencies or, at the very least, show that they are not opposed to them or the sexual ideology of the democracy. The hero's romantic quest does not usually entail any kind of personal transformation within the confines of the plot.[94] Rather,

[91] For the ability "to live as one pleases" as quintessentially democratic, see, e.g., Arist. *Pol.* 1317b10–14; Thuc. 2.37.2–3.

[92] In Menander's *Plokion*, the wealthy heiress completely controls the household and its occupants (296, 297 K.-A.). Cf. on marrying an *epikleros* 805 K.-A. Cf. Pl. *Laws* 6.774c; Foxhall 1989, 34, 39; Golden 1990, 175; V. Hunter 1994, 39.

[93] For the politics of gender in the tragic household, see Maitland 1992.

[94] An exception to this rule occurs in *Epitrepontes*, in which the resolution of the rape plot leads not to societal change (by uniting real or perceived socioeconomic opposites) but to a

the transformative dimension of the plot occurs on the societal level in an imagined but unrepresented future. The protagonist's love changes how society will reproduce, because it creates a more egalitarian union or because he has been democratically selected for reproductive success over and against an oligarchic opponent (as in the *Aspis* and *Sikyōnioi*).

Although Menandrian plays generally allow little scope for depicting the process of change at the level of individual character, one plot pattern hinges on issues of personal transformation and resocialization. Plays of this type depict the ethical transformation or reform of the male protagonist within the context of the romantic relationship itself. This more radically transformative and politically trenchant dynamic occurs in the "plays of reconciliation."[95] In the three fragmentary specimens of this plot pattern (*Perikeiromenē*, *Misoumenos*, and *Epitrepontes*), the narrative emphasis is on repairing an already-established relationship rather than on building a marriage from scratch. In each case, the hero oversteps the bounds of propriety, committing a real or imagined harm against the comparatively powerless heroine. The emphasis of the plot then focuses not on redressing the harm per se, but on remaking the relationship on terms that prevent the perpetration of similar harms in the future. In each case, the message is the same: the superior power and privileges of the male protagonist do not entitle him to trample on the rights or feelings of his partner.

This ethical trajectory is made possible by two conventional devices. Comedy's fidelity to the gender ideology of democratic citizenship requiring that respectable citizen women be neither seen nor heard generally forecloses a depiction of the relationship dynamics between lover and beloved. But the reconciliation plays skirt the ideology of sexual separation by featuring heroines who are lost or displaced citizens or, as in the *Epitrepontes*, already respectably married women. These conceits allow the heroine to act outside the constraints of female respectability. In each case, the protagonist's passion for the unusually autonomous heroine gives her the power to domesticate and educate her unruly partner. Thus, while the male protagonist has infinitely more social and political power than the heroine, his love causes him to cede this power, at least in the temporary effort to win the heroine back. Conveniently, the heroine remains immune to love's debilitating effects. Although Menander's come-

---

transformation in the values and beliefs of the romantic hero. Nevertheless, the change in the hero's belief system constitutes an assault on the gender ideology of the democratic polis; see further chapter 8. Sostratos in the *Dyskolos* does undergo a transformation of sorts, since his romantic success is correlated to his willingness to perform manual labor. But the play presents this less as a transformation than as a disclosure of Sostratos's natural egalitarianism; see further chapter 4.

[95] For this plot pattern, see Webster 1960, 3–25.

dies manipulate female social identity in the interests of plot, they never sacrifice the ideology embodied in Athenian law that denied female citizens an autonomous sexual desire.

The reconciliation plays portray the heterosexual romantic relationship as a site in which the play of power is urgently at stake. This emphasis has a special political significance in the *Perikeiromenē* and *Misoumenos* because the protagonists in these works are mercenaries. These plays (along with the *Sikyōnioi*) depart from New Comedy's conventional construction of the romantic protagonist as defined primarily by his eros rather than by attributes of social position. Although this convention tends to make Menandrian protagonists rather flat, not to say boring, characters, hardly deserving of the label "protagonist" at all, they nevertheless operate as potent figures of wish fulfillment and identification. Precisely because they are so neutral, Menander's protagonists also usually lack the social attributes that would interfere with the audience's investment in their cause.[96] They become figures of identification more because of their position in the narrative as the romantic winners than because of any traits or redeeming qualities they possess in their own right.[97] But Menander's mercenary protagonists are hardly blank slates capable of absorbing myriad fantasy projections: in fact, they are burdened with a too-recognizable social identity. They are associated with the Hellenistic rulers and, by default, with the threats that the mercenary was seen to pose to the life and values of the Greek polis community.[98] Accordingly, like the flatterers and parasites that sometimes attend them, Menander's mercenaries stand out as political figures within the ostensibly domestic space of comedy.[99]

When a mercenary plays the romantic lead in Menander's comedy, he alienates the heroine by overly aggressive and assertive behavior—in

[96] Frye 1957, 167.

[97] For identification with a character on the basis of his or her narrative position (rather than because of the character's specific traits or attributes), see Jeffords's discussion of structural and spectacular identification in filmic representations of Vietnam (1989, 17).

[98] In Terence's *Eunuch*, the soldier Thraso (whose character is probably drawn from Menander's *Kolax*), boasts of being the close confidant of the king (397–407). In Plautus's *Miles Gloriosus*, Pyrgopolynices is a mercenary recruiter for Seleucus (75); in Menander's *Kolax*, the soldier Bias is compared to Alexander himself and, implicitly, to Demetrius Poliorcetes (Sandbach 2 = Athen. 434c, Sandbach 4 = Athen. 587d). Cf. Terence, *Self-Tormentor* 117. Elderkin (1934) argues that the soldier Therapontigonus, "servant of Antigonus," in Plautus's *Curculio* is modeled on Demetrius Poliorcetes. In Menander's *Perikeiromenē*, Polemon is identified by his rank as a chiliarch (294); and in Menander's *Misoumenos*, Thrasonides seems to have been serving the kings of Cyprus in their effort to ward off Ptolemy I (Sandbach 5).

[99] For comic flatterers and parasites as political figures associated with the Hellenistic courts, see P. G. Brown 1992b.

other words, by acting too much like a mercenary. In each case, the mercenary's romantic reconciliation requires that he disavow and distance himself from his offending behavior and that he act like a citizen rather than a soldier. Comedy thereby encloses the contemporary political confrontation between military kingdoms and the Greek cities within the romantic relationship. In these transnational or transpolis comedies, the protagonist's acquisition or display of ethical and cultural competencies takes precedence over the democratic parochialism associated with romantic success in the more nationalistic homosocial plots.[100] By portraying the mercenary as passionately attached to the heroine, comedy employs eros to civilize the mercenary through self-interest rather than coercion. In the end, the mercenary willingly gives up his transient life of violence to become a citizen husband. With this narrative pattern, comedy offered a script enacting and ensuring the survival of the Greek cities before they had actually escaped the Hellenistic rulers. But insofar as the power of love in comedy turns out to be the city's power, it is also a woman's power.

Reproduction and Resistance

It seems that in some cases at least, there is a price for enclosing political conflicts within the romantic relationship. In the reconciliation plays, women seize new authority as the domesticators and educators of unruly and uncivilized men. Although comedy developed the convention of deploying displaced female citizens as ethical exemplars to reproduce polis culture by containing and transforming the Hellenistic threat in the romantic relationship, the very use of the convention cuts in two directions. By depicting women—who stand in for all those without full membership rights, and who assist in reproducing both citizens and civic competencies—it allows figures normally excluded from political consideration to resist that exclusion (if only tacitly).[101]

On one level, the empowered heroines of Menander's reconciliation plays have the functional role that Froma Zeitlin attributes to female characters in Athenian tragedy. She states:

[100] For comedy's transnational audiences and contexts, see LeGuen 1995; Handley 1997.

[101] The unsettling of the gender system in comedy can also upset the boundaries between free persons and slaves and between Athenian citizens and noncitizens of all statuses because comedy's empowered heroines are often initially believed to be of foreign or servile status. Similarly, the ceding of moral authority to a foreign *hetaira* in the *Samia* and the partial empowerment of a slave *hetaira* in the *Epitrepontes* calls into question the multiple forms of exclusion on which the democratic polis was based.

> Even when female characters struggle with the conflicts generated by the particularities of their subordinate social position, their demands for identity and self-esteem are nevertheless designed primarily for exploring the male project of selfhood in the larger world. These demands impinge on men's claims to knowledge, power, freedom, and self-sufficiency—not, as some have thought, for woman's gaining some greater entitlement or privilege for herself and not even for revising notions of what femininity might be or mean. Women as individuals or chorus may give their names as titles to plays; female characters may occupy center stage and leave a far more indelible emotional impression on their spectators than their male counterparts (Antigone, for example, with respect to Creon). But functionally women are never an end in themselves, and nothing changes for them once they have lived out their drama on stage.[102]

Comic heroines may ultimately be empowered to suit male purposes and needs, as in tragedy. Yet it is possible to draw a distinction between the immediate needs informing comedy's literary choices and the ideological effects of those choices. In other words, that comic heroines are empowered at all has a significance that exceeds the motivations or plot requirements responsible for that empowerment.

In any case, we cannot simply assume that comedy's ideological effects mirror those of tragedy (however repressive or liberatory we might believe them to be), because comedy is informed by very different generic conventions and historical circumstances. In contrast to the aristocratic heroines of tragedy, the heroines of Menander's reconciliation plays are depicted as ordinary "girl next door"–type figures. Unlike the actual female citizen next door, however, the heroines of the *Perikeiromenē* and *Misoumenos* are in disguise; their true social and political identities are temporarily held in abeyance. Here again the parallel with tragic convention is illuminating. Tragic "displacement plots" focus on aristocratic women, once free, who have lost their status by being enslaved in the aftermath of war. According to Edith Hall, these plots express "the Athenians' desperate dependence on recognized membership of the polis."[103] In comedy, by contrast, the loss of social identity does not render its heroines primarily objects of pity but rather provides the crucial enabling condition for their agency. By masking the heroine's true civic identity, comic displacement plots make it possible for their heroines to evade the constraints of their conventional social position.[104] This re-

[102] Zeitlin 1996, 347. For the representation of women in tragedy, see also Rabinowitz 1993; Wohl 1998; Ormand 1999; McClure 1999; Foley 2001.

[103] E. Hall 1997, 98.

[104] The ideological effects produced by the deployment of disguised but empowered heroines in Menander's comedy are similar to those achieved by the "disguised" crossed-dressed heroines of Shakespearean comedy. According to Belsey (1985), the motif of female

lease—temporary though it may be—exposes the arbitrariness of traditional female social roles.

It should be clear that I am not framing questions of comedy's ideological work in a theoretical rubric that posits subversion versus containment as mutually exclusive models.[105] Rather, I treat comedy as a participant in the complex political and cultural negotiations of its times. Because comedy is composed of narrative impulses that reproduce as well as resist the civic status quo, it can straddle both sides of the subversion/containment fence. It is true that comedy's formulaic closure in marriage seems to temper the subversive energies unleashed by the temporary empowerment of female characters. Yet the fact that comic heroines ultimately become wives, assuming a traditionally subordinate female position, in no way erases or cancels out their prior depiction in the narrative. Rather, it is precisely the safe restoration of the empowered women of the reconciliation plays to the traditional gender system that allows comedy to get away with turning over more authority to these women than was culturally available to them. In other words, the conservatism of the marriage plot form allows comedy to contest prevailing gender categories in a way that seems not to be subversive. For despite the emphasis on containment built into its generic end—marriage—the means by which comic narratives sometimes achieve this end effectively installs the figure of the empowered woman in the cultural imaginary.

It is, of course, difficult to demonstrate how such instantiations might have achieved concrete effects in the social world, given the nature of our evidence. But anyone with doubts about the power of dramatic representations to reshape existing gender categories has only to recall Lycurgus's fifty-five-line citation of Euripides' *Erechtheus* in his speech against Leocrates (1.100; cf. Demades 1.37). Lycurgus recites the speech of Praxithea, wife of Erechtheus, who willingly sacrificed her virgin daughter to defend the city against invasion. According to Peter Wilson, with this citation (and others) Lycurgus is appropriating tragedy and its generic prestige to construct models for contemporary political behavior.[106] Yet if Lycurgus is using tragedy, tragedy is also using him. His appeal to Praxithea, a woman, as a paragon of civic virtue and a positive exemplar for

---

transvestism in Shakespeare's comedies provides a way for comic heroines to forge friendships with the men they love (paving the way for romantic and companionate marriages) in advance of the social conditions enabling women to form such friendships.

[105] The question of whether literary texts are mainly conservative or subversive is a central area of contention between cultural materialists and New Historicists. See Greenblatt 1988, 21–66, for Shakespearean drama as ultimately recontaining the radical doubts it promotes. For the cultural materialist position, see, e.g., Belsey 1985. For a critique of these "either-or" models as reductive, see Howard 1994.

[106] Wilson 1996, 310–31.

citizen men is unparalleled in extant Athenian oratory.[107] Thus, tragedy's depiction of a heroine endowed with superior civic loyalty and patriotism paved the way for a woman—albeit a fictional and noble one—to enter into democratic civic discourse as a political exemplar for citizen men.

Similarly, as I will argue in later chapters, comedy's empowerment of female characters in the service of civic ends effectively depicts women as standing in relation to the sociopolitical order "as what calls to be included within its terms, i.e., a set of *future* possibilities for inclusion, what Mouffe refers to as part of the not-yet-assimilable horizon of community."[108] Previous commentators have identified a utopian tendency in Menander's comedy, arguing that the creation of emancipatory possibilities is an immanent feature of literary and artistic practice.[109] *Reproducing Athens* will show, however, that there are specific historical factors animating comedy's contradictory propensities to reproduce and resist the civic status quo. I began this chapter by suggesting that Lycurgus's histrionic reference to Hyperides' "tragic" proposal to free the slaves and to enfranchise the metics and *atimoi* reveals important information about the constitutive role of internal status boundaries in the making of Athenian democratic identity. For Lycurgus, these internal boundaries—maintained through strict rules of sexual reproduction—were the sine qua non of Athenian identity. But Lycurgus is, of course, making this claim as part of an attempt to revise the Athenian defeat at Chaeronea to make it less devastating, less final. To that end, he makes Hyperides' proposal, which was passed but never implemented, the worst consequence of the defeat. While this was no doubt an effective rhetorical strategy, it may concede more than Lycurgus would have wished. His appeal to the necessary Athenianness of the citizen body is inscribed within a context that bears witness to the democratizing effects created by the rise of an external enemy larger and more powerful than the polis. That Hyperides' proposal was made at all testifies to the democratic and

[107] Lycurgus's emphasis on Euripides' wisdom and the nobility in his iambic lines (1.100)—rather than in the character of Praxithea—may reflect an attempt to diminish or disguise the emancipatory implications of his citation. It should be stressed that the liberatory significance of Praxithea's speech does not stem from the contents of what she says; after all, she defends a position that completely cedes female reproductive labor to the polis. Rather, what is important is that Lycurgus attributes civic virtue to a woman and appeals to a woman as an exemplar for men in the context of democratic discourse.

[108] Butler 1993, 193. For effective politicization as the generation of new political inclusions, see Laclau and Mouffe 1985; Mouffe 1992.

[109] Konstan states: "The comedy of Menander, like that of Aristophanes, betrays a tension between a universalizing or utopian impulse and the constraints of social practices, which surfaces symptomatically as lapses in the logic of the action or as the overdetermination of personal motives" (1995, 10; cf. 166–67). Wiles (1991) links the dual trajectories of comedy to the cosmopolitanism of the Hellenistic period.

inclusionary possibilities elicited by the international transformations taking place. The pressing external threat effectively, if temporarily, diminished the significance of internal status boundaries between citizens and noncitizens of all types.

To be sure, these changes were much more pronounced in Menander's time than in the previous Lycurgan generation. The existence of Macedonian military kingdoms had become a more or less ineradicable feature of the international landscape. So too the decline of the polis as an independent or viable military power had become a reality impossible to ignore. While these circumstances did not bring an end to Athenian democratic culture, they did create a new urgency to define and redefine civic identity in ways attentive to the polis's new conditions of possibility. The rise of large-scale autocratic military kingdoms at least partially reoriented the coordinates of civic identity: it suddenly became important to define and distinguish polis inhabitants from the Macedonian outsiders, and it became correspondingly less crucial to maintain rigid internal status distinctions between citizens and everyone else.

The constitutive coexistence of opposing impulses within Menander's comedy is a product of this transitional historical epoch.[110] The paradigmatic marriage plot performs the reproduction of the citizen body, and with it the status distinctions separating citizens from everyone else. At the same time, however, the formal and thematic conventions that bring about the performance of this paradigmatic narrative resist the reproduction of the civic status quo. The use of eros to forge unions across status barriers and the empowerment of displaced female citizens raise the possibility of alternative social arrangements, of doing away with the divisive and exclusionary internal status boundaries.[111] The dynamic tension between these competing reproductive and transformative trajectories attests to comedy's negotiation of the stresses and strains that the tumultuous Hellenistic period placed on traditional democratic cultural arrangements.

Although comic narratives simultaneously reify and rebel against the constraints of citizen status, the manner in which and extent to which they do so are conditioned by whether a specific play is more heavily national or transnational in its orientation and outlook. In nationalistic comedy (plays with a pronounced Attic or Athenian setting), the status-conserving impulse is stronger than in the transnational or transpolis plays.[112] Because the orientation is internal to the polis, internal status

[110] I borrow the phrase "constitutive coexistence" from Moglen 2001, 1.

[111] See Konstan 1995, 10; Wiles 1991, 30; A. Masaracchia 1981.

[112] Menander's extant plays and fragments with a nationalist emphasis include the *Aspis*, *Geōrgos*, *Dyskolos*, *Epitrepontes*, *Samia*, and *Sikyōnioi*. Although the presence in the *Aspis* and

divisions between citizens and slaves as well as gender divisions retain a strong constitutive importance in defining the privileged status group of male citizens. Yet even in the most nationalistic plays, an implicit critique of the arbitrariness of internal status and gender boundaries often accompanies the reproduction of civic norms. For instance, the plot devices that enable slaves and courtesans to act as surrogates for female citizens in the *Epitrepontes* and *Samia* expose the conventional and permeable boundary separating citizens and noncitizens.

By contrast, plays with a pronounced transnational coloring powerfully upset the conventional gender hierarchy.[113] Because these plays are more explicitly concerned with defining and reproducing polis culture against the Hellenistic kingdoms, gender difference assumes less importance as a constitutive axis of male civic identity within the polis community. In fact, in the *Perikeiromenē* and *Misoumenos* the traditional gender system is significantly undermined in the service of rebuilding polis culture against the Hellenistic "mercenary" kingdom. These plays temporarily release their heroines from the constraints of civic respectability so that they may assist in the mercenary's civic education. In so doing, the works call attention to the artificiality of existing gender asymmetries within the organization of polis culture.

In my reading of the plays, I attend to comedy's countervailing tendencies to reproduce democratic and civic culture against various Hellenistic threats and to subvert internal status boundaries between citizens and noncitizens and between men and women. This dual focus will enable us to consider comedy's work and meaning in its own historical epoch and to consider what comedy tells us about classical democratic culture. For by adapting the norms of citizen status to its own narrative patterns, comedy offers important evidence of the interconstitutive relationship

Sikyōnioi of mercenary characters lends these works a transnational orientation, in each play the nationalist perspective predominates. In the *Aspis*, Kleostratos becomes a mercenary specifically to obtain funds to give his sister a proper dowry for her marriage, and thus the play annexes Hellenistic mercenary service to the reproductive needs of the polis. Nevertheless, the moral of the story warns against such a creative adaptation, since mercenary service leads to Kleostratos's presumed death. In addition, that his sister inherits his mercenary booty threatens to undermine rather than to ensure her reproductive future, because it leads a greedy old man to manipulate the laws of the epiklerate in order to marry her for her newfound wealth rather than for purposes of procreation (see further chapter 3). Terence's *Self-Tormentor*, based on Menander's *Heauton Timoroumenos*, similarly blends the national and the transnational in the context of ruling out mercenary service as a legitimate activity for young citizens. Although a seeming foreign mercenary plays the romantic lead in the *Sikyōnioi*, that play, as I argue in chapter 7, is a quintessential specimen of democratic nationalist comedy.

[113] Transnational plays include Menander's *Perikeiromenē*, *Misoumenos*, and *Kolax* and Terence's *Eunuch*, based on a Menandrian original.

between the public and private in democratic Athens, the role of gender and sexual ideologies in sustaining the norms and ideology of democratic citizenship, and the immanent tensions and instabilities within the citizenship system. Comedy's very ability to deploy conventions involving displaced female identity, harms to female citizens, and role reversals between female citizens and courtesans of slave and foreign status tells us something about the logic and possibilities of classical democratic culture. By deploying courtesans as stand-ins for female citizens, comedy reveals the underdetermination of the citizenship system as well as its latent potential to include rather than exclude outsiders.

Before turning to the comedies, in the next chapter I consider the historical setting in which Menander's plays were performed. This will set the stage for interpreting comedy's cultural and political poetics in subsequent chapters. In addition, I clarify what I mean by the "reproduction" of democratic culture—for to elaborate the ways in which democratic culture was reproduced in the early Hellenistic era is not to claim that things went on exactly as before, as we will see. Rather, I chart the negotiation between received democratic practices and principles and changed historical circumstances that enabled the Athenians to assert the continuity of democratic culture in the midst of radical change.

2

Reproducing Democracy in Oligarchic and Autocratic Athens

The Reproducibility of Athenian Democracy

Although Athens suffered a major military blow at the battle of Chaeronea, the city did not passively accept the defeat or the consequent reality of Macedonian supremacy. Rather, in the years following the battle, the Athenians prepared to refight it. Under the leadership of Lycurgus, the Athenians fortified the city and navy; stockpiled weapons, armor, and gold on the acropolis; and perhaps most significantly, nationalized hoplite service. When news of Alexander the Great's death reached Athens, the Athenians instigated a general rebellion against Macedonian power in Greece. They authorized Leosthenes to hire an experienced mercenary force and sent ambassadors to the Greek cities to enlist support for their cause. They presented the revolt as a struggle for Greek freedom against the forces of barbarian despotism, likening the coming contest to the famed Persian Wars of the previous century.[1]

The war initially went well for the Greek forces, but Antipater eventually received reinforcements and defeated the Greek cities. The war that contemporary sources called "the Hellenic War" had come to a close. And, as if to reinforce the demise of the Greek forces and their perceived ethnic solidarity, the war has come to be known as the Lamian War.[2] Antipater's own policies also seem to have been geared to erode any lingering sense of "Hellenic" unity. He imposed peace terms on each city separately, leaving Athens for last. The Athenians nervously sent ambassadors—but to no avail. Antipater did not destroy the city that had masterminded the revolt and declared itself inimical to Macedonian rule, but his terms were severe enough to make the Athenians long for the days of

[1] For Athenian preparations for the Lamian War, see Diod. 18.9.4–5; [Plut.] *Vit. X Orat.* 841d; Plut. *Mor.* 852c; for the war as a campaign against the forces of barbarian despotism, see Diod. 18.10.3; Hyp. 6, passim. For some recent discussions of the Lamian War, see Gehrke 1976; Schmitt 1992; Lehmann 1988; Ashton 1984; Morrison 1987; Habicht 1997, 36–42.

[2] Ashton (1984) argues that the name "Lamian War" originates with the historian Hieronymus of Cardia, who chose not to offend the Macedonian authorities in the aftermath of the Chremonidean War by referring to the conflict as the "Hellenic War."

Philip and Alexander (Plut. *Phoc.* 29.1). Antipater could not afford to be generous in victory—as Philip and at times Alexander could—because in 322 the fate of the Macedonian Empire was far from secure.

Because Antipater's first objective was to solidify the unsteady Macedonian Empire, he imposed severe and subjugating conditions on the Athenians. Foremost among these was the demand that they reinstate the "ancestral constitution" (*patrios politeia*) in accordance with the "laws of Solon" (Plut. *Phoc.* 27.3; Diod. 18.18.5). Although the sources describe the constitutional change in the traditional rhetoric of Athenian conservatism, in all likelihood this language represents the Athenian translation of the Macedonian requirement, since it was Antipater's general policy to install oligarchies in the defeated Greek cities.[3] Athens was forced to limit the franchise to men possessing at least 2,000 drachmas. This requirement, disfranchising either 12,000 or 22,000 citizens, reduced the citizen body to the more easily controllable size of 9,000.[4]

The purpose of the disfranchisements was to weaken the polis and to undermine democratic resistance to Macedonian rule.[5] This is probably the reason why Antipater resettled many of those who lost their citizen status in remote Thrace and called for the deaths of leading democratic politicians, including Demosthenes and Hyperides.[6] By executing the former democratic leaders, Antipater also eliminated a key source of anti-Macedonian opposition in the city. Finally, and most egregiously according to Plutarch, Antipater installed a garrison of Macedonian troops in

[3] For the rhetoric of *patrios politeia* in the settlement of 322, see Gehrke 1976, 90–91; Wallace 1989, 207 n. 77. Antipater's installation of oligarchies in many of the Greek cities, not only in Athens, after the Lamian War seems to refute Hackl (1987), who argues that the elimination of Athenian democracy in 322 was the product of immanent instabilities within the democracy itself. For Antipater's policies after Alexander's death, see further Heckel 1992, 1999.

[4] Plut. *Phoc.* 28.4; Diod. 18.18.4–5. Hansen (1986) accepts Diodorus's figure of 22,000 disfranchised, while Sekunda (1992) argues that Plutarch's estimate of 12,000 must be correct. For an overview of the demographic question, see Sekunda 1992. According to Diodorus, the poor were removed from the citizen body because they were perceived to be warmongers accustomed to receiving their pay from military service for the state. It is doubtful, however, that pro- and anti-Macedonian sentiment within the polis was so neatly tied to economic divisions.

[5] According to a report in the *Suda*, Demades, acting on Antipater's orders, suspended the law courts and rhetorical contests as part of the Lamian War settlement in 322 (*Suda*, s.v. "Demades"). Gehrke (1976, 93 n. 38) states that whether or not Antipater issued an order to this effect, the courts would have been closed for all practical purposes, given the enormous number of citizens disfranchised by the imposition of a 2,000-drachma property qualification.

[6] According to Plutarch (*Dem.* 28.3), Antipater sent his soldiers under the command of Archias the "exile hunter" to execute Demosthenes, Himeraeus (brother of Demetrius of Phaleron), Aristonicus, and Hyperides.

the city to ensure Athenian compliance with Macedonian rule (Plut. *Phoc.* 28.1). Although Antipater's settlement disabled and undermined the leadership, institutions, and demographic basis of the democratic city, shortly after his death in 319 the Athenians were emboldened to restore the democracy, despite lacking the capability to defend it against the military power marshaled by the successors.[7]

The democratic restoration of 318 marks the beginning of a pattern of democratic restorations and suspensions that was to persist in Athens throughout the transition to the Hellenistic age, and throughout the more limited period of Menander's dramatic career. The Athenian constitution was changed in 322, 318, 317, 307, 301, 294, 287, and again in 260. Paradoxically, these constitutional alternations demonstrate not the instability of democratic culture but rather its steadfastness—its seemingly inevitable reproducibility. In the introduction, I argued that this resilience is owed in part to the interconstitutive relationship between sexual and political reproduction in democratic Athens; the Macedonians did nothing to interfere with the matrimonial and attendant cultural sources of democratic culture, so far as we know. Although it is impossible to determine whether and to what extent the marriage and gender system picked up in producing ideology after the political institutions were suspended, the emergence of comic narratives celebrating the democratic marriage system certainly contributed to the robustness of democratic and polis culture. This chapter examines the historical context—the Macedonian-backed assault on Athenian democracy and the emergence of the successor kingdoms—against which Menander's democratic family romances and the tenacity of democratic culture must be understood.

The first half of the chapter considers the regime of Demetrius of Phaleron, the Athenian who managed Athens on behalf of Antipater's son Cassander between 317 and 307. In general, Demetrius's oligarchic regime has been considered to be much less detrimental to democratic culture than both Antipater's oligarchy, which preceded it, and the Antigonid sponsorship, which followed it.[8] This is because the oligarchy was mild—the 1,000-drachma property qualification did not drastically deplete the citizen body as Antipater's 2,000-drachma requirement had—and because political institutions—the Assembly, Council, and the courts—continued to function throughout Demetrius's ten-year rule. Yet, contrary to what one might expect, the operation of political institutions served to impair rather than restore democratic practices and be-

[7] The Athenians were counting on receiving military support from the Macedonian Polyperchon, who issued an edict calling for a return to the pre–Lamian War status quo (Diod. 18.56). Unfortunately for the Athenians, Polyperchon proved to be an incredibly incompetent general.

[8] See, e.g., Tracy 1995, 2000.

liefs. Demetrius's reforms not only limited the scope and possibilities of political participation but also promoted principles antithetical to traditional democratic ideals.[9]

That the Athenians perceived Demetrius's regime as damaging is well attested by the events of 307, when their hostility forced him to flee the city in fear for his life. After fifteen or so years of authoritarian rule, the Athenians were ready to negotiate for a better deal. The Antigonids (Antigonus Monophthalmos and his son Demetrius Poliorcetes) encouraged this negotiation by announcing themselves to be the champions of Greek freedom, effectively assuming an identity in keeping with Athens's hereditary role in Greece. In the second half of the chapter I discuss the various ups and downs of Athens's relationship with the second Demetrius, considering the precarious and ultimately impossible coexistence of democracy within the wider context of external autocracy between 307 and 302 and briefly sketching the period of tyranny and oligarchy that ensued. I argue that comedy played a crucial role in making Athens's dependency on foreign autocrats like Demetrius less offensive to civic and democratic sensibilities. By recasting autocrats like Demetrius as braggart soldiers and romantic rivals, comedy translates the international conflict between polis and kingdom into a romantic contest—that is, into a contest the polis can win. With recurring stories of the braggart soldier's romantic defeat and ridicule, comedy offered the Greek cities allegorically coded tales commenting on the barrenness of the emergent Hellenistic kingdoms.

The Policies and Politics of Demetrius of Phaleron: Law, Power, and Prior Restraint

Just a few months after restoring the democracy in 318, Athens was forced to come to terms with Cassander, Antipater's son. Like his father, he employed occupation troops and an oligarchic constitution to ensure Athenian compliance with his "alliance." According to Diodorus, however, he promised that the troops were a temporary measure to be removed as soon as he ended the war against Polyperchon, his rival for the Macedonian throne, whom Antipater had made guardian (*epimelētēs*) of the two kings (Philip's son Arrhidaeus and Alexander's young son). In

[9] It has often been argued that Demetrius's political reforms were driven by his philosophical commitments (J. Williams 1987, contra Gehrke 1978). While it seems clear that Demetrius was well acquainted with Aristotle's political philosophy, it is impossible to determine whether philosophical concerns did indeed drive his politics. My interest is in the practical effects of Demetrius's policies rather than in his personal motivations for implementing them.

addition, although Cassander insisted that the Athenians adopt an oligarchic constitution, he allowed the new government to employ a relatively low wealth requirement for citizenship.[10] While Cassander seems to have been more lenient in his treatment of Athens, he was no less anxious than his father to keep the city firmly under his control. If anything, his own need in this regard was far more urgent than Antipater's had been because he lacked an official position and could therefore be regarded as an illegitimate usurper by Macedonians and Greeks alike.[11] The seizure of Athens was Cassander's first step in winning Greece and Macedon away from Polyperchon—the general to whom his father had bequeathed the regency.

Because it was of such crucial importance for his own project to secure and maintain his hold on Athens, Cassander appointed his personal friend, the Athenian citizen Demetrius of Phaleron, to oversee the domestic affairs of the city.[12] For the next ten years, Demetrius ruled Athens as a virtual regent, probably under the title of *epimelētēs*.[13] During this time, Demetrius made numerous changes in Athenian legal, political, and administrative culture. Although in his own writings he claimed to have corrected the democracy, later writers labeled him a monarch or tyrant.[14] In what follows, I review the evidence for Demetrius's reforms, considering in particular what effects they had on traditional democratic practice and ideals.[15]

The reform that had the most direct impact on the production of comedy and that emblematizes the way in which Demetrius wielded power in

[10] For Cassander's settlement with Athens, see Diod. 18.74.1–3; cf. Plut. *Phoc.* 31.1–2, 33.2. The number of citizens disfranchised by the 1,000-drachma requirement is unknown. According to Ktesikles' *Chronicles*, Demetrius of Phaleron conducted a census and counted 21,000 Athenians (Athen. 272c = 51 F.-S. = Wehrli 31 F = *FGrH* 245 F 1; on the census, see Hansen 1986, 29–36; Sekunda 1992, 320). If there were only 22,000 citizens at the beginning of the Lamian War, as some scholars (e.g., Sekunda 1992) contend, then the property qualification had only a small impact on the size of the citizen body. Shipley (2000, 128), however, suggests that about 5,000 citizens were disfranchised under Demetrius's regime; see also Habicht 1997, 58.

[11] For the struggle between Cassander and Polyperchon, see Heckel 1992, 193–204.

[12] Demetrius may have been elected to his position (see Diod. 18.74.3), but he was certainly preselected or approved by Cassander (Lehmann 1997, 62–63 with n. 75).

[13] Diodorus is the only ancient source to report the title *epimelētēs* (18.74.3; ἐπιμελητὴν τῆς πόλεως). Tracy (1995, 43–45) provides a review of the controversy regarding Demetrius's official title.

[14] For Demetrius as a monarch, see Plut. *Demetr.* 10.2–3; as a tyrant, see Paus. 1.25.6. For Demetrius's claim to have corrected the democracy, see Strabo 9.1.20.

[15] There is a vast bibliography on Demetrius of Phaleron's regime. I have consulted Ferguson (1911a, 38–94), Bayer (1969), Mossé (1992a), Gehrke (1978), Wood and Wood (1978, 249–52), J. Williams (1987, 1997), Green (1990, 36–51), Tracy (1995, 36–51), Habicht (1997, 53–66), Lehmann (1997, 62–85), and the essays in Fortenbaugh and Schütrumpf (2000).

the city is his creation or transformation of the *agōnothesia*.[16] Under the democracy, every comedy and tragedy was sponsored by a wealthy citizen assigned to perform the choregic liturgy.[17] At dramatic contests, these citizen sponsors competed against each other to win honor and prestige by putting on the best or most lavish production. By assigning wealthy citizens the task of financing dramatic performances, the democracy harnessed elite resources and agonistic instincts for the public good, at least according to the conventional story. Instead of allowing several citizens to finance dramatic productions, Demetrius employed a single elected contest official (the *agōnothetēs*), who, with a combination of public and private funds, had the task of producing all of the choruses.[18] Modern opinion is divided as to the significance of this reform: it has been viewed both as a "democratization of festivals" and as an extension of the fourth-century choregic liturgy allowing for the further cultivation of elite prestige and democratic dependence.[19]

What needs to be emphasized, however, is that the interpretations referred to above are based on an inscription commemorating Xenocles, the *agōnothetēs* of 306 (IG II^2 3073). In other words, commentators have based their claims about the operation and politics of the *agōnothesia* under Demetrius's oligarchic regime on evidence from the restored democracy.[20] Like most aspects of Demetrius's regime, the *agōnothesia* is strikingly unattested by epigraphic evidence.[21] The fact that publication on stone—a hallmark of democratic policy—falls off almost completely under Demetrius's regime is in itself compelling evidence for the antidemocratic nature of his rule.[22] While only two Assembly decrees dating from Demetrius's regime survive, more than one hundred decrees from

[16] Pickard-Cambridge 1988, 91.

[17] For the choregic system, see Pickard-Cambridge 1988, 86–93; Csapo and Slater 1994, 139–57; Wilson 1997, 2000. For the democratic and civic context of Athenian dramatic festivals, see Goldhill 1990, 2000.

[18] According to Wilson (2000, 271), the most profound change in the shift from *khorēgia* to *agōnothesia* was that competition between *khorēgoi* was removed.

[19] On the *agōnothesia* as democratic, see Mikalson 1998, 55; as elite patronage, see Parker 1996, 268; Wilson 2000, 273–74.

[20] This measure—apparently in contrast to the majority of Demetrius's innovations—was preserved by the democracy in 307.

[21] There are only two extant Assembly decrees from the period between 317 and 307, IG II^2 450 and IG II^2 453. For the lack of preserved inscriptions dating from Demetrius's regime, see Tracy 1995, 39, and 2000, 338; Hedrick 2000.

[22] Although Tracy may be correct in suggesting that Demetrius curtailed inscribing for financial reasons (2000, 338 n. 32), the measure seems to have been viewed as antidemocratic, judging by the flurry of inscribing undertaken by the restored democracy immediately after Demetrius's expulsion. Hedrick (2000, 333) suggests that the democracy's concern to publicize official information may have been a reaction to the repressive policies of Demetrius of Phaleron.

the period between 307 and 301 have been recovered.[23] It is in this context of epigraphic and democratic fervor that Xenocles' monument belongs. Consequently, this inscription tells us more about democratic sensibilities after Demetrius's expulsion than about how the *agōnothesia* operated or was intended to operate during his oligarchic regime.

One of the striking features of this inscription is Xenocles' claim that the "demos was *khorēgos*" (ὁ δῆμος ἐχορήγιε, meaning that the demos financed the festival). What ideological significance should be attached to this break with the liturgical tradition according to which the liturgist claimed credit in his own name for dramatic sponsorship? Although Jon Mikalson sees this shift as signaling a democratization of festivals, irrespective of what Demetrius of Phaleron intended, Peter Wilson is more skeptical. He comments on the inscription,

> The demos now takes the first place epigraphically (as the subject of the verb ἐχορήγει), . . . in the honorific position once occupied by the *khoregos*. Yet even if the demos now holds pride of place, there is a decided formalism about its role as "*khoregos*." The demos may now be the provider of basic funds for the *agones*, but unlike its classical predecessors, it is not a victor; the lustre of agonistic victory cannot belong to the demos as such.[24]

While it may be true that the demos as a collective could not assume the prestige of agonistic victory formerly awarded to elite citizen liturgists, this does not necessarily reduce Xenocles' attribution of festival sponsorship to the demos to a formalistic piety. In the Hellenistic city, democratic ideology was produced and sustained by Athenian opposition to Macedonian power, as well as in the context of mass–elite negotiations.[25] By the very act of declaring that the demos was *khorēgos* after a period of Macedonian oligarchic rule, Xenocles' monument asserts the legitimacy and primacy of the democratic government.

Although Demetrius may have condemned the choregic liturgy as a debilitating waste for elite families, if we view the *agōnothesia* solely as a financial or economic reform we may well miss an important aspect of its

[23] Habicht states: "Of the surviving decrees from this period, no less than twenty-six stem from him [Stratocles] (only two of them after 301), and these must represent only a small part of the actual total. Evidence of such intense activity by the ekklesia exists for no earlier or later period" (1997, 71).

[24] Wilson 2000, 273. Cf. Mikalson 2000, 273.

[25] This, of course, raises the large question of how "democratic" ideology changed in response to the international environment. For present purposes, let it suffice to say that with Habicht (1997), I do see democracy in the early Hellenistic city as a meaningful political ideology rather than as (only) a patriotic or anti-Macedonian slogan; cf. Gabbert 1986.

intended or effective purpose.[26] During the free democracy, the *khorēgia* did more than serve as a vehicle of elite self-promotion: it could also provide an opportunity for conveying the political ideas and goals of the *khorēgos* himself. In some cases from the fifth century it is possible to detect a connection between the political commitments of the *khorēgos* and the content of the play he sponsored.[27] By centralizing dramatic sponsorship in a single state official, the *agōnothesia* gave the state—which for all practical purposes meant Demetrius—sole, if tacit, control over the content of all dramatic productions. This is not to say that Demetrius actually censored plays on a case-by-case basis, as the tyrant Lachares may have done at the Dionysia in 300.[28] The very knowledge that a single state official financed all the tragedies and comedies would in itself have had a chilling or implicit censoring effect on playwrights who knew in advance that their works would have to meet with the approval of one of Demetrius's officials.[29] The idea that the *agōnothesia* operated as a vehicle of implicit censorship during Demetrius's rule is consistent with his general policies of censoring political and social behavior. Although Demetrius neither removed nor evacuated political institutions, he regulated or corrected them, as he later put it, by changing the prior rules that defined what counted as legitimate political practice.

One of the first things Demetrius did upon entering office was to give new laws to the Athenians.[30] Apart from certain restrictions on burial practices, however, there is little surviving evidence regarding the con-

[26] According to Plutarch, Demetrius described the choregic tripod as a "final libation for dissipated fortunes, and the cenotaph of extinct households" (Plut. *Mor.* 349a = 136 Wehrli). Gehrke (1978, 173), however, argues that Demetrius's elimination of the *khorēgia* should be seen as an attempt to inhibit a key source of elite display and prestige, and thus to curtail alternative sources of power in the polis.

[27] Pickard-Cambridge 1988, 90.

[28] According to a summary of Menander's plays, the tyrant Lachares prevented the performance of his *Imbrians* at the Dionysia (52 test. K.-A.).

[29] Menander's own activity and success during this period may account for the suspicion that he fell under in the aftermath of Demetrius's expulsion (see Philoch. *FGrH* 328 F 66). According to Diogenes Laertius, Menander was almost brought to trial, simply because he had been a friend of Demetrius (5.79). He escaped prosecution through the intervention of Telesphorus. On the possible identity of Telesphorus as a relative of Demetrius of Phaleron, see Potter 1987. For the many impeachments following Demetrius's expulsion, see Philoch. *FGrH* 328 F 66.

[30] IG II^2 1201 lines 12–13 seems to praise Demetrius for giving good laws to the Athenians (see F.-S. 16b). According to the Parian Marble, Demetrius gave laws to the Athenians in the archonship of Demogenes, or in 317/6 (F.-S. 20a = Wehrli F 15). Syncellus calls Demetrius the third lawgiver of the Athenians (20b F.-S. = Wehrli F 17). The evidence associating Demetrius with the passage of new laws is collected and discussed in Gagarin 2000, 348–54; cf. Dow and Travis 1943.

tent of these laws. Accordingly, it has recently been argued that Demetrius did not, in fact, overhaul the entire legal system as W. S. Ferguson maintained in several studies.[31] Though we cannot gauge whether Demetrius deserves to be known as the "third lawgiver" of the Athenians, after Draco and Solon, there is evidence that he implemented significant changes in legal practice and law enforcement that were not only strongly at variance with previous democratic practice but also worked to instill fundamentally antidemocratic beliefs and practices.

During his tenure as *epimelētēs*, Demetrius created (or re-created) two magisterial boards, the *nomophylakes* (guardians of the laws) and the *gynaikonomoi* (the supervisors of women). Taken together, these institutions had broad and unprecedented policing powers, enabling them to intervene in aspects of life not traditionally subject to legislative restraint under the democracy. According to Philochorus, the *nomophylakes* "compelled the magistrates to obey the laws, and they sat in the Assembly and Council with the *proedroi*, preventing the enactment of things that were illegal or inexpedient for the city" (*FGrH* 328 F 64B.a).[32] The report in the *Suda* adds that the *nomophylakes* also prevented the enactment of decrees that seemed illegal to them (*FGrH* 328 F 64B.b).

Most commentators take these reports to mean that the institution of the *nomophylakes* replaced the procedure of the *graphē paranomon*, or at any rate rendered it effectively obsolete.[33] Under the classical democracy, the *graphē paranomon* entitled any citizen to object to a speaker's proposal on the grounds that it was against existing laws or in some way contravened democratic principle. The *nomophylakes* therefore eliminated a principal source of the citizen's political power. By employing a body of expert (or at least officially designated) legal interpreters, Demetrius undermined the participatory and egalitarian principles of democratic politics.[34] At the same time, the operation of the *nomophylakes* articulated a new and fundamentally antidemocratic separation between the government and the citizens. Whereas under the democracy entire juries were

[31] Gagarin 2000, 351 with n. 11; cf. Ferguson 1911a, 412–47; 1911b.

[32] Although Philochorus attributes the creation of this magistracy to Ephialtes (*FGrH* 328 F 64B.a), there is no certain evidence for its existence until Demetrius's regime. Gehrke (1978, 188–91) and J. Williams (1987, 1997) argue that Demetrius first instituted the *nomophylakes* in Athens. Wallace (1989), however, links the institution to Antipater's oligarchic regime; see also O'Sullivan 2001.

[33] Ferguson 1911a, 44; Hansen 1991, 211.

[34] According to one report, the name of the Eleven (the magistrates who supervised the prison, carried out sentences in public cases, and had the power to carry out summary executions for certain offenses) was changed to *nomophylakes* under Demetrius's regime (Pollux 8.102 = Wehrli F 32 = 52 F.-S.). Whether or not the *nomophylakes* actually took over the duties of the Eleven, the tradition that they did so may attest to their broad police powers.

conceived as the guardians of the laws, under Demetrius's regime this vital role was restricted to a small policing body.[35]

In addition to being able to censor political speech, the *nomophylakes* may also have controlled the agenda in political institutions, thus imposing prior restraints on political speech.[36] This capacity is hinted at visually: the *nomophylakes* sat with the *proedroi*, the group of citizens who set the agenda for political deliberation in the Assembly. The seating arrangement suggests, but by no means proves, that the *nomophylakes* also absorbed the capacity of the *proedroi* to preapprove the topics for political discussion, thereby ensuring that no subject either at variance with Demetrius's laws or subversive to his regime could be considered. This interpretation is supported by Aristotle's recommendation that oligarchic regimes employ *nomophylakes* to maintain the appearance of popular participation while in reality foreclosing the very possibility of subversive political discussion:

> In oligarchies it is advantageous either to elect additionally certain persons from the multitude [to serve as officials], or to establish an official board of the sort that exists in some regimes, made up of those they call "preliminary councilors" or "law guardians," (*nomophylakes*) and [to have a popular Assembly that will] take up only that business which is considered in the preliminary council; for in this way the people will share in deliberating but will not be able to overturn anything connected to the regime. (*Pol.* 1298b26–31)[37]

During Demetrius's regime political institutions associated with the democracy continued to function, though no longer staffed according to the democratic principle that deemed a man's economic status politically irrelevant. But this institutional continuity operated to erode rather than engender democratic practice and habits of thought, because the rules of political engagement had been fundamentally transformed.[38] That Demetrius increased the size of juries in impeachment (*eisangelia*) cases has sometimes been seen as evidence for the democratic character of his regime.[39] Yet the impeachment procedure was primarily used to prosecute treason and subversive activity, suggesting instead that institutional proprieties were doing no more than protecting Demetrius's power and po-

[35] For democratic juries as guardians of the laws, see, e.g., Aes. 3.7.

[36] According to Dahl (1989, 112–14), control of the agenda is necessary for authentic democratic deliberation.

[37] Trans. Lord 1984. Elsewhere (*Pol.* 1323a7–10) Aristotle distinguishes the *probouloi* and *nomophylakes* on the grounds that the former institution is a feature of oligarchic regimes, the latter of aristocratic polities.

[38] Contra Tracy 1995, 2000.

[39] Tracy 2000, 339. Demetrius reportedly increased the number of jurors in impeachment cases from 1,000 to 1,500; see Pollux 8.53 = 96a F.-S.; see also *Lex. Rhet. Cant.*, s.v. *eisangelia* = 96b F.-S.

sition. Similarly, by preventing the enactment of illegal measures, the *nomophylakes* safeguarded the specific laws and policies that he, Demetrius, deemed legitimate while fostering an antiparticipatory political practice by separating officials and citizens.

The prior restraints Demetrius imposed on political speech and participation seem to have been complemented by analogous legal constraints on behavior in the private sphere. Demetrius employed a board of *gynaikonomoi*, magistrates empowered to superintend the behavior of women and their morals, or so the name of the magistracy suggests.[40] As the institution is attested in the ancient sources, however, it appears that *gynaikonomoi* had a variety of functions with no necessary competency or moral orientation. For instance, in the *Politics*, Aristotle asserts that the *gynaikonomos* is a magistrate specifically appropriate to aristocratic rather than democratic regimes—a claim premised on the assumption that the *gynaikonomos* had as his primary duty controlling women. According to Aristotle, the institution could not be implemented in a democracy because there was no way to prevent the wives of poor men from going outside to work (*Pol.* 1300a4–7).[41] In practice, however, the institution did not have so limited a purview. In Syracuse, the *gynaikonomoi* regulated the dress of women in all public contexts and restricted the nocturnal movements of men as well as women (Phylarchus *FGrH* 81 F45 = Athen. 521b–e). In the majority of cases (in cities other than Athens and Syracuse), the most frequently attested spheres of activity for *gynaikonomoi* are funerary and festive. For instance, in Gambreion, the *gynaikonomos* was chosen by the people to supervise the purifications performed before the Thesmophoria and to pray for the celebrants abiding by the law.[42]

In every case attested, the *gynaikonomoi* regulate appearances and maintain order in the *public* sphere, often but not exclusively in ritual contexts. Aristotle supports this evidence insofar as he assumes that the *gynaikonomos*' duty is to keep women inside the home—in other words, out of the public sphere. But in Demetrius's Athens, the *gynaikonomoi* had different or at least additional duties. In fact, we never hear anything about the *gynaikonomoi* monitoring public appearances or policing ritual

[40] That Demetrius is known to have implemented the magistracy has sometimes been considered evidence for philosophical influence on his policies (J. Williams 1997, 337; 1987, with references cited; see also Mossé 1992 for philosophical influence on Demetrius's other reforms). But Gehrke (1978) convincingly argues that there is no evidence linking Demetrius's institution of the *gynaikonomoi* to any specific philosophical agenda.

[41] Aristotle's remark indicates that women had more freedom of movement under the democracy than the official ideology allowed or acknowledged. See further Ober 2000; Schaps 1998; and on women's freedom and work, M. H. Jameson 1997; Brock 1994.

[42] Sokolowski 1955, #16 lines 17–25. For the *gynaikonomos*'s duties in other cities, see, e.g., Plut. *Solon* 21; Pouilloux 1954–58, 1: #141; Ogden 1996, 367–69.

correctness. Under Demetrius's regime, they seem to have been primarily concerned with what went on within the house rather than outside it, and with the behavior of men rather than of women.[43] At any rate, these are the only competencies or habits attributed to the *gynaikonomoi* in Athens.[44] In the seventh book of his *Atthis*, Philochorus lists their duties: "The *gynaikonomoi*, in cooperation with the Areopagites, used to watch meetings in private homes—during both wedding parties and other sacrificial occasions" (*FGrH* 328 F65 = Athen. 245c).

Philochorus's report that the *gynaikonomoi* monitored private citizens in the context of weddings and sacrificial occasions is corroborated by evidence from comedy. A speaker in a fragment from Menander's *Kekruphalos* refers to a specific law that the *gynaikonomoi* enforced regarding the number of guests at weddings:

> Learning at the office of the *gynaikonomoi*
> that a list had been drawn up, of all the cooks
> who cater weddings, in accordance with a certain new law (*nomon kainon tina*),
> in order to determine whether anyone happens to be entertaining more
> guests than the law permits, he went . . .
>
> (208 K.-A.)

In this work, Menander is acknowledging Macedonian power in Athens, if only in the form of Demetrius's new law and institutional reform. Unfortunately, it is impossible to determine the dramatic force of the reference or the date of the play in which it occurred. In Timocles' *Philodikastēs*, however, the speaker is openly critical of the *gynaikonomos* and the new law:

> Open the front door at once, so that we may be
> more conspicuous in the light in case the *gynaikonomos*, as he strolls by,
> wants to count the number of guests,
> as he is accustomed to do in accordance with new law (*ton nomon ton kainon*).
> He ought to do just the opposite
> and scrutinize the houses of the dinnerless.
>
> (K.-A. 34 = Athen. 245a)[45]

[43] Some commentators have argued that the institution of the *gynaikonomoi* was implemented already in Lycurgan Athens (Garland 1981, 1–54). The argument is based on a report that Lycurgus passed "democratic" sumptuary legislation ([Plut.] *Vit. X Orat.* 842a–b). The only Lycurgan sumptuary law we actually know of forbade women to travel to Eleusis in carriages. If *gynaikonomoi* were employed to enforce this law, they would have been regulating the public sphere, rather than private homes as under Demetrius's regime.

[44] On the basis of a votive depicting a dinner party dedicated by the *gynaikonomos* in Thasos, Pouilloux suggests that the *gynaikonomoi* there monitored general sacrificial occasions in a private context (1954–58: 1:366 n. 4, 408). There is no evidence (aside from the votive) to support this claim.

[45] The exact dates of Timocles' career are uncertain. According to Dover, "the latest

Athenaeus, who preserves these passages about the *gynaikonomoi* in Athens, reports that they also scrutinized guests at symposia, citing Lynceus of Samos's report that the legal limit was thirty participants (245a). Taken together, the evidence indicates that under Demetrius the *gynaikonomoi* habitually monitored the private sphere, diligently keeping tabs on the number of guests at all private communal gatherings. But the comic evidence points to this duty being regarded as somewhat absurd or at any rate pointless. This may, of course, be the reason why comedy could refer to the *gynaikonomoi* with apparent impunity. By satirizing the *gynaikonomoi* for spying on citizens guilty of nothing more than trying to attend a good dinner party, comedy suggests that there was no need for the institution, that Athenian citizens were too busy entertaining themselves to be plotting against the state.

Whether comedy's parodic references to Demetrius's new law and the *gynaikonomoi* were meant to be subversive or were simply intended to allay his fears of subversion, the evidence is strong that Demetrius was at the very least anxious about the security of his regime. In every other city where the magistracy is attested, its officials monitor the public rather than the private sphere and focus on the activities of women rather than solely on those of men. Exceptionally in Athens, the *gynaikonomoi* monitored private activity and sought to inhibit civic solidarity (and therefore potential resistance) by limiting and regulating collective activities. Plutarch's report that in 307 Demetrius was more afraid of his fellow citizens than Demetrius Poliorcetes seems to indicate that his fears were well founded (*Demetr*. 9.3).

Athens and the Antigonids: The Failed Foundation of Hellenistic Democracy

According to tradition, the Athenians erected 300 or more statues of Demetrius of Phaleron during his ten-year rule. When they were liberated, they are said to have melted down these statues.[46] While it is impossible to determine the veracity of these reports, their very existence speaks to the deep animosity his regime provoked. Athenians were angry not only because he passed insidiously antidemocratic reforms but also, and perhaps more significantly, because he betrayed Athenian identity

datable reference (fr. 34.3) in [Timocles'] work is mention of the *gynaikonomoi* . . . instituted (317–307 B.C.) by Demetrius of Phaleron" (1996, 1528).

[46] For Demetrius's statues, see 24a F.-S. = Wehrli F 21; 24b, 24c F.-S. = Wehri F 23; 25a F.-S. = Wehrli F 22; 25b F.-S. = Wehrli F 53, F 54.

and heritage.[47] For instance, Demochares bitterly attacked Demetrius for priding himself on contemptible economic measures while forfeiting the honor and glory of Greece to the commands of Cassander.[48] Similarly, Duris of Samos condemned Demetrius for—inter alia—using the vast state surplus to finance his insatiable lusts rather than to pay troops to defend the city:

> Demetrius of Phaleron, when he had gained control over an income of twelve hundred talents a year, spent only a little out of this income on the army and the administration of the city; the remainder he completely squandered through his innate lack of self control: every day he organized splendid parties with a great number of guests; in the costs of the dinners he surpassed the Macedonians; in their refinement (he surpassed) the Cyprians and Phoenicians. Showers of perfume fell on the ground and many of the floors in the men's quarters were decorated with flowers, arranged in colorful patterns by craftsmen.
>
> There were also secret meetings with women and nocturnal love affairs with young men. And thus Demetrius who was laying down laws (*thesmoi*) for other people and regulating their lives, organized his own life with utter freedom from law.
>
> His personal appearance was also a matter of concern to him: he dyed the hair on his head blond, and touched his face with rouge, and rubbed himself with other anointing-oils. For he wanted to make a cheerful and pleasing impression by his outward appearance on all who met him[.] (Athen. 542c–d)[49]

Duris's critique is generally regarded as a bit of histrionic editorializing, in keeping with the conventions of Hellenistic historiography and the trope of characterizing the tyrant as ruled by insatiable appetites, rather than as a historically accurate assessment of Demetrius or his rule.[50] Nevertheless, the correlations Duris draws between Demetrius's person and his policies hint at why the Athenians found his regime so oppressive. For instance, the claim that Demetrius dared to pass laws (*thesmoi*) regulating the private conduct of others while living his own life with

[47] There is also a tradition denying that Demetrius was a genuine citizen himself. According to Aelian, Demetrius was born of a slave in the house of Timotheus and Conon (4 F.-S. = Wehrli F 2b). For this topos, see chapter 1, note 22.

[48] See Plb. 12.13.8–11 = *FGrH* 75 F 4, 89 F.-S.; Marasco 1984, 181–90. For Demochares' critique of Athenian flattery of Demetrius Poliorcetes, see *FGrH* 75 F 1, 2 = Athen. 252f–253d.

[49] Trans. F.-S. 43a = Wehrli F 34 *FGrH* 76 F 10; for the tradition that Demetrius allowed himself to be called Lampito, a woman's name, see Athen. 593f = Wehrli F 37; D.L. 5.76 = Wehrli F 38.

[50] For the anti-Macedonian bias in Duris's work, see Kebric 1977, 25–28; for Duris and the conventions of Hellenistic historiography, see Kebric 1977, passim. For the traditional depiction of the tyrant as driven by appetitive needs, see McGlew 1993.

utter freedom from law (*anomothetēton*) seems to refer to the restrictions that the *gynaikonomoi* placed on personal freedom. More significant may be Duris's rendering of Demetrius's personal effeminacy as both the emblem and cause of his de-masculinizing nonmilitary policies. Whether or not we believe that Demetrius wore makeup and colored his hair and incessantly arranged sexual assignations, his perceived failure to effectively militarize the state seems to be at the heart of critiques of his rule.[51]

Although the restored democracy passed a plethora of decrees in honor of their liberators in 307, they also passed one decree in honor of a native hero, Lycurgus, the leading democratic statesmen between Chaeronea and the Lamian War. The timing and content of the decree suggest an attempt both to reverse or erase Demetrius's subjugating policies by contrasting them with those of the last leader of the free democracy and to resurrect the military manhood of the citizenry.[52] The decree was exceptional in two respects: it was the first time a grant of *sitēsis* was ever passed posthumously and it was the first time the honor was awarded for services not pertaining to bravery in war.[53] The narrative begins with a commendation of Lycurgus's lineage, specifically the democratic loyalty he inherited from his ancestors, men who themselves were privileged to have received public burials for their military efforts on behalf of the city ([Plut.] *Vit. X Orat.* 852a). The emphasis on Lycurgus's inherited goodwill or love (*eunoia*) for the democracy seems to be an implicit dig at Demetrius of Phaleron—a citizen who, despite the conspicuous use of his "democratic" deme name, was notable chiefly for his disloyalty to democratic tradition. In a second dig Lycurgus, far from collaborating with Macedonian rulers, is described as so aggressive in militarizing the polis that Alexander demanded that the Athenians surrender him to Macedonian authorities; the Athenians, however, refused (852c–d). Finally,

[51] Tracy states that "it is to his [Demetrius's] credit that he appears to have reinstated, no doubt in the face of strong Macedonian intransigence, a year-long course of military training for the youth of Athens" (1995, 47). This alleged reinstatement, however, is based on an argument from silence; there is no certain evidence indicating whether the *ephebeia* was in operation during Demetrius's regime (Tracy 1995, 40 n. 24).

[52] The decree is preserved in [Plut.] *Vit. X Orat.* 851f–852e and from an inscription, IG II 2 457. M. J. Osborne (1981) has identified IG II^2 513 as another copy of the decree. See also Habicht 1997, 68; Kralli 2000; Hedrick 2000. For Lycurgus's programs of civic and cultural renewal, see Mitchel 1970; Mossé 1982; Humphreys 1985a; Bosworth 1988, 204–15; Faraguna 1992; Habicht 1997, 22–30. On relations between Athens and Alexander during this period, see Heisserer 1980; Will 1983; Schwenk 1985. On the nationalization of hoplite service after Chaeronea, see Sekunda 1992.

[53] According to Gauthier (1985: 107–8), the decree for Lycurgus attests a shift in the conception of *sitēsis* as an award for a military feat or act of bravery to a more general award for civic duty. He describes the new conception as a shift from honors for *erga* to honors for *logoi*. See also M. J. Osborne 1982, 162 and n. 28.

the contrast with Demetrius is also pointed in the characterization of Lycurgus as an important lawgiver (852b). While the restored democracy did away with Demetrius's laws and reforms, they moved that all of Lycurgus's decrees should be valid and republished on the acropolis (852e). The total effect of the decree, according to one modern commentator, was to transform Lycurgus into "a symbol of Athenian democracy and national aspirations."[54]

Athens could not defend itself against the military power of the Hellenistic kingdoms, but maintaining domestic autonomy, which for all practical purposes meant democratic government and some semblance of military power, was of vital importance to the Athenian self-image. The overall effect of Demetrius of Phaleron's regime, I suggest, was to allow the Athenians to come to terms with the fact that they could neither defend nor feed themselves without accepting some support from the Hellenistic rulers. In other words, the intractable authoritarian policies of Antipater and Cassander gave birth to a new spirit of negotiation and compromise.[55] In 315 Antigonus took advantage of the great hostility generated by Cassander's authoritarian policies among the Greeks. He denounced Cassander before a Macedonian army assembly for his crimes against Macedon and, in a seeming non sequitur, declared that all the Greeks should be free, without garrisons, and autonomous (Diod. 19.61.3). Despite nominally reconciling with Cassander in 311, Antigonus adhered to his policy of freeing the Greeks, eventually sending his son Demetrius to undermine Cassander's control in central Greece and the Peloponnese.[56] While his sincerity and the motives underlying this policy have been questioned, Antigonus and Demetrius did live up to their word, at least initially.[57] By freeing the Greeks, and Athens in particular, Antigonus sought to win allies and support by engendering *eunoia* (goodwill), which, according to one report, he regarded as a more secure source of rule than force and slavery (Plut. *Demetr.* 8.2).[58]

[54] Habicht 1997, 68.

[55] On Antipater's policy of ruling the Greek cities by installing garrisons and oligarchies, see Diod. 18.18. 8, 55.2, 57.1, 69.3, with Heckel 1999.

[56] On the peace of 311, see *RC* 1, Antigonus's letter to Skepsis; Diod. 19.105.1.

[57] For discussions of Antigonus's policy toward the Greek cities, see Simpson 1959; Billows 1990, 189–236, and 1995. Burstein (1980) argues that Antigonus's decree forms the immediate backdrop of Menander's play the *Halieis* and the sympathy for the exiles it contains.

[58] Billows argues that Antigonus's policy of freedom for the Greek cities paved the way for the development of a new relationship between the cities and the kings based on reciprocity; he sees Antigonus's policy as enabling the Greek cities "to exploit the manipulative element in their traditional system of honors and euergetism with the Hellenistic kings" (1995, 73). By contrast, in a study of the Greek cities in Asia Minor, Ma (1999, 179–219) argues that euergetism was exploited by rulers and cities alike to legitimate and restrict the

Whatever Antigonus's true feelings about Greek freedom may have been, he seems to have regarded an alliance with Athens as crucial to justifying his own imperial aims. According to Plutarch, Antigonus considered Athens "the beacon tower of the inhabited world which would speedily flash the glory of their [Antigonus's and Demetrius's] deeds to all mankind" (*Demetr*. 8.2).[59] But by using Athenian ideals to legitimize their position in Greece, Antigonus and Demetrius were, intentionally or not, declaring themselves to be the inheritors of Athens's traditional role as guardians of Greek freedom.[60] In so doing, they invited the Athenians to receive them on their—that is, Athenian—terms. This seems to be precisely what happened. The honors the Athenians voted for their liberators in 307 resemble nothing so much as an attempt to transform Antigonus and Demetrius into traditional democratic heroes, modified to meet the needs of the Hellenistic polis.

In 307 Demetrius successfully freed Athens from Cassander's and Demetrius of Phaleron's control. He razed Cassander's fort on Munychia hill, restored Athens's ancestral constitution (*patrios politeia*), and promised grain and timber for ships.[61] In return, the Athenians voted unprecedented honors for both Demetrius and his father. Their images were woven into Athena's sacred *peplos*, two new tribes were created in their honor, and an altar was dedicated to Demetrius *Kataibatēs*.[62] In addition, golden statues of Demetrius and Antigonus were placed alongside those of Harmodius and Aristogeiton in a place where it had been previously unlawful to erect a statue (Diod. 20.46.2). Taken together, these honors and awards seek to incorporate the Antigonids into preexisting civic forms and, perhaps more important, to evoke the historical foundation of the democracy. W. R. Connor suggests that by echoing earlier cultural patterns, the Athenians may have been drawing a parallel between their

---

rulers' power. According to Ma, the cities' language of euergetism influenced the reality of empire by encouraging the rulers' to abide by moral norms and by reinscribing Hellenistic officials into the fabric of the city. In addition to adapting the traditions of euergetism, Athens and the other Greek cities also employed ruler cult to forge relationships with the Hellenistic rulers. Habicht (1956, 222–29) argues that ruler cult offered the cities a vocabulary to express the fact that they were unable to maintain themselves without the benefactions of the kings. On ruler cult as part of the cities' attempt to create a social memory of recent events to preserve polis coherence in the face of radical disruptions see also Price 1984, 30; Ma 1999, 219–26.

[59] As Ferguson puts it, "Athens itself would have been the chief jewel in the crown of any monarch" (1911a, 69).

[60] The Athenians described the Lamian War as a war against Antipater in the name of Greek freedom (see Ashton 1984).

[61] Plut. *Demetr*. 10.1–2; Diod. 20.46.1–4.

[62] See Plut. *Demetr*. 10.2–4. According to Plutarch, the new alliance was also sealed with a marriage exchange. Demetrius married Euthydike—a descendant of Miltiades, a man known for his own aristocratic marriage practices—to create a tie of reciprocity (*kharis*) with the city (*Demetr*. 14.1–2).

liberation from Demetrius of Phaleron and the overthrow of the Peisistratids: "The revisions in the tribal system making two additional tribes that could be named after Demetrius and his father may not only be compliments to the Macedonian liberators but also allusions to the change in the tribal system that account for an earlier Athenian liberation from tyranny."[63]

The Athenians so readily accepted Demetrius and Antigonus as their champions because along with the democracy, they also revived the military manhood of the city and its citizens. Under Demetrius of Phaleron's rule, the Macedonian commander in the Piraeus controlled military actions and decisions. Although Athenian citizens were at various times called on to fight, they were not fighting for honor or for Athens but rather to aid Cassander in his personal struggle for power.[64] By contrast, the Antigonids allowed the city to reestablish its military power in its own name and for its own sake. After the liberation in 307, Antigonus promised materials for one hundred triremes. A year later Demetrius sent twelve hundred suits of hoplite armor to the city after winning a major battle against Ptolemy I.[65] In addition to receiving these benefactions, the Athenians immediately began remilitarizing the city; for instance, they reinforced the walls of the city and harbor and the long walls between them.[66]

This military preparedness was a virtual necessity because by leaving the city without its promised garrison, Demetrius also left it vulnerable to renewed attack and capture by Cassander. Indeed, Cassander immediately tried to regain the city, initiating a conflict known as the Four Years' War. He was perilously close to retaking it when the Athenians finally persuaded Demetrius to come to their aid for a second time. With Demetrius's help, the Athenians managed to recapture their outlying fortresses from Cassander and to drive him beyond Thermopylae.[67] During this period, the Athenians clearly envisaged Demetrius as the city's advocate and protector in the struggle for Greek freedom and democracy.[68] In

[63] Connor 1989, 19; Hedrick 2000.

[64] For instance, Cassander demanded that the Athenians send twenty ships to aid *him* in his war against Antigonus (Diod. 19.68.3).

[65] Plut. *Demetr.* 10.1–2, 16.3. Habicht describes Demetrius's dedication of 1,200 hoplite arms as a "grand gesture, far exceeding the 300 arms Alexander had sent after the battle of Granicus" (1997, 77).

[66] For discussion, see Habicht 1997, 70.

[67] For the Four Years' War, see Habicht 1997, 74–76.

[68] Habicht sums up the epigraphic evidence for the Four Years' War: "According to Athenian documents from these years, Cassander represented pure evil, and the aim of his offensive was the 'enslavement' of Greece. The Athenians, on the other hand, under the leadership of King Demetrius and his allies, saw themselves as fighting for deliverance, freedom, and democracy—for their own city and for the rest of Greece" (1997, 75).

the aftermath of Cassander's defeat, a statue of Demetrius was even placed alongside the personified *Dēmokratia*.[69]

But prolonged contact strained the "special" relationship between Athens and Demetrius. Plutarch places the blame for the tragic turn in this relationship entirely on Athens. By incessantly flattering Demetrius, the city eventually corrupted his mind, leading him into delusional enterprises and inducing him to make disastrous decisions (*Demetr.* 10.2–3). In reality, the tensions probably began to accrue simply because Demetrius—who became King Demetrius in 306—spent too much time in the city during the Four Years' War and its aftermath, treating it as the capital of his own kingdom and making it abundantly clear that he could not live up to democratic idealizations.

A particularly notorious incident occurred in 302, when Demetrius informed the Athenians that he wanted to be initiated into the Mysteries all at once and at the wrong time of the year. Although the chief priest of the Mysteries refused, Stratocles, the speaker who most vigorously catered to Demetrius's requests and demands, found a way around the problem that preserved a semblance of ritual correctness.[70] He proposed a decree to change the name of the current month to Anthesterion, the time for initiation into the Lesser Mysteries. Immediately afterward he had the name of the month changed again, enabling Demetrius to be initiated into the Greater Mysteries (*Epoptika*; Plut. *Demetr.* 26; Diod. 20.110.1). Although this use of the Assembly decree might be taken as demonstrating the performative power of democratic speech to enact a new (chronological) reality, it was viewed as a travesty of ritual and politics, producing considerable discontent within the democratic citizenry. Demochares, who initially played a leading role along with Stratocles in the restored democracy, was eventually exiled for indiscreetly voicing his hostility to Stratocles' sycophantic behavior (Plut. *Demetr.* 24.5). The comic poet Philippides voluntarily went into exile for similar reasons. In one of his comedies he openly attacked Stratocles for giving Demetrius honors that should have been reserved for the gods. Plutarch preserves the following verses:

> He who abbreviated the year to one month,
> used the acropolis as an inn,
> and introduced *hetairai* to the virgin,
> it's because of him, the frost blasted the vines,
> because of his impiety, the *peplos* was torn down the middle,
> because he gave divine honors to men.

[69] *ISE* 7 lines 14–15.

[70] For Stratocles, see Habicht 1997, 71–73.

These things destroy democracy (*dēmos*), not comedy.
(*Demetr*. 12.4 = Philippides 25 K.-A., lines 4–7;
Demetr. 26.3 = Philippides 25 K.-A., lines 1–3)[71]

This passage posits a correspondence between the reproductive and political effects of Demetrius's ritual and sexual improprieties and Stratocles' role in facilitating them. According to the speaker, such behavior not only threatens the reproductive life of the city (Plutarch also notes that the grain was destroyed) but also undermines the democracy. The defense of comedy in the final line may indicate that either Demetrius's abuses or the fawning and sycophantic behavior of Athenian politicians toward him had been previous targets of comic abuse.[72] Whatever the case, Athens's dependence on Demetrius was too deep and too precarious for this kind of explicit political criticism.[73] Shortly after the comedy was performed, if indeed it was performed, Philippides went exile; he did not return for more than a decade.[74]

"Romantic" Resistance: Comedy and the Sterility of Empire

Within a matter of a few years, Demetrius was routinely exerting the kind of authoritarian power over Athenian domestic politics that he was supposed to have eradicated in 307. Instead of installing censors in political institutions to see that his wishes were carried out, Demetrius sent letters that had the force of commands and the power to negate the speech acts of the democracy. After a certain Cleaenetus used his personal connection with Demetrius to dissolve a debt, the Assembly passed a decree forbidding any citizen to introduce a letter from Demetrius into its proceedings. Demetrius was reportedly so angered by this show of independence that the Assembly repealed the measure and passed a new decree declaring that anything Demetrius requested in the future was to be considered just toward men and the gods (Plut. *Demetr*. 24.3–4). This ostensibly democratic decision to surrender all decision-making power

[71] In the *Amatorius*, Plutarch quotes another verse that probably came from the same comedy (*Mor*. 750e = Philippides 26 K.-A.).

[72] See Webster 1970, 106.

[73] The point is not that political criticism no longer had a point or place in comedy, but rather that it had to be in keeping with the aims and purposes of the regime in power. The comic poet Archedikos—recently identified by Habicht (1993) as a pro-Macedonian politician under Antipater's oligarchy—maligned the ardent democrat Demochares for, inter alia, acting as a male prostitute (4 K.-A.). This criticism of an anti-Macedonian politician certainly recalls Aeschines' attack on Timarchus, the profligate but prolific anti-Macedonian politician of the previous generation (see Dem. 19.286–87). In all probability, Archedikos's attack on Demochares was launched when the oligarchy was in power.

[74] Ferguson 1911a, 124–26.

vividly demonstrated the impossibility of democracy within the context of Demetrius's rule. It should come as no surprise that the Athenians rejected Demetrius just as they had their former oppressors. In this case, however, rejection took the form of a declaration of neutrality—what Ferguson calls their "Phaeacian policy"[75]—rather than military insurrection. After the Antigonid kingdom was all but destroyed in 301, the Athenians denied Demetrius (and the other kings) entrance to the city (Plut. *Demetr.* 30.3).

Although a monumental setback, the defeat of Demetrius and Antigonus at Ipsus in 301 did nothing to deter either Demetrius's or his adversaries' desire for empire. His absence from Athens simply created a power vacuum that allowed Lachares, an Athenian apparently supported by Cassander, to establish a tyranny there. Lachares may have remained in power until 295, when Demetrius seized control of the city for a second time.[76] During the second tenure of his rule, Demetrius no longer postured as either a liberator or a champion of Greek freedom; instead, he seems to have taken his cue from the by then defunct Antipatrid dynasty, employing oligarchic political measures coupled with military power to control the city.[77] Nevertheless, after nearly two generations of despotic and oligarchic rule, the Athenians were willing to fight yet again to regain their freedom and democracy. In 287, with material assistance from Ptolemy I and Lysimachus, the Athenians defeated Demetrius's forces and reestablished the democracy.[78] Epigraphic evidence dating from the next twenty-five years or so attests that there followed an intensely democratic and nationalistic period in Athens's history.[79] Although it came to an abrupt end in the aftermath of the Chremonidean War, what is of interest for present purposes is not Athens's irrevocable defeat in 260 but rather the city's ability to withstand the domination of Demetrius Poliorcetes and its dependence on external autocratic rulers with its democratic spirit intact.[80]

In this chapter, I have discussed the remarkable stability of Athens's

[75] Ferguson 1911a, 126.

[76] The chronology of Lachares' tyranny is disputed; for a review of the evidence, see Habicht 1997, 81–87; M. J. Osborne 1981–83, 2:144–53.

[77] Just as in Antipater's oligarchy of 321–318, a registrar (*anagrapheus*) replaced the secretaries (*grammateis*) of the council in 294. For the character of Demetrius's rule between 295 and 287, see Habicht 1997, 87–94.

[78] Key sources for these events are the decrees honoring Kallias and Phaedrus of Sphettos, Athenians in Ptolemaic mercenary service; see Shear 1978 for the documents and discussion. See also M. J. Osborne 1979; Habicht 1997, 95–97 and references cited in n. 99.

[79] See Habicht 1997, 138–39.

[80] For continuing Athenian and Greek resistance to Macedonian rule after the Chremonidean War, see Kurke 2002 on Machon's subversive poetry.

democratic ethos or mentality throughout a period characterized by unprecedented discontinuities on the institutional and practical levels. Although anti-Macedonian sentiment catalyzed this democratic fervor to some extent, it alone does not account for the entrenched democratic commitment that led the Athenians to restore the democracy again and again, despite their lack of effective military power. It is my argument in this book that their resiliency was also practically promoted by the continuous production of cultural narratives that enacted and naturalized Athens's democratic identity. Comedy's reproductive romances performed and secured the survival of Athenian democratic and Greek civic culture. By way of conclusion here, I want to sketch out how comedy's romantic plots also—in some cases—provided imaginary solutions to the real problems posed by the domination and demands of rulers like Demetrius Poliorcetes. By the end of the fourth century, there was no denying the reality that the Hellenistic kingdoms monopolized both military and economic power and that neither Athens nor any of the Greek cities could survive without their assistance. While comedy could not do away with this situation, its narratives could transfigure it, offering alternative ways of understanding contemporary realities that made them seem less damaging to the culture and traditions of the city-state.

The first thing that should be noted is that although New Comedy is well known for its lack of explicit political content and commentary, references to Demetrius Poliorcetes are surprisingly common.[81] In Alexis's *Knight* (*Hippeus*), a speaker extols Demetrius along with the Athenian lawmakers for expelling the philosophers from the city (99 K.-A. = Athen. 610e).[82] The reference here is to a decree—passed in the democratic furor following the expulsion of Demetrius of Phaleron—that required philosophical schools to obtain licenses from the state.[83] In the comic fragment, Demetrius is perceived as working with and supporting the democratic lawmakers. A fragment from Alexis's *Krateia* or *Pharmakopōlēs* contains a similarly positive reference to Demetrius (116 K.-A. = Athen. 254a). The speaker toasts Antigonus, Demetrius, and Demetrius's wife Phila for an Antigonid naval victory won against Ptolemy in 306. The positive attitude evinced here is clearly in keeping with the buoyant mood immediately following the democratic restoration, the period in which the interests of Demetrius and the democracy briefly coincided.[84]

[81] There may be many additional indirect or implied references to Demetrius—such as is the case in Philippides 25 K.-A.

[82] For Alexis's play and the decree of Sophocles of Sunium, see Arnott 1996a, 858–59.

[83] Sophocles' decree did not actually expel the philosophers; rather, it made philosophical schools subject to state regulation. See Ferguson 1911a, 103–7.

[84] A later work of Alexis's (246 K.-A. = Athen. 502b; cf. 92 K.-A. = Athen. 369e) con-

But Demetrius's penchant for ostentation and excess also provided ample material for the comic poets. According to Plutarch, Demetrius's well-known weakness for women induced the comic poets to declare his courtesan Lamia rather than his monumental siege tower the real "city-taker" (*Helepolis*; *Demetr.* 27.2).[85] Alexis's *Demetrius*, also known as *Philetairos*, may have similarly lampooned Demetrius's erotic adventures (46–51 K.-A.).[86] In addition, the siege of Rhodes from which Demetrius took the epithet "Poliorcetes" ("the Besieger") probably inspired the title of Diphilus's play *The City-Wall-Taker* (*Hairēsiteikhēs*; 4 K.-A.).[87] Such praise of Demetrius or joking references to his larger-than-life exploits were possible only when things were going well between Athens and Demetrius. When the honeymoon ended, when Demetrius started living in Athens in the winter of 304, it was obviously neither safe nor expedient for individual poets to censure him directly or explicitly.

Comedy, however, was able to bypass the difficulties posed by implicit and explicit censorship by adapting potentially sensitive political materials to its own seemingly nonpolitical narrative patterns.[88] Instead of mocking the grandiose military aspirations and endeavors of Alexander's successors, comedy inserts the Hellenistic ruler—or rather his surrogate, the braggart soldier—into its romantic plot lines. It is true that the braggart soldier figure has its roots in Old Comedy, but New Comedy gives this conventional type a historically specific spin by linking the soldier with the Hellenistic kingdoms.[89] Although the soldier is not explicitly

---

tains a similar laudatory toast to Ptolemy II, his sister-wife, and their *homonoia* (so Arnott 1996a, 691 ad 5). The speaker seems to be extending the quality of feeling and attitude structuring the conjugal bond to the structure of international relations. Given the fact that Ptolemy II's marriage to Arsinoe was incestuous, an ironic meaning may also be in play (cf. Arnott 1996a, 688 n. 1). It is impossible to determine whether this habit of toasting the successors when they performed some benefaction for the city or otherwise aided it was idiosyncratic to Alexis or was more widespread. At any rate, the references to Seleucas's gift to the city, a tiger probably sent sometime after 306, seem to be more in the spirit of humor rather than a compliment to the king; for the tiger, see further Alexis 207 K.-A. = Athen. 590b; Philemon 49 K.-A. = Athen. 590b; Arnott 1996a, 590.

[85] For this type of humor, see Men. *Pk.* 482–85.

[86] Arnott (1996, 157), however, does not think that the title *Philetairos* refers to a man's passion for a *hetaira* or that the Demetrius in question is Demetrius Poliorcetes.

[87] Diphilus's *Hairēsiteikhēs* was also called the *Eunuch* and the *Soldier*; see Athen. 469e; Diphilus *Test.* 6 K.-A. Wartenberg (1973, 17) suggests that Diphilus changed the name of the play for political reasons.

[88] Cf. Aristotle's comments on the contrast between Old and New Comedy, *E.N.* 1128a22–24.

[89] In Menander's comedy, the soldier type is generally named for some martial attribute or association: Polemon, Thraso, Stratophanes, Kleostratos, Bias. For a complete listing, see Wartenberg 1973. In adapting Greek New Comedy for Roman audiences, Plautus sometimes makes the soldier's connection with the Hellenistic rulers more explicit by giv-

identified as Demetrius Poliorcetes or any of the other kings, the link is there.[90] For instance, a speaker in Menander's *Kolax*, in all probability Strouthias, flatters the braggart soldier by remarking that he (the soldier) has slept with all the famous *hetairai* of the day, including two known consorts of Demetrius Poliorcetes.[91] And in Plautus's *Miles Gloriosus*, the soldier boasts of his service to and intimacy with Seleucus (*M.G.* 75ff.).

By casting the surrogate soldier as a rival in the contest for a courtesan or prostitute, comedy encloses and transfigures the conflict between the city and ruler in its own romantic frame. The fact that these romantic rivals stand in, on some level, for the Hellenistic rulers lends their depiction as inept failures in love and war a pointed political edge.[92] How threatening could the Hellenistic rulers be if they were like or depended on braggart soldiers routinely ridiculed and outwitted by parasites and slaves? Comedy's derision of the braggart soldier recalls the political humor found in Old Comedy. According to pseudo-Xenophon (an author critical of Athens's democracy), poets of Old Comedy mocked the rich, the wellborn, and those seeking to have more than the demos (2.18). Reviewing Aristophanic specimens of Old Comedy, Jeffrey Henderson finds pseudo-Xenophon's assessment to be basically correct, concluding that comedy ridicules perceived enemies of the demos.[93] Accord-

---

ing them names that recall the epithets of Demetrius "Poliorcetes": e.g., Therapontigonus, Pyrgopolynices.

[90] There is additional evidence associating the Macedonian rulers with censorship. In his treatise *On the Differences of the Comedies*, the Hellenistic writer Platonius claims that the comic poets were so afraid of offending the Macedonian rulers that "they deliberately constructed the masks with greater comic distortion . . . so that the appearance of the mask would not coincide by some chance with the features of some Macedonian ruler and the poet incur the penalty because he was thought to have acted deliberately. At any rate we see the shape of the brows on the masks of Menander's comedy and how the mouth is distorted and not of human proportion" (trans. Csapo and Slater 1994, 174).

[91] Athen. 13.587e = Men. *Kol.* fr. 4 Sandbach. The same speaker also praises the soldier for drinking more than Alexander (Athen. 434b–c = fr. 2 Sandbach). Elderkin (1934) argues that Therapontigonus in Plautus's *Curculio* is modeled on Demetrius Poliorcetes. In Plautus's *Bacchides* 900ff., Chrysalus announces that one of the Bacchis sisters is visiting the newly opened Parthenon, a comment that may refer to the opening of Parthenon after Demetrius left in 302. In Terence's *Eunuch*, the soldier Thraso (whose character is probably drawn from Menander's *Kolax*) boasts of being the close confident of the king (397–407); In the *Miles Gloriosus*, Pyrgopolynices acts as a mercenary recruiter for Seleucus. The "braggart cook"–type figure also sometimes identifies himself with the Hellenistic rulers. In Demetrius's *Areopagite*, performed sometime after 294 B.C., the cook, lording his own art over the lowly art of acting, claims to have cooked for Seleucus, Agathocles, and Lachares—the Athenian tyrant (1 K.-A.); see also chapter 1 n. 98.

[92] The political reference of comedy's romantic innuendo may have been particularly near the surface in Menander's *Androgunos*. See 51 K.-A.; Wartenberg 1973, 22–23.

[93] Henderson 1990, 296. For politics and humor in Aristophanes, see also Carey 1994;

ing to this view, laughter operated to make democratic community and to sustain democratic values by disciplining and chastening those perceived to be of stepping out of line. New Comedy adapts this technique, using ridicule and romantic defeat to challenge the power of the Hellenistic kingdoms in ways that were safe precisely because they appeared not to be political.

At the same time, the emphasis on the braggart soldier's vulnerability to flattery places the contemporary circumstances that compelled the Greek cities to flatter the Hellenistic rulers in a new and less devastating register. While Athenian politicians were condemned for betraying their heritage by flattering Demetrius, in comedy the negative emphasis falls on the susceptible recipient of such deceptive speech—that is, the braggart soldier himself.[94] In comedy, flattery often operates as a weapon of the weak that more than levels the playing field between rich and powerful braggart soldier and relatively powerless citizens and slaves.

But comedy's most potent weapon is its conventional narrative form. By casting the braggart soldier as a rival and loser in its own romantic scripts, comedy revises the narrative of contemporary affairs in order to allow the citizen (and the city he stands for) to come out on top. Stories of the soldier's inevitable romantic defeat offered a face-saving if fantastic means of rendering subordination to the Hellenistic rulers less ruinous to the civic self-image. There is, however, one exception to the general rule that deserves mention here. In Terence's *Eunuch*, the braggart soldier is granted the right to share the courtesan (*meretrix*) with a citizen at the end of the play. Significantly, he does not win this right on his own but rather through the auspices of his parasite. Although Terence's play is adapted from Menander's *Eunouchos*, it borrows the characters of the soldier and parasite from Menander's *Kolax*. Given that Menander's *Eunouchos* does not survive and only one hundred or so lines of the *Kolax* have been recovered, it is impossible to determine with certainty what effect the insertion of these replacement characters had on the plot of the *Eunuch*, or indeed what role they played in the *Kolax*.[95] What is worth noting here is that in Terence's *Eunuch*, the concluding agreement between the citizen and soldier to share the courtesan Thais comes as a jarring surprise in the context of a play in which the courtesan had previ-

Edwards 1993; Halliwell 1991b; on the uses of laughter in Greek culture more generally; see Halliwell 1991a.

[94] For criticism of Athenian flattery of Demetrius Poliorcetes, see Demochares, Athen. 253a–b = *FGrH* 75 F 1; Athen. 253b–d = *FGrH* 75 F 2; Plut. *Demetr*. 24.5; Duris, Athen. 253d–f = *FGrH* 76 F 13; Theopompus, Athen. 254b = *FGrH* 115 F 280. For the political implications of the comic flatterer, see also P. G. Brown 1992b.

[95] On this question, see Barsby 1999, 17–19.

ously enjoyed autonomy over her own romantic liaisons.[96] We do not know whether this final compromise has a Menandrian antecedent (in the *Kolax*, for instance), but in Terence's play it seems to represent an accommodation between the city and the Hellenistic kingdoms in which the city, once again, triumphs. The soldier—depicted as too offensive to be a real contender for Thais's affection—is allowed to remain in the picture to finance the pleasures and needs of everyone else in the new society.[97]

With the citizen-versus-soldier plot pattern, comedy provides an imaginary solution to the problematic play of power between Hellenistic autocrats and the less powerful city. Because the love interest is always a courtesan rather than a female citizen, these comedies do not, on the surface, seem to preserve the correspondence between sexual and political reproduction embedded in the plays featuring the marriage plot.[98] Nevertheless, stories of a soldier's proclivity for commodified sexual relationships do allegorically comment on the barrenness of the kings and kingdoms that the soldier represents. The sterility of comedy's braggart soldiers presages the mortality and transience of the Hellenistic ruler and kingdom.[99]

[96] This kind of compromise solution obviously could not have occurred in Menander's *Eunouchos* because, inter alia, there was no soldier in that play (insofar as we know). On the relationship between the ending of Terence's *Eunuch* and that of the Menandrian version, see Ludwig 1968, 172–73, and 1973; J. C. B. Lowe 1983; Steidle 1973; R. L. Hunter 1985, 94; Barsby 1999, 282–83.

[97] Because the heroine in Menander's *Kolax* was enslaved to a pimp—rather than being a free and autonomous courtesan who needed wealth to finance her household—some commentators have suggested that there was no motivation for a final accommodation between the citizen and soldier in the *Kolax* such as we find in Terence's play (see Ludwig 1973; Barsby 1993). While this speculation may be right, the fact remains that we have no certain evidence for the ending of the *Kolax* and thus cannot rule out a Menandrian precedent for the accommodation that ends Terence's *Eunuch*.

[98] Plautus's *Miles Gloriosus* draws a correlation between political control and sexual control. In the Latin play the soldier is characterized as a *moechus*, a man who particularly delights in stealing other men's women. The Athenian courtesan he kidnapped from "Athens in Attica" is rescued in an adultery scheme. The soldier is foolishly convinced that the wife of his neighbor in Ephesus has conceived a mad passion for him. When he enters her house, her irate husband seizes him as an adulterer and subjects him to the traditional Athenian punishment for such offenders (although the play is set in Ephesus); on the punishment, see chapter 3, note 46.

[99] Comedy may subtly mock the Hellenistic rulers by rendering their comic counterparts sterile romantic losers, but the comic tradition more explicitly comments on the nonreproductive amorous exploits of Demetrius Poliorcetes. Machon, a New Comic poet from Corinth or Sikyon, collected and rendered into verse the witty sayings of famous courtesans. While ostensibly displaying clever repartee, these sayings in several cases make Demetrius of Poliorcetes (or, more specifically, his nonreproductive sexual escapades) the joke. Machon's *Chreia* contains an anecdote in which Demetrius masturbates for his courtesan

Although the infertility of the braggart soldier is usually tacit, an implicit corollary of romantic defeat, in one case comedy makes this consequence explicit by highlighting the braggart soldier's desperate desire for a son to continue his line and power. Plautus's *Truculentus*, perhaps the least sentimental of all New Comedies, achieves this effect by exploiting and exposing comedy's usually unspoken reproductive codes.[100] In the play, the greedy courtesan Phronesium passes off an exposed infant as her own son by a Babylonian soldier. The soldier is so eager for a son that he has promised her all of his possessions if only she will consent to raise the baby (*Truc.* 399–400). It is later discovered, however, that one of Phronesium's other lovers, the Athenian citizen Diniarchus, fathered the child when he raped a female citizen. Unlike other rapists in New Comedy, Diniarchus really does not want to do the right thing by marrying his victim, desiring nothing but to maintain his nonreproductive commodified relationship with the insatiable Phronesium. Eventually, of course, in keeping with the laws of the genre, Diniarchus does marry the female citizen, uniting the fragmented citizen family. Yet though the play preserves the marriage plot pattern, it strips it of the conventions and conceits that make closure in citizen marriage seem like the right and inevitable ending. Diniarchus agrees to the marriage solely to avoid being taken to court by the rape victim's irate father, and promises to reenter the relationship with Phronesium at some future time. By failing to channel Diniarchus's desire toward a marriageable woman, the play exposes heterosexual marriage as an arbitrary and artificial closure.

This unusual resolution, unsatisfactory if judged against comedy's customary happily-ever-after endings, stems from the play's deployment of two incongruent narratives: a marriage plot and a citizen-versus-soldier rival plot.[101] According to the proprieties of the marriage plot, Diniarchus ought to be in love with the female citizen he has raped and with whom he has fathered a child. Although Diniarchus remains bound to the marriage plot, the play channels his erotic and reproductive energies into the rival plot for Phronesium. His insertion in the rape/marriage plot serves only to produce a child to assist Phronesium in her scheme against the soldier. In other words, Diniarchus's implication in the marriage plot

Lamia (Athen. 13.577e–f = Gow 13). In another vignette, he asks to sodomize the courtesan Mania (Athen. 13.579a = Gow 15). The association of the notoriously womanizing Demetrius with nonreproductive sexuality in these stories may obliquely figure his power as similarly "nonreproductive" or short-lived. For the anti-Macedonian political thrust of Machon's *Chreia*, see Kurke 2002.

[100] Konstan (1983, 160) notes that this is one comedy in which love and marriage are not reconciled.

[101] There is a third plot line, not relevant here, that centers on Strabax, yet another contender for Phronesium's favors.

paradigm hinders his prospects in the rival plot against the soldier by furnishing Phronesium with exactly what she needs to keep the soldier ensnared. Of particular interest in the play's attempt to fuse two discrepant plot patterns is its disclosure of comedy's ordinarily unstated reproductive politics and policies. Diniarchus cannot opt out of the marriage plot, because rape in New Comedy always leads to the birth of a child. By contrast, the soldier's frustrated desire for a successor and heir seems to represent his own attempt to evade the inevitable reproductive impoverishment associated with his character and narrative position.

No extant Menandrian comedy exposes the politics of reproduction so forthrightly, yet the conventions are clear and consistent: braggart soldiers in comedy are always infertile, losing out in both the romantic and reproductive contest. In this way, comedy emphasizes in the sexual register the ephemeral power of the Hellenistic rulers and their kingdoms. The ideological power of these conventions is clarified by the contrast they form with the unwitting reproductive success of comedy's citizen heroes in the marriage plot, a convention that leads to an emphasis on the resilience and reproducibility of the democratic city. The next chapter examines the various plot devices and strategies that lead to romantic triumph and the promise of the city's perpetuation that such triumph enacts.

3

Making Citizens in Comedy and Court

Gender and Democratic Identity

Menander's comedy is deeply and emphatically political. By casting braggart soldiers, representatives of the Hellenistic rulers and their kingdoms, as inevitable losers in romantic contests against citizens, comedy comments on and undercuts the new Hellenistic structures that were challenging the culture and traditions of the Greek cities. And, in many cases, the heterosexual unions to which the plays give rise instantiate key democratic principles, paving the way for the reproduction of the social order along new, more egalitarian terms. In addition, comedy's valorization of the laws of civic membership constitutes a form of democratic resistance in its own contemporary context. Although Macedonian-backed oligarchies intermittently held power in Athens and made the possession of wealth a necessary requirement for citizenship, extant comedy never acknowledges the relevance of economic considerations to the questions of citizen status that so often drive its plots, but instead presents the traditional birth-based norms as if they were the only ones in operation. With these conventions, comedy resists, and indeed one might say erases, the reality of Macedonian power in Athens.

What remains to be considered, however, is whether comedy, at least in some cases, conveys distinctively democratic political information that is neither allegorically coded nor simply a default position emerging from its tacit opposition to oligarchic rule. For comedy seems to valorize nominal norms of citizenship without remarking on the substantive values, principles, and practices of the democratic political order made accessible by those norms. Although the distinction between nominal and substantive norms of citizenship is often of heuristic value in modern political theory, in the Athenian context it obscures rather than illuminates the culture of citizenship.[1] Because the Periclean law employed a norm for civic membership that was directly and indirectly tied to various social practices, these practices themselves became invested with the aims and ideology of the democratic political order. In other words, the nativity requirement for civic membership produced practices of citizenship that,

[1] For the listinction between nominal and substantive norms of citizenship, see Bauböck 1992.

over time, helped generate the substantive values of the democratic political order.

The first half of the chapter provides the background for this claim by examining some of the practical and ideological effects of the citizenship law, with a particular focus on the cross-fertilization of gender and politics its operation encouraged. There is a pressing need for this exposition because, as Marilyn Katz observes, the relevance for democratic theory of the exclusion of women from political rights has received no scholarly attention to date.[2] Although this chapter is in part an attempt to redress that omission, the analytic focus is on gender rather than on women per se. More precisely, it elaborates some of the ways in which the gender system (the organization of men and women defined with reference to the reproductive arena) was implicated with the citizenship system (the organization of men defined with reference to the political arena), and consequently with the production of democratic political ideology.[3]

The implementation of the Periclean citizenship law did not, in itself, make gender pertinent to democratic civic identity or ideology. For instance, in Aeschylus's *Oresteia* trilogy (first performed in 458 B.C., several years before the law was passed), citizen identity is constituted almost exclusively in terms of gender. This democratic foundation story insistently links the emergence of the political order to the political, social, and reproductive subordination of women to men.[4] Yet, though conceptions of gender difference and hierarchy were always important to the constitution of the democratic male self, the gender regime was not always the same: no gender system, even one so apparently intransigent as the Athenian, is immune to change over time. While it is probably possible to detect many shifts in gender ideology over the course of Athenian history, the Periclean citizenship law produced perhaps the most pro-

[2] Katz 1999. There have been several important studies of gender and democratic ideology. See Loraux 1993; Winkler 1990a; Halperin 1990; M. H. Jameson 1997.

[3] For the concept of gender used in this study and a discussion of the articulation of gender in other forms of social and political organization, see Connell 1987; Pateman 1988; Scott 1988; Stevens 1999. My argument that the citizenship law assisted in producing the Athenian gender system is parallel to Stevens's argument that modern political societies produce gender through the specific rules of membership they employ. She states, "Marriage and kinship rules, instrumental to the reproduction of political societies in their particularity, which is to say, as political societies, produce the sex/gender dichotomies of femininity and masculinity through controlling not women per se, but the processes of reproduction that interpellate the bearers of children and those who cannot bear children into particular relations with each other" (Stevens 1999, 12; cf. 210).

[4] For gender in the *Oresteia*, see Zeitlin 1996. On the importance of class and status issues, see P. W. Rose 1992. For a New Historicist reading that argues for the trilogy's preservation of the aristocratic status quo, see M. Griffith 1995. For a reading of the trilogy arguing that the dramatic foundation of the democratic order is tied to the destabilization, rather than the entrenchment, of gender polarities, see Rocco 1997.

found changes.[5] By identifying native women of free birth as the sole bearers of legitimate children and citizens, the law effectively inaugurated a new chapter in the gender history of Athens's democracy.

Before the passage of the law, Athenian men could marry and produce legitimate children and heirs with free women of foreign or native descent. Afterward, however, citizens were no longer permitted to marry and produce heirs with women from other *poleis*. If a citizen chose to live with a nonnative woman, any offspring were regarded as bastards (*nothoi*), children without a legitimate place in either family or state. Accordingly, the implementation of the law not only invested marriage and the family with new significance as institutions and practices of citizenship: it also redefined what counted as a marriage and a legitimate family. Since marriage and the institution of citizenship now depended on female nativity (among other things), the identity of a citizen's wife became the focus of unprecedented attention and emphasis. This can be attested in the material culture by the sudden appearance of women on Athenian funerary monuments and vases associated with burial dating from the second half of the fifth century B.C. Whereas women are very infrequently represented on earlier grave monuments, from the mid–fifth century onward they dominate the "symbolic language" in which the dead are commemorated.[6] Robin Osborne links this change in representation to the significance that Pericles' citizenship law attached to wives and mothers:

[5] Although Loraux observes that the Periclean law might have produced changes in democratic gender ideology by making space for maternal inheritance, she concludes that it did not ultimately unseat the existing regime. For Loraux, there is no such thing as a "female citizen," any more than there is a "female Athenian" (1993, 119; cf. 120). In fact, "female citizen" (*politis*) is attested; see [Dem.] 59.107. According to Loraux, Athenian women were always only regarded as members of the gender-race of women. While this is certainly an important and enduring strand in Athenian gender ideology, it is possible to detect the emergence of alternative, often contradictory, views. For instance, though the idea of a race of women persists in the fifth and fourth centuries, the Periclean citizenship law clearly did foster a belief in maternal inheritance, suggesting that women had rather more in common with men than a view of women as a separate race would allow. The nativity requirements for citizen status encouraged the view that women, just like men, passed important traits onto their children. Thus, after the implementation of the citizenship law, one way of impugning a citizen's credentials, loyalty, or claims to political leadership was to insist that he inherited "foreign" blood from his mother or grandmother. The orator Demosthenes was said to have inherited disloyalty to the state and wickedness from his Scythian grandmother; see Aes. 2.78, 93, 180, 3.171–72; Din. 1.15 (on this topos, cf. see Connor 1992, 168–70; Harding 1987; Ober 1989, 268–70; V. Hunter 1990; Lape forthcoming). This example suggests that change in gender (as well as racial) ideology was a consequence of the citizenship law's correlation of sexual and political reproduction. For the connection between political change and change in a culture's gender system, see especially Scott 1988.

[6] R. Osborne 1997, 12. There is a fifty-year break in the practice of putting monumental markers on graves beginning around 500 B.C., perhaps due to sumptuary legislation. See further R. Osborne 1997, 14.

> Formal exclusion of non-Athenian mothers from Athenian political society led to an emphasis on Athenian wives and mothers, and brought women literally into the public eye: men secured their own claims to citizen status by advertising that their wives and mothers conformed to the ideals of Athenian womanhood, and that their homes were models of domestic regularity, unsullied by the exotic.[7]

As the Periclean citizenship law directed new political attention to the citizen's wife and his marriage, it of necessity directed similar attention to all of his relations with women, in part because it was suddenly imperative to determine whether a given relationship was a marriage or something else.[8] For this reason, the law encouraged the creation of an environment in which a citizen's real or alleged relationship with a wife, courtesan (*hetaira*), prostitute (*pornē*), foreigner, or slave could be presented as a gauge of his political identity and commitments.[9] The first half of the chapter maps this "democratic" gender ideology, elaborating the ways in which relations between men and women could be constructed to sustain or subvert supposed egalitarian norms between men, or to attest a citizen's civic loyalty or his lack thereof.

There is a need for this exposition not only because the importance of gender to Athens's democracy remains understudied, but also because various permutations of this ideology inform comedy's ostensibly "nonpolitical" romantic plots. By using compliance with laws of citizenship as its privileged narrative outcome, Menander's comedy depicts the Periclean citizenship law in action. In so doing, it dramatizes, albeit in a generically mediated way, the law's effective yoking of marriage, sexuality, and the gender system to the practice and ideology of democratic citizenship. This is not to say that comic narratives passively reflect either legal norms or the historical reality of how actual citizens complied with those norms. Although the laws of citizenship constitute its generic rules, comedy enacts law and makes citizens by deploying its own formal conventions, themes, and devices, which often alter the meaning of the civic norms they enact. In some cases, the agonistic structure of the plot

[7] R. Osborne 1997, 32. For the depiction of women on grave stelae and lekythoi, see also Humphreys 1993, 104–8; Stears 1995; Leader 1997. For the Periclean citizenship law as an attempt to subject maternity to the rule of law, see Bassi 1998, 198–200.

[8] For the dangerous attention that a citizen's relationship with a *hetaira* could elicit, see further chapter 5.

[9] In this respect, the law fostered a preexisting cultural tendency to attach political import to relations between men and women. This tendency can be attested already in Homer and in Solon's reforms. I have argued elsewhere (Lape 2002–03) that Solon banned bastards from the family and polis in order to put every citizen on the same reproductive footing and to discourage men from keeping *pallakai* (concubines), and in that way using women as material markers of male prestige.

rewards a character with the qualities and characteristics associated with a democratic belief system. Plays of this type implicitly transform the birth-based norms of civic membership into specifically democratic entrance criteria. In addition, the majority of the plays present eros or love, rather than law, as the motivation for citizen marriage. With this convention, comedy transforms the city's laws into innate principles of citizen identity or biology, thus masking highly political messages in stories that seem not to be political at all. Yet in many cases, the literary strategies that comedy employs to achieve the narrative end of complying with the norms of citizenship undercut the very civic outcomes they impose.

The Importance of Acting Athenian

By defining exactly who was and was not eligible for democratic citizenship, the Periclean law offered the city and its citizens a powerful statement of civic identity. Athenian citizens, it said, were natives, men born from a native father and a native mother. This statement thus appears to be descriptive rather than performative; that is, because eligibility for citizenship was determined at birth, the citizenship law designated who was always already eligible to be a citizen, effectively making citizenship an ascribed status rather than defining what it meant to be a citizen. For several reasons, however, the practical realities were far more complex. By recognizing all those with bilateral parentage as citizens, the law also tacitly defines citizens as men who marry and produce legitimate children in accordance with the law.[10] In other words, the law's birth requirement enjoins a range of social practices, or, as Nicole Loraux puts it, it makes parentage both an obligation and a right.[11] And the very nature of the birth requirement added to the normalizing force of these injunctions: translated into practical and cultural terms, it made a citizen's status dependent (inter alia) on the sex act of his conception. Barring eyewitnesses or modern DNA testing, however, it was obviously not possible to be certain about the circumstances surrounding that event. Consequently, since the identity of a citizen's birth parents could never be established beyond question, neither could a man's claim to citizen identity ever be verified once and for all, at least by the men who composed and sought access to the citizen group. Although women were in a better

[10] For the tacit social performatives contained in speech acts, see Bourdieu 1991, 122; Butler 1997. In Butler's terms (1997, 141–59), the Periclean law produced long-term social and political effects because of the tacit or social performatives it compelled—namely, the sexual and matrimonial corollaries that were implied by the law but did not need to be spelled out for knowledgeable social actors.

[11] Loraux 1993, 17 n. 26.

position to know and state with certainty who the fathers of their children were, and hence to buttress and secure male claims to status and identity, they were normally not consulted on such questions.[12] Indeed, that a woman's role in the reproductive process gave her superior knowledge of, and even control over, male identity appears as a source of anxiety for Greek men from the earliest literature onward.

By establishing a requirement for citizenship that could never really be verified beyond question, the citizenship law made the status of every citizen vulnerable to challenge. This made it all the more important to maintain the appearance that one was exactly who one claimed to be—or, in W. R. Connor's words, "to look and act like an Athenian in every possible way."[13] Therefore the demonstrable practices of citizenship, including marrying a native woman and fathering legitimate children, became crucial visible corollaries to the supposed invisible "essence" of Athenianness. It was of vital importance to maintain appearances, because the impossibility of ever establishing a citizen's parentage beyond doubt did not deter the Athenians from scrutinizing it throughout his life. Before he was formally inducted into the deme and citizen body, the citizen-to-be's parentage was evaluated at various phratry and (in some cases) genos rites. The major scrutiny came when he reached eighteen and the demesmen voted to determine whether he was free, had attained the right age, and was born according to the laws, a stipulation that after 451/0 meant from a native woman given by *enguē* to an Athenian citizen.[14] This formal recognition, however, was far from the end of the process. The citizen's parentage was inspected every time he was allotted a public position and at periodic special scrutinies.[15] Just as there was no one act by which a father definitively acknowledged and established his paternity, so too there was no one act by which a citizen could secure his civic legitimacy once and for all.[16] Accordingly, acting Athenian—that is, con-

[12] See, however, the exceptional case involving Plangon in Dem. 39, 40.

[13] Connor 1994, 41.

[14] [Arist.] *A.P.* 42.1–2. For the deme scrutiny, see Whitehead 1986, 97–104, and Robertson 2000, emphasizing the importance of the recruit's physical appearance and age.

[15] On the scrutiny for public office, see [Arist.] *A.P.* 55.3. For the special scrutiny of the entire body of citizens held in 346, see the references cited in chapter 1, note 20. For the possibility that the Egyptian grain episode prompted a similar scrutiny in the fifth century, see Philoch. *FGrH* 328 F 119; Diller 1937, 93; Patterson 1981, 95–96; Whitehead 1986, 97–98.

[16] Rudhardt (1962, 59) demonstrates that paternal recognition is established by an accumulation of individual acts of recognition performed at rites of passage and festal occasions (the Amphidromia, the tenth-day ceremony, phratry festivals, etc.), no one of which is sufficient in itself to establish legitimacy once and for all. For these festivals and ceremonies, see further Golden 1990.

forming to communal expectations of exactly who one was supposed to be—was a central, if implicit, practice of democratic citizenship.[17]

Engendering Egalitarianism

Just as the Athenian cultural context in which the Periclean citizenship law was installed shaped its practical and ideological meaning, so too the democratic context that authored the law interacted with the already operative cultural practices it tacitly enjoined. Although Athenian marriage and gender practices were not intrinsically democratic, their very invocation by the law to regulate access to a democratic political environment lent them new democratic salience. What is important for present purposes is that the law created the conditions that made relations between men and women a newly significant venue for generating and sustaining political relations between men. In what follows, I elaborate some of the ways in which relations between men and women could either engender or endanger the values and norms of democratic citizenship.

Democratic citizenship was based on a principle of egalitarianism.[18] Under the developed classical democracy, all adult male citizens (those with the proper birth requirements and who had been accepted by their demes) were considered equals, both politically and legally. In principle, they all had an equal opportunity to vote, to make important political and judicial decisions, and to speak in the political arena, and all enjoyed equality with respect to the law. Finally, most political offices were filled by sortition from the entire citizen body. These practices imply a belief in citizen equality, for as the democratic theorist Robert Dahl points out, it is hardly likely that a group would implement and continue to use democratic procedures without having or developing a corresponding belief in citizen equality.[19] If Dahl is correct about the relationship between principles and practice, then we need to consider what sources or practices produced and sustained the Athenian commitment to the belief that all citizens were in fact equal.

This is an especially pressing question for a number of reasons. While the norm of equality does seem to be implicit in democratic practices,

[17] The importance of public recognition encouraged citizens to gather witnesses for all important events, see Humphreys 1985b; Scafuro 1994.

[18] On the centrality of egalitarianism to Athenian democracy, see, e.g., Morris 1996, 19–48; Rauflaab 1996, 139–74; Ober 1989.

[19] I am here paraphrasing Dahl's comments on what he calls the "strong principle of equality," and "principle of equal consideration of interests" (1989, 31, 97–98). Morris (1996, 2000) applies these concepts to the Athenian democracy, arguing that an egalitarian belief system based on a principle of equality was a necessary precondition for the establishment of democracy in late-sixth-century Athens.

the evidence shows that egalitarianism never attained the status of blindly held conviction or foregone conclusion; egalitarianism was a dominant ideology but by no means an uncontested one. To cite just one example: in the aftermath of the Peloponnesian War, a period generally characterized by an intense democratic backlash in response to the manifold abuses of the Thirty Tyrants, a measure was proposed to limit citizenship to property holders.[20] Although the proposal was defeated, its very existence demonstrates that the democratic brand of egalitarianism was far from axiomatic. The most significant challenge to it came from various forms of social hierarchy that some felt ought to receive political weight.[21] The social order was characterized by significant inequalities in the distribution of wealth and perceived inequalities among the citizens with respect to ability, talent, birth, and status. Accordingly, it took an enormous amount of work to prevent these social inequalities from being converted into political inequalities, or to make political egalitarianism seem appropriate despite the existence of social hierarchy.[22]

The operation of the citizenship system generated a foundation for democratic egalitarianism. By defining citizenship with reference to the processes of biological reproduction, the law—drawing on and adapting processes that can be traced back to Solon's family legislation—implicitly annexed the asymmetry of the gender system to foster the construction of symmetrical relations between male citizens. The superior position of each male citizen in the gender hierarchy provided a common basis for his egalitarian status with respect to other citizens, regardless of his place in the social hierarchy.[23] Reworking Joan Scott's formulation, we might say that the law caused politics to construct gender and gender to construct politics in significant new ways.[24] For the law implicitly constitutes each citizen as an equal exchange partner whose equality is defined by his ability to enter the matrimonial economy (and to adhere to the city's sexual mores).[25] Thus marriage and sexual practices provided a common

[20] For the decree of Phormisios to limit citizenship to property holders, see Lys. 34.

[21] For tensions between social and political norms in Athens, see Ober 1989; Ober and Strauss 1990.

[22] As Walzer puts it: "since dominance is always incomplete and monopoly imperfect, the rule of every ruling class is unstable. It is continually challenged by other groups in the name of alternative patterns of conversion" (1983, 11).

[23] The argument that some form of sex inequality is foundational to egalitarian socio-political arrangements for men has been made by many feminist political theorists; see MacKinnon 1989, 3–12; Pateman 1988; Squires 1999.

[24] Scott (1988, 27) outlines a method of historical research attuned to the ways in which "politics constructs gender and gender constructs politics."

[25] The Periclean citizenship law constructed the male citizen body as a group of equal exchange partners. Their equal status depended on citizens having access to the same sphere of exchange. In practice, the dowry system ranked and valued women in economic

ground between citizens, a material domain for the generation of an egalitarian belief system.

While the Periclean citizenship law emphasized the matrimonial and reproductive equality of male citizens, it did not lessen existing economic differences between citizens that allowed for inequalities of sexual opportunity. Several measures, however, suggest that the state attempted to offset this differential sexual access. For instance, price controls were put on the fees that certain kinds of female prostitutes could charge.[26] One of the duties of the *astynomoi* (city controllers) was to prohibit "flute girls, harp girls, and lyre girls" from charging more than two drachmas for a night. If more than one man wanted the same woman, the *astynomoi* determined who would get the girl by a casting of lots, the quintessential democratic method of selection ([Arist.] *A.P.* 50.2).[27] According to a speaker in a New Comic play by Menander's slightly younger contemporary Philemon, the democratic forefather Solon himself passed a law instituting state-sponsored prostitution to channel the erotic energies of young men into a socially acceptable format.[28]

σὺ δ' εἰς ἅπαντας εὗρες ἀνθρώπους νόμον·
σὲ γὰρ λέγουσιν τοῦτ' ἰδεῖν πρῶτον, Σόλον,
δημοτικόν, ὦ Ζεῦ, πρᾶγμα καὶ σωτήριον,
(καί μοι λέγειν τοῦτ' ἐστὶν ἁρμοστόν, Σόλων·)
μεστὴν ὁρῶντα τὴν πόλιν νεωτέρων
τούτους τ' ἔχοντας τὴν ἀναγκαίαν φύσιν
ἁμαρτάνοντάς τ' εἰς ὃ μὴ προσῆκον ἦν,
στῆσαι πριάμενόν τοι γυναῖκας κατὰ τόπους
κοινὰς ἅπασι καὶ κατεσκευασμένας.
ἑστᾶσι γυμναί, μὴ 'ξαπατηθῇς· πάνθ' ὅρα.
οὐκ εὖ σεαυτοῦ τυγχάνεις ἔχων, ἔχεις
<ἐρωτικῶς> πῶς. ἡ θύρα 'στ' ἀνεῳγμένη.
εἷς ὀβολός· εἰσπήδησον. οὐκ ἔστ' οὐδὲ εἷς
ἀκκισμός, οὐδὲ λῆρος, οὐδ' ὑφήρπασεν,

terms, encouraging marriages between families of equal economic status and thus fostering social stratification rather than egalitarian norms. On the dowry system and the intergenerational reproduction of inequalities, see further chapters 1 and 4. Here it can be noted that the common subordination of all men to erotic desire, irrespective of their economic status, also leads to an egalitarian emphasis in the marriage plot (see *Thesauros* 176 K.-A.).

[26] I am describing the general category of prostitutes referred to as *pornai*. On this designation, see further Davidson 1997, 73–108.

[27] It was possible to use the "impeachment" procedure (*eisangelia*), a public indictment for treason and the attempt to overthrow the democracy, to try men who hired flute girls for a higher price than the law allowed (Hyp. 4.3).

[28] Athenaeus (13.569d) cites Philemon and Nikander of Kolophon to show that Solon passed such a law. On Nikander's report, see Halperin 1990, 186 n. 89; Kurke 1999, 196 n. 51.

ἀλλ' εὐθύς, ἣν βούλει σὺ χὢν βούλει τρόπον.
ἐξῆλθες· οἰμώζειν λέγ', ἀλλοτρία 'στί σοι. (3 K.-A.)[29]

But you found a law for all mankind:
for you were the first, Solon, they say, to discover
this practice, a democratic one, by Zeus, and a saving one
(and it's fitting for me to say this, Solon):
seeing the city teeming with young men
who, having their necessary nature,
were erring with respect to what didn't belong to them,
you bought and stationed women in various locations,
equipped as common possessions for all men.
They stand there naked, so you won't be deceived: you can see everything.
You don't happen to feel quite yourself,
you're feeling erotic perhaps? The door's open.
One obol: jump right in. There's no
coyness or nonsense, and she doesn't back away from you, but immediately,
whichever one you want and in whatever way you want.
You come out: tell her go to hell, she's nothing to you.

Although a comic fragment can hardly be taken as certain evidence that Solon passed such a law, the passage importantly, if parodically, attests to the conceptual associations between democratic ideology and prostitution, as David Halperin and Leslie Kurke have each discussed.[30] As Halperin puts it, "it shows that at least some people in classical Athens could look on prostitution as an intrinsic component of democracy."[31] Athenaeus quotes this passage along with similar excerpts from the Middle Comic poets Eubulus and Xenarchus.[32] Eubulus and Xenarchus praise the use of female prostitutes as a prophylactic against adultery and the pursuit of expensive *hetairai*. These activities frequently had political connotations insofar as they were associated with the wealthy and leisured—that is, the class of citizens usually suspected of harboring antidemocratic sentiments, as I discuss in more detail below. The speaker in Eubulus's *Nannion* flatly states that men commit adultery (have secret affairs) for the sake of *hubris* (outrage) rather than desire (ὕβρεος οὐ πόθου χάριν). The speaker in Philemon, however, claims that Solon de-

[29] The text is Kassel-Austin's except for the reading of νόμον instead of μόνον, the transposition of νόμον (2) and Σόλον (1) (Kock), and the reading of <ἐρωτικῶς> πῶς in 12 (Edmonds 1961). I am following Kurke's modifications of Kassel-Austin (Kurke 1999, 196–97).

[30] Halperin 1990, 101; Kurke 1999, 197.

[31] Halperin 1990, 101.

[32] Athen. 568e = Eubulus 82 K.-A.; Athen. 568f–69a = Eubulus 67 K.-A.; Athen. 569a–d = Xenarchus 4 K.-A.

tected a natural propensity in all young men to act inappropriately because of their sexual urges. This declaration of common male nature and hence equality (at least with respect to sexual impulse) receives added emphasis from the construction of female prostitutes as "common possessions for all," an objectification enhancing the perceived commonality of their purchasers.

"Solon's law" is conceptually democratic because the construction of women as interchangeable and available objects produces a corresponding equality of sexual opportunity in their male customers. According to the speaker, by giving up the "freedom" to err with regard to "what didn't belong to them," the citizens gained the right to employ and enjoy inexpensive prostitutes. Whether or not every citizen could afford a "cheap" prostitute, the fiction that he could helped define his status as a free and equal democratic citizen. At the same time, the speaker constructs the sexual economy of the brothel in accordance with fundamental democratic ideals. The classical democracy prided itself on making important knowledge publicly available, especially with regard to financial affairs. In the realm of prostitution, the democratic emphasis on full disclosure translates into the full nudity of females.[33] The speaker praises the prostitutes' exposure as a safeguard against deceit or unfair business practices (ἑστᾶσι γυμναί, μὴ ’ξαπατηθῇς· πάνθ’ ὅρα). By holding out the lure of viewing nude females to incite male desire, the speaker implicitly correlates sexual desire with the desire for democratic practice: one energizes the other.

This reading of Philemon 3 K.-A. builds on David Halperin's and Leslie Kurke's elaborations of the ideological implications of prostitution in Athens's democracy. Halperin considers the establishment of inexpensive female prostitutes as conceptually analogous to various measures ensuring the male citizen's bodily integrity, including the interdiction on prostitution for citizen men.[34] On this interpretation, the availability and penetrability of female prostitutes structurally counterbalances the protected bodily boundaries of citizen men while underscoring their status as penetrators. Kurke traces the comic (and democratic) construction of female prostitutes as completely interchangeable and alienable to the contest between elite and emergent civic culture in the archaic and early classical periods. Whereas the *hetaira*, an invention of elite culture, was

[33] Significantly, the emphasis on complete nudity occurs only in the Philemon passage valorizing the democratic utility of Solon's provisioning of cheap female prostitutes. In Eubulus's *Nannion* and *Pannukhis* (67, 82 K.-A.), the *pornai* are veiled, albeit in transparent garments, while in Xenarchus's *Pentathlum* (4 K.-A.), the *pornai* are described as sunbathing with bare breasts. The significance of these comic passages in Athenaeus's text is discussed in Henry (1992).

[34] Halperin 1990, 102–3.

associated with gold and gift exchange, the *pornē* celebrated by democratic culture was linked with coinage and commodity exchange. Like the state's regulation of coinage, the regulation of prostitutes can be viewed as

> a civic intervention into the circulation of goods and services to equalize the status of all citizens. For, as coinage breaks down the aristocratic monopoly on precious metals and top-rank goods and provides a standard against which all labor can be measured, these state-subsidized prostitutes (at least in the Athenian imaginary) endow all citizens with an equal phallic power. If *hetairai* function like metals in the fantasy of the aristocratic symposium, the *pornē* circulates like money in the agora.[35]

It should be clear from my own reading of Philemon that I agree with both of these interpretations; indeed, a main aim of this chapter is precisely to demonstrate the relevance of gender to democratic theory and practice. Yet though the passage from Philemon provides a particularly explicit gloss on what might be called the "the democratic ideology of prostitution," I do not believe the comedy from which this key passage has been culled (*Adelphoe*) endorsed that ideology. On the contrary, my suspicion is that the comedy, like Menander's comedy generally, implicitly challenged the commodification of the female body (as well as male desire) by championing heterosexual relations based on bonds of passion, male friendship, or both. It is true that the celebration of imagined naked female prostitutes in Philemon recalls the display of mute female nudes, very possibly *hetairai*, in Aristophanic Old Comedy.[36] The key point, however, is that in Philemon we are in the realm of the imagined rather than the real.[37] In contrast to Old Comedy, New Comedy employs narrative patterns that preclude the frank celebration of random and undirected male sexual passion (as I discuss further below). While the speaker in Philemon's *Adelphoe* is clearly recommending anonymous sexual relations with female prostitutes, in accordance with the conventional democratic gender ideology, the main narrative of the play almost certainly undercut this injunction by depicting a young citizen seeking a specific

[35] Kurke 1999, 198.

[36] See further Zweig 1992.

[37] The narrative perspective of the speaker makes it clear that these prostitutes were not actually paraded on the stage during his speech. Kock (1880–88, 2:479) suggests that a pimp was the speaker. If that was the case, we can safely assume that the comedy as a whole undercut his view of prostitution, because pimps are generally the most maligned figures in comedy. Alternatively, if, as Kurke speculates (1999, 197 n. 54), a young citizen who had recently enjoyed a cheap prostitute is the speaker, we can also be fairly certain that he was not the play's "hero," given comedy's conventional narrative patterns.

woman rather than casual sex with a stranger.[38] One suspects that the conventional gender ideology is so bluntly expressed in Philemon precisely because it was no longer so obvious or unquestioned that it could go without saying.

The gender ideology of democratic citizenship discussed so far might be summed up as follows. The egalitarian status of each male citizen was founded on and sustained by his sex right and sexual control over his female family members and prostitutes. No matter what his place in the social hierarchy, each citizen could afford sexual pleasure, given the plethora of inexpensive female prostitutes. While it is impossible to determine whether this equality of sexual opportunity translated into equality in practice, the important point is that Athenian ideology insists on the principle. Speakers in civic discourse often describe prostitutes and *hetairai* as common and available to "anyone who wished," even though a fee was attached to their services, with *hetairai* generally being more "costly" than prostitutes (*pornai*), as I discuss below.[39]

A striking example of the conflation of *hetairai* and *pornai* occurs in Isaeus's speech *On the Estate of Pyrrhus*. At issue in the speech is whether or not the mother of a rival claimant for Pyrrhus's estate (Phile) was Pyrrhus's legitimate wife or a *hetaira*. The speaker insists that the woman was a *hetaira* because she brought no dowry, or at least none that could be attested by witnesses. But when it comes to distinguishing the wife and the *hetaira*, the speaker does not, as might be expected, appeal to economic considerations (i.e., pointing out that a wife brought income into the household while the *hetaira* was presumed to extract it). Rather, he constructs the opposition primarily in terms of sexual availability. Phile's mother, he contends, was a *hetaira* because she was "common," and "available to all comers" (literally, "to whoever wanted"; Is. 3.11, 13, 16, 77). By denying the *hetaira*'s cost and her autonomy, in effect presenting her as no different from a *pornē*, the speaker diminishes the class resentment that a democratic jury might harbor against Pyrrhus and his

[38] Unfortunately, it is not known whether Philemon routinely constructed his comedies around a marriage plot. The *Trinummus*, a certain Plautine adaptation of Philemon's *Thesauros*, which employs a marriage plot (one in which the erotic energy is entirely sublimated into the bond between the young men), critiques the dowry system and the pursuit of expensive *hetairai* and thus conveys a general critique of commodified romantic and matrimonial relations. My guess is that the *Adelphoe* contained a similar critique. For comedy's challenges to the conventional gender ideology, see further chapters 5, 6, and 8.

[39] According to Kurke (1999, 180ff.), the conflation of the *hetaira* and the *pornē* in fourth-century civic discourse represents the triumph of egalitarian ideology. In many cases this is true, but it is important to note that the *hetaira* is not always assimilated to the *pornē* in Athenian lawsuits. Democratic citizens had good reasons for keeping the traditional elitist ideology of the *hetaira* alive and well, inasmuch as it provided precisely the contrast needed to underscore their own impeccable civic credentials; for examples, see further below.

relatives for their perceived ability to enjoy a lifestyle not open to everyone. In other words, the speaker contributes to the fiction that both prostitutes and *hetairai* were easily accessible to all citizens, irrespective of their economic circumstances. The conceit that any citizen could enjoy a prostitute was strengthened by the corresponding precept that every citizen had a right and a duty to marry an Athenian woman and to maintain exclusive sexual access to that woman.[40] Thus, marriage and prostitution can be seen as complementary structures: each practice delineates the citizen's rights and privileges while simultaneously figuring his egalitarian status.

The egalitarian work of gender, however, was challenged by deep-seated economic inequalities that, though not directly translatable into inequities of power and entitlement, could be used to forge status distinctions in the sexual sphere and to encroach on the sexual privileges of others. While sexual access was in theory "democratized" by the state's provisioning of inexpensive prostitutes, or at least by the fiction that prostitutes were available to anyone who wished, not all prostitutes were "equal" (despite the leveling depictions contained in Athenian lawsuits such as Is. 3). There were a variety of "sex workers" in ancient Athens: flute and lyre girls, streetwalkers, prostitutes who worked in brothels, *hetairai*. Yet the precise differences intended by these designations are often hard to pin down, especially with respect to the distinction between the *hetaira* and *pornē*.[41] For instance, in Menander's *Epitrepontes*, Habrotonon is described as a *hetaira*, a *pornē*, and a harp girl. In this case, it is not Habrotonon's actual status that determines her title but rather the attitudes of the male characters describing her.

Yet though the terms *hetaira* and *pornē* can be used interchangeably by male speakers, they were not exactly random designations. According to James Davidson, it is possible in the classical period to detect a difference between the *hetaira* and the *pornē* along an axis of gift and commodity exchange.[42] On this argument, the *pornē* or common prostitute exchanged a certain amount of time and specified sexual services for a fixed price, while the *hetaira* went to great lengths to obfuscate the terms of her dealings with men, exchanging unspecified favors and gifts with friends

[40] Although some commentators have argued that the Periclean citizenship law benefited native Athenian women by giving them a better chance at marriage (Hignett 1952, 346), according to Apollodorus ([Dem.] 59) this provision also served the needs of Athenian men. In his view, the Periclean law gave Athenian men the right, or at least the expectation, of being able to marry their daughters off without having to provide exorbitant dowries.

[41] On the variety of sex workers in Athens, see Davidson 1997; on their fees, see Halperin 1990, 107–12.

[42] Davidson 1997, 109–36. Cf. Kurke 1999, discussed above, and Kopytoff 1986, on the ideologies of commodity exchange.

in lasting relationships.[43] Although the *hetaira* may have successfully concealed her fees, or her conversion of companionship into gifts and favors whose value was not easily calculated in precise economic terms, she could not and did not attempt to conceal the fact that she was not readily available to just anyone. Everyone knew that the upkeep of a *hetaira* was in some way "expensive" and thus not an option for every citizen. Accordingly, a man known to be having a relationship with a *hetaira* was—to some extent—publicizing the comfort of his economic circumstances.

For this reason, having an affair with a *hetaira* cut two ways: it offered a way of asserting a status distinction but it also left a citizen vulnerable to envy and even judicial assault. A citizen who flaunted an affair with a *hetaira* while keeping a legitimate wife could be accused of using women as a material and quantitative gauge of status. In Athenian lawsuits, consorting with a *hetaira* is frequently characterized as a political liability linked to certain types of antidemocratic or anti-Athenian behavior. For instance, Demosthenes' attack on the orator Apollodorus assimilates his irregular sexual relationships to a general pattern of antidemocratic display and conduct: "You wear an expensive cloak and have freed one *hetaira* and married another . . . and you take three slaves about with you and live so licentiously that everyone knows about it" (36.45).[44]

A man's character could be blackened as antidemocratic or generally antipatriotic for having multiple affairs with *hetairai*—or even for having a relationship with one *hetaira* if he chose to reside with her instead of with a citizen wife. In his speech against Leocrates, Lycurgus is careful to mention that Leocrates deserted the city together with his *hetaira* as though his preference for a *hetaira* rather than a wife were in itself a testimony to his treason (Lycur. 1.17; cf. 21–22). In addition, the *hetaira* herself is sometimes constructed as the enemy of male and female citizens alike. Not only was the *hetaira* perceived as taking citizens away from female citizens in "need" of husbands, an issue Apollodorus harps on in his prosecution of Neaira, but also her adornment was seen as coming at the expense of female citizens. Thus, Callistratus attempts to elicit the jurors' rancor at his brother-in-law by disclosing that Olympiodorus lives with a *hetaira* rather than a wife, and by emphasizing that he allows her to lord her riches over allegedly less wealthy female family members:

[43] Socrates' encounter with the *hetaira* Theodote (Xen. *Symp.* 3.11.4ff.) is the locus classicus for the mystification surrounding the *hetaira*'s services; see further Davidson 1997, 128–30; Goldhill 1998.

[44] For a discussion of this passage and the antidemocratic associations of display, see Ober 1989, 206–8.

> This Olympiodorus, judges, has never married a native woman in accordance with your laws. He has no children and he has lost none. He does, however, have a *hetaira* in his home whose freedom he bought, and it is she who has brought ruin to all of us, turning his mind to greater madness. . . .
>
> It is not just for myself that I am engaged in this lawsuit, but for his sister, born of the same father and mother, who lives with me as my wife, and for his niece, my daughter. For they too are suffering injury no less than me, but even more. How are they not being injured or how are they not suffering terribly whenever they see this man's *hetaira* going out in splendid procession, showing off a great mass of gold and fine clothes beyond the limits of propriety, and committing *hubris* at our expense, while they are too poor to afford any of it? (Dem. 48.53, 54–55)

The speaker problematizes his brother-in-law's behavior in several ways. First, Olympiodorus's decision to opt out of the state matrimonial system in order to live with a *hetaira* is presented as a misdeed too shameful for his brother-in-law to mention (though that embarrassment is somehow overcome before the jurors).[45] But more significant than this affront to the cultural mores is the injury done by Olympiodorus's behavior to the female members of the family—his sister and her daughter. The harm to their status is specifically described as a form of *hubris*: the *hetaira*'s ostentation implicitly reduces the status of respectable but less well dressed female citizens.

The Politics of Seduction

In the competitive arena of democratic politics, egalitarian status was often figured in negative terms: no man was supposed to have more than his share of political power. Just as relationships with women could fortify the citizen's egalitarian status among men, so too could they lead to an emphasis on inequality and hierarchy. There were two especially problematic ways of using relationships with women to antidemocratic effect: taking more than one's share of women (by, for instance, keeping *hetairai*) and taking women who "belonged" to other citizen men. The latter could mean committing adultery with another man's wife or seducing his mother, his sister, or (worse yet) his virgin daughter. If caught in the act, the culprit could be summarily killed, or bound and subjected to the "radish" torture or any other punishment the citizen chose to inflict short of using a knife.[46] Moreover, any properly entitled citizen, not only

[45] For the shame-incurring aspect of relations with a *hetaira*, see chapter 5.

[46] Apollodorus states that the male victim could torture the accused *moikhos* in court in "democratic fashion": that is to say, he could do whatever he wanted, provided that he

the "injured" husband or father, could prosecute the accused with a *graphē moikheias*, possibly leading to the punishment of death.[47]

The law and ideology of *moikheia* have received a great deal of attention in recent years. In large part the credit for this upsurge in interest is owed to the important studies by David Cohen on law, social values, and ideology in democratic Athens.[48] One of Cohen's more controversial points, however, centers on the meaning of *moikheia*—what I translate as "seduction." Cohen contends that *moikheia* is equivalent to adultery and thus that it specifically refers to a violation against the marriage bond. But as many scholars have noted, the sources clearly attest that a man could commit *moikheia* with an unmarried woman.[49] For example, Apollodorus includes the solicitation of *moikheia* by fraud or entrapment among Stephanos's many offenses against the sociosexual mores of Athenian citizenship. He reportedly contrived to apprehend a certain Epaenetos from Andros as a *moikhos* with Neaira's unmarried daughter Phano (Dem. 59.64–65). Although Epaenetos initially agreed to pay the blackmail money, as soon as he was released he filed an indictment against Stephanos for false imprisonment. Epaenetos admitted to having sex with Phano but denied that he was a *moikhos*. According to Epaenetos, Phano did not have the status to support a prosecution for *moikheia*—not because she was unmarried, but rather because she belonged to the class of women who sit in a "brothel" (*ergastērion*; Dem. 59.67). This example attests that a woman's civic sexual status, rather than her marital status, is tied to the sexual prohibition in the legal construction of *moikheia*.

Cohen, however, points out that nearly all societies, especially Mediterranean societies, have a category of sexual prohibition specific to the marriage bond.[50] He defines *moikheia* as adultery because he assumes that the Athenians must have also had a concept and word for adultery. This

---

refrain from using a knife ([Dem.] 59.66). On the radish torture and depiliation, see Ar. *Nub*. 1083; Carey 1993; and on the punishment of the *moikhos*, see now Kapparis 1996, and Omitowoju 2001: 107–9.

[47] For the *graphē moikheia*, see [Arist.] *A.P.* 59.3. For other legal procedures that could be applied in cases of seduction, see further Harrison 1968–71, 1:35–36, and Omitowoju 2002: 109–15.

[48] D. Cohen 1990, 1991a, 1991b.

[49] For *moikheia* as applying to all Athenian women, irrespective of their marital status, see Harrison 1968–71, 1:36; Cole 1984; Cantarella 1991, 292–95; Foxhall 1991; Carey 1995; Omitowoju 2002, 72–115. For examples in Menandrian comedy, see Men. *Sik*. 209–10; *Pk*. 357, 370, 390, 986; *Sam*. 589–91.

[50] D. Cohen states, "Whether in ancient Near Eastern or Biblical Codes, in Byzantine, Roman, or Canon Law, in the laws of Manu, in the statutes of all early modern European states, or for that matter in the customary law of groups as diverse as the Nuer, the Trobriaders, the Bedouin, or the Sarakatsani nomads of Modern Greece, virginity and the marital relationship both represent distinct categories of sexual prohibition" (1991a, 102 with n. 91).

idiosyncratic interpretation is also related to Cohen's global thesis that Athenian law articulates a "democratic" conception of the private sphere, which, he argues, means an unregulated one. Cohen maintains that Athenian law did not regulate sexual behavior for moral reasons, but only when it represented a threat to the purposes and aims of the political community. Accordingly, he rejects the authenticity and existence of the *graphē moikheias*, a statute regarded as genuine by other scholars.[51]

Although I do not agree with Cohen's interpretation, his work is important in shoring up the exceptional nature of the Athenian conception and law of *moikheia*. The unique statutory provision can be explained, I believe, by the historically specific gender ideology of Athens's democracy. The restriction of sexual access to all "respectable" Athenian women reflects the state's interest in the reproductive integrity of all potential "bearers" of citizens. Since any sexual act was potentially a reproductive act for women, all nonmarital sexual activity had to be prohibited—in principle, if not in actual practice. This attitude underlies Euphiletos's oft-quoted claim that the *moikhos* commits a worse crime than the man who uses "force" (i.e., the rapist):

> Thus, men of the jury, the lawgiver believed that men who use force deserve a lesser penalty than those who use persuasion; for the latter he condemned to death, whereas for the former he doubled the damages, considering that those who achieve their ends by force are hated by those they have assaulted; while those who use persuasion corrupt the victims' minds, thus making the wives of other men more closely attached to them than to their husbands; they get the whole house into their hands, and make it unclear whether the children are the husband's or the seducer's. Accordingly, the lawgiver made death their penalty. (Lys. 1.32–33)[52]

The restriction of sexual access to unmarried women can be explained by the fact that they were eventually going to be married. Since the Athenians regarded past behavior and character as a reliable predictor of future behavior, ensuring the chastity of Athenian women before and after marriage was of the utmost importance. A woman's premarital sexual activity could, if it became known, call into question her perceived ability to bear legitimate children. This principle underlies the comic convention whereby a woman with known premarital experience can be married only to the man with whom she has had that experience, even if he has raped her.

The ideology of legal statutes can be uncovered by considering whom or whose interests a law protects, and also by considering whom or

[51] For the authenticity of the *graphē moikheias* ([Arist.] *A.P.* 59.3), see Todd 1993, 108.
[52] Trans. adapted from Todd 2000.

whose activities the law forbids. In the case of the *moikheia* statute, the law protects the sexual integrity of female citizens in the interests of citizen men. The law and ideology of *moikheia* also seems to be oriented to protecting Athenian men from the predatory behavior of other men. Lin Foxhall offers a Foucauldian interpretation of the Athenian ideology of *moikheia* based on the isomorphism between sexual and social relations.[53] According to this view, the prohibition of *moikheia* is geared less to protecting Athenian women than to protecting the authority of Athenian men over them. Since the citizen male was supposed to be able to control the sexuality of his household members, a sexual assault on a woman under his supervision would have undermined his authority in the household and hence the political authority and access his domestic supervision underwrote.[54] She further suggests that an attack on another man's women could be perceived as an attack on his standing as a democratic citizen, particularly in cases in which a significant socioeconomic disparity existed between the offender and victim: "[T]he infringement of another man's fundamental source of control over his female relatives created an uncomfortable tension between the egalitarian political ideology and the stratified and hierarchical socio-economic reality of classical Athens."[55]

Any attempt to impose a unitary explanation on Athenian attitudes and laws pertaining to *moikheia* is probably doomed to failure. K. A. Kapparis has shown that laws with implications for "adultery" were passed over several centuries and were accordingly shaped by varying concerns and attitudes specific to the period in which each was enacted.[56] Nevertheless, over time a democratic ideology of *moikheia* emerged as paramount. Aristotle, for instance, simply assumes without elaboration that *moikheia* is a "class crime" and therefore a political act. In the *Rhetoric*, he associates it specifically with the newly wealthy and remarks that no one would think that a poor or ugly man was guilty of *moikheia* (1372a23, 1391a19). The correlation of seduction and wealth may reflect the purely practical consideration that only someone with wealth would have the time and opportunity to seduce women in other men's households—this is certainly the assumption underlying the initial conflict between the impoverished

[53] Foxhall 1991, 299–300.

[54] Foxhall 1991, 299.

[55] Foxhall 1991, 300. According to Foxhall, Stephen Todd argues (in a forthcoming work) that the *moikhos* appropriated the political authority and power of his cuckolded victim specifically when he was of higher socioeconomic status. The idea that a man's poverty made his women vulnerable to wealthy predators appears to have been an important theme in Menander's *Plokion*; see 298 K.-A. with Gell. 2.23.14–20.

[56] Kapparis 1995, 120–21. The implementation of the Periclean law of citizenship also lent new democratic significance to the offense of *moikheia*.

Gorgias and wealthy Sostratos in the *Dyskolos*, as we will see in the next chapter.

In fourth-century lawsuits, *moikheia* is sometimes presented as a general form of reprehensible behavior. For instance, Diocles, the villain in one of Isaeus's inheritance cases, is characterized as someone whose greed leads him to trample on the rights of others by cheating heiresses, arranging murder, and committing *moikheia* (Is. 8.40–44). What is perhaps most shameful and outrageous about Diocles' perpetration of *moikheia* is that he persists in the practice even after having suffered the customary punishment for such offenders caught in the act. In a speech on Phormio's behalf, Demosthenes impugns the orator Apollodorus's democratic credentials by speaking of his ostentatious display with multiple *hetairai* (Dem. 36.45). In a speech against one of Phormio's witnesses, Apollodorus responds in kind. He accuses the "rich, wicked, and greedy" Phormio not only of living in an "adulterous" union, but also of having seduced the wives of many men. Significantly, Apollodorus rhetorically assimilates Phormio's serial seductions with his habit of using citizen men as prostitutes and depriving them of their civic rights (Dem. 45.79).

According to Euphiletos, the speaker of Lysias 1, *moikheia* is the only offense that is regarded with equal severity in democracies and oligarchies alike (Lys. 1.2). Nevertheless, there is evidence linking *moikheia* with antidemocratic or oligarchic ideology that, in fact, comes from this very case.[57] There are two speeches in the Lysianic corpus titled *Against Eratosthenes*. In Lysias's first speech, Euphiletos, a man who contrived to catch the adulterous Eratosthenes in bed with his wife, is defending his action in killing or executing the seducer. In second *Against Eratosthenes* (Lys. 12) Lysias himself is denouncing the oligarchic member of the Thirty Tyrants who reportedly had a hand in killing Lysias's brother and confiscating his property. In 404/3, in the aftermath of the Peloponnesian War, the members of this Spartan-backed regime abolished the law courts and the rule of law, and systematically confiscated the property of

[57] Whereas I emphasize that the democratic context invested the offense of *moikheia* with specific political connotations, Cohen argues that the honor/shame code was paramount in the construction of *moikheia* and accordingly interprets the offense through the rubric of Mediterranean anthropology. He describes the *moikhos* as a quasi–Don Juan figure, a man of honor who augments his status by the sexual conquest of women attached to other men (D. Cohen 1990, 163–64; cf. 1991a, 61–63). While the analogy may be apt, there is absolutely no evidence for it. Far from being a man of honor, the *moikhos* is described as an abject and womanly man (Davidson 1997, 165). In a democratic context it would not have been possible to acknowledge openly the status won by the citizen's sexual conquests, as such a claim would have diminished the collective standing of the citizen body. *Moikheia* can be considered antidemocratic because it represents taking more than one's share of women. The Don Juan syndrome may be better invoked in the context of aristocrats competing among each other for young men.

as many rich citizens and metics as they could. The Thirty were notorious for breaking into other men's homes in the night, abducting and murdering them, and stealing their possessions. Although it has been argued that the Eratosthenes in both speeches is one and the same man, some scholars object to the identification because there is absolutely no hint in Lysias 1 that Eratosthenes the adulterer was involved with the Thirty, or with politics at all.[58] The omission, it is argued, is telling because Lysias would surely not have passed up an opportunity to further demonize the adulterous Eratosthenes. Yet the omission can be explained in another way, taking into account the assumptions regarding the association between sexual activity and political activity in democratic culture. In this light, the narrative of Eratosthenes' sexual exploits reads like a political allegory of the crimes of the Thirty Tyrants.[59]

In democratic rhetoric, the Thirty were associated with a pattern of behavior that might be described as the political equivalent of *moikheia*. While the *moikhos* stealthily infiltrates other men's homes, appropriating sexual access to other men's women (Eratosthenes is said to have made the seduction of other men's wives his *tekhnē*—his special skill or craft), the Thirty were notorious for wrongfully entering the homes of other men and appropriating their property (e.g., Lys. 12.19). Though the Thirty advertised a program of civic reform and morality, they effectively abolished the rule of law, putting as many as 1,500 men to death without trial.[60] In Euphiletos's defense speech, Euphiletos embodies the return of the democratic rule of law. As Euphiletos presents it, Eratosthenes' most egregious offense was penetrating and outraging the physical space of the house (Lys. 1.4). While Eratosthenes' passion for the sexual conquest of other men's wives led him to wantonly break the city's laws, Euphiletos, on finding Eratosthenes naked and in bed with his wife, calmly declared before clubbing him to death: "It is not I who am killing you, but the city's laws" (Lys. 1.27).[61]

[58] The most recent review of the question can be found in Kapparis (1993), who concludes that the identification of the two men is impossible; see also Avery 1991.

[59] Perotti (1989–90) and Porter (1997) argue that Lysias 1 is a fictional case. According to Perotti, Lysias 1 is an allegory, with the relationship between Euphiletos and his wife standing for the relationship between the polis and the democracy. Eratosthenes thus alienates Euphiletos's wife in the same way that the Thirty estranged the polis and democracy. Porter, however, sees the case as a comic adultery story. While I propose that the rhetorical strategies of Lysias 1 suggest a translation of the Thirty's politics into the sexual domain, I make no claims as to the authenticity of the speech; for ideology in Lysias 1 see now Wolpert 2001.

[60] On the moral-legal program of the Thirty, see Lys. 12.5; [Arist.] *A.P.* 35.2–3; Xen. *Hell.* 2.3.12.

[61] For Euphiletos's repeated characterization of his action as a state-sanctioned execution rather than a killing or murder, see Herman 1993.

During the second half of the fourth century B.C, the associations between sexual behavior and political ideology become newly explicit in civic discourse and, I would argue, newly important for the purpose of constituting democratic civic identity. In this period, a kind of collective democratic morality seems to be forming, as attested by the rhetoric of family values that pervades political discourse.[62] It was fueled, in large part, by the changes in Athenian circumstances, including the city's diminishing military stature. Although I discuss this moralization of democratic civic identity in more detail in chapter 7, here I want to call attention to one prong of the process, visible in the Athenian statesman and finance minister Lycurgus's vigorous projects of democratic cultural renewal.[63] In order to remake democratic culture in the aftermath of Athens's catastrophic military defeat in 338, he made frequent and innovative use of the courts and legal procedures to articulate and enforce democratic ethics and values. In one prosecution, known primarily from Hyperides' speech on the defendant's behalf, Lycurgus impeached an Athenian citizen for *moikheia*. Lycurgus argued that by sleeping with other men's wives and freeborn virgins, the defendant was overthrowing the democracy (Hyp. 1.12.).[64] The defendant responded by parroting Lycurgus's tragic rhetoric, charging that he was the one subverting the democracy:

> Also, you accuse me in the impeachment of undermining the democracy by breaking the laws; yet you yourself overrode all the laws when you submitted an impeachment concerning matters where the laws prescribe public actions before the *thesmothetai*. Your primary motive was to enter into the trial at no risk; but in addition you wanted the opportunity to write melodrama into the impeachment—as indeed you have now done—by charging that I am making many women stay indoors and grow old unmarried, while forcing many others into unsuitable and illegal marriages. (Hyp. 2.12)[65]

By making visible Lycurgus's rhetorical and judicial ploys, the speaker seeks to neutralize and belittle his charges. The *eisangelia* procedure was a form of impeachment that could be used to prosecute anyone accused of attempting to overthrow the democracy as well as to prosecute cases of bribery and treason.[66] Lycurgus used it to prosecute Leocrates for fleeing the city after Chaeronea, and here to prosecute Lycophron for undermining the democracy by seducing freeborn women. Although the

[62] For the emergence of morals discourse as a key component of citizen identity in the second half of the fourth century, see further chapter 7.

[63] For the Lycurgan project, see references cited in chapter 2, note 52.

[64] Cf. Lycur. *Against Lycophron*, fr. 2 Burtt.

[65] Trans. Whitehead 2001.

[66] See Hyp. 4.7–8, with Hansen 1991, 213.

speaker calls attention to Lycurgus's tragic language to suggest that the accusation is a ridiculous rhetorical overstatement, the use of tragedy was probably crucial to the logic of his case.[67] Lycurgus's prosecution of Lycophron, like his prosecution of Leocrates, belongs to his project of political and cultural refashioning. To that end, Lycurgus seems to have used his prosecutions to find scapegoats on whom to shift the blame for the decline in the city's affairs.[68] For instance, in the speech against Leocrates, Lycurgus characterizes Leocrates as a brute lacking in the normal feelings of kinship for the city and its citizens, thereby implicitly attributing responsibility for the defeat to Leocrates and citizens like him and removing it from the mass of citizens. That Lycurgus uses tragic diction to describe the effects of Lycophron's supposed adultery suggests a similar tactic of attributing the tragic turn in the state's affairs to internal outsiders, here blaming the "immoral" Lycophron rather than the unfeeling Leocrates.[69]

Although Lycurgus's characterization of *moikheia* as a dangerous antidemocratic offense is shaped by a postdefeat historical setting and by his immediate rhetorical needs, his very ability to explicitly and directly make such an argument attests to the preexisting association between *moikheia* and antidemocratic behavior. What is novel in Lycurgus's prosecution is that *moikheia* is presented as an urgent threat requiring political attention. This urgency is probably related to the general moralization of democratic identity taking place in the second half of the fourth century, a process that I discuss more fully in chapter 7. For present purposes, what is important to note is that the conventions of comic romance uphold the democratic ideology of *moikheia* articulated by Lycurgus. In comedy, seduction or *moikheia* rather than "rape" is depicted as the most serious sexual offense.

This overview has presented some of the ways that gender structured and was structured by democratic ideology. Far from being removed from politics, relations between men and women in the putatively private sphere were a constitutive axis of democratic civic identity and ideology.

[67] The same logic likely accounts for Hyperides' use of comedy in defending Lycophron; see Hyperides' second speech in defense of Lycophron.

[68] Lycurgus also prosecuted Lysicles, one of the Athenian generals at Chaeronea, and Autolycus, a member of the Areopagus who removed his wife and children from the city to protect them from the Macedonians.

[69] His creation of official texts of the works of the canonical three tragedians and his rebuilding of the theater of Dionysos in stone demonstrate the importance of tragedy to Lycurgus's political-cultural project ([Plut] *Vit. X Orat.* 841f). For the strategic use of tragedy in his speeches, see Wilson 1996, 312–14. Yunis (2000), on the use of tragedy as a mode of historical explanation in Dem. 18, is also relevant.

The Periclean citizenship law, and the laws and procedures that supported it (the *graphai* for *xenia*, *moikheia*, and *hubris*), encouraged a dynamic interaction and cross-fertilization between gender and politics. In the remainder of the chapter, I consider how comedy's stories of citizen-making evoke, reinforce, and in some cases transform this cultural complex. For, as I noted above, although comedy is scrupulously faithful to the laws and norms pertaining to citizenship, it nevertheless employs its own conventions, themes, and narrative patterns to depict the citizenship law in action.

To cite one example: because of the strong antidemocratic associations attached to seduction, comedy often uses an act of rape rather than a seduction to motivate its ultimately law-abiding citizenship plots. In so doing, comedy sends an ideological message that both supports and subverts the democratic gender system. By casting the heroine as the victim of rape, usually imagined as an act of overwhelming passion, comedy invests the female citizen with a newly explicit source of sexual value for Athenian men. It thereby subtly undermines the external and internal boundaries of the citizenship system: the emphasis on the female citizen's sexual value blurs the boundary between female citizens and noncitizens while simultaneously paving the way for reconstructing power relations between male and female citizens. But this is to anticipate matters discussed later. For the remainder of this chapter, I review some of the most prominent strategies with which comedy dramatizes the citizenship law in action, considering how they produce effects that enhance the ideology of citizenship and how they also subvert and transform it.

Passionate Protagonists and Practical Citizens

Comic characters generally conduct their romantic lives in accordance with the dictates of private passion rather than legal norms.[70] In Menander's *Dyskolos* and *Aspis*, the protagonists immediately seek to marry for what seem to be purely personal considerations of desire and love. It is generally agreed, however, that these plays place an unusually explicit emphasis on love or eros as the proper foundation for a legitimate citizen marriage.[71] More frequently, comedy establishes the correlation between love and marriage covertly or retrospectively: citizen marriages come

[70] For *eros*—which can mean both desire and perhaps "love"—in Menandrian comedy, see Flury 1968; Gomme and Sandbach 1973, 24; A. Masaracchia 1981, 213; Anderson 1984; Walcot 1987; Wiles 2001, 43; P. G. Brown 1993; Konstan 1995, 93–95. On tradition and originality in Terence's depiction of love, see Barsby 1999, 5–29. For more general discussions, see Rudd 1981; Thorton 1997; Calame 1999.

[71] See also Terence's *Phormio* and *Andria*.

about as if by accident, as happy coincidences of private passion and civic law.[72]

In many plays, the protagonist is able to marry the heroine only when, at the last minute, she is by chance found to be a lost citizen. In plays following this pattern (the recognition plot), emotional and erotic attraction are presented as the true basis for the relationship.[73] For instance, in Menander's *Perikeiromenē* and *Misoumenos*, the protagonists consider and treat their respective mistresses as wives even though neither woman seems to be eligible for marriage. The protagonists in these plays seem content to remain indefinitely in nonmarital relationships. They decide and desire to marry the heroine only when circumstances make that possibility available, that is, after the heroine's true citizen status is recovered.[74] The same pattern recurs in every recognition plot: a last-minute discovery of the heroine's true identity allows an already-established romantic relationship to be normalized in citizen marriage.[75] While these plays ultimately uphold the norms of Athens's matrimonial citizenship system, they nevertheless send the message that the real reason for the marriage is the young citizen's passion, not his sense of obligation to the state's law.

A similar emphasis on the personal motivation for marriage occurs in plays structured according to a rape plot.[76] In this pattern, a young Athenian citizen usually rapes and impregnates a female citizen prior to the opening of the play. The plot focuses on normalizing the rape and its consequences by bringing about the happy ending of the marriage of the rapist and victim. Although the conventions of this plot type reveal a

[72] See Konstan 1983, 160.

[73] For the recognition motif, see Menander's *Heros*, *Karkhēdonios*, *Kitharistēs*, *Misoumenos*, *Sikyōnioi*, and *Phasma*; Terence's *Andria*, *Eunuch*, and *Self-Tormentor*. Menander's *Epitrepontes* and Terence's *Hecyra* deploy a variation on the recognition motif. See further Webster 1974, 57–67; Fantham 1975, 56–59; Goldberg 1980, passim; Zagagi 1994, 23–26, 51–64. On the ideological effects of the recognition motif, see Konstan 1995; on recognition as the paradigmatic device of naturalistic comedy, see McCarthy 2000.

[74] See Konstan 1995, 107–19, for the lack of motivation for the marriage in Menander's *Perikeiromenē*.

[75] In Terence's *Andria*, however, the protagonist is willing to marry the heroine by fraud—i.e., before her true status has been retrieved. The hero in the *Cistellaria* may plot a similarly fraudulent marriage, though it is not clear whether the marriage laws in Sikyon were precisely the same as those in Athens.

[76] For the rape plot, see Menander's *Geōrgos*, *Epitrepontes*, *Heros*, *Kitharistēs*, *Plokion*, *Samia*, *Phasma*, and *Fabula Incerta*; Terence's *Adelphoe*, *Eunuch*, *Hecyra*, and *Phormio*; Plautus's *Aulularia*, *Cistellaria*, and *Truculentus*. For the use of Roman comedy as evidence of Athenian law and judicial or pretrial practice, see Paoli 1976, 76–77; Fraenkel 1960, 399; Fantham 1975, 44–45; Ogden 1996, 175; Scafuro 1997, 16–19. For rape in Menandrian comedy, see Fantham 1975; Konstan 1995, 141–52; Pierce 1997; Scafuro 1997, 238–78; Rosivach 1998, 113–50; Sommerstein 1998; Lape 2001; Omitowoju 2002.

great deal about the gender ideology of democratic citizenship and the ideological work of comedy, for present purposes I will consider only one facet of the rape motif.[77] Most often, rape in New Comedy occurs at a nighttime religious festival,[78] a context so common that even the characters know the convention. A slave in Menander's *Epitrepontes* remarks: "a nighttime festival and women. It's likely that a girl was raped" (451–53). The citizen rapists are portrayed as young, drunk, and excessively passionate (e.g., Ter. *Ad.* 470–71). Although the rape is presented as a random, anonymous, and unpremeditated act, the scenario is always implicitly constructed according to civic specifications.[79] Comic protagonists always rape female citizens who are eligible for citizen marriage; although noncitizen women are generally present at these nighttime festivals, they are never targeted. These conventions lead to the tacit conclusion that the rape and the marriage it compels are motivated by the protagonist's desire for a female citizen. Thus, while the rape and recognition plot patterns represent two different generic strategies by which comedy portrays the citizenship law in action, in each case the catalyst for making the marriage is the same—namely, male desire for a female citizen.

This emphasis on the passionate basis for citizen marriage is striking because in the Athenian civic context, marriage was not conceived as an institution geared toward satisfying either the emotional or the sexual needs of citizens. The primary (though not the only) purpose of Athenian marriage was the procreation of legitimate heirs and citizens. The Athenian orator Apollodorus succinctly states the official ideology:

> τὰς μὲν γὰρ ἑταίρας ἡδονῆς ἕνεκ' ἔχομεν, τὰς δὲ παλλακὰς τῆς καθ' ἡμέραν θεραπείας τοῦ σώματος, τὰς δὲ γυναῖκας τοῦ παιδοποιεῖσθαι γνησίως καὶ τῶν ἔνδον φύλακα πιστὴν ἔχειν. ([Dem.] 59.122)[80]

[77] For the ideological work of the rape motif, see chapter 1 and Lape 2001.

[78] In the *Epitrepontes*, the rape is said to have occurred at the previous year's Tauropolia; in the *Phasma*, at the Brauronia or Adonia (95, 97); in Plautus's *Cistellaria* (based on Menander's *Synaristosai*), at a festival to Dionysus in Sikyon (156); in the *Aulularia*, at a festival to Ceres (36, 794–95); in the *Plokion*, at an unidentified nocturnal festival (Gell. 2.23.15). The festival setting is not specified in Terence's *Adelphoe* (470–71). No information concerning the rape scenario is attested in the extant fragments of Menander's *Geōrgos* or *Heros*. The circumstances of the rape in Terence's *Hecyra* (the street, 822–28) and *Eunuch* (in the home of a courtesan) are exceptional.

[79] The exception occurs in Terence's *Eunuch*: Chaerea stalks a woman he believes to be a slave and contrives a plot to gain sexual access to her. The young man in the *Heros* also rapes a presumed slave or noncitizen (the circumstances of the rape are not given in the extant portions of the play).

[80] For discussion of this passage and its perceived value as a source for social history, see Wolff 1944, 74; Vernant 1980; Just 1989, 52–53.

For we have courtesans for pleasure, concubines for the daily service of our bodies, and wives for the production of legitimate offspring and to have a trusty guardian of our household property.

In recent discussions of this passage, scholars argue that the various criteria Apollodorus employs to delineate female social identities are not (in every case) meant to be mutually exclusive.[81] According to this view, Apollodorus is not denying that Athenian men received sexual satisfaction from their wives, but rather is making the point that wives were the only women entitled to bear legitimate heirs. It is not my intention to enter into the debate regarding where and with whom Athenian men actually found sexual pleasure. Rather, I want to elaborate the implications of the distinctions actually drawn by Apollodorus. He defines female social identity on the basis of the sexual significance attached to the female body in the context of a lawsuit in which he is explicitly trying to show that being a *hetaira* or *pornē* is absolutely incompatible with being a citizen wife. He does not mention or admit that wives provided a source of sexual pleasure to their husbands, precisely because his rhetorical strategy is to argue that Neaira cannot be a citizen wife not only because she has been sexually available to many men, but also because she has been an object of sexual pleasure "often times and in numerous and disgraceful ways" ([Dem.] 59. 114). Although Apollodorus largely agrees with the speaker in Isaeus 3, who distinguishes wives and *hetairai* primarily on the basis of their sexual availability to Athenian men, he emphasizes that being sexually available means being a slave to the lusts of men. He assumes that there is something inherently demeaning and shame-incurring in being made to serve the sexual needs of another. Given this conception, there are good grounds for thinking that Apollodorus intended to draw a firm distinction between *hetairai* and wives as possessing, respectively, sexual versus reproductive utility. In any case, his complete lack of explanation or apology in offering his schema of female identity suggests that he regarded it as relatively uncontroversial. It

[81] P. G. Brown 1990b, 247–28 with n. 35; Thorton 1997, 166. By contrast, Sealey (1984, 118) dismisses this statement as nonsensical precisely because he understands Apollodorus to be identifying the services and activities that define and distinguish wives, *hetairai*, and concubines. He finds it absurd that the *pallakē* was limited to providing "nonsexual massage." While Sealey may be perversely literal in this interpretation, Apollodorus's description of the province of the *pallakē* is undeniably awkward; on this issue, see further Vernant 1980, 47–48; Mossé 1989; Davidson 1997, 73–77. My own view is that Apollodorus stumbles when it comes time to identify the concubine's role because the institution of concubinage was rare, if it existed at all, in the classical polis, see especially Patterson 1991b; Mossé 1991; Cox 1998. Significantly, Stephanus's defense was going to hinge on the claim that he kept Neaira as a *hetaira* rather than a *pallakē* or wife (118–19). For the implicit bias against the keeping of concubines articulated already in Solon's laws, see Lape 2002–03.

seems reasonable, therefore, to accept Apollodorus's statement as an expression, perhaps even the official version, of a dominant ideology.[82]

The production of legitimate children was a matter of both religious and political concern in democratic Athens.[83] In a study of marriage patterns in Isaeus, Signe Isager concludes that "nearly every man and woman in Athens got married."[84] Isaeus's inheritance cases also make it clear that the procreative imperative of marriage overrode considerations of emotion or sentiment. Even a marriage based on male friendship and a purportedly deep affection between husband and wife ended in divorce because the couple remained childless for several years.[85] Furthermore, the state could intervene in the lives of married couples, separating them and uniting each with different partners, in the interest of maintaining the number of *oikoi* in the polis (or in the interest of maintaining the legitimacy and "purity" of the civic group, as [Dem.] 59 makes clear). The heiress or *epikleros* could be compelled to divorce her husband and marry her nearest relative within the *ankhisteia*.[86] The speaker in Isaeus 3 remarks that it has often happened that husbands have been deprived of their wives because of the laws governing the heiress (Is. 3.64). In addition to the interlocking religious, procreative, and political aspects of Athenian marriage, economics also weighed heavily in marriage strategies.[87] The partibility of Athenian inheritance meant that exogamy or marriage beneath one's economic class could result in the fragmentation of estates.[88] Like other agrarian societies in which estates are divided equally among male heirs, the Athenians used kinship endogamy (combined with strategic exogamy) to consolidate property and to prevent the dissolution of family holdings.[89]

[82] Actual social practices may have contradicted the official ideology; see Bourdieu 1977; Giddens 1979; Winkler 1990a; Cohen 1991a; Roy 1997.

[83] Thompson 1981, 20–21; Just 1989, 90. Rubinstein (1993) suggests that Athenian litigants may present a distorted or exaggerated view of the imperative to produce heirs and perpetuate the *oikos* since claims about the disaster of allowing an *oikos* to die out are made in very self-serving contexts.

[84] Isager 1980–81, 89.

[85] At least this is how the speaker explains his divorce; see Is. 2.7–8. On the reasons for divorce, see Cohn-Heft 1995.

[86] On the epiklerate, see Gernet 1921; Harrison 1968–71, 1:132–38; Schaps 1979, 25–47; and below. Roy (1999) describes the *ankhisteia* as a legally instituted kinship group that came into being for the limited functions of determining rights of inheritance and duties. On the composition of the *ankhisteia*, see further Harrison 1968–71, 1:143–48.

[87] Male friendship and politics were also important considerations in marriage strategies; see Is. *Menecles* 2.4 and Lys. 19. For the political strategies underlying the marriages of fifth-century political figures, see Humphreys 1993, 25; Cox 1998.

[88] Cox 1998, 34.

[89] Cox states, "a rough estimate from the known or inferred marriages in Davies's listing, for instance, indicates a proportion of endogamous unions of 19 percent—not a terribly

The Comic Romance Narrative: Marrying Interest and Necessity

It is not clear whether comedy's emphasis on the "romantic" basis of marriage represents an entirely novel conception. But clearly the possibilities of what could be said in public discourse about the reasons why ordinary citizens married had changed. In comedy, Athenian men not only passionately desire their wives and wives-to-be, but they also (implicitly or explicitly) see passion for a specific woman as the primary basis for the marital relationship.[90] By contrast, while the Athenian orators mention a variety of motives for marriage (friendship, kinship, economics, etc.), they never mention passion as a consideration in selecting a marriage partner.[91] Thus, there is a discrepancy between the official purpose for making a marriage—namely, to produce children—and the romantic motives that characters favor in comedy. In general, comedy's emphasis on romantic marriage is taken to signal a real historical shift not only in attitudes toward marriage but also in conceptions of identity.[92] By marry-

---

high figure compared to other agrarian societies that practice kinship-in-marriage" (1998, 32, with n. 96). For marriage and kinship loyalty, see Is. *Apollodorus* 7.11–12; Thompson 1967; Just 1989, 80–81. On kinship endogamy as an Athenian marriage strategy, see R. Osborne 1985, 135–36; Gallant 1991, 42–46; Cox 1998, 31–37.

[90] While the romantic and sexual elements of citizen marriage are vividly portrayed in Aristophanic comedy, most especially in *Lysistrata*, Old Comedy does not depict eros as a *motivation* for making a marriage. The only literary evidence (to my knowledge) imputing a sexual motive for citizen marriage is the concluding passage of Xenophon's *Symposium*. When the dinner party was nearing its close, two actors enacted the mythological marriage of Dionysus and Ariadne. The speaker states: "When the guests eventually saw them in each other's arms and going off as if to bed, the unmarried men swore they would get married and the married men mounted their horses and rode away to their own wives with the same end in view" (Xen. *Symp*. 9.2–7). Since Xenophon was a critic of Athenian democracy, his works cannot be taken as objective reporting on democratic culture. In the *Symposium*, as in the *Oeconomicus*, Xenophon is, in part, engaged in a project of refashioning aristocratic social practices to make them less threatening to democratic culture. Thus the symposium, usually associated with aristocratic nonmarital sexualities including pederasty and various forms of prostitution, is here celebrated as a prelude to civic marriage. For the antidemocratic associations of sympotic culture generally, see O. Murray 1990. For Xenophon's portrayal of aristocratic and gender ideology, see Johnstone 1994; Murnaghan 1988.

[91] This absence may simply reflect the nature of the sources, in which even to mention an Athenian woman by name was enough to call her respectability into question. For the avoidance of naming respectable women in the Athenian lawsuits, see Schaps 1977.

[92] Recent work both in and out of classics acknowledges that romantic love is a modern construct with no necessary counterpart in other historical epochs (cf. Belsey 1994). That said, questions as to whether comedy attests a link between love and marriage in Athenian culture, or perhaps signals the emergence of a new romantic ideal of marriage, remain contentious. Part of the problem, as noted above, is the difficulty of determining the se-

ing for love, comic characters privilege their own autonomy and capacity for personal choice. For this reason, several commentators have seen the comic love plot as presaging the emergence of the "individual."[93] At one time, such a claim would not have been subject to scrutiny, as such emergence was considered an unproblematic part of an evolutionary and even teleological process. Nowadays, however, the "individual" is often considered a contingent social construct manufactured in precise historical circumstances to meet specific historical needs. Before considering what the emphasis on passionate marriage *for men* does within the framework of comic plots, I want to consider whether there are grounds for associating it with the rise of "individualism" as it has come to be understood.

Since the Enlightenment, the individual has been viewed as a self that stands apart from, and exists prior to, all social formations. In Alisdair MacIntyre's definition, "I am what I myself choose to be. I can always, if I wish to, put in question what are taken to be merely contingent social features of my existence."[94] This conception has its roots in the transition from monarchy and rule based on hereditary privilege to the rise of the state based on "universal citizenship." Social contract theorists provided a founding ideology for the modern state by creating a new type of inhabitant: the individual. By making those in the state "individuals" before they were citizens, social contract theorists beginning with Hobbes were able to subordinate prior identities based on family, class, and status to a new form

---

mantic range of the Greek word *eros*. P. G. Brown argues (1993, 189–205) that New Comedy supports a love-marriage link. Davidson's suggestion (1997, 127–128) that the very lack of access to respectable women may have served to spark male desire for them supports this thesis. Walcot (1987), however, argues that New Comic love plots do not show that a romantic ideal of marriage existed or was developing, whereas Rudd (1981) sees at least the lineaments of romantic love emerging in Greek New Comedy. In the most recent book-length study of eros, Thorton states that Menander's comedies "clearly indicate a recognition that in Hellenistic Greece, at least among the middle class reflected in comedy, love should have been or least often was a precondition for marriage." He undercuts this claim, however, by concluding that comedy alone cannot be used "to support the attribution of 'romantic love' or 'romantic marriage' to the Hellenistic Greeks" (Thornton 1997, 175). Wiles (2001, 52, 50) considers romantic love in comedy as a discourse employed to negotiate changing relations between the individual and the state and to reconcile "many of the basic oppositions and contradictions in Greek democratic life." It is worth repeating that Menander's comedy does not portray romantic love as a mutual bond or attraction between two people, but rather portrays the hero's idealization and objectification of the heroine (see P. G. Brown 1993, 198). Although the heroines in the *Epitrepontes* and *Misoumenos* are clearly attached to their respective partners, it is only in Roman versions of New Comedy that we find heroines who vividly express romantic feelings for their lovers; see, e.g., Plautus's *Cistellaria*.

[93] Wiles 2001, 52, and 1991, 30; Hofmeister 1997.

[94] MacIntyre 1984, 220.

of discrete identity. In this way, they were able to forge a group out of a disparate and fragmented population. Inhabitants of the state were linked by a shared construct of individual identity that needed protection from the state.[95] There is no trace of this form of individualism in the world of comedy. Comic protagonists may temporarily reject social conventions, but they in no sense perceive themselves as having a presocial identity.

While the Enlightenment ideology of the individual is not in evidence in comedy, the emphasis on marrying for love might well be an index of the emergence of a historically specific brand of individualism linked to the particular circumstances of Hellenistic Athens. The period in which Menander wrote was marked by catastrophic change on both the domestic and international fronts. Since transformations on the political and international level can provoke transformations of self-identity and new forms of intimate relationships, it is certainly possible that the backhanded valorization of marrying for love in comedy is a symptom of wider cultural and historical processes.[96] In a matter of a decade, Alexander the Great had completely changed the shape of the world, sometimes toppling in the span of mere days empires that had stood for centuries. Moreover, large-scale demographic shifts were occurring throughout the period, bringing people from different *poleis* and regions into contact with unprecedented frequency. At the same time, traditional sources of civic identity were rapidly evaporating. Citizens had once been defined by their military role as protectors of the city, but in the Hellenistic period the citizen army could no longer protect the city from various foreign powers.[97]

Viewed from this perspective, the emergence of an ideal of romantic marriage and the individualist ethic that it implies might be seen as a response to the general uncertainty of the times. In other words, the valorization of marrying for love in Menander's comedies need not be viewed in negative terms as a "rejection of politics" but rather may signal the formation of a new site on which identity could be anchored in a rapidly changing era. Whether there is anything political or polis-oriented about this new source of identity remains to be seen. That the individual protagonist seems to act on his preferences rather than on considerations of the polis and civic community does not really tell us anything. In a seminal essay on nationalism, Etienne Balibar states that the forging of national identities "is not a matter of setting a collective

[95] This ideological negotiation is the reverse of the process that enabled the transition to democracy in Athens. Solon and Kleisthenes used law to create a concept of citizenship based on membership in the polis rather than in the family or in any other social group.

[96] Giddens (1991) traces the effects of globalization and modernity on conceptions of the self and intimate relationships.

[97] See Ridley 1979 and chapter 7 below.

identity against individual identities. *All identity is individual*, but there is no individual identity that is not historical or, in other words, constructed within a field of social values, norms of behavior and collective symbols."[98]

What must be considered, then, is how the comic hero's privileging of a romantic motivation for marriage sits with the broader purposes and aims of civic community. It is undeniably true that the erotic basis for citizen marriage in comedy leads to an emphasis on personal rather than political considerations: protagonists marry for what seem to be egoistic reasons of personal passion. On closer inspection, however, the opposition between the personal and political (or the individual and the communal) collapses. Whatever putative reason Menandrian characters offer for their matrimonial decisions, in making marriages in accordance with the Periclean law they are necessarily supporting that law and its ideology. In other words, although comedy individualizes its heroes, it always does so in accordance with civic norms. Thus, far from posing a threat to the marriage system, the emphasis on the passionate motive for marriage leads to the naturalization of the city's contingent norms of citizen status. It grounds the principles of civic membership on the seemingly nonpolitical desire of male citizens for female citizens. In so doing, comedy portrays the democratic civic body as self-regulating, and for that reason entirely immune from the vagaries of political circumstance.

Staging a Biopolitics of Democratic Citizenship

The Periclean law granted a kind of political recognition to women: women were recognized as members of the civic community on the basis of their role in the reproductive process. This produced changes that simultaneously enhanced and worsened the status of women—at least in the realm of ideology. The need for a native woman to bear legitimate and "Athenian" heirs led to the implicit recognition of women as bearers and carriers of "Athenianness." Yet this gain was counterbalanced by the knowledge that any nonmarital sexual activity on the part of a woman necessarily called the paternity and hence legitimacy of a citizen's children into question. As one Menandrian speaker puts it: "a mother loves her child more than the father; she knows it's hers, he only thinks so" (657 Kock). Consequently, the implementation of the Periclean law fostered an ideology of female sexual control.[99] Since women embodied both the integrity and contours of the citizenship system, their sexual activity

[98] Balibar 1991, 94.

[99] For the politics of the citizen's control over the sexuality of the members of his household, see Foxhall 1991.

became a matter for more direct political concern and supervision: nonmarital female sexual activity was, in effect, legally proscribed.[100] This is not to say that Athenian women refused to participate in nonmarital sexual activity. The very risks attached to such behavior may have made it seem that much more interesting and inviting.[101] But with the passage of the Periclean law, a norm of female sexual integrity was attached to the official ideology of the Athenian citizenship system (which, of course, may bear little resemblance to what women actually did).

In dramatizing the law in action, comedy converts the official ideology of female sexual integrity into an unassailable generic convention. Although traumatic circumstances such as shipwreck and kidnapping frequently obscure the identity of female citizens and lead to situations that imperil their chastity, the civic constraints of the genre demand that they enact their proper status. This means two things. First, female citizens only ever have one sex partner, their husbands or eventual husbands. And second, Athenian women must always have a husband. Lost female citizens are found less to reunite fragmented families than to enable the women themselves to assume their proper roles as bearers of citizens.[102] These conventions are especially clear in plays in which a rape is resolved in the second generation. In such plays, a citizen rapes and impregnates a woman. After giving birth, the woman exposes the child and unknowingly marries the very man who violated her. The action generally takes place when the exposed child reaches sexual maturity and must either resume her true identity or risk losing the sexual respectability entitling her to that identity.[103]

Menander's *Heros*, a play known from a short plot summary and about one hundred verses, vividly and exceptionally portrays the dangers facing heroines in plays following this pattern.[104] Before the action of the play begins, Myrrhine gave birth to twins, a boy and girl, as a result of a rape. Rather than exposing the children, she gave them to a shepherd to raise and subsequently married Laches, apparently without realizing that he was very man who had raped her. When the shepherd dies, the twin children are forced to work off the debt their shepherd father owed Laches. In turn, one of Laches' slaves falls in love with the "heroine," and thinking her of similar status, asks his master to be allowed to live

[100] This prohibition is implicit already in the Draconian law of justifiable homicide (Dem. 23.53–54) and explicit in the *graphē moikheias*. On the dating of these provisions, see Kapparis 1995.

[101] See Roy 1997; D. Cohen 1990.

[102] The exception is Plautus's *Epidicus*, in which family reunion replaces romance.

[103] The normalization of a rape in the second generation seems to have occurred in Menander's *Heros*, *Kitharistēs*, *Phasma*, *Hiereia*, *Synaristosai*, and probably in the *Hypobolimaios*.

[104] For the plot, see Gomme and Sandbach 1973, 385.

with her in the equivalent of marriage. This arrangement, impending when the play begins, would obviously disqualify the heroine from resuming her rightful status (42–44).[105] In fact, it is the only case in Menander's extant comedy in which we find a slave in love with a citizen.[106] The union is ruled out from the start, however, because a young citizen has already raped and impregnated the heroine. And in accordance with the conventions of comic rape, it is this man—the heroine's one and only sex partner and a citizen—whom she must eventually marry.

While female citizens are constructed less as characters in their own right than as placeholders of the reproductive sexuality required of female citizens in Athenian law and ideology, Athenian men do not fare much better. Menander's young citizen protagonists are the least developed or individuated characters appearing in the plays. This is, to be sure, partly explained by the fact that their "real," adult lives begin only after the comedies end.[107] But the genre's deployment of relatively character-less protagonists also stems from the purely instrumental role in which they are cast. Although male and female citizens in comedy seem to be differentiated on the basis of their sexuality—the male is active and the female passive—male characters are no more in control of their passions than female citizens are in control of their bodies. Young citizens in love envision themselves as slaves compelled to do eros's bidding rather than as masters of their desires.[108] More important, the difference between male and female sexual autonomy collapses in the reproductive arena: citizen men are also destined to preserve and enact their civic procreative status.

[105] The heroine and her twin brother do not seem to have been technically enslaved, but rather are in the process of working off debts incurred by their foster father.

[106] Some commentators see this as exceedingly transgressive insofar as it shows that love can dismantle status barriers supposed to separate citizens and noncitizens (A. Masaracchia 1981, 219–20). The fact that eros has already done its work—i.e., the heroine has been raped by a citizen before the play begins—softens somewhat the transgressive effects of eros in the comedy. The critical thrust of the play lies in the implied ethical contrast between the slave and citizen in love. Whereas the slave acts with exemplary self-restraint and decorum, the citizen, by virtue of the rape he commits, is portrayed as lacking ethical mastery. What is more, according to the plot summary, the slave volunteered to take the blame for the citizen's action, and thus "marry" a woman with prior sexual experience.

[107] Frye states, "We are simply given to understand that the newly married couple will live happily ever after. . . . That is one reason why the character of the successful hero is so often left undeveloped: his real life begins at the end of the play, and we have to believe him to be potentially a more interesting character than he appears to be" (1957, 169). The exception occurs in Menander's *Epitrepontes* (see further chapter 8). Kharisios's maturation and apparent development may be possible precisely because he is already married and living his life, as it were, rather than suspended on the threshold of adulthood as is more frequently the case with comic heroes.

[108] *Dys.* 345–47; *Sam.* 621–32; *Thesauros* 176 fr. K.-A.

Comic protagonists are notorious for the rapes they commit during their drunken escapades at anonymous nighttime festivals. Although they rape in mixed company—that is, in contexts in which citizens and noncitizens are present—they never accidentally rape women of noncitizen status. In comedy's carefully constructed rape scenarios, Athenian men seem predestined to desire only female citizens. If civic sexuality is irresistible, so too is civic reproduction. Pregnancy and childbirth inevitably result when female citizens are raped in comedy, as the young democratic citizen acquires the sexual and reproductive potency previously reserved for the gods in myth.[109] The hyperfertility of rape constructs the female citizen as a passive and reproductive being—exactly the ideological construction embodied in Athenian law. At the same time, it also emphasizes the civic reproductive sexuality of the citizen male. The ideological significance of this construction is clarified by a peculiar generic injunction: in Menandrian comedy, Athenian men never inadvertently impregnate women of noncitizen status.[110] This is striking because male citizens in Menander's plays often have affairs with noncitizen women (courtesans, mistresses, and slaves). In other words, the hyperfertility of comic rape is matched by the corresponding sterility of all nonpolitically productive sexuality. Athenian men in comedy are incapable of fathering real bastards (children whose status cannot be legitimated by the retrospective marriage of their parents).

The corollary to the convention forbidding the birth of true bastards is the rule requiring that all legitimate or potentially legitimate children survive. In Menander's *Perikeiromenē* and *Heauton Timoroumenos*, male citizens expose legitimate children for economic reasons. In each case, however, the children survive and are eventually reunited with their families in the working out of the love plot. Just as in many of the rape plot

[109] See, for instance, Euripides' *Ion*, where the foundation of the citizenship system, and thus the transition from autochthony to sexual reproduction, is catalyzed by Apollo's rape of Creousa.

[110] There are some exceptions to this rule in Roman versions of Greek New Comedy. In Terence's *Phormio* (based on a play by Apollodorus), Chremes, an older Athenian citizen, seems to have been a bigamist, keeping a secret Lemnian wife and child in addition to his Athenian family. Since Athenians could intermarry with Lemnians, this secret marriage did not actually disturb the nationalist orientation of the citizenship system (see further Ogden 1996, 178–79). It did, however, violate the principle that a man was supposed to have only one wife at a time (except perhaps for a brief period during the Peloponnesian War). The play papers over the bigamy issue by having the Lemnian woman conveniently die upon arriving in Athens. The action focuses on normalizing the status of her daughter by Chremes, which means arranging a proper citizen marriage for her. The play that clearly violates the rules of the comic love plot is Plautus's *Epidicus*. Although the heroine is restored to her family, she turns out, exceptionally, to be a real bastard. The play substitutes the conventional closure of the marriage plot with a new form of closure—i.e., freedom for the slave.

plays, mistakes and transgressions made by men in one generation are revised or corrected by the following generation.

A near exception to comedy's generic ban on bastardy occurs in the *Samia*. Demeas, a wealthy older Athenian citizen, has a live-in Samian mistress. Before the action of the play begins, his adopted son Moschion raped or seduced Plangon, the neighbor's daughter, who subsequently became pregnant and gave birth to an illegitimate child. Moschion promises the girl and her mother that he will confess to his father and arrange to marry the girl as soon as Demeas returns from a business trip, but he breaks his promise and delays. He decides to take the easy way out and allows Chrysis to pass off Plangon's child as her own for the time being—by an amazing coincidence, Chrysis happened to become pregnant with Demeas's child at exactly the time that Plangon conceived. Unfortunately, the crucial lines in which Moschion relates the information about Chrysis's pregnancy are badly damaged. It is certain that Chrysis was actually pregnant because Demeas later sees her breast-feeding Moschion's child (*Sam.* 265–66). We do not know what happened to Chrysis's baby, beyond its failure to survive. In his recent notes on the text, W. Geoffrey Arnott concludes that line 57 contained a statement "to the effect that Chrysis herself had borne a child at about the same time as Plangon but that it had died, been stillborn, or even perhaps exposed."[111] On the basis of comedy's generic ban on bastardy, I would argue that Chrysis child was miscarried or stillborn, but not exposed (a crucial point).

By allowing Chrysis to conceive but rendering the pregnancy nonviable, the comedy gets to have it both ways: it preserves the prohibition against bastardy while exploring issues of bastardy and the limits of male knowledge. This situation is made possible by Demeas's irregular living arrangements. He is the only citizen in all of extant comedy to install successfully a former *hetaira* in his home, choosing to live with her rather than with a citizen wife (see chapter 5). Although such arrangements were not technically illegal, they were nonetheless dangerous because they created the appearance of a "fraudulent" marriage. It is precisely this perception that Demeas seeks to ward off by insisting that Chrysis expose the baby he supposes is their child. It is as if the very act of bringing Chrysis into his house threatens to transform her into a wife—that is, a woman with a reproductive sexuality (*Sam.* 130). Her pregnancy

[111] Arnott 1998a, 39. Some scholars have argued, however, that Demeas was mistaken and did not actually see Chrysis breast-feeding the baby. For the view that Chrysis did not bear a child, see Dedoussi (1988b). This argument does not fit with the rest of the play as we now have it, since the plot hinges on the fact that Chrysis was known to have been pregnant and on her ability to breast-feed (84–85). See further West 1991 and chapter 5 below.

underscores the pragmatic and dangerously permeable distinctions of sexual status that separate wives from "all the rest," to borrow Davidson's useful phrase.[112] At the same time, the stillbirth of the child conceived by Chrysis vividly preserves and reinforces that differentiation. But disturbingly, it is as if the polis has appropriated Chrysis's maternal, if not reproductive, capacity. Although she cannot bear children for the polis, she can care for them. Her failed pregnancy allows her to act as a surrogate, to feed but not produce a citizen child.[113]

In using adherence to the citizenship law as its central generic convention, comedy grants the law more constraining force than it could have had in practice. The polis did not make it illegal to father bastards. Rather, it discouraged men from fathering bastards by making bastardy a socially and politically abject status. Bastards could not inherit from their fathers and conversely were not obliged to support their parents in old age.[114] Comedy eliminates the potential for conflict between law and lived realities by granting the democratic polis a monopoly on the reproductive capability of the citizen. Thus, the comedies construct the citizen's body as a "corporeal abbreviation" of the arbitrary norms of citizen status.[115] Characters uphold the law and its ideology not out of deliberate choice but simply as a matter of generically predetermined biological necessity. With the transformation of citizenship from a pragmatically enacted status into a bodily destiny, comedy passes off its own intensely ideological valorization of the citizenship system as no more than natural biology.

Although comic plots reinforce the exclusive norms of democratic citizenship, in many cases the narrative entertains the fiction that a real or imagined violation of civic ideology has occurred. As various plots within the plays unfold, characters expose the unfair arbitrariness of the state kinship system that made legitimacy the sine qua non of family and polis membership. For instance, in the *Samia* Moschion tries to convince Demeas to raise the child that Demeas mistakenly believes he has fathered with Chrysis. Demeas indignantly refuses, justifying his position by emphasizing that the child was born out of wedlock, as it were. In other

[112] Davidson 1997, 74, 76.

[113] On the maternal dispositions of Menander's courtesans, see Henry 1986 and chapters 5 and 8 below.

[114] If recognized by his father, a *nothos* could receive a small inheritance (*notheia*) from his father's estate of either 1,000 drachmas, according to Harpocration (s.v. *notheia*), or 500 drachmas, the figure given in Ar. *Birds* 1650ff. According to Plutarch (*Sol.* 22.4), Solon passed a law releasing children born from courtesans (*hetairai*) from the responsibility of caring for their parents. On Athenian bastards, see Patterson 1990; Ogden 1996; Hartmann 2000.

[115] I borrow this phrase from Bourdieu 1977, 93–94.

words, although Chrysis is a Samian, the play does not problematize her status, or the status she transmits to her supposed child, in ethnic terms.[116] Rather, the problem with the baby's status is presented solely in terms of its bastardy: Demeas insists that he is not the sort of man to rear a bastard.[117] In response, Moschion first asks:

τίς δ' ἐστὶν ἡμῶν γνήσιος, πρὸς τῶν θεῶν,
ἢ τίς νόθος, γενόμενος ἄνθρωπος;

(*Sam.* 137–38)

Who of us is legitimate, by the gods,
or a bastard, being a human being?

It seems as though Moschion is appealing to a universalizing conception of human nature that trumps the polis's arbitrary and irrelevant kinship statuses. He continues:

οὐθὲν γένος γένους γὰρ οἶμαι διαφέρειν,
ἀλλ' εἰ δικαίως ἐξετάσαι τις, γνήσιος
ὁ χρηστός ἐστιν, ὁ δὲ πονηρὸς καὶ νόθος[.]

(140–42)[118]

I don't think birth makes a difference;
if one examines the matter justly, the good man is
legitimate and wicked man a bastard.

With this statement, Moschion challenges the state's ability to assign fixed social identities based on its own rules of sexual reproduction. According to Moschion, the true source of social identity is to be sought in the "individual" himself, or more precisely in his ethical status. Accordingly, his overall argument might be taken as indicating that an emergent conception of human nature was beginning to replace the narrow kinship statuses privileged by the democratic polis. The power of this alternative vision is undercut, however, by the dramatic circumstances in which Moschion offers it. When Moschion defends the bastard child's right to life, he knows full well that the child is his own (rather than his father's) and that it will soon become legitimate by his own marriage to its mother. In

[116] That the barrier to Chrysis and Demeas's marriage centers on her status as a *hetaira*, rather than as a foreigner in Athens, is a tacit critique of ethnicity or nationality as a basis for civic exclusion.

[117] ἄλλωι με θρέψειν ἔνδον ὑὸν προσδοκᾶις / νόθον; [. . . .]ν γ' οὐ τοῦ τρόπου τοὐμοῦ λέγεις (135–36).

[118] These lines are attributed by Stobaeus in "On Good Birth" to Menander's *Knidia* rather than the *Samia*. It is possible that the lines occurred in both plays.

other words, Moschion's critique of the state kinship system operates on a dramatic level to preserve and reinforce that system.[119]

Democratic Reproduction in the *Aspis*

The means by which comic characters obey democratic civic norms in Menander's plays reveal the polis not as a place "out there," absent from the comedies, but as the prior framework structuring the romantic plots and inhabiting the bodies of comic characters. Thus, far from representing a retreat from the political domain, comedy insistently (and insidiously) adheres to its norms. But it remains to be considered whether there is anything particularly or markedly democratic in how comedy promotes civic norms. By way of conclusion, and to pave the way for the next two chapters, I will discuss one way in which comedy's support for the laws of democratic civic membership is in some instances linked to an affirmation of the substantive values of the democratic political community. By portraying the law in action, Menander's plays deploy a romantic narrative that makes the Periclean correlation between political and biological reproduction seem natural. Such narratives are particularly well suited to promoting an ideological agenda because they cast marriage (and getting the girl) as the reward that some characters get and others do not.[120] The marriage plays thereby send the message that certain behaviors and attitudes lead to sexual and romantic success and hence political reproduction. Just as comedy allows only state-sanctioned reproduction, so too only characters whose actions are properly democratic (or at least not nondemocratic) obtain sexual and reproductive success. Since comic protagonists are generally one-dimensional characters whose civic behavior consists precisely in their appropriately directed sexual desire and reproductive capacity, the democratic emphasis in the comedies often emerges most clearly in plays that feature a rival lover who lacks a properly democratized character.

Smikrines in Menander's *Aspis* is the most villainous rival in the extant fragments and plays. When his niece suddenly seems to become a wealthy

[119] In one Menandrian fragment (835 K.-A.) a speaker criticizes his mother's interest in *genos* (family). He concludes, like Moschion, that character rather than kinship is what makes a man wellborn. An important difference, however, is that while Moschion's critique of kinship is directed at the state kinship system and its privileging of legitimacy, the speaker in the fragment seems to be disparaging notions about kinship based on national and ethnic origins. Without knowing the context in which this passage occurred, it is obviously impossible to assess its impact and meaning.

[120] Thus Frye likens the action in comedy to a lawsuit "in which plaintiff and defendant construct different versions of the same situation, one finally being judged as real and the other as illusory" (1957, 166).

heiress (*epikleros*), Smikrines demands to marry her, despite her having already been promised to a young citizen who is deeply in love with her. To make matters worse, as the oldest living male relative (her brother is mistakenly presumed to be dead) he seems to have the legal privilege, though not as he claims the obligation, to do so.[121] It is clear to all, however, that it is the girl's new wealth, and not the girl herself, that has fired Smikrines' sudden passion for marriage (e.g., *Asp.*139–43). The divine speaker of the prologue specifically reports that Smikrines cares for money and wealth rather than people (117–20, 123). Thus the marriage plot is framed as a contest between competing matrimonial motivations of love and money. In Athens, this competition would have had a marked political inflection. Smikrines' obsessive love of wealth, coupled with his lack of regard for social relationships and ethical considerations, implicitly stigmatizes him as an oligarch. The link between wealth and oligarchic ideology was pervasive in Greek thought and enjoyed heightened prominence in Menander's day, thanks to the Macedonian policy of controlling Athens through the imposition of oligarchic regimes (see chapter 4). Consequently, the struggle for the girl, a struggle about who gets the marriage and who gets to reproduce, is also a contest between oligarchic and democratic political norms—and hence a contest over the terms of political reproduction.

It is as if Smikrines is so offensive to comedy's civic ethical norms that his ultimate defeat must be overdetermined. His adversaries stage a play within a play in order to trick him out of his matrimonial pretensions by placing another, seemingly more wealthy, pseudo-heiress before him. At the same time, the heroine's brother unexpectedly returns alive and well from a mercenary campaign, voiding Smikrines' claim on both the girl and the property. Interestingly, Smikrines' defeat is prefigured on the biological level, too: his overvaluation of wealth, a marker of oligarchic ideology, is implicitly tied to his waning potency and questionable fertility. His brother Khairestratos pleads with Smikrines to have the decency not to make a marriage he is obviously too old for:

(Kh.) ὢν τηλικοῦτος παῖδα μέλλεις λαμβάνειν;
(Sm.) πηλίκος;
(Kh.) ἐμοὶ μὲν παντελῶς δοκεῖς γέρων.

(*Asp.* 258–59).

Khairestratos: Are you planning to marry a young girl at your age?
Smikrines: My age?
Khairestratos: I think you're really an old man.

[121] The legal issues in the *Aspis* are examined in Karabelias (1970), Gomme and Sandbach (1973), Karnezis (1977), MacDowell (1982), and P. G. Brown (1983).

At first glance, Khairestratos's emphasis on Smikrines' age seems very odd, inasmuch as Athenian men normally married much younger women. Because it is the only instance in all of New Comedy in which age difference is presented as a relevant barrier to marriage, Adele Scafuro suggests that Khairestratos's argument is a case of "special pleading."[122] But Khairestratos is not alone in focusing on the question of Smikrines' age. Khairestratos, Daos, and the divine prologue speaker each describe Smikrines not merely as older than his intended bride, but specifically as an extremely aged man (γέρων), at least within the confines of comedy's generic youth culture.[123] Although Athenian men had considerable latitude as to their age at marriage, Isager concludes in her study of marriage patterns in the private lawsuits of Isaeus that "a man could become so old that public opinion would be against his marriage. If there was reason to think he was too old for siring children, he ought to refrain from marrying."[124]

When a man married an *epikleros*, the official procreative purpose of marriage and the man's perceived ability to sire children had an added importance.[125] It was the legal duty of the man who married an heiress to father a child to inherit the estate that "went with the woman." A law attributed to Solon required that the husband of the heiress have intercourse with her three times a month (Plut. *Sol.* 20.2–3). This stipulation draws attention to the purpose of the *epiklerate*: namely, to allow a man to pass on his estate through a daughter or a sister. Thus, on coming of age, the heiress's children inherited the estate and were to be adopted into their maternal grandfather's or uncle's household (*oikos*). According to the prevailing interpretation, these Solonian provisions were calculated to maintain the number of households in the polis rather than to allow estates to fall into the hands of relatives. In other words, the law concerning the *epikleros* privileges the reproduction of families over the familial accumulation of wealth. The matrimonial conflict in the *Aspis* portrays exactly this tension.

By repeatedly emphasizing Smikrines' advanced age, the characters appear to be hinting that he will not be up to meeting his conjugal obligations. The servant Daos seems to question Smikrines' potency when he incredulously asks: "Marry her? . . . Will he be able?"[126] The lack of an

[122] Scafuro 1997, 288–93.

[123] *Asp.* 114, 142–43, 259, 351. Although Smikrines' age is never actually specified, he is older than his brother Khairestratos, who is married with grown children (255).

[124] Isager 1980–81, 86. See Is. 2.6, 6.22–24.

[125] The following brief overview of the epiklerate draws on Gernet (1921), Harrison (1968–71, 1:132–38), Schaps (1979, 25–47), Just (1989, 95–98), V. Hunter (1994, 13–15, 22–23), and Cox (1998, 94–99).

[126] (Kh) μέλλει γαμεῖν γὰρ αὐτός. / (Da) εἀπέ μοι, γαμεῖν; / δυνήσεται δέ; (*Asp.* 310–11).

infinitive in line 311 leaves it unclear what kind of ability Daos is asking about. Khairestratos answers Daos's query: "That's what the 'fine and noble' gentleman *says*" (311).[127] It is no accident that Khairestratos refers to Smikrines with a term for an aristocrat and an oligarch—ὁ καλὸς κἀγαθός—at precisely the moment his sexual and reproductive prowess are being questioned.[128] In its characterization of Smikrines, the comedy slyly relates oligarchic ideology, here marked by Smikrines' overvaluation of wealth, to impotency and infertility.

This association is supported by the evidence of other Menandrian comedies: Smikrines is not the only rival character to have political affiliations undermined in sexual terms. For instance, Moschion in the *Sikyōnioi* is stigmatized as an oligarchic seducer of questionable masculinity, a characterization that stands in pointed contrast to the hero's commitment to the norms of democratic matrimonial and political practice. Thus in some instances at least, comedy joins its naturalization of democratic civic and sexual norms to a corresponding critique of oligarchic political and sexual ideology. The next chapter pursues this idea in more detail, considering the critique of oligarchic ideology contained in the marriage negotiations in the *Dyskolos*, the sole complete specimen of Menander's comedy recovered to date. Whereas the *Aspis* affirms the democratic ideology of marriage by impugning the rival's economic motives for marriage, the *Dyskolos* not only condemns oligarchic ideology but also explicitly affirms the egalitarian values of the democratic political order.

[127] This interpretation of the text was first suggested to me by R. L. Hunter.

[128] For the association of the label *kalos k'agathos* with elitist ideology, see Lys. 12.86; Isoc. 8.133; Ober 1989, 259–61; Bourriot 1995.

4

The Ethics of Democracy in Menander's *Dyskolos*

The Politics of Love at First Sight

Although Menander's comedy persistently correlates male romantic passion (eros) with Athenian citizen marriage, as I discussed in chapter 3, the plays usually establish and affirm this link only retrospectively.[1] In some cases, marriages based on male erotic attraction for a female citizen come about as if by accident, as chance events made possible by the last-minute discovery of the heroine's true citizen identity. In other cases, the need to repair an act of rape leads to the formation of a citizen marriage implicitly based on male passion.[2] The romantic plot in Menander's *Dyskolos*, however, significantly deviates from these conventional patterns. In the prologue, the god Pan explains (37) that he has made the protagonist Sostratos fall madly in love with the heroine to reward her for carefully tending his shrine and the nymphs.[3] The action opens with Sostratos explaining to his incredulous friend, the parasite Khaireas, that he has just seen a girl, fallen irrevocably in love, and decided to marry her.[4] After listening to Sostratos's story, Khaireas describes the services he usually provides for friends in love.

> . . . παραλαμβάνει τις τῶν φίλων
> ἐρῶν ἑταίρας· εὐθὺς ἁρπάσας φέρω,
> μεθύω, κατακάω, λόγον ὅλως οὐκ ἀνέχομαι·
> πρὶν ἐξετάσαι' γὰρ ἥτις ἐστί, δεῖ τυχεῖν.
> τὸ μὲν βραδύνειν γὰρ τὸν ἔρωτ' αὔξει πολύ,
> ἐν τῶι ταχέως δ' ἔνεστι παύσασθαι ταχύ.
> γάμον λέγει τις καὶ κόρην ἐλευθέραν·
> ἕτερος τίς εἰμ' ἐνταῦθα· πυνθάνομαι γένος,
> βίον, τρόπους.
>
> (58–66)[5]

[1] See chapter 3, note 70.

[2] For the recognition motif and rape plot pattern, see chapter 3.

[3] The heroine "flatters" Pan and the nymphs, *Dys*. 39–44.

[4] On the identification of Khaireas as a parasite in the cast list, see Handley 1965a, 138–39 ad 48.

[5] The text of this play quoted throughout is Sandbach; translations are adapted from Arnott.

Suppose one of my friends conceives
a passion for a courtesan; right away I snatch her,
I get drunk, I set fires, I don't endure reason.
It's necessary to seize her before you find out who she is.
Delay greatly increases passion,
but a quick beginning means a speedy conclusion.
Say a man suggests marriage with a freeborn girl;
I'm a different man; I make inquiries about her family,
economic status, and character.

In effect, Khaireas rehearses the conventional parts that he, the comic parasite, knows how to play. In so doing, he suggests that Sostratos has gotten his plots mixed up, that he is treating a freeborn girl like a courtesan. Khaireas does not, of course, succeed in convincing Sostratos of the error of his ways. Rather, the sole point of his brief appearance in the play seems to be to call attention to the unusual romantic plot about to unfold.[6] While the first scene underscores the novelty of Sostratos's immediate decision to marry for love, by the conclusion of the play the romantic basis for a male citizen's marriage is cast as an unquestioned orthodoxy: Sostratos's father simply states that eros makes a young man's marriage more secure (788–90). Thus, rather than following the more typical comic strategy of retrospectively linking desire and marriage, the *Dyskolos* deploys eros specifically and explicitly to generate a citizen marriage.

The *Dyskolos* differs from every other extant comedy in which a citizen desires to marry for love in that Sostratos conceives this desire before he meets the heroine or even learns her identity.[7] The "love at first sight" strategy neutralizes the implicitly political considerations of kinship, class, and social status that normally went into the making of Athenian marriages. At the same time, by basing marriage on love rather than law, it constructs the marriage system as natural and self-generating. Remarkably, the *Dyskolos* employs this ideologically potent marriage strategy at precisely the time when marriage had lost its special status as the privileged institution of citizenship and political reproduction.[8]

According to the didaskalic notice, the *Dyskolos* won first prize at the

[6] See further Konstan 1995, 93–94.

[7] Cf. Men. *Asp.*, Ter. *An.*

[8] Although a few commentators have noticed the discrepancy between comedy's interest in issues of citizen status and the reality of the contemporary political situation, there has been little attempt to interpret or explain this curious phenomenon. Davies (1977–78, 113–14) argues that comedy's interest in issues of citizen status is pure escapism. Modrejewski (1981, 247) and Vérilhac and Vial (1998, 60) use the evidence of Menandrian comedy to argue that the Macedonian intervention did not affect the—matrimonial—citizenship system. Ogden (1996, 174) mentions the fact that New Comedy essentializes the citizenship system during the period of Macedonian domination.

Lenaia in January of 316 B.C., about one year into Demetrius of Phaleron's oligarchic regime.[9] During this time, wealth was required for citizenship—1,000 drachmas, to be exact—rather than bilateral Athenian parentage alone (Diod. 18.74.3). Although there is no direct evidence that Demetrius's regime suspended the democratic matrimonial norms of citizen status, they were without question subordinated to an overarching wealth requirement.

By rooting the norms of citizen marriage in male sexual desire and love, the *Dyskolos* deploys a seemingly nonpolitical and innocuous strategy of reasserting the democratic citizenship system while resisting the norms of oligarchic political membership. In this way, the play invests the city with symbolic if not actual control over its political identity. In addition to reaffirming and reproducing democratic membership norms, the play also produces and asserts the primacy of democratic political values. This dual political emphasis results from the play's use of gender and ethical strategies to remake social bonds. By emphasizing that Sostratos's love for the heroine outweighs her seemingly impoverished status in the making of their marriage, the *Dyskolos* constructs the heroine as innately desirable and valuable in her own right. The play thereby deploys a construction of gender capable of subordinating and subtly critiquing the social and political significance of economic status.

In addition to recruiting gender to remake the membership norms of the (suspended) democratic constitution, the *Dyskolos* also deploys an innovative ethical strategy to reconstruct social relations in accordance with the egalitarian values customarily associated with political institutions. In keeping with comedy's Athenian cultural conventions, there is no possibility that the heroine herself can forge a cross-class friendship with Sostratos or in any way serve as an ethical exemplar for her elite husband-to-be. As we will see in chapter 6, this trajectory is possible only when the heroine is in disguise or when she is already respectably married. Consequently, the play confers the didactic role on the heroine's half-brother Gorgias, an impoverished but moral farmworker. In the course of the action, Gorgias unexpectedly usurps the role of comic hero, solving the problem that proved insurmountable for Sostratos. After a heroic act of altruism, Gorgias is made *kurios* of his sister and thus arbiter of Sostratos's matrimonial fate. Because Sostratos's romantic success depends on his ability to orient his behavior and attitudes to the expectations of the egalitarian Gorgias, the marriage plot provides a format for an unusually explicit statement and affirmation of democratic ethical values. After being awarded the heroine, Sostratos arranges to have Gorgias marry his own wealthy sister: this is the only certain case in

[9] On the date of the play, see Handley 1965a, 123–24.

which a poor man is allowed to marry up without suffering the consequence of being mastered by an economically superior wife.

In this chapter, I examine the constructions of gender and ethics that lead to the successful resolution of the marriage plot with two economically and sociologically mixed marriages. I argue that these strategies operate in tandem to project and affirm democratic values and, at the same time, to criticize oligarchic political ideology. The plot takes on an anti-oligarchic inflection because economic considerations are rendered irrelevant to the question of matrimonial eligibility—which in comedy serves as the marker of citizen status. Since wealth was considered to be the most salient factor in determining citizenship in the oligarchic polis, this dethroning of the primacy of economic status has direct political relevance.[10]

Yet though the play unequivocally privileges democratic values over the oligarchic alternative, it does so in the social rather than the political realm. This shift in the site of ideological production and contestation has a double-sided effect, reproducing democratic values while simultaneously subverting the exclusionary norms of the democratic political order. For to justify democratic values in the social milieu—that is, without recourse to the political—characters in the play appeal to the common condition of human nature and propose that ethical rather than economic status is the most important determinant of a person's worth and identity. With these arguments, the play makes available a discourse that implicitly challenges not only forms of exclusion based on economic status but also "democratic" forms of exclusion based on Athenian nativity and legitimacy. Accordingly, in my reading of the play I attend to the subversive as well as the reproductive trajectory of the double marriage plot.

The Democratic Logic of the Comic Plot

Before the action of the play begins, Sostratos stumbles on the unattended and apparently impoverished heroine in a remote country setting. Under the influence of Pan, a god notoriously associated with rape, he conceives an immediate and intense attraction to the girl. Although the

[10] Although my reading of the play agrees in many respects with that of Rosivach (2001), our approach to social and economic issues is very different. Rosivach concludes, "The play's happy ending thus leaves the impression, by its allocation of rewards, both that wealth is a good thing and that everyone in the play who is wealthy deserves to be" (2001, 134). I argue that by making everyone wealthy, the play dismantles the very idea of a status quo characterized by economic disparities and instead presents the utopian fantasy that social and economic differences can be transcended.

stage seems to be set for rape, Sostratos refuses the act that his comic counterparts undertake so casually. Instead, he immediately determines to marry her, his desire already seeking legitimate channels. While this might seem to be a point in his favor, it in fact positively impedes the making of his marriage. Precisely because Sostratos has not made his marriage a matter of necessity by raping the girl in advance, he must prove to his highly suspicious social and economic "inferiors" that he is actually worthy of the marriage. By requiring that the elite citizen gain the consent and win the approval of the heroine's impoverished family members, the play supplies a context in which egalitarian values and ideals can be articulated, affirmed, and privileged against elite alternatives.[11]

The problem, however, is that to gain the consent of the heroine's family, Sostratos must first find some common ground with them: without an act of rape to make an economically mixed marriage a matter of civic necessity, the socioeconomic and cultural gulf between Sostratos's family and the heroine's remains intact. Although he anticipates that his wealth will make him eminently suitable husband material, it initially serves to call his character into question. Members of his beloved's family, like impoverished citizens in comedy generally, regard the activities of the rich with suspicion and distrust.[12] Sostratos himself never finds a release from his initial social position; the comic problem supplies a way around it.

The heroine's father is presented as an extreme misanthrope who refuses to give his daughter out in marriage.[13] Knemon acts this way not because he is wicked or cruel but rather because he believes himself too virtuous to live in a society in which all bonds of social reciprocity have been eroded by rampant self-interest and greed. Rather than repudiating his misanthropic behavior after it nearly causes his death, Knemon claims that the polis would be a far better place if everyone behaved like him: there would be no prisons, law courts, or wars (718–21). But paradoxically, in his efforts to escape human vice, Knemon becomes, in his own

[11] The heroine's father is not, of course, "poor." He leads a frugal and ascetic life as a matter of moral choice rather than economic necessity. The important point is that when Sostratos falls in love with the girl and determines to marry her, he believes that she and her father are poor (*Dys*. 130, 604–6). On Knemon's wealth, see Gomme and Sandbach 1973, 186–87 ad 327; Handley 1965a, 278 ad 842–44. In any case, the heroine's half-brother, Sostratos's reluctant partner in the matrimonial quest, is undeniably impoverished. He is repeatedly described as a beggar in the play (296, 795).

[12] In comedy and democratic culture, poverty seems to have led to an introjected sense of shame among the poor. On poverty and shame, see further chapter 5.

[13] Gorgias explains that Knemon has vowed not to give his daughter out in marriage until he finds someone like himself (ὁμότροπον αὑτῷ, *Dys*. 336–37). This means never, since Knemon is said to be unique in all of human history (324–25).

way, as unfit for society as those whose corruption he so vigorously condemns. By opting out of society, Knemon regresses to a Cyclopean state of presocial savagery that effectively removes him from the play.[14] He is a vivid though ultimately static presence whose most important dramatic function lies in the opportunity he provides for Sostratos to forge a relationship with Gorgias, the heroine's half-brother. That function is crucial because, as the play seems at pains to emphasize, Gorgias and Sostratos have absolutely nothing in common. While Sostratos is rich, urbane, articulate, leisured, and in love, Gorgias is poor, rustic, and too overworked to experience or comprehend "love" (24–29, 39–42, 343–44). Yet the need to overcome the obstacles posed by Knemon's character collapses this social distance: the seemingly impossible task of gaining his consent creates an imperative for collaborative action that would have been otherwise unthinkable.[15] In other words, Knemon's ethical position brings about the conditions that enable Gorgias and Sostratos to forge a relationship not defined by their prior social identities. This plot structure, in essence a homosocial triangulation that dispenses with the female altogether, makes it possible to remake social relations while bypassing preexisting barriers of social and economic status.[16]

The Class Politics of Sexual Conduct

Although Sostratos evidently enjoys social and economic advantages over Gorgias in Athenian society, in the narrower context of the play it is Gorgias who has all the power. The structure of the plot emphasizes this dynamic by repeatedly placing Gorgias in situations in which he is called on to evaluate Sostratos's sexual conduct or matrimonial worth. The first arises when Gorgias's slave Daos reports that he has seen a young man stalking his sister. Daos's failure to intervene prompts Gorgias to contrast

[14] Throughout the play, Knemon is described as refusing and avoiding speech (*Dys.* 10–12, 334–35) the characteristic that, according to Aristotle, distinguishes "man" from animals and insects, and makes him fit to inhabit a polis (*Pol.* 1253a10–19). The extent of Knemon's regression is vividly demonstrated by his threats of cannibalism (467). For the Cyclopean elements of Knemon's character, see R. L. Hunter 1985, 173. Giglioni (1982, 89) links Knemon's savagery and misanthropy to the *apragmosunē* associated with Athenian aristocrats under the democracy; cf. Carter 1986; Christ 1998.

[15] Although Wiles (1984) and Hoffmann (1986) call attention to the factionalized social universe of the play, they overlook the role of Knemon's character in creating a context for building a new more cohesive society.

[16] While most marriage plots are driven by what Sedgwick (1985) calls homosocial desire—a social force that operates within the structural context of heterosexuality but aims at forging social bonds between members of the same sex—in the *Dyskolos* the homosocial triangulation serves to form and transmit specifically democratic political structures and values.

his own sense of familial duty with Knemon's obvious neglect. Castigating Daos, he warns him not to imitate Knemon's *dyskolic* disposition (242–43). In this way he puns on the dual dramatic and ethical applicability of the concept of *mimēsis*. By calling attention to the process of imitation, he establishes the importance of the paradigmatic moral example as the guide to action in this social reality. Accordingly, when he and Daos find Sostratos lurking about Knemon's house, he performs in an exemplary fashion.

Gorgias first confirms that Sostratos is the suspected sexual predator by identifying him as the one wearing the expensive *khlanis* (cloak), as if that in itself were a sign of moral opprobrium and criminality (257). By mentioning the cloak, Gorgias both calls attention to the disparity in his and Sostratos's economic positions and signals the democratic framework through which he views that disparity.[17] This framework emerges as he gradually subordinates the precise nature of Sostratos's actions to the overarching fact of his elite status. He first accuses Sostratos:

ἔργον δοκεῖς μοι φαῦλον ἐζηλωκέναι,
πείσειν νομίζων ἐξαμαρτεῖν παρθένον
ἐλευθέραν, ἢ καιρὸν ἐπιτηρῶν τινα
κατεργάσασθαι πρᾶγμα θανάτων ἄξιον
πολλῶν.

(289–93)

I think you've set your mind on a vile action,
intending to persuade a freeborn girl to make a mistake,
or watching for an opportunity to
perpetrate an act for which you deserve to die many times over.

Since Gorgias is not exactly sure what Sostratos is up to, he makes his charges appropriately vague. As commentators have remarked, his accusation seems to be a euphemistic way of contrasting rape and seduction.[18] But establishing Sostratos's precise intentions is not Gorgias's particular concern. Although he initially draws a strong distinction between the two acts, judging rape to be far worse, his subsequent threat of judicial retaliation conflates them, characterizing both as acts of hubris:

οὐ δίκαιόν ἐστι γοῦν
τὴν σὴν σχολὴν τοῖς ἀσχολουμένοις κακὸν
ἡμῖν γενέσθαι. τῶν δ' ἁπάντων ἴσθ' ὅτι
πτωχὸς ἀδικηθείς ἐστι δυσκολώτατο[ν.

[17] For the elitist associations of the *khlanis*, see Dem. 21.133, 36.45.

[18] Fantham 1975, 53; P. G. Brown 1991, with reference to Harris 1990.

πρῶτον μέν ἐστι᾽ ἐλεινός, εἶτα λαμβάνει
οὐκ εἰς ἀδικίαν ὅσα πέπονθ᾽, ἀλλ᾽ εἰς [ὕβριν].

(293–98)[19]

At any rate, it's not fair that
your leisure should be a harm to those who have none.
Know that a beggar who has been wronged
is the most *dyskolic* of all men. At first, he's just pitiful,
but later he considers his injuries not just
as a harm but specifically as [hubris].

With this threat, Gorgias describes what Sostratos's predatory sexual behavior toward his half-sister means for him. Deploying strongly marked sociopolitical terms, he renders Sostratos's sexual misconduct in terms of politically inflected class conflict. Accordingly, the sexual and physical aspects of the "crime" are subordinated to considerations of status. In this cultural landscape, Sostratos's attempted sexual exploitation becomes a form of socioeconomic exploitation. By warning that a beggar is an especially bitter enemy because he considers his injury not just a crime but specifically an act of hubris, Gorgias discloses the democratic lens through which he views the situation. In democratic discourse, the legal action and rhetoric of hubris operated to maintain and protect the ideal of citizen equality by making virtually any assertion of a status distinction, from physical assault to the ostentatious display of wealth, liable to judicial redress.[20] Gorgias characterizes Sostratos's apparent sexual misconduct as a form of political misconduct by drawing on the democratic perception of hubris as abuse perpetrated by the wealthy against the poor. Although he personally views the violence of rape as more reprehensible, from a legal standpoint the act itself is less important than its social context. In other words, the fact that an ostentatiously wealthy citizen seems to be taking advantage of a poor man has more judicial significance than the precise form that the exploitation takes.

Sostratos is not, of course, planning to commit an act of hubris against the girl and her family. In his efforts to dispel the charge, he not only denies any criminal intention but also endorses a properly democratic attitude to wealth by offering to marry the girl without a dowry (303–9).

[19] For the restoration of ὕβριν in *Dys.* 298, see Handley 1965a, 186 ad 297, citing Philippides 27 K.-A. as a parallel; Gomme and Sandbach 1973, 182–83 ad 298.

[20] For the role of the law and rhetoric of hubris in counterbalancing political equality and socioeconomic inequality, see Halperin 1990, 88–112; Ober 1996, 86–106. On the concept of hubris in Greek thought more generally, see Fisher 1992, arguing that hubris arises from a deliberate attempt to dishonor, and Cairns 1996, arguing that the agent's overvaluation of his own honor is the central factor.

This gesture suggests that Sostratos does not overvalue wealth or privilege it as a fundamental determinant of social identity.[21] In fact, the marriage he seeks will dissipate the very social conditions that make hubristic assertions of superiority possible. Thus, Sostratos acquits himself of harboring the intentions that Gorgias initially attributes to him. Nevertheless, in Gorgias's eyes the external signs of his social identity—the opulent *khlanis*—enact the antidemocratic attitude that he seems to disavow.

After Sostratos's explanation, Gorgias immediately apologizes for his accusations and declares himself an ally in Sostratos's cause. But it soon becomes clear that his assistance will be of little practical use. Gorgias paints a grim picture of Knemon's misanthropy, explaining that no one can get through to him, family member or not. When Sostratos refuses to be deterred, Gorgias impatiently characterizes the problem very differently:

> σὲ δ' [ἄγοντ' ἂν] ἴδηι
> σχολὴν τρυφῶντά τ', οὐδ' ὁρῶν γ' ἀνέξεται.
>
> (356–57)

> If he sees you in your leisure and luxury he won't even
> endure looking at you.

It is odd that Gorgias should suddenly worry about Sostratos's appearance, given that he has just described the situation as hopeless, warning that Sostratos faces an insurmountable task not because of any problem of his own but because Knemon is a uniquely hostile and misanthropic old man who avoids all human contact without regard for claims of family or economic status (326–37). In this situation, the question of Sostratos's ostentatious display would seem to be secondary, if not completely irrelevant. By calling attention to Sostratos's leisure and luxury, however, Gorgias reveals his lingering suspicions about Sostratos's character. He distrusts Sostratos not because he is wealthy per se, but rather because he seems to be using his wealth to assert a status distinction. As Leslie Kurke remarks, in the speeches of the orators *truphē* is stigmatized because it implies an antidemocratic attitude. It involves, among other things, "sashaying through the agora in a cloak that reaches to one's ankles (Dem. 19.314)."[22] By describing Sostratos as "τρυφῶντα" (elegant and extravagant), Gorgias virtually accuses him of perpetrating hubris by other means.[23] In his character portrait of Meidias as the paradigmatic hubristic and antidemocratic man, Demosthenes draws a direct connec-

[21] Marrying a girl without a dowry, like providing dowries for the daughters of impoverished citizens, could be considered a form of public benefaction akin to a liturgical donation; see Is. 10.25–26 with Just 1989, 40–41.

[22] Kurke 1992, 105.

[23] For the connection between hubris and *truphē*, see Fisher 1992, 111–17; cf. Men. *Geōr.* fr. 2 Sandbach, and 840 K.-A. = 616 K.-T.

tion between Meidias's *truphē* and his acts of insolence against ordinary citizens: "I do not see how the mass of Athenians are benefited by all the wealth that Meidias retains for personal luxury (*truphē*) and display, but I do see how the acts of hubris he commits because he is exalted by his wealth affect many citizens" (Dem. 21.159).

By problematizing Sostratos's *truphē* immediately after subtly accusing him of hubris, Gorgias calls his democratic credentials into question. In effect, Gorgias identifies a second obstacle to Sostratos's marriage that operates in tandem with the ostensible comic problem of Knemon's character.[24] Along with having to win the consent of a figure who has regressed to a state of savagery, Sostratos also has to prove that he does not harbor the antidemocratic attitude his conspicuous extravagance suggests. Thus, we might say that the problem posed by Knemon's misanthropic character provides a cover for the more politically sensitive problem of socioeconomic inequality explored in the context of the relationship between Gorgias and Sostratos.[25]

That there are essentially two comic problems in this play becomes clear when Gorgias and Daos come up with an impromptu plan to aid Sostratos in his matrimonial quest. Although the situation has been described as futile, they nevertheless encourage Sostratos to make a good impression on Knemon. To that end, they advise him to impersonate a hardworking farmer.[26] Sostratos readily agrees to conceal the signs of his social status and soft life by spending a day digging ditches in a field. Yet despite his zealous application to the work, the plan fails.[27] In itself, this is not very surprising, since there never was any reason to think that

[24] On the multiple plot lines in the *Dyskolos*, see Schäfer 1965, 91–95; M. Anderson 1970, 213; Zagagi 1979, 1994, 156–68; Goldberg 1980, 73; Brown 1992a; Konstan 1995, 99.

[25] Konstan argues that Menander "resolves the class issue in *Grouch* by displacing it onto the theme of the misanthrope's idiosyncratic unsociability. . . . [A] potential story of social inequality and tension is overridden by an alternative narrative that is fanciful or wishful in character" (1995, 105).

[26] It may actually be Daos who suggests that Sostratos impersonate a laborer; see Gomme and Sandbach 1973, 190 ad 366.

[27] Thus this plan, like the others previously deployed, suggests an outcome that fails to materialize. Throughout the play, the action of the plot produces the expectation that the problem is going to be resolved in a conventional and scripted way, only to frustrate that expectation. For instance, when the action begins, Sostratos is busy trying to gain the assistance of a figure identified in the cast list as a parasite. Although this suggests that the parasite is going to have a hand in the ensuing romantic drama, he disappears from the play after the opening scene. A short time later, Sostratos decides to gain the help of his father's clever and practical slave (*Dys*. 181–85), producing the expectation that the cunning slave–type figure is going to play his conventional role of facilitating a young lover's romantic intrigue. This repeated emphasis on a conventional outcome focuses attention on the significance of how the plot is in fact eventually resolved. See further Ireland 1983; Zagagi 1979; P. G. Brown 1992a. On Getas's role, see Arnott 1964.

Knemon would notice, let alone be impressed by, a farmer. But the reason for the failure is that Knemon never makes his anticipated appearance to witness the performance, suggesting that the point of the intrigue scenario was not really to win his approval.

Just when it seems that Sostratos will never even meet Knemon, a completely unanticipated turn of events neutralizes Knemon's opposition to his daughter's marriage. He suffers a near fatal accident that finally brings home to him the unviability of his social isolation and dream of self-sufficiency. When he falls down a well on his property he finds he has no friend or neighbor or family member to assist him. Although Gorgias has never received even the most basic social courtesies from Knemon, he nevertheless unreservedly comes to the injured man's rescue. In return for this completely unselfish act, Knemon adopts him and gives him the task of seeing to his sister's marriage. Thus it is Gorgias—not the romantic hero or the cunning slave—who solves the problem that was beginning to seem insurmountable.

Through his actions, Gorgias provides the moral example that restores normalcy to Knemon's household. According to Knemon, the significance of Gorgias's actions consists not in the result they achieved (i.e., saving his life) but in the underlying attitude that they demonstrate:

ἀλλὰ μὰ τὸν Ἥφαιστον—οὕτω σφόδρα <δι>εφθάρμην
  ἐγὼ
τοὺς βίους ὁρῶν ἑκάστους τοὺς λογισμούς <θ'> ὅν τρόπον
πρὸς τὸ κερδαίνειν ἔχουσιν—οὐδέν' εὔνουν ᾠιόμην
ἕτερον ἑτέρωι τῶν ἁπάντων ἂν γενέσθαι· τοῦτο δὴ
ἐμποδὼν ἦν μοι. μόλις δὲ πεῖραν εἷς δέδωκε νῦν
Γοργίας, ἔργον ποήσας ἀνδρὸς εὐγενεστάτου.

(718–23)

By Hephaestus, I thought nobody on this earth could
show goodwill to another, that's how corrupted I was,
by seeing men's ways of life and calculation, how they're
disposed to gain. That was my one obstacle, but now Gorgias alone
has given me proof [of *eunoia*] by performing
the deed of an especially wellborn man.

Although Sostratos—a young man who hunts with dogs, wears expensive clothing, and has leisure and a father with the aristocratically overdetermined name of Kallippides—seems to be the "wellborn" aristocrat in this play, here Knemon praises Gorgias, the poor farmer elsewhere described as a beggar, for performing the deed of the "especially wellborn man" (cf. 296, 795).[28]

[28] The democratic transvaluation of *eugeneia* seems to underlie Knemon's praise; see further Loraux 1986, 193–94; Ober 1989, 259–66, esp. 261.

Performing Egalitarianism

While Gorgias unexpectedly usurps the role of comic hero to solve one prong of the problem, the play is far from over at this point. After Knemon speaks in defense of his own character and in praise of Gorgias, Gorgias is given the opportunity to resolve the second part of the comic problem: he must decide whether Sostratos is the hubris-prone aristocrat his luxurious appearance so strongly suggests. This scene is the thematic and ideological corollary of that in which he initially misjudged Sostratos's romantic intentions. Because both scenes dramatize a kind of judicial activity, they introduce a forensic setting into the comic plot. In each case, Sostratos's economic power is subordinated to Gorgias's power to determine his romantic fate. In this way, the unusual plot configuration in the *Dyskolos* replicates the sociopolitical dynamic between elite litigants and jurors in the democratic law courts. In democratic Athens, the law courts operated as powerful instruments of democratic social control precisely because the behavior of elite citizens was scrutinized by juries composed of middling citizens.[29] The relationship between Gorgias and Sostratos reproduces this institutional configuration in the private sphere and on the interpersonal level.[30] Unlike an actual litigant, Sostratos is not seeking to defeat a rival; he is contending on his own behalf, for personal satisfaction and, implicitly, to ensure the continuity of his household.

In the end, Gorgias accepts Sostratos as a suitable husband for his sister, offering the following justification for his decision:

οὐ πεπλασμένωι γὰρ ἤθει πρὸς τὸ πρᾶγμ᾽ ἐλήλυθας,
ἀλλ᾽ ἁπλῶς, καὶ πάντα ποιεῖν ἠξίωσας τοῦ γάμου
ἕνεκα, τρυφερὸς ὢν δίκελλαν ἔλαβες, ἔσκαψας, πονεῖν
ἠθέλησας. ἐν δὲ τούτωι τῶι μέρει μάλιστ᾽ ἀνὴρ
δείκνυτ᾽, ἐξισοῦν ἑαυτὸν ὅστις ὑπομένει τινὶ
εὐπορῶν πένητι· καὶ γὰρ μεταβολὴν οὗτος ṭύ̣χ[ης
ἐγκρατῶς οἴσει. δέδωκας πεῖραν ἱκανὴν τοῦ τρ̣όπου.
διαμένοις μόνον τοιοῦτος.

(764–71)

[29] Ober 1989, 1996.

[30] The play's re-creation of the law court setting is especially significant because the democratic law courts were not in operation when the comedy was performed; see chapter 2, note 5. The reduced property qualification imposed by Cassander in 317 certainly raised the population of citizens to a level sufficient to operate the courts, but the oligarchic political context in which the courts were embedded necessarily altered their function. To take the most obvious point: during the democracy, the courts provided a format in which "middling" citizens could hold elites accountable to egalitarian expectations, thereby counterbalancing social and economic inequalities with judicial power (Ober 1989). By disfranchising the poorest of the citizens, the oligarchic regime diminished the socioeconomic gap between litigants and jurors, eliminating the conditions that had rendered the courts powerful sites of ideological production.

You came to this affair honestly, without fabricating your character,
and were ready to do anything for the sake of the marriage.
Although you're extravagant, you took a mattock and dug
and were willing to work. In this way especially a man reveals himself,
if, although rich, he is prepared to treat the poor man as his
equal. He will bear changes of fortune with composure.
You've given sufficient proof of your character. Only see
that you remain the same.

Thus, it turns out that the intrigue plot is successful, although not in the way and for the audience originally intended. Gorgias takes Sostratos's willingness to play the other, so to speak, as an indication that he does not consider external signs of socioeconomic status to constitute essential or meaningful differences between persons. In this way, Sostratos's romantic and reproductive success is linked to an egalitarian ideology. Yet the logic of that conclusion is strikingly odd. Gorgias rewards Sostratos for revealing his true character in the context of a plot based on deception and impersonation; his one day of hard labor was little more than a dramatic performance that entailed elaborate staging, costuming, performance, and an audience.

How then are we to understand Gorgias's evaluation? It must be remembered that Gorgias is not rewarding Sostratos for successfully deceiving Knemon. Rather, his comment is based on how he himself, the architect of the plot as well as its internal audience, perceived Sostratos's actions. With the seemingly perverse assertion that Sostratos revealed rather than concealed his character, Gorgias calls attention to the metadramatic (or metasocial) meaning and effect of Sostratos's performance. But whereas metadrama generally reveals the artifices and conventions that enable theater, Sostratos's performance operates here to expose social rather than theatrical conventions.[31] It is significant in this respect that his costuming is, in part, an undressing.[32] His one day of hard labor is calculated to remove all traces of his elite status, from his clothing to his skin color. This simultaneous process of unmasking and concealment does not expose the conventions of dramatic illusion per se. Instead, in Gorgias's estimation, it discloses the arbitrary and manufactured nature

[31] On metadramatic play in Menander's comedy, see Blänsdorf 1982; Gutzwiller 2000. In discussing this scene, Gutzwiller (2000, 117) also draws attention to the use of metadrama, but emphasizes its role in securing the comic happy ending rather than its work in producing and reinforcing the egalitarian message of the play. As in the *Sikyōnioi*, the *Dyskolos* tailors metatheatrial techniques to the specific themes of the play. See chapter 7.

[32] In Sostratos's mother's dream, Pan puts chains on Sostratos, gives him a "goatskin" and a mattock, and orders him to dig (*Dys.* 412–17). For this reason, some scholars have suggested that Sostratos wore the *diphtheron* in the intrigue plot, although there is no evidence one way or another in the text; see Keuls 1969, 211–12.

of social and economic distinction. By shedding the trappings of his elite status to work as a laborer, Sostratos inadvertently reveals the nonessential nature of the conventions that define a citizen's place in the social hierarchy. His performance exposes elite identity as no more than a dramatic illusion produced by the props issuing from the inequitable distribution of wealth.[33]

Ethical Identity and the Democratization of Social Relations

While the mechanism of dramatic resolution in the *Dyskolos* offers a potent, if tacit, criticism of social hierarchy, it also offers a strategy for remodeling the social arena in accordance with egalitarian norms. The plot places Gorgias in the rather unusual situation of having to determine whether an elite citizen is worthy of marrying his sister. An initial difficulty arises from Gorgias's operating assumption that the wealthy tend to use their social position to abuse others. Although it becomes clear that Sostratos is not guilty of such abuse, the structure of the plot, which links matrimonial success to a favorable judgment, requires a more positive basis for rewarding him. Moreover, Gorgias must make this positive evaluation without undermining his own social status or calling into question his egalitarian commitments. It is the tension between these two requirements that creates the conceptual space in which a democratization of social relations can occur within a domain already organized according to hierarchical norms. In other words, it is Gorgias's need to reach a face-saving accommodation with Sostratos that clears a terrain on which social relations can be reconstructed on a more egalitarian footing.

First, Gorgias attributes Sostratos's romantic triumph not to the impact of his actions within the internal drama itself, but rather to the implied belief underlying them. This subtle distinction (also made by Knemon in his interpretation of Gorgias's heroics) provides the key to the egalitarian ideology promulgated by the play. In Gorgias's view, by demonstrating a willingness to work, Sostratos treats a poor man as his equal.[34] The crucial component of this assessment is the unquestioned assumption that all men (which in the context of comedy means "citi-

[33] Sostratos's performance in the intrigue plot highlights the material basis of social distinction.

[34] ἐν δὲ τούτωι τῶι μέρει μάλιστ᾽ ἀνὴρ / δείκνυτ᾽, ἐξισοῦν ἑαυτὸν ὅστις ὑπομένει τινὶ / εὐπορῶν πένητι (*Dys.* 767–69). Gorgias's word order, which brings together εὐπορῶν and πένητι at the end of the sentence, adds emphasis to the idea of equality being promulgated in the speech; cf. Gomme and Sandbach 1973, 251 ad 767.

zens") are fundamentally equal, despite the existence of socioeconomic inequalities.[35] In other words, Gorgias rewards Sostratos for enacting, through his performance, a principle of citizen equality. By treating this principle as an incontrovertible fact, Gorgias—and indeed the play as a whole—establishes and promotes a democratic conception of the human condition and of human nature within the citizen body. Such a view transforms the egalitarian status associated with democratic citizenship into a fundamental identity that does not require political institutions for its activation. It thereby offers a means of promoting egalitarianism within a social arena structured by long-standing inequalities of wealth and social status. By rooting equality in human nature, the play presents it as prior to all forms of socioeconomic inequality. At the same time, it constitutes a powerful critique of the prevailing conditions of inequality: if citizens are essentially and fundamentally equal, then signs of social and economic status are unreliable and ultimately meaningless markers of social identity.

On one level, the *Dyskolos*'s essentialization of Athenian citizen identity is not exceptional in comedy. The central "citizen marries girl" narrative generally operates to this effect. By repeatedly portraying the triumph of citizen marriage over all obstacles, comedy constructs the citizenship system as self-generating and -regulating, and Athenian citizens as biologically destined to enact their status. Through sheer repetition of this narrative pattern, comedy offered its audience a myth of civic identity as essential and inevitable. Yet in producing this civic myth, the plays use a variety of strategies. Some deploy the recognition motif, for example, constructing citizen status as an embodied identity that trumps and triumphs over other markers of social identity. In Terence's *Andria*, the heroine's true citizen identity manifests in her appearance and physical bearing. She is described as "noble and free" (*honesta ac liberali*, *An.* 123) by a character who believes that she is a slave. In the *Eunuch*, the citizen rapist disguises himself as a eunuch to get access to the girl in question. While he successfully conceals his masculine identity, his true citizen identity confounds the disguise (*Eun.* 473, 683). In the Terentian examples (based on Menandrian originals), the body and its surfaces operate as signifiers of citizen identity. In Menander's *Epitrepontes*, in contrast, the emphasis is less on the body as a bearer of identity than on character. In the arbitration scene, Syros argues that an exposed child should be allowed to keep the tokens that were found with it precisely because the child might later act like a citizen, aspiring to hunt and practice athletics

[35] For citi: en perspective as dominant in comedy, see Treu 1981.

(*Epit.* 320–37). Citizen identity, here conceived in unmistakably aristocratic terms, is again shown as something that cannot be suppressed by nurture or circumstances. In the *Dyskolos*, the emphasis shifts once more, to democratic identity rather than the naturalness of Athenian civic identity per se. The "recognition scene" in which Gorgias interprets the true meaning of Sostratos's actions gives substantive content to an Athenian civic identity based on a fundamental concept of equality while undermining the social significance of economic difference.

Of course, it is one thing to call into question the significance and validity of social hierarchy and another thing to dismantle that hierarchy. In itself, the transformation of democratic equality into a principle of human identity seems a weak foundation on which to effect a democratization of social relations: it posits egalitarianism as a blind faith without offering a material or practical foundation to sustain it. But Gorgias does establish a kind of practical basis for egalitarian identity in the way that he judges Sostratos on the basis of his character (*ethos*). He privileges a conception of character that operates as a common currency available to all citizens irrespective of their place in the social hierarchy.[36] His seemingly paradoxical claim that Sostratos demonstrated his true character while attempting to deceive Knemon reveals how this construction detaches an individual's social identity from the traditional signs of identity based on socioeconomic status. According to Gorgias, Sostratos's willingness to work revealed his true egalitarian disposition despite the signs of his wealth and status that apparently pointed to an antidemocratic disposition. In fact, all the major turning points in the play involve a character assessment based on the conduct rather than the social status of the individual in question.[37]

This conception of character clearly owes a great deal to Aristotelian ethical thought.[38] In Aristotle, and implicitly in the *Dyskolos*, a person's

[36] In some Menandrian fragments we do find the idea that socioeconomic status affects a person's character (in particular, that poverty made it difficult to maintain a good character).

[37] Cf. *Dys.* 718–23, 764, 770, and implicitly 815–16. Knemon's remark that Gorgias performed the deed of a wellborn man attests the thoroughly performative or pragmatic conception of character deployed in the *Dyskolos* (721–23).

[38] While it is widely agreed that there is Aristotelian influence on the conception and construction of Menandrian plots and characters, there is no agreement regarding its significance. Important studies of Menander and Peripatetic philosophy include Tierney (1936); Barigazzi (1965a), arguing that all of Menander's plays can be interpreted with reference to a philosophical program; Gaiser (1967), critiquing Barigazzi and discussing the ironic and comic treatment of philosophical themes in the plays; Webster (1960, 195–219), a general review; Lord (1977), on Terence's *Adelphoe*; and R. L. Hunter (1985, 147–51). Recent studies emphasize the aesthetic and social influence of Aristotelian thought on Menander's

state of character is disclosed through actions (and emotions) involving choice (Arist. *E.N.* 1106b36–1107a4). Yet though the *Dyskolos* draws on an Aristotelian conception of character, the play does not promote a recognizably Aristotelian ethical doctrine. What it means to have a "good" character in Menander's *Dyskolos* bears little resemblance to Aristotelian ideas about moral virtue. Rather, the play presses an "Aristotelian" conception of character into service on behalf of a democratic value system. Accordingly, having a good character means treating other men as equals.[39] While this ethical norm is obviously democratic in the context of Athenian democracy, its availability to every citizen in every position in the social hierarchy gives it an added emphasis. In the *Dyskolos*, prior social and economic disadvantages do not operate as barriers to democratic ethical virtue. Poverty and wealth are both envisaged as potential but surmountable obstacles to maintaining the recommended ethical norms. In addition to valorizing a kind of equality, the *Dyskolos* also promotes an ethic of work and agricultural labor.[40] Finally, happiness, the reward and reason for cultivating one's character, is linked to erotic pursuits rather than to moral virtue. Happiness, insofar as it is mentioned, is getting the girl one loves and reproducing the democratic citizen body (381–89).

It is worth noting that the *Dyskolos*'s ethicization and naturalization of egalitarianism operate in tandem with another important democratizing strategy. The *Dyskolos* renders the female citizen sexually desirable as well as reproductively necessary. This construction has a powerful "democratizing" effect (for men) because it liberates marriage exchange from the constraints of economic status by neutralizing the power of the dowry system to reproduce socioeconomic stratification. A woman's dowry was expected to be proportional to her husband's patrimony.[41] Accordingly,

---

plays rather than the ethical; on the tragic flaw, see M. Anderson 1970; on Aristotelian dramaturgic metaphors, Gutzwiller 2000; on the common elitist critical ideology, von Reden 1998; on the sociological, Patterson 1998.

[39] Ramage (1966, 205) argues that the dominant value in the play is *philanthropia* or *philia*—"friendship or friendliness in the broadest sense, ranging from love for the opposite sex through intense loyalty to courtesy and consideration." While the play does promote friendship, friendliness, and love, it does not do so in a value-free or ideologically neutral way. Rather, it constructs these social institutions according to a specifically egalitarian logic.

[40] *Dys.* 754–55, 766–67, 775, 862–65. On this theme in the *Dyskolos*, see Keuls 1969; Rosivach 2001; and in Menander generally, see Arnott 1981, 220.

[41] On the size of a woman's dowry, see Foxhall 1989, 34; Schaps 1979, 74–75. Cf. V. Hunter 1994, 15–18; Cox 1998, 117–20; chapter 1, note 75. In the resolution of the *Dyskolos*, Knemon instructs Gorgias to give the unusually high portion of one-half of his estate as his daughter's dowry (763). Based on this passage, Paoli (1961) suggests that there was a law requiring that a daughter be given one-half of a man's estate in cases in which he adopted a male heir.

the dowry system helped perpetuate existing patterns of socioeconomic differentiation within the citizen body. In the *Dyskolos*, however, Sostratos falls irresistibly in the love with the heroine before he knows who she is or her family's economic background. By deploying the device of love at first sight, the play subordinates the economic considerations of the dowry system by making them irrelevant.

The *Dyskolos*'s strategy of preventing the intergenerational reproduction of inequality depends on the construction of the heroine as desirable in her own right. The heroine's appeal in this respect is emphasized toward the end of the first act when she comes onstage and laments her inability to get water from the well. Sostratos, who happens to be in the neighborhood, seizes the opportunity to appraise her beauty and, addressing the spectators, invites the male viewers to share in his voyeurism (192, 194).[42] Later in the play, when reporting a second voyeuristic incident, Sostratos describes her as an *agalma*, or precious object. *Agalmata* are specifically associated with aristocratic gift exchange and refer to a type of object whose value resists quantification in economic terms.[43] Thus, by referring to the heroine as an *agalma*, Sostratos calls vivid attention to the work of gender in investing the heroine with a source of value that transcends ordinary considerations of economic status. Yet the egalitarian effects of this strategy are distributed unequally, by gender. The heroine's value dismantles hierarchies based on wealth and status between male citizens while leaving intact the subordination of women to men within the gender system itself.

Although the play does not question the reigning gender hierarchy, it does raise the possibility of lessening or neutralizing it. Sostratos emphasizes that the heroine is desirable both because of her beauty and because of her character (as he imagines it). As he puts it:

> ἐλευθερίως γέ πως
> ἄγροικός ἐστιν.
>
> (201–2)
>
> She is a rustic,
> but yet with a kind of free or liberal bearing.

The use of the adverb ἐλευφερίως to describe the heroine's rustic character suggests that she shares the kind of liberal poise or demeanor more frequently associated with citizen men or youths than with women. Ac-

[42] On Sostratos's address to the audience, see Handley 1965a, 165 ad 194.

[43] See *Dys*. 677, cf. 682–83. On *agalmata* and gift exchange ideology, see Gernet 1981; Kurke 1991. On money and marriage exchange in Menander's comedy, see Lape 2001, 105–11. On the general tension surrounding the commodification of civic symbols (outside the matrimonial economy), see von Reden 1998.

cording to Sostratos, she has acquired a character that can be praised in the language of ethical approval usually reserved for male citizens because of the upbringing she received with her reclusive father. After Gorgias describes her education and confinement, Sostratos becomes even more eager for the marriage:

> ὦ πολυτίμητοι θεοί,
> οἷς ἀποτρέπεις νυνὶ γάρ ὡς οἴει με σύ,
> τούτοις παρώξυμμ' εἰς τὸ πρᾶγμα διπλασίως.
> εἰ μὴ γὰρ ἐν γυναιξὶν ἐστιν ἡ κόρη
> τεθραμμένη μηδ' οἶδε τῶν ἐν τῶι βίωι
> τούτων κακῶν μηδὲν, ὑπὸ τηθίδος τινὸς
> δειδισαμένη μαίας τ' ἐλευθερίως δέ πως
> μετὰ πατρὸς ἀγρίου μισοπονήρου τῶι τρόπωι,
> πῶς οὐκ ἐπιτυχεῖν ἐστι ταύτης μακάριον;
>
> (381–89)

> O much-honored gods! The means you've used
> to turn me away now, as you think,
> have spurred me doubly for the affair.
> If the girl hasn't been raised among women,
> if she doesn't know any of the evils in this life, all
> the fears trumped up by aunts or nurses,
> but has been raised somehow freely with a fierce father
> who hates wickedness—
> how wouldn't it be pure happiness to get her?

Being raised "liberally," or as befits a free citizen, turns out to mean being raised without women. Although this comment represents a male fantasy of controlling social as well as sexual reproduction, it also reveals that gender difference is (at least to some extent) a social construct dependent on socialization and education.[44] According to this logic, the attributes for which men traditionally condemn women turn out to be products of culture rather than nature and so are contingent rather than essential. The subversive force of this disclosure probably accounts for the deployment of conventional negative gender stereotypes against other women in the play.[45] This is not to say that Sostratos is aware of the

[44] Handley (1965, 197 ad 384–89) adduces Antiphanes' 159 K (*Misoponēros*) as a parallel. In that passage, the speaker praises the Scythians for giving their children the milk of cows and mares and not bringing wet-nurses, slave tutors, or nannies into their houses. While these passages both emphasize the negative influence of servants (along with women generally) in the context of child-rearing, in the *Dyskolos* only the upbringing of the young heroine is in question. Sostratos's endorsement of novel child-rearing practices is not part of a general social critique but rather operates to characterize his own (and the male audience's) fantasy of gaining a wife designed to male specifications.

[45] That Getas condemns the servant women for their licentious and lying ways while

emancipatory implications of his own statement. As far as he is concerned, the recognition that some female gender characteristics are social artifacts means only that women can be made better objects for men to control. Yet in calling attention to the teachability of virtue or character, the play raises the possibility that women might be evaluated using the same ethical criteria applied to men, rather than solely in the terms supplied by the gender system.

Marriage Exchange and the Critique of Ideology

The romantic plot involving Sostratos's desire for Gorgias's sister encloses and resolves the class conflict, and the political conflict that it signals, within a homosocial relationship. The privileging of Gorgias's egalitarian values in that relationship constitutes an implicit critique of oligarchic ideology—a critique that is deepened in the context of the argument Kallippides and Sostratos have concerning the question of whether Gorgias should be allowed to marry into the family. Immediately after Kallippides approves of Sostratos's marriage, Sostratos insists that Gorgias must be married to his sister. Rather than automatically consenting to the marriage—the typical pattern when comic plays conclude with multiple marriages—Kallippides strenuously objects, and a debate between father and son ensues. The long-standing democratic use of marriage as an institution of citizenship lends this debate political significance as a question about whether to include or exclude Gorgias from the group of entitled citizens. Initially, Kallippides flatly refuses Gorgias because, as he puts it, he does not want two beggars (*ptōkhoi*) in the household (794–96). That Gorgias's matrimonial eligibility and, implicitly, his civic standing, are assessed solely in economic terms by Kallippides renders this debate a democratically coded commentary on the oligarchic ideology of citizenship.[46]

I have been describing the confrontation between Sostratos and his father as a debate, but it is, in fact, curiously one-sided. After voicing his economic objections, Kallippides falls silent, appearing less as an active participant in a debate than as a sounding board for a lecture designed to undermine the economic criteria of oligarchic citizenship.

περὶ χρημάτων λαλεῖς, ἀβεβαίου πράγματος.
εἰ μὲν γὰρ οἶσθα ταῦτα παραμενοῦντά σοι

Kallippides jokingly refers to the bibulousness of all women offsets the extravagant praise of the heroine's character (*Dys*. 402–4, 459–69, 858). Knemon, however, is abused for hating women (932).

[46] For the link between economic status and oligarchic citizenship, see, e.g., Pl. *Rep*. 550c–d; Arist. *Pol*. 1279b8–9, b18–19, 1279b40–1280a1, 1290b17–20, Ostwald 2000a:27.

εἰς πάντα τὸν χρόνον, φύλαττε μηδενὶ
τοῦ σοῦ μεταδιδούς· ὧν δὲ μὴ σὺ κύριος
εἶ, μηδὲ σαυτοῦ τῆς τύχης δὲ πάντ' ἔχεις,
μή τι φθονοίης, ὦ πάτερ, τούτων τινί.
αὕτη γὰρ ἄλλωι, τυχὸν ἀναξίωι τινί,
παρελομένη σοῦ πάντα προσθήσει πάλιν.
διόπερ ἐγώ σε φημὶ δεῖν, ὅσον χρόνον
εἶ κύριος, χρῆσθαι σε γενναίως, πάτηρ,
αὐτόν, ἐπικουρεῖν πᾶσιν, εὐπόρους ποεῖν
ὡς ἂν δύνηι πλείστους διὰ σαυτοῦ. τοῦτο γὰρ
ἀθάνατόν ἐστι, κἂν ποτε πταίσας τύχηις,
ἐκεῖθεν ἔσται ταὐτὸ τοῦτό σοι πάλιν.
πολλῶι δὲ κρεῖττόν ἐστιν ἐμφανὴς φίλος
ἢ πλοῦτος ἀφανής, ὃν σὺ κατορύξας ἔχεις.

(797–812)

You are talking about money, an unstable substance.
If you know that it will stay with you forever, guard it and
don't share with anyone. But where your control's
not absolute, and all's on lease from fortune, not your own,
why grudge a man some share in it, Father? Fortune
might take it all away from you, hand it to someone else who
perhaps doesn't deserve it. So, as long as you control it, Father,
you yourself, I say, should use it generously, aid everyone,
and by your acts enrich all whom you can.
This is immortal. If by chance you ever stumble,
it will yield to you a like repayment. A visible friend is far
better than hidden wealth kept buried.

In this lengthy entreaty on Gorgias's behalf, Sostratos never once mentions Gorgias. Instead, he argues from general principles, transforming the marriage question into an examination of Kallippides and the fundamental significance of his economic status. This strategy enables him to launch a twofold attack on the social and political importance of wealth. He argues that the possession of money or material prosperity is inherently unstable: a person enjoys wealth not because of his deserts, or his skill at managing and manipulating money and resources, but simply because he has a loan from Fortune. By insisting that the control of money is solely a matter of chance, and emphasizing the point through the repetition of *tukhē* and its cognates, Sostratos denies that there is a meaningful connection between money and the person who has it, thereby striking directly at the oligarchic ideology of citizenship (801, 803, 809). By rendering wealth a random and contingent possession, he also tacitly asserts that wealth, the oligarchic criterion for citizen status, is arbitrary and hence politically irrelevant.

According to Sostratos, wealth in itself is worthless: it acquires its value only by being put to use to help others.[47] The generous use of wealth converts unstable economic capital into symbolic capital that can be drawn on in times of crisis. It might appear that Sostratos's argument for "enlightened self-interest," as E. W. Handley puts it, is no more than an exhortation to practice symbolic domination. For the giving of a gift that cannot possibly be repaid creates a ranking by placing the recipient in symbolic and social debt to the giver.[48] According to this logic, far from creating a more egalitarian society, by "marrying up" Gorgias will simply exchange one form of social subordination (economic) for another. The kind of social debt Sostratos encourages his father to create, however, is not based on a straightforward relationship of domination and subordination. Rather, he urges his father to invest in social relations as a defensive measure because all men, rich and poor alike, inhabit a social universe that is, in his estimation, entirely capricious. Sostratos warns that economic prosperity is inherently insecure in a universe controlled by fortune, an assessment that is borne out by the events of the play.[49] The state of contingency common to the lives of all men produces a natural leveling effect.[50]

Sostratos's appeal draws its coercive power by tapping into the ideology of public expenditure in democratic Athens. He concludes (811–12) by contrasting the possession of "a visible friend" (ἐμφανὴς φίλος) with "invisible wealth" (πλοῦτος ἀφανής). These terms recall and rework a distinction between two kinds of property: "visible property" (φανερὰ οὐσία), land and assets that are known to the community, and "invisible or hidden wealth" (ἀφανὴς οὐσία), assets whose existence is hidden from neighbors and community.[51] This contrast is most frequently associated with the assessment of public liturgies. In democratic Athens, there was a loophole in cases of compulsory liturgical donations—a citizen assigned

[47] Sostratos urges his father to make as many people as possible "*euporous*." Given the association of *euporoi* with oligarchic citizenship (Arist. *Pol.* 1279b8–9), Sostratos might be urging Kallippides "to make citizens" by giving Athenians the resources to meet the financial requirements of citizenship under Demetrius's regime.

[48] For symbolic domination, see Bourdieu 1977, 183–97. See also Handley 1965a, 273 ad 807–10.

[49] Gomme and Sandbach (1973, 256 ad 801) note that *tukhē* in 801 is close to being a personification.

[50] Sostratos's speech is a counterpart to Gorgias's speech at 271–87 (Arnott 1964, 1980), but their construction of fortune differs. Gorgias depicts fortune as operating according to a predictable pattern, rewarding those who respect the status of others and punishing those who look down on or despise the poor; Sostratos figures it as a more random principle. In each case, the speaker adapts the construct to suit the rhetorical needs of an argument animated by democratic or egalitarian values.

[51] On the distinction between visible and invisible wealth, see Finley 1952, 54; Gernet 1981, 343–48; Gabrielsen 1986; Kurke 1991, 225–39.

the contribution in question could plead insufficient funds, provided he could identify another wealthier citizen to perform the service. If this second citizen in turn refused to meet the financial expense, a formal inquiry was held to determine whose assets were greater, and hence who would perform the liturgy.[52] According to Vincent Gabrielsen, in the ensuing trials "each party sought to inflate the value of the opponent's property by mobilizing a host of arguments designed to demonstrate that besides his φανερὰ οὐσία (visible wealth) the latter owned a sizable store of ἀφανὴς οὐσία (invisible wealth)."[53]

The accusation that an opponent possessed a store of invisible property seems to have been a topos in the orators.[54] The charge served to cast aspersions on an opponent's character by suggesting that he was attempting to evade public social obligations for selfish and antidemocratic reasons. By likening Kallippides' refusal to give his daughter in marriage to the practice of hiding wealth, Sostratos draws on this stereotypical perception, with all its opprobrious connotations.[55] But in this matrimonial context, the power of a democratic jury to give or withhold favorable judgment does not motivate individuals to keep their assets visible and make generous expenditures. Rather, the inherent precariousness of the social universe that Sostratos describes encourages acts of largess. Here, one who conceals his property suffers removal from the fabric of social relations. Sostratos's alteration of the technical distinction between visible and invisible wealth to a contrast between "invisible wealth" and a "visible friend" emphasizes this point. If he is willing to incur the financial loss entailed by accepting Gorgias as a son-in-law, Kallippides will remain embedded in social relations. He will acquire the most valuable form of currency in a social reality in which individuals are continually threatened by fortune.[56]

While Sostratos's speech contains a striking, if democratically coded, critique of oligarchic ideology and an attempt to use social relations to

[52] On the antidosis challenge and trial see Gabrielsen 1987; Christ 1990.

[53] Gabrielsen 1986, 101.

[54] Finley 1952, 54–55; Kurke 1991, 226–27.

[55] The force of Sostratos's speech derives in part from its the application of a formerly "public" ideology of expenditure in the context of ostensibly private social relations. His attempt to ethicize of the ideology of liturgical donation is significant because Demetrius of Phaleron abolished the choregic liturgy, and perhaps others as well, see Wehrli fr. 136 = *FGrH* 228 F 25 = 115 F.-S.; see also chapter 2, above.

[56] Sostratos's rhetoric implicitly links Kallippides with Knemon. Knemon's refusal to give his daughter in marriage—a decision motivated by moral rather than economic considerations—symbolizes his withdrawal from social relations. In Knemon's case, this detachment proves literally life threatening. Kallippides is not, of course, so problematic a figure. His refusal to exchange his daughter is figured as a potentially rather than actually dangerous withdrawal from the support network of social relations.

compensate for the absence of democratic state institutions, its subversive edge is somewhat blunted by its ironic reception: Kallippides simply refuses to take it seriously. Rather than explicitly acknowledging the content of the speech, he attacks its form, castigating Sostratos for presuming to speak to him in gnomes (817).[57] The inversions of speech protocols involved in Sostratos's pompous moralizing to his father is undoubtedly meant to be humorous, but it would be a mistake to dismiss the speech on that account. It is a commonplace that humor is a way of having it both ways, a way of saying and yet not saying what cannot be expressed under ordinary circumstances. And most important, Sostratos's speech works—it succeeds in bringing about its professed intentions. Gorgias is, in the end, accepted and even welcomed into the family. This inclusion amounts to an admission of his citizen status that implicitly challenges the oligarchic correlation of wealth and citizenship. Indeed, the exaggeration of Gorgias's poverty—he is described as a beggar throughout the play—suggests a deliberate emphasis of this point.[58]

Kallippides' acquiescence to Sostratos's demands does produce an ideological rapprochement between oligarchic father and democratic son. He acknowledges the general point that social relations, specifically friendship, should not be limited by economic factors. However, in a crucial regard he corrects Sostratos, claiming that the friendship at stake is not his own but Sostratos's. Kallippides describes Sostratos's speech as a pretense for his own purpose of cementing a friendship with Gorgias (813–16).[59] By displacing the politically charged points of the speech onto the relationship between Gorgias and Sostratos, Kallippides can acknowledge the general principle expressed without losing face or caving in to his son's democratic rhetoric. The mutually acceptable agreement that the oligarchic parent and democratic son forge lessens the ideologi-

[57] According to Aristotle (*Rhet.* 1395a1–5), the speakers of gnomes should be older and should speak only on subjects in which they are experienced. For proverbs and poetics in the *Dyskolos*, see Tzifopoulos 1995.

[58] On the exaggeration of Gorgias's poverty, see Gomme and Sandbach 1973, 181 ad 285.

[59] The emphasis on forming and consolidating the friendship between Sostratos and Gorgias differs from the conventional Menandrian comic representation of male friendships in that they are not already friends. The play's focus on the formation of an "egalitarian" friendship between two socioeconomic unequals operates in tandem with the creation of economically mismatched marriages. In both cases, the *Dyskolos* restructures social relations in order to build democratic culture from the ground up. There is a similar congruence between friendship and marriage exchange between the rich and poor in Menander's *Samia*, but in that play the old men Demeas and Nikeratos are already friends and the wealthy Demeas seems to have more power in the relationship (see further chapter 5). According to Konstan (1997, 60–67), friendship played a marginal role in Athenian democratic politics. For friendship in comedy, see Zucker 1950.

cal gap between them by affirming that they both really want the same thing: namely, a tightly knit and inclusive community.

Egalitarianism and Inclusion

The *Dyskolos* moves from a sterile and fragmented social order to an inclusive and fecund comic community. The play begins with Pan's description of the barren landscape of Phyle, where men are forced to work rocks rather than soil, and of Knemon's fragmented household (1–4, 13–27).[60] The sterility of Knemon's land and house is depicted as the outgrowth of his character: Knemon's misanthropic dream of seceding from social relations leads to an obsessive concern with physical boundaries (108–10, 115, 161–68, 444–47, 482–85). In his efforts to isolate and detach himself from the outside world, he even ceases to work parts of his land (161–65). Significantly, Sostratos's romantic success hinges specifically on his own willingness to prepare the land for cultivation (367–70, 525–29). The regeneration of community, scripted in the agriculture sphere, is linked to the creation of a new kind of community. The matrimonial unions produced in the play create the conditions not only for reproducing families but also for producing a more egalitarian society. By linking together rich and poor and town and country, they generate a new social formation in which both economic and social differences are diminished.[61]

The *Dyskolos* promotes the principle of equality associated with democratic political practices and institutions in the social arena. In marked contrast to the ideology and practice of the historical democracy, however, the *Dyskolos* links the principle of natural equality to a norm of inclusivity. Under the classical democracy, civic egalitarianism was associated with and perhaps sustained by the normative exclusivity of the citizen body.[62] At best, the body of fully entitled male citizens constituted only about one-tenth of the population.[63] When the *Dyskolos* was per-

[60] The play's conspicuously marked setting in the Attic deme of Phyle is also central to the democratic significance of the play; see Wiles 1984. Phyle was the seat of democratic resistance to the oligarchic regime of the Thirty in 404/3. For the democratic "men from Phyle," see Aes. 3.187–90; Krentz 1982, 112–13. It seems no accident that Sostratos, the pampered youth from the city, receives his democratic education in Phyle.

[61] The sacrifice to Pan also plays a key role in uniting city and country.

[62] According to Ober and Strauss, "Exclusivity was a principle as central and sacred to the existing political order as equality" (1990, 267).

[63] Hansen's figures show about 30,000 citizens in the fourth century, which "represented no more than a tenth of the whole population of Attica" (1991, 94; cf. 90–94). Other scholars, however, argue that there were only 20,000 citizens in the fourth century; see Sekunda 1992; see further chapter 2, note 4.

formed in 316, the criteria of Athenian citizenship had become even more narrow. A man wishing to qualify not only was required to be a freeborn native adult whose status and legitimacy had been confirmed by the demesmen; he also had to possess a minimum of 1,000 drachmas.

According to the ideology of oligarchic rule, wealth rather than birth alone was what made a man fit for membership in the political community. The *Dyskolos* insistently undermines this oligarchic correlation by questioning the significance of economic status and wealth. In the context of its action, all men are held accountable to the same moral standards irrespective of their socioeconomic position. The play neutralizes wealth's ability to operate as a positive social advantage by portraying the human condition as inherently egalitarian because always contingent: wealth is an accidental and arbitrary attribute with no intrinsic connection to the person who possesses it. It thus emphasizes that wealth is meaningless as a basis for social hierarchy or exclusion. At the same time, the precarious human condition in the *Dyskolos* engenders communal solidarity, for social relations are the only remedy for the manifold dangers of social existence.

Though the double marriage plot in the *Dyskolos* comes down firmly on the side of democratic rather than oligarchic political membership qualifications, it does so outside traditional institutions of political participation. The play offers an argument against the use of one form of inequality—economic status—to determine social and political membership where there are deep-seated inequalities in status and gender. Accordingly, it seems only a small step to the further claim that other forms of inequality are also politically and socially meaningless. In fact, the play does seem to blur or lessen the distinction between freemen and slaves. Gorgias treats Daos like a family member rather than a family slave; it is as if his own marginal social position, his exclusion from Knemon's family and low socioeconomic status, collapses the distance between them. This is not to say that Gorgias's status has been in any way compromised by his social circumstances: rather he raises Daos to his own level, demanding that the slave follow the same ethical norms that he sets for himself. The normative distinctions between men and women and freemen and slaves also seem to be blurred in the erotically charged prenuptial festivities with which the play concludes (935–39, 946–53).[64]

[64] The komastic ending of the comedy in Pan's cave may also be tacitly subversive. Demetrius of Phaleron imposed new laws for the regulation of private life, a policy that seems a direct affront to the ideology of democratic freedom (Arist. *Pol.* 1317a40–b14). He is known to have regulated funerals and the size of grave monuments (Cic. *Leg.* 2.64–66 = 53 F.-S.) and to have created a board of *gynaikonomoi*. Aristotle describes *gynaikonomoi* as instituted to enforce morality (*eukosmia*) and to keep women in the home (*Pol.* 1322b38–1323a8, cf. 1300a4–7). Under Demetrius's regime, however, the institution seems to have

But not everyone is seamlessly incorporated into the new egalitarian and inclusive society. In the last act, the action returns to Knemon, the blocking character who has been neutralized but (a crucial point) not socialized.[65] The two slaves whom he had abused abduct him and subject him to precisely the rituals of social reciprocity he had earlier refused.[66] From one perspective, the violence perpetrated by the slaves against a citizen seems to take the egalitarian logic of the play to its extreme. Their ability to get away with violating the autonomy and corporeal integrity of a citizen suggests that egalitarianism in the economic sphere has spilled over into the status distinctions separating free men from slaves. And, in fact, the slaves justify their actions as a duty of kinship. The marriage unions produced in the play make Knemon a kinsmen—*oikeios*—of the slaves (238–40, 903–4).[67] However, the violent but ultimately incomplete incorporation of Knemon also points in another direction: it casts him as the remainder that resists assimilation into the new dominant order. By exposing the inability of the democratic society to accommodate and include everyone, the play acknowledges the particularity of the social order it founds and subtly questions the inclusivity it otherwise seems to promote. Although the *Dyskolos* privileges democratic culture over oligarchic or hierarchical alternatives, it does not do so in an unequivocal way. Democratic culture appears as an inevitably partial and imperfect solution to the problem of community.

been used to monitor private social gatherings and sacrifices and to limit their size to thirty persons (Philoch. *FGrH* 328 F 65; Men. 208 K.-A.; Timocles 34 K.-A.; Athen. 245ab); see further chapter 2, notes 40–45. The celebration in Pan's cave must have exceeded the legal limit, or come perilously close to doing so, but the characters celebrate in blissful or willful ignorance of any impropriety or law prohibiting such activity.

[65] On the significance of the fifth act in Menandrian comedy, see W. S. Anderson 1972; Nicastri 1978; R. L. Hunter 1985, 40; P. G. Brown 1990a, 37–61; see further chapter 9.

[66] For this scene, see Dedoussi 1988a.

[67] *Oikeios* usually refers to members of the same household, family, kinsmen, or close friends, but not to slaves (see LSJ, s.v. *oikeios* II). In Is. 6 a citizen's *oikeioi* are specifically distinguished from the household slaves, *oiketai* (6.15, 16, 39).

5

The Politics of Sexuality in Drama and Democratic Athens

THE CASE OF MENANDER'S *SAMIA*

The Father-Son Romance

By the end of the first act in Menander's *Samia*, everything seems to be set for the marriage plot to proceed to its predestined end. In the opening monologue, Moschion, the wealthy young hero, confesses to having fathered a child with the girl next door and to desiring to marry her. The only thing standing in his way is the small matter of gaining his father's consent. For nine months at least, Moschion's deep shame before his adoptive father Demeas has prevented him from owning up to his behavior. Nevertheless, he resolves to confront his father about the marriage—or to act like a man, as his slave puts it—as soon as his father returns from abroad. This anticipated father–son confrontation never materializes, however, because unbeknownst to Moschion, Demeas has taken it upon himself to arrange his son's marriage with his friend Nikeratos's daughter: the very young woman who has already borne Moschion a child. Thus, in the space of the first act the problem seems to be solved, all obstacles removed.

To a certain extent, this scenario resembles the opening of the *Geōrgos*, another work that begins after a wealthy young man has raped and impregnated an impoverished female citizen. Although the hero's father in that play also arranges and prepares his son's wedding in the first act, the intended bride-to-be is not the rape victim but rather the hero's homopatric half-sister. According to the conventions of comedy, the planned marriage is wrong for two reasons: comedy neither allows its violated heroines to avoid marrying their rapists nor tolerates half-sibling marriage.[1] In all probability, the protagonist's father planned a half-sibling marriage specifically to preserve the household wealth. Accordingly, we can assume that the successful resolution of the plot with the marriage of

[1] On comedy's avoidance of half-sibling marriage, see chapter 1, notes 84, 85.

wealthy rapist and the impoverished victim involved neutralizing the perceived economic barrier to the marriage.

In the *Samia*, by contrast, the anticipated economic impediment to interclass marriage has been neutralized in advance. Although we never learn in the play as it is now preserved exactly why Demeas is so keen to marry his son to the dowryless daughter of his poor neighbor, it is clear that his friendship with Nikeratos counteracts the traditional bias against marriage between the rich and the poor. Nikeratos may have been less enthusiastic at first because he is "poor but proud," as Eva Keuls describes him,[2] but he quickly agrees to the marriage. While the use of male friendship as a kind of social solvent to dismantle the stratifying effects of economic difference is also the strategy underlying the homosocial romance plot in the *Dyskolos* (discussed in the previous chapter), again, there is a crucial difference in *Samia* that underscores how exceptional its seemingly problemless plot is.

The *Dyskolos* vividly depicts the vast sociocultural gulf separating the wealthy city sophisticate protagonist and the impoverished rustic who eventually becomes the heroine's guardian (*kurios*). In order for marriage to be an effective means of forging a new social solidarity, the plot must first create a point of contact between the participants in the exchange, some common ground between the patently diverse social constituencies represented by the hero and heroine's brother. For this reason, the *Dyskolos*'s story of heterosexual romance, one-sided though it may be, is displaced by a story of homosocial friendship. In the *Samia*, however, a common space between the rich and poor neighbors already exists. The prior friendship between Demeas and Nikeratos makes it unnecessary to reroute the marriage plot into a story of male friendship in order to establish a basis for interclass marriage. This is not to say that the democratic "class" politics of marriage and sexuality are absent in the *Samia*; they are, as I discuss below, transferred to a new location. The barrier to Moschion's marriage actually arises from its extraordinary overdetermination. Though the traditional route to maturation in comedy involves the triumph of a young man's passion in the face of initial paternal and or social protest, both of these paths are closed to Moschion. By arranging Moschion's marriage, Demeas precludes the one arena in which comedy grants its protagonist the illusion of autonomy within the existing civic constraints of the genre. That Moschion impregnated the heroine in advance of his father's planning can be seen as his own preemptive response to the too stringent dictates of paternal authority.

Although the need for Moschion to achieve a tentative maturity is part of the comic problem, it is not an issue that the narrative actually re-

[2] Keuls 1973, 9.

solves. Rather, his immaturity allows his own story to be displaced by a second romantic plot. When Demeas returns home and confronts Moschion about his impending marriage, Moschion fails to tell his father that he has already made the marriage a matter of necessity by fathering a child with Plangon. Instead, he allows Chrysis, Demeas's Samian mistress, to pass off the child as her own bastard son by Demeas. Presumably, once safely married he was going to reclaim and legitimize his son. In the midst of the wedding preparations, however, Demeas discovers that Moschion is the true father of the child without also discovering that Plangon, rather than Chrysis, is actually the mother. In this way, the play places Demeas in the position of believing that his *hetaira* and adopted son have produced a child behind his back. In response to this situation, the ever-controlling Demeas takes it upon himself to conduct an impromptu trial to discover who is at fault, his live-in *hetaira* or his adopted son. He acquits Moschion on the basis of his character, while condemning the woman he seemed to love as a whore and a pestilence.

In the process of clearing Moschion of committing an imagined seduction, Demeas appropriates, or at least claims a share of, his son's status as romantic hero while distracting attention from his ineligibility for the role. For Demeas is an anomaly within the surviving corpus of Greek and Roman New Comedy: He has the distinction of being the only *senex amator* (old man in love) to enjoy a successful romantic relationship.[3] Moschion himself hints at Demeas's status as the real romantic lead in his opening monologue by telling the story of Demeas's infatuation with Chrysis before offering a truncated version of his own romantic exploits. Perhaps even more exceptionally, Demeas is the only character granted a permanent reprieve from the normalizing constraints of civic matrimony in order to reside with a *hetaira*. Although affairs with *hetairai* were tolerated in comedy and society, such relations were supposed to be the stuff of youth. And, at any age, such affairs could inflame class resentments, as Attic lawsuits attest.

The problematic nature of Demeas's affair with Chrysis is revealed in Moschion's opening monologue. According to Moschion, Demeas was ashamed even to admit to having conceived a passion for Chrysis (*Sam.* 23, 27). But his shame is precisely what allows him to have it both ways.[4] Being ashamed enables Demeas (and Moschion) to violate normative sociosexual practices while simultaneously reinforcing the very value system their passions have breached. In this way, shame (in comedy, at least)

[3] On Demeas as a *senex amator*, see also Grant 1986, 180; Zagagi 1994, 116.

[4] Similarly, in *Sikyōnioi* the evidence of a character's shame mitigates his attempted violation of civic sexual proprieties; see further chapter 7. On shame (*aiskhunē*) in the *Samia*, see Jacques 1971, xxxviii with n. 4; W. S. Anderson 1972, 156–57; Henry 1985.

makes possible a dissonance between social practice and ideology, opening up a space for agency and autonomy. It is precisely because Demeas feels shame for his attraction for Chrysis, a psychic and somatic sign of his internal obedience to the prevailing sexual orthodoxies, that he can take the extremely subversive step of actually installing Chrysis within the house in the place that was supposed to be the privilege of the citizen wife. It is surely significant that Moschion claims credit for the idea, thereby (in some small measure) allaying the scandalous and elitist implications of Demeas's actions. Living with a *hetaira* carried overtones of elitism because it was an arrangement not available to every citizen and, at the same time, because it suggested an untoward privileging of personal preference over civic communal norms. Thus, just as Moschion's marriage plot is to some degree dislocated by Demeas's romantic plot, so too the issue of class politics, the expected barrier to Moschion's marriage, is displaced onto Demeas's story.

Demeas's claim to romantic heroism consists not in his ability to form a new relationship but rather in his ability to diminish the subversive significance of his prior romantic attachment. Within comedy's civic value system, a permanent live-in relationship with a *hetaira* could never be fully or directly sanctioned. Accordingly, Demeas's romantic plot is a story about the end of an affair. When forced to choose between his adoptive son and his *hetaira*, he unequivocally sides with his son. By disciplining his desire and suppressing it in favor of his only civic attachment—the legally created kinship bond with his son—he proves that his relationship is not a threat to either moral or sociopolitical norms. Paradoxically, it is Demeas's decision to throw Chrysis out of his house that "legitimizes" the affair; that is to say, Demeas is able to resume the relationship in the end precisely because he performs the devaluation of it required by the dominant ideology.

In this chapter, I examine the politics of sexuality in this unconventional father–son romance, or rather in their interwoven romantic plots. Because the play casts both father and son as passionate but guilty protagonists, it brings the norms of civic sexuality into unusually sharp focus. At the same time, to salvage the credibility of both characters as citizen protagonists the play deploys various strategies that neutralize the opprobrium of their situations. Chief among these is a dramaturgic idiosyncrasy unique in the surviving corpus: the extensive use of monologue.[5] Demeas and Moschion speak more to the audience than to each other, a technique that enables them to reveal their inner convictions, to show

[5] According to Blundell's estimate (1980, 44), monologue accounts for about 370 lines in a play of about 900 lines. On the importance of monologue, see also Jacques 1971, lix–lx; Bain 1983, xxi; Arnott 2000b.

their internal compliance with civic proprieties despite contradictory surface appearances. This emphasis lends the play a forensic focus. By explicitly and implicitly inviting the audience to evaluate their personal dramas, the protagonists treat the theatrical audience as jurors and democratic citizens; they thus use the power of drama to transform theater into court.[6] While it is impossible to determine at present whether the *Samia* was performed during a period of democracy or one of oligarchy, in either case the play provides a compelling demonstration of comedy's ability to act as an institutional surrogate for participatory democratic politics.

Yet, as is common in comedy, the very strategies that produce civic outcomes tend to be double-edged, subtly subverting the civic status quo they seem to secure. In order to acquit Moschion, Demeas deprecates his relationship with Chrysis and Chrysis herself. To these ends, he draws on the stereotype of the "immoral" prostitute found in democratic legal narratives.[7] Although Demeas draws on this stock figure to defend his son and salvage his own compromised civic credentials, the play's narrative offers no role for such a character. Rather than acting like an immoral prostitute, Chrysis is characterized by her maternal disposition and reproductive sexuality—that is, exactly like a female citizen. By acting too much like the respectable and reproductive women from whom she was supposed to differ, Chrysis contradicts Demeas's words and the cultural cliché on which they rest. By dramatizing the dissonance between Chrysis's actual character and the negative stereotype, the play undermines traditional gender assumptions. At the same time, by calling attention to cultural fictions of female identity, the play exposes the constructed nature of traditional gender categories, opening a space in which they might be transcended or remodeled. Finally, because Chrysis is of Samian extraction, the critique of the gender system also implicitly calls into question the supposed racial difference between citizens and noncitizens.

Forensic Theater: Staging Comedy as Court

The typical Menandrian prologue is expository in nature; the speaker explains the background of the plot, usually with a genealogical story,

[6] On the cross-fertilization of theatrical and oratorical plots and themes more generally, see Ober and Strauss 1990, 248–49; E. Hall 1995; Scafuro 1997. On the institutional parallels between court and theater in democratic Athens, see Pickard-Cambridge 1988.

[7] Although Chrysis is technically a *hetaira* or former *hetaira*, Demeas condemns her as a prostitute (χαμαιτύπη), a term with more derogatory force than *pornē*; see note 65.

and forecasts the happy ending that will inevitably unfold.[8] While such a disclosure might seem to undercut the play's dramatic suspense, the irony and humor in comedy often depend on the discrepancy between the awareness of the audience and that of at least some of the characters. The audience can enjoy various situational incongruities and mistaken assumptions precisely because they know more than the characters on stage. For this reason, the prologue speaker is often either a god or a personification of a key dramatic principle, such as Chance or Ignorance. The *Samia*, however, departs from this convention, opening with a prologue-like monologue delivered by Moschion.[9]

Although Moschion does not have the omniscience possessed by other prologue speakers, he is able to supply the necessary background information as he tells the story from his inevitably subjective and obviously interested perspective. Initially, it appears that the story he is introducing will be his own, for he begins with a confession. Like so many other comic heroes, Moschion has perpetrated a harm. But the story of his error is not the only story he tells. Instead of explaining exactly what he has done to justify his remorseful and defensive posture, he first describes his adoptive father's character, his own generosity in public and private, and, eventually, the story of his father's passion for a Samian *hetaira*. When it finally comes time for Moschion to confess to what he has done, he defers yet again. Although he admits that a girl became pregnant and bore his child, he leaves it the audience to infer what came before (*Sam.* 49–50).

Moschion's digressive narrative turns out to be his way of confessing to a rape or seduction; although comedy often uses a rape plot to generate the narrative, this is the only case in Menander's extant comedy in which the protagonist both problematizes his own behavior from the outset and expresses remorse for it.[10] This unusual perspective effectively transforms the genre of Moschion's monologue, converting a comic prologue into a forensic defense speech. The generic intertextuality is signaled not only by Moschion's defensive posture but also by his employment of specific forensic tropes. Most conspicuously, he offers a liturgical catalogue, or

[8] On Menandrian prologues generally, see Del Corno 1970; Holzberg 1974; R. L. Hunter 1985, 24–30, and 1987 (on New Comic prologues more generally); Vogt-Spira 1992, 75–92; Zagagi 1994, 142–68.

[9] There is a lacuna of about ten lines in the opening of the play. For Moschion's monologue as a prologue, see Blume 1974, 2; Jacques 1971; Gomme and Sandbach 1973; Sisti 1974; Bain 1983; Blume 1974; Lamagna 1998.

[10] Kharisios in the *Epitrepontes* may express remorse for raping Pamphile. In the text as we have it, however, he condemns himself for fathering a bastard rather than for committing the rape (894–99). See further Konstan 1995, 148–51.

enumeration of public benefactions—a staple of an Athenian defendant's legal narrative.[11]

ὃς γέγον]α μέντοι, νὴ Δί', ἀθλιώτερος·
παχεῖς] γάρ ἐσμεν. τῶι χορηγεῖν διέφερον
καὶ τῆι] φιλοτιμίαι· κύνας παρέτρεφέ μοι,
ἵππο]υς· ἐφυλάρχησα λαμπρῶς· τῶν φίλων
τοῖς δεομένοις τὰ μέτρι' ἐπαρκεῖν ἐδυνάμην.
δι' ἐκεῖνον ἦν ἄνθρωπος. ἀστείαν δ' ὅμως
τούτων χάριν τιν' ἀπεδίδουν· ἦν κόσμιος.

(12–18)[12]

And I've become more wretched
because we're [rich]! I distinguished myself by serving as
a chorus master [and] by my zealous ambition. He raised dogs
for me and [horses]. I starred as a commander of my tribe's cavalry.
I could give modest help to friends in need.
On account of him, I was a man. But I repaid
him decorously: I used to be well-disciplined.

No doubt there is some humor in Moschion's rhetorical pretensions: he was probably too young to have served as both a *khorēgos* and a phylarch (commander of his tribe's cavalry).[13] What is important, however, is that by using the catalogue in a context in which he is seeking to defend his behavior and establish the propriety of his character, Moschion demonstrates his knowledge of the topos; whether he successfully and skillfully deploys it is another question.[14] By claiming to have made lavish and generous outlays in public and private, Moschion assumes the stance of a defendant seeking special consideration from a jury. Wealthy litigants

[11] For the liturgical catalogue as primarily a feature of defendants' stories, see Johnstone 1999, 94–96. On the institution of public liturgies in Athens, see chapter 4. For the association of *philotimia* with the system of liturgies, see chapter 6 with notes 39–41.

[12] The text cited here is Arnott; trans. adapted from Arnott.

[13] Gomme and Sandbach (1973, 546–47 ad 13) suggest that the discrepancy between Moschion's age and the age requirements for these offices (40 and 30) stems from changes in the functions of, and requirements for, these offices by Menander's time. It seems more likely that we are meant to perceive the discrepancy between Moschion's age and his posturing as a civic and social benefactor.

[14] Moschion seems to be an inept negotiator of the class politics associated with elite litigation and liturgical donation. By emphasizing their generous benefactions, actual defendants sought to diminish class resentment and obtain *kharis* from the jurors. But Moschion wants to have it both ways, to be seen both as an ordinary citizen and as a member of a conspicuous elite. For Moschion's deme enrollment, cf. *Sam.* 10. Arnott supplies "παχιε͂ς" at the beginning of line 13. If this is correct, Moschion deploys a topos meant to garner demotic sympathy in tandem with a complaint about the burdens of wealth.

seem to have viewed liturgical donation as a kind of legal insurance. According to Josiah Ober,

> Litigants . . . quite naturally asked jurors to take into consideration the good things they had done for the state in the past and would be likely to do in the future. The performers of liturgies who mentioned their contributions in court hoped that the common people would feel a sense of gratitude (*charis*) for service rendered them. Indeed, the hope for gratitude from the demos and especially from jurors was the motive behind many liturgists' acts of public generosity to the state, and some of them were not reticent about admitting it. Lysias's client (25.12–13), for example, states plainly that he had undertaken liturgies so that he would be thought better of by "you jurors" if he were ever summoned into court (cf. Lys. 18.23, 20.31, 21.15).[15]

In his own defense before the theatrical audience, Moschion is obviously not trying to win a favorable verdict, but he is seeking to repair his character and his credibility as romantic protagonist. His need to do so stems in part from the unusual nature of his "mistake." Unlike other comic protagonists, Moschion seems to have seduced the heroine rather than committing the judicially neutral act of rape favored elsewhere in comedy, fathering a bastard (*nothos*) in the process.[16] As I noted in chapter 3, seduction, not rape, was considered the paradigmatic sexual offense in ancient Athens.[17] In such offenses, law and ideology constructed juridical injury by assessing not the presence or absence of consent between the parties involved but the offender's intent and the perceived effects of his actions on the male who controlled sexual access to the victim.[18] For these reasons, seduction was considered a quintessentially antidemocratic crime, a crime thought to be characteristic of the newly rich and hubris-prone aristocrats. That Moschion is wealthy and his victim poor adds just this dangerous dimension of class politics to his own behavior, regardless of his intentions.

Although Moschion does not actually confess to his crime, several factors, including the assumptions of other characters, suggest that he seduced rather than raped the heroine.[19] The context in which he commit-

[15] Ober 1989, 228.

[16] For a more detailed discussion of the construction of sexual offenses in law, ideology, and comedy, see chapter 3.

[17] See D. Cohen 1990, 148.

[18] For the politics of consent in democratic Athens, see now Omitowoju 2002, which unfortunately became available too late to be fully considered in the present study.

[19] Moschion's apparent seduction of the heroine is an exception to the generic bias against the seduction of virgins in Menander's extant plays and fragments. The titles of several plays whose plots are unknown may indicate that such seductions occurred elsewhere in comedy: Alcaeus's *Adelphai Moikheuomenai* (*Seduced Sisters*, 1 K.-A.), Amipsias's *Moikhoi* (*Se-*

ted the act is itself ambiguous. Although it was a nighttime festival, the usual setting for comic rape, the festival was the Adonia being held in his own home; and the home (albeit usually the victim's, not the perpetrator's) is the regular context for acts of seduction.[20] In cases of New Comic rape, alcohol and passion often diminish the transgressive significance of the rapist's action, but these mitigating factors are not relevant here. Although Moschion was probably overcome by eros on the night in question, as New Comic rapists generally are, he does not say as much. More significant, he lacks the alibi of intoxication.[21] He was sober and knew his victim, indicators of seduction rather than rape. Moreover, neither his own father nor Nikeratos hesitate to label him a seducer (*moikhos*, 588–92). At one point, Nikeratos even threatens to apply the self-help remedy allowed for seducers caught in the act (612, 717–18).[22] Finally, although Moschion never confesses to his crime, his name probably announced it. Elsewhere in comedy, "Moschion" often plays the rival and would-be seducer rather than the romantic protagonist–rapist.[23]

Moschion's forensic posture—which sets the tone for the dramaturgy of the entire play—stems as much from his shame at violating social and political mores as from his shame before his father.[24] This triangulation between father, son, and community is established in the prologue-apolo-

---

ducers, 12–14 K.-A.), Antiphanes' *Moikhoi* (*Seducers*, 159 K.-A.), and Philemon's *Moikhos* (*Seducer*, 45 K.-A.). The titles may, however, refer to an incident of real or pretended adultery (an offense against the marriage bond) rather than the seduction of a virgin. Plautus's *Miles Gloriosus* and *Bacchides* (based on Menander's *Dis Exapaton*) contain adultery plots in which a *hetaira* poses as a married woman: in the *Miles*, to punish an overbearing soldier; in the *Bacchides*, to extort money from a wealthy citizen. On adultery scenarios in comedy, see further Scafuro 1997, 232–35.

[20] For the *oikos* as the scene of *moikheia*, see Paoli 1976.

[21] For the unusual features of the rape/seduction scenario in the *Samia*, see further Jacques 1971, xxix–xxx.

[22] In both cases, Nikeratos uses the technical language for apprehending a seducer: μοιχὸν λαβών (see C. Austin 1970, 100). Scafuro has noted the tension between Nikeratos's description of Moschion as a *moikhos* (717–18) and the fact that he is supposed to have committed an act of rape. She suggests that *moikhos* in those lines probably means rape (1997, 197 n.12), but the technical sense in which Nikeratos uses the term seems to rule against this conflation.

[23] The "Moschions" in the *Perikeiromenē* and *Sikyōnioi* are both characterized as losers and seducers. Choricius, however, may refer to an association of the name with "rape": "Is it really the case, of the masks created by Menander, 'Moschion' has taught us to rape virgins?" ("Speech on behalf of those acting in plays of Dionysus," quoted and discussed in MacCary 1970; Wiles 1991, 92–94). On the name Moschion, Wiles (1991, 94) states: "Moschion (*moschion* = young shoot, or little calf) suggests the age and sexuality of the mask, with an echo of *moicheia* (adultery, debauchery)." On the contrast between Moschion's delicate mask and his attempt to act like a mercenary in the fifth act, see Blume 1998.

[24] Many commentators call attention to the importance of the father–son relationship in

gia by Moschion's deliberate intermingling of his father's story with his own. Even his deployment of the liturgical catalogue is conditioned by this three-way interdependence. His ostensible reason for enumerating his public and private benefactions is to illustrate the nature of his relationship with Demeas. Moschion's participation in the liturgical contract and civic life depends on a prior contract with his father. In exchange for providing him with the means to win honor in the eyes of the community, Moschion gave his father "disciplined behavior": he used to be *kosmios*.[25] In this way, Moschion makes the family, or more precisely the father–son bond, the ultimate source of democratic mores and norms.

Moschion is ashamed to confess his illicit sexual conduct both to the law court audience he constructs and to his father. This is, in fact, one of the insufficiently resolved strands of the comic problem and plot. From beginning to end, Moschion is too dependent on his father's judgment and approval. In his need to appear "good" (*kosmios*) before his father, he is willing to harm the woman he claims to love, her mother, and his own bastard son. Yet Moschion's shame before Demeas also is an important link with his adoptive father. Demeas too fell victim to a transgressive passion that he was ashamed to admit to his son.[26] He was seized by an intense desire for a *hetaira*, a condition more appropriate for a youth than an old man (in comedy and society). Despite his effort to conceal

---

the *Samia* and (in New Comedy generally). See the commentaries Jacques 1971; Gomme and Sandbach 1973; Sisti 1974; Bain 1983; Blume 1974; Lamagna 1998. Lloyd-Jones (1990) and Blume (1974, 8) identify the father–son relationship and reconciliation as the play's dominant theme. See also E. Masaracchia 1978–79, arguing for Moschion's need to shake off paternal authority; Grant 1986, arguing that idiosyncrasies and inversions in the father–son relationship between Demeas and Moschion arise from the characterization of this relationship as a friendship; and Weissenberger 1991, on the deficit of trust between father and son. See also Keuls 1973, Henry 1985, and Zagagi 1994, who emphasize the importance of Chrysis's role, in addition to the father–son motif. On the father–son theme in comedy generally, see Wehrli 1936; R. L. Hunter 1985, 95–109, with 103–5 on the *Samia*; Fantham 1971; and below on the refused "Hippolytus plot."

[25] Cf. *Sam.* 273, 344, and Blume 1974, 11–12. On the moral connotations of *kosmios*, see Mette 1969; Blume 1974, 11; Jacques 1971, xxx–xxxi. West (1991: 20) suggests that Moschion's much-stressed *kosmiotēs* might be seen as a "bourgeoisification" of Hippolytus's *sōphrosunē*, but it may also obliquely refer to his quasi-ephebic status. One of the officials in charge of the ephebes was specifically called a *kosmētēs*. And in honorary decrees, ephebes are praised for their *eukosmia* (orderliness and discipline); for the inscriptions, see Reinmuth 1971. On the moral component of ephebic education, see Ober 2001, 203–4, and chapter 7 below.

[26] Goldberg states that "Moschion is simply projecting his own sense of shame onto Demeas" (1980, 94). While Moschion may well be "projecting" in his monologue, Demeas certainly does behave as though his relationship with Chrysis is problematic, if not shame-producing, in his own efforts to keep the workings of his household secret. See further below.

the affair, Moschion discovered it and even abetted it. In his opening monologue, he claims credit for convincing Demeas to install Chrysis in their home to ward off competition from younger rivals.[27] By disclosing Demeas's secret sexual shame along with his own, Moschion establishes a basic parallelism between himself and his adoptive father. To underline this unusual father–son sexual symmetry, the play emphasizes their reproductive synchronicity as well. In his opening monologue, Moschion refers to the striking coincidence that their bastard sons were born at exactly the same time.[28]

This "like father, like son" pretense is, of course, the device that generates the comic problem: Demeas's mistaken belief that Moschion fathered a child with Chrysis. By replacing the real seduction with this pseudo-seduction plot, the play puts Demeas's relationship on trial, deftly sidestepping the convention requiring that the protagonist be youthful.[29] At the same time, the illicit sexual passion of father and son invests them each with forensic features. Because both characters must explain and justify their behavior, they plead their cases to the audience rather than speaking to each other, a device that accounts for the extensive use of monologue in this play.[30] In so doing, they speak more like defendants concerned to profess and perform ideologically correct views of the social order than like comic characters. This focus is so pervasive that it disrupts the linear trajectory of comedy's conventional narrative pattern: scenes of forensic reasoning and farcical misunderstanding highjack the teleology of the romantic plot.

The Consequences of Nonconjugal Cohabitation

While Moschion's need to adopt a forensic disposition is readily apparent, the need for Demeas to do so may seem less compelling to a modern reader. After all, the only thing Demeas is actually guilty of is violating comedy's internal age requirement for successful romance. In contrast to Moschion, whose sexual behavior has harmed Plangon and her father, Demeas's flamboyant romantic life does not seem to be harming anyone. At worst, by maintaining a Samian *hetaira* in a luxurious lifestyle, Demeas is doing damage to himself, as he is engaging in just the kind of

[27] The key lines are damaged, but it is clear that Moschion claimed some responsibility for bringing her into the house.

[28] On the fate of Chrysis's baby, see chapter 3 and note 111.

[29] Although Moschion mentions that Demeas needed to defend against younger competitors (*Sam.* 26), Demeas may not have actually been so old. The key point is that his status as a father makes him ineligible for the protagonist role within comedy's conventions.

[30] For the preponderance of monologue in the *Samia*, see above note 5.

behavior that, according to recent commentators, Athenian law tended to permit rather than prohibit. They see the relative absence of legislation regulating the private sphere as indicating the classical democracy's interest in protecting the personal freedom and negative liberty of its citizens.[31] In particular, the catchphrase "living as one likes," deployed by both democrats and their critics to characterize the culture of democracy, is adduced to support the existence of an alleged domain of personal freedom.[32] While recent historians are probably correct to revise the view of Athens as a liberty-less polis, they nevertheless run the risk of mistaking ideologically charged statements for descriptions of the sociopolitical reality. The dialectic of freedom and unfreedom in democratic Athens is highly complex and conditioned by more than the presence or absence of legislation or rules.[33]

There was no law either compelling the Athenian citizen to marry or prohibiting him from living with a woman whom he did not marry. Yet citizenship's definition with reference to marriage and legitimate procreation had a strong normalizing force.[34] The laws of citizenship, like the laws governing male prostitution, regulate and shape social practice not by issuing "orders backed by threats" but rather by delineating the boundaries within which it was possible for the "citizen" to act.[35] By living with a foreign woman and a former *hetaira*, Demeas was implicitly bucking the norm: he was acting un-Athenian and asserting a personal preference at odds with the ethos of monogamy enshrined in Athenian law and ideology. Indeed, living with a *hetaira* rather than a wife was apparently so "not done" that one Athenian litigant professes to be ashamed even to have to report that his brother-in-law never married a native woman in accordance with the laws but installed a former slave *hetaira* in his house (Dem. 48.52–53). Finally, the fact that such behavior was class-specific—not every citizen could afford the extravagance of living with a former *hetaira*—only made Demeas's behavior appear worse.

Although living with a *hetaira* was an offense against democratic cultural mores rather than law, Demeas's behavior potentially crossed a judi-

[31] See D. Cohen 1991a; Wallace 1995, 1996. Although his arguments are not couched in the vocabulary of political liberalism, Foucault (1985, 23 and passim) is also relevant to the question of the "regulation" of sexual conduct in Athens.

[32] See Thuc. 2.37.2–3; Pl. *Rep.* 557b; Isoc. 12.131, 7.20; Arist. *Pol.* 1317a40–b14. According to Socrates in Plato's *Republic*, there is so much freedom in democratic states that it trickles down, infecting even the animals (557c).

[33] For a critique of the tendency to posit freedom as an absolute rather than a relational and contextual practice in modern liberal political philosophy, see W. Brown 1995: 6.

[34] On the instituting and norming power of Athenian laws pertaining to citizenship, see further chapters 1 and 3.

[35] See Carey 1998 for a discussion of the applicability of H. L. A. Hart's conception of law as "orders backed by threats" to Athenian law.

cial and legal line when Chrysis conceived and bore his child. Any child born to Demeas and Chrysis would have been a "true" *nothos* (bastard): a child whose status could never be normalized by the belated marriage of its parents and who would therefore have been a permanent outsider, excluded from family, inheritance, citizen status, and civic religion.[36] The Athenian state never prohibited the generation of such outsiders; in fact, despite the link between citizen status (both its possession and transmission) and state-designated rules of sexual reproduction, the state passed no explicit laws either to encourage the production of a democratic population or to limit the production of internal outsiders.[37] The normalizing force of democratic culture was tacitly rather than overtly coercive.

The problem for Demeas consists not in his having fathered a bastard but rather in what the presence of such a child in his household might be taken to mean. Although the Athenian state used marriage as an institution of civic membership, it took no steps to manage citizen marriage practices. There were no marriage licenses, no matrimonial archives, and no special officials empowered to designate a given relationship as a marriage. The failure to regularize and define marriage practices might seem a curious oversight, if not downright negligence, on the part of a polis that constituted itself through strict rules of sexual reproduction within the marriage context. Yet this very absence of bureaucratic policing seems to have had a strong chilling effect on nonconjugal forms of cohabitation. It is not that the Athenians had difficulty recognizing a citizen marriage when they saw one; rather, the difficulty lay in proving that a live-in heterosexual relationship was something other than a marriage. The closest thing to a legal definition of marriage in Athens is "living together for purposes of producing legitimate children."[38] This meant that the act of fathering a child with a woman with whom one lived was itself sufficient to create the appearance of a marriage. The potential legal burden for a citizen in Demeas's position would be to prove that his relationship with Chrysis was something other than a counterfeit citizen marriage. In other words, the danger of refusing the conjugal norm consisted not in opting out of the system but its opposite: seeming to be illegally opting in. In fact, the only extant lawsuit for *xenia* (impersonating a citizen) hinges on precisely this problem. In this case, the Athenian orator Apollodorus accused Neaira, a former Corinthian *hetaira*, of impersonating a citizen by living in marriage with Stephanos, Apollodorus's political enemy. To show that the relationship between Stephanos and Neaira was being passed off as a citizen marriage, Apollodorus harps on

[36] See chapter 3, note 114, for references.

[37] See Roy 1999.

[38] E.g., [Dem.] 59. 122. See also chapter 1, note 48, on the *enguē* formula.

the existence of children in their household. He anticipates that Stephanos will claim that Neaira is his mistress, a former *hetaira*, rather than his wife. Apollodorus instructs the jurors to refuse this defense as specious because he was living with children. Apparently, the idea that a citizen might rear bastards was virtually inconceivable—at least in the context of civic discourse. Accordingly, Apollodorus was able to argue without qualification that the presence of children in Stephanos's household demonstrated an intent to pass off his arrangement with Neaira as a marriage (see chapter 3, above).

In the *Samia*, Demeas certainly seems to be aware of the judicial jeopardy in which the existence of Chrysis's child places him. On learning that Chrysis is rearing the child against his wishes, he sarcastically remarks that she has become his "married *hetaira*" (130). He realizes that the existence of a child in his household is sufficient to signal the presence or pretense of a marriage. This probably accounts for one facet of his forensic characterization. In addition to enjoying a special intimacy with the audience in the trial of Moschion and his own romantic relationship, Demeas is especially concerned about the possibility of litigation. He alone of all the characters vigilantly strives to manage appearances so as to present a harmonious facade to the outside world of neighbors, friends, and enemies. Believing himself betrayed by his son and mistress, he determines to be a man by concealing his misfortune (351, 355–56). He forces himself to appear suitably festive on the supposedly happy occasion of his son's marriage, despite the havoc in his household (446–50). He twice speaks of anonymous witnesses, keen observers eagerly scrutinizing his private life in the hopes of finding judicial ammunition (473–75). And finally, when Moschion publicizes the false charge that Demeas leveled against him, Demeas castigates him for summoning witnesses to his mistake.[39]

Demeas's Defense: Revising the Tragic Family Plot

Although Demeas responds with appropriate civic indignation when he learns that Chrysis is rearing his bastard child, the play does not allow him to directly confront the politically sensitive nature of his living arrangements. Rather, it places him in a situation that enables him to neutralize its anticivic implications. In a sense, Moschion paves the way for this move by emphasizing that Demeas is the real sponsor behind nu-

[39] The knowledge that the legality of Moschion's adoption could easily be challenged by any supposed relative also surely contributes to Demeas's sensitivity to his judicial position. According to Keuls (1973), Moschion's adopted status accounts for the basic lack of trust or insecurity in the father–son relationship; see also Blume 1974, 140.

merous acts of civic largess. The stress on Demeas's communal expenditures alleviates the suspicion that his decision to reside with a *hetaira* reflects a selfish dedication to private ostentation. More important, the play allows Demeas to prove that he does not privilege the relationship with a *hetaira* over his politically sanctioned bond. Although relations with *hetairai* normally stand in opposition to civic matrimony, in this case the contest is between *hetaira* and adopted son.

Demeas begins the third act with a disclosure that a sudden catastrophe has interrupted his good fortune. Instead of jumping to the obvious conclusion, Demeas invites the audience to review the facts together with him.

> ἦ 'στ[ὶ] πιθανόν; σκέψασθε πότερο[ν εὖ φρονῶ
> ἢ μαίνομ', οὐδέν τ' εἰς ἀκρίβειαν [τότε
> λαβὼν ἐπάγομαι μέγ' ἀτύχημα[
>
> (216–18)

> Is this plausible? Consider whether I am reasoning well,
> or whether I'm crazy, whether by not ascertaining the exact truth
> I bring a great misfortune upon myself.

Demeas's language and emotional tone characterize him more as a litigant than as a jilted lover and betrayed father. His concern to argue from probability is, of course, a staple of forensic reasoning. Similarly, Demeas's desire to think rationally rather than be carried into madness seems to underline a generic contrast between oratory and tragedy in the emotional register. Finally, his second-person address to the audience, "σκέψασθε" (consider), frames his own story as a legal narrative and the theatrical audience as jurors or judges.[40] In keeping with this forensic frame, he reports the facts as he knows them to be. First, during the rushed preparations for Moschion's wedding, he heard Moschion's former nurse coddling "Chrysis's" baby and naming Moschion as the father. Shortly afterward he witnessed Chrysis breast-feeding the child. From these events, he concludes (wrongly) that Chrysis is the mother of the child but refuses to conclude on the basis of mere hearsay that Moschion is the father.

> αὐτὴν δ' ἔχουσαν αὐτὸ τὴν Σαμίαν ὁρῶ
> ἔξω διδοῦσαν τιτθίον παριὼν ἅμα,
> ὥσθ' ὅτι μὲν αὐτῆς ἐστι τοῦτο γνώριμον
> εἶναι, πατρὸς δ' ὅτου ποτ' ἐστίν, εἴτ' ἐμὸν

[40] The second-person invitation σκέψασθε is a common exhortation in oratory (Dem. 18.252.9; 19.4.3, 148.1, 166.2, 251.1, 300.6; 21.58.1, 73.1, 88.2, 143.2) but occurs only here in Menander's extant comedy. Similarly, the adjective ἀκρίβειαν (exact) is found only here in the extant comedies but is common in the Athenian orations.

εἶτ'—οὐ λέγω δ', ἄνδρες, πρὸς ὑμᾶς τοῦτ' ἐγώ,
οὐχ ὑπονοῶ, τὸ πρᾶγμα δ' εἰς μέσον φέρω
ἅ τ' ἀκήκο' αὐτός, οὐκ ἀγανακτῶν οὐδέπω.
σύνοιδα γὰρ τῶι μειρακίωι, νὴ τοὺς θεούς,
καὶ κοσμίωι τὸν πρότερον ὄντι χρόνον ἀεὶ
καὶ περὶ ἔμ' ὡς ἔνεστιν εὐσεβεστάτωι.

(265–74)[41]

I saw the Samian herself holding the child,
nursing it outside as I went by,
so it's known that the baby is hers,
but who the father is—whether it's me,
or whether—gentlemen, no I won't tell
you that! I've no suspicions, but I bring
the facts and what I've heard out on the open. I'm
not angry, yet! I really know my boy—
That he was always well-disciplined in days
gone by, and showed the greatest possible piety to me.

This passage might be seen as a commentary on the citizen male's desire to uncover the secrets of maternity and paternity, to use reason to disempower women in the one arena in which biology gave them the edge over men dependent on them for knowledge and indeed identity. It is no small irony that female physiology—Chrysis's ability to nurse a child not her own—vividly exposes the limits of male knowledge, or what Demeas thinks can be known (γνώριμον).[42] Nevertheless, Demeas's flawed reasoning is crucial for what it reveals about his character and commitments.

Directly addressing the audience members as "gentlemen" (ἄνδρες), Demeas hesitates even to voice the suspicion that Moschion has fathered a child with Chrysis. Commentators point out that Demeas's proclivity for this form of address signals his special rapport with the audience.[43] While this observation is certainly correct, Demeas's terminology has an additional dramatic and thematic significance: it clarifies how he conceptualizes the audience, and in turn provides the lens through which he views his family crisis. Here and elsewhere in the play, monologue enables a character to reveal his thoughts and inner life, but Demeas

[41] The text quoted in 266 is Arnott.

[42] On the sense of γνώριμον here, see Gomme and Sandbach 1973, 569 ad 267. For the problem of knowledge in the *Samia*, see Stoessl 1973.

[43] See *Sam.* 269, 329, 447, 683; J. Blundell 1980, 41. Bain (1977, 190–92) assembles all the evidence for this form of address in Menander's comedy, noting that it often serves an exclamatory function. The verb—σύνοιδα—implies having knowledge about a person, "especially as a potential witness" (LSJ, quoted in Gomme and Sandbach 1973, 569).

chooses to address not himself but members of the audience.[44] By calling on them as ἄνδρες and including them in his deliberations, Demeas makes the audience into a character in his domestic drama: he transforms the theatergoers into jurors or judges.[45] A single term might not in itself be sufficient to establish this reframing, but the point is clinched by the deliberative and forensic contexts in which he deploys it, coupled with his use of oratorical diction. For instance, his expression "to put the matter before you" (τὸ πρᾶγμα δ' εἰς μέσον φέρω) is a common oratorical collocation, used only once elsewhere in Menander's extant comedy (*Pk.* 522) in a markedly oratorical context.[46]

Demeas not only speaks like a litigant, he also acts like one. To conduct his impromptu paternity test, he does what any truth-seeking litigant would do: namely, call for the torture of the household slave. Upon pain of branding, Parmenon is forced to confirm that Moschion is, in fact, the father of the child. This disclosure elicits Demeas's second monologue in this act.

> ὦ πόλισμα Κεκροπίας χθονός,
> ὦ ταναὸς αἰθήρ, ὦ-τί, Δημέα, βοᾶις;
> τί βοᾶις, ἀνόητε; κάτεχε σαυτόν, καρτέρει.
> οὐδὲν γὰρ ἀδικεῖ Μοσχίων σε. παράβολος
> ὁ λόγος ἴσως ἐστ', ἄνδρες, ἀλλ' ἀληθινός.
> εἰ μὲν γὰρ ἢ βουλόμενος ἢ κεκνισμένος
> ἔρωτι τοῦτ' ἔπραξεν ἢ μισῶν ἐμέ,
> ἦν ἂν ἐπὶ τῆς αὐτῆς διανοίας ἔτι θρασὺς
> ἐμοί τε παρατεταγμένος. νυνὶ δέ μοι
> ἀπολελόγηται τὸν φανέντ' αὐτῶι γάμον
> ἄσμενος ἀκούσας.
>
> (325–35)

> O Citadel of Kekrops's land,
> O thin-spread ether!
> O—why are you shouting, Demeas? Restrain yourself.
> Bear up! Moschion has done you no wrong.
> This a paradoxical thing to say, gentlemen, but it's true.
> If he had done what he has done willingly,
> or because of infatuation or out of hatred
> for me, he would still be brazening it out and opposing me.

[44] On Demeas's use of self-address elsewhere in the play, see J. Blundell 1980, 68.

[45] In the *Sikyōnioi* ἄνδρες is also used in a specifically legal context. In the assembly scene (reported in the text) the romantic protagonist addresses the "jurors" as ἄνδρες in 240, 269 (and as conjectured, 225). When Moschion, the oligarchic romantic rival, concedes defeat he too addresses the audience as ἄνδρες. See further chapter 7.

[46] Gomme and Sandbach (1973, 569) adduce Dem. 28.139 as a parallel.

As it is, he's acquitted himself. He was glad
to accept the marriage once I suggested it.

Demeas's first line is a quotation from Euripides' *Oedipus*. The allusion to a story about a son who kills his father and fathers children with his mother might seem to offer a close, though hardly exact, parallel to Demeas's imagined family betrayals. Yet the point of the citation is precisely to deny the parallel and to refuse the tragic situation. Forcing himself to restrain his wayward emotions, he abruptly switches genres, dispensing with the pathos of tragedy for the presumed rationality of democratic rhetoric.[47] Demeas signals the generic shift by addressing the theatrical audience as ἄνδρες, once again drawing the spectators into his forensic illusion. In this monologue, however, Demeas no longer asks for deliberative assistance but rather seeks to impose his own interpretation of past events on the audience-jurors. After concluding to his own satisfaction that Moschion and Chrysis have produced a child together, Demeas attempts to convince the audience (and himself) that Moschion is innocent of wrongdoing and disloyalty.

To that end, he leads the audience step-by-step through his reasoning in order to justify a conclusion that even he regards as paradoxical. According to Demeas, Moschion's eagerness for the marriage with Plangon and the evidence of his former character preclude the possibility that he seduced Chrysis with either amorous or malicious intent—in other words, that he seduced her at all.

οὐδενὶ τρόπωι γὰρ πιθανὸν εἶναί μοι δοκεῖ
τὸν εἰς ἅπαντας κόσμιον καὶ σώφρονα
τοὺς ἀλλοτρίους εἰς ἐμὲ τοιοῦτον γεγονέναι,
οὐδ' εἰ δεκάκις ποητός ἐστι, μὴ γόνωι
ἐμὸς ὑός.

(343–47)

It's simply not credible that Moschion who was
so well-disciplined and *sōphrōn* in dealing with others (strangers)
would behave in such a way to me,
not even if he's ten times my adopted son,
not my son by birth.

If Moschion is innocent, then, by Demeas's reasoning, Chrysis must be entirely at fault. He assumes that she took advantage of Moschion's youth and got him drunk (338–42).[48] The very same factors that elsewhere ex-

[47] On the forensic coloring of this monologue, see J. Blundell 1980, 38. Goldberg (1980, 100), in contrast, sees comedy as the dominant genre.

[48] Lamagna (1997, 139) discusses the significance of Demeas's characterization of Mosch-

culpate the comic protagonist from having committed an act of rape are invoked here to excuse Moschion for falling victim to a woman's sexual allure. Demeas's explanation is, of course, no more than a figment of his imagination, since Moschion and Chrysis have not had a child together. But that is precisely the point: Demeas's interpretation is significant for what it says about his imagination and deepest beliefs.[49] By exonerating Moschion at the expense of Chrysis, Demeas creates the impression that he possesses all the inner convictions of a middling democratic citizen.[50] Although Demeas is the character most at pains to conceal the workings of his psychic and domestic life, he turns out to have absolutely nothing to hide—from the standpoint of the official ideology, at any rate.[51]

Demeas's middling credentials are also brought out by his refusal to identify with the aristocratic cultural narrative the play offers him. His situation, as many commentators have observed, comments intertextually on the Hippolytus plot known best from Euripidean tragedy.[52] Like the

---

ion's offense as an *atukhēma* rather than an *adikēma*. For the importance of the Aristotelian classifications of harms in characterizing the protagonist's actions, see further chapter 6 with note 27.

[49] On the use of monologue to enable a character to disclose inner convictions and feelings, see Bain 1983, xxi.

[50] According to Zagagi (1994, 124, 126), Demeas's rejection of Chrysis attests to the subordination of individual interest to the needs of the household. While I agree with this interpretation, I argue that Demeas's behavior is portrayed as ideologically correct rather than "realistically," as Zagagi contends. In her treatment of the *Samia*, Zagagi seems to use the term "realism" to denote the comedy's faithful depiction of the actual historical reality, but we need a more fine-grained model to map the relationship between the two. The narrative conventions of comedy shape and indeed distort how it presents the laws and ideology pertaining to citizenship. In the *Samia*, Demeas performs an ideologically correct privileging of the father–son relationship over his relationship with a *hetaira*. In so doing, he offers the kind of idealized depiction of his household relationships usually found in the law courts (see Humphreys 1993, 5). Thus, we might say that in this case comedy realistically portrays the official ideology.

[51] There is a certain irony in Demeas, the one character who gives the illusion of having an inner life at odds with his social position, having internalized exactly the set of responses necessary to reproduce the democratic state. In this respect, Demeas is akin to Kharisios in the *Epitrepontes*, the romantic protagonist who similarly suppresses his love in order to remain faithful to the official ideology of citizenship. On the complex interconnection between Kharisios's actions and beliefs and the needs of civic ideology, see the subtle analysis of Konstan 1995, 151–52, and chapter 8 below.

[52] Cf. Wehrli 1936, 64; Katsouris 1975, 131–35; West 1991; Lamagna 1998, 64–67, and 1997–98; Gutzwiller 2000, 109–11. On comedy's use of tragedy, as elaborating tragic plot patterns in comic situations, see Katsouris 1975; on tragic forms and meters, Webster 1974, 56–67; on the production of comic plots out of a mixture of modes, Goldberg 1980, 13–28; on the dramatic effects of the use of tragic devices and allusions, R. L. Hunter 1985, 114–36; analyzing the forms of tragic intertextuality and their role in shaping comedy's realistic scenarios, Hurst 1990; elaborating the metatheatrical effects produced by tragic intertexts, Gutzwiller 2000; see also Porter 2000. For comedy's domestication of tragic sacrifice, see

aristocratic Theseus, Demeas is confronted with evidence that his formerly well-behaved son has slept with his own domestic partner, in each case a woman of foreign descent and dubious moral pedigree. Their responses, however, could not be more different. Theseus immediately believes the accusations contained in his wife's suicide note, condemning and cursing his hypocritically puritanical son for rape.[53] By contrast, when confronted with compelling evidence of sexual intimacy between his *hetaira* and son, Demeas interprets the facts like a socialized citizen—that is, he conducts a trial and condemns the woman. Accordingly, rather than disowning his son, he disowns his mistress, preserving a manly silence about his own injuries.

> Δημέα, νῦν ἄνδρα χρὴ
> εἶναί σ'· ἐπιλαθοῦ τοῦ πόθου, πέπαυσ' ἐρῶν,
> καὶ τἀτύχημα μὲν τὸ γεγονὸς κρύφθ' ὅσον
> ἔνεστι διὰ τὸν ὑόν, ἐκ τῆς δ' οἰκίας
> ἐπὶ κεφαλὴν ἐς κόρακας ὦσον τὴν καλὴν
> Σαμίαν.
>
> (349–54)

> You must be a man, Demeas.
> Forget your passion. Stop loving her!
> As far as you can, keep the present misfortune secret.
> Do it for your son's sake. Drive the beautiful
> Samian headfirst from your house.

Shame, Poverty, and Anger: The Politics of Affect

Interestingly, Demeas conceives of his rejection of Chrysis as a form of manliness. In his view, "being a man" is a matter of controlling his emotions (under whose purview the Greeks placed erotic desire).[54] Manliness, then, is a matter of being *sōphrōn*, of containing and mastering emotions rather than being driven by them or even extinguishing them. Demeas's acquittal of Moschion can be seen as the triumph of rational control over emotion, of manhood over desire, and (most important) of *sōphrosunē*, a central virtue of democratic citizenship, over its opposites, *akrateia* and *akolasia*.[55] Though civic manhood for Demeas is a completely interiorized

---

also Scodel 1993. In this study, I treat tragedy as an embedded genre. For the poetics of embedded genres, see Martin 1984.

[53] The possibility for such a forgery probably underlies the bias against the use of written documents in court, see Humphreys 1985b; Scafuro 1994.

[54] Foucault 1985.

[55] For *sōphrosunē* as a cardinal civic virtue, see Whitehead 1993, 65.

state, it is just the opposite for his poor friend and neighbor. Nikeratos deems Demeas's self-control in the face of sexual betrayal a sign of servility rather than manhood. He chastises Demeas for failing to assume an anger (*orgē*) appropriate to the situation (498–500). If it were his bed that had been disgraced, he claims, he would have sold his concubine and son, as well as prepared a suit for murder. Thus, while Demeas sees his situation as calling for the suppression of desire and anger (*eros* and *orgē*), in Nikeratos's imagination it demands rage rather than restraint, the expression of emotion rather than its containment (350, 447). Indeed, he seems to embody Demeas's rage for him, as he nearly explodes with anger in reaction merely to Moschion's presence (519).

Unlike Demeas, Nikeratos cannot experience his masculinity by feeling his emotions. Rather, it is only by acting on his anger that he can acquire the necessary external support of his manhood. As he puts it:

> ἀνδράποδ[ον εἶ, Δημέα
> εἰ γὰρ ἐμὸν ἤι[σχυνε λέ]κ̣τρον, οὐκ ἂν εἰς ἄλλον ποτὲ
> ὕβρισ' οὐδ' ἡ συ̣γ[κλ]ι̣θεῖσα· παλλακὴν δ' ἂν αὔριον
> πρῶτος ἀνθρώπω̇ν ἐπώλουν, συναποκηρύττων ἅμα
> ὑόν, ὥστε μηθὲν εἶναι μήτε κουρεῖον κενόν,
> μὴ στοάν, καθημένους δὲ πάντας ἐξ ἑωθινοῦ
> περὶ ἐμοῦ λαλεῖν λέγοντας ὡς ἀνὴρ Νικήρατος
> γέγον' ἐπεξελθὼν δικαίως τῶι φόνωι.
>
> (506–13)

> [You're acting] like a slave,
> [Demeas]. If he'd shamed my bed, neither he nor his partner
> would commit hubris against anyone again. I'd have been the first man to
> sell off my *pallakē* the next day and I'd disinherit my son at the same time.
> Then no place would have been empty, barbershop or stoa—
> all the world would have been sitting in their seats from dawn's first light
> gossiping about me, saying that Nikeratos had turned out
> to be a real man, justly prosecuting for murder.

Although Nikeratos's reaction may be exaggerated for comic effect, it should not be viewed as foolish for that reason.[56] Elsewhere in the play, Nikeratos indulges in a similarly excessive emotional response to sexual dishonor. When he learns that Moschion has seduced and fathered a child with his daughter, he is unable to control his anger. Being a self-willed (*authekastos*) and unsocialized type, in Demeas's reckoning, he responds with characteristic extremity by trying to burn the child alive

[56] Commentators sometimes dismiss Nikeratos's heavy-handed hypothetical because, after all, Moschion and Chrysis were free persons rather than slaves and no murder was committed; but his hyperbolic response characterizes his own conception of manhood.

(550–51, 553–55).[57] By acting on his anger, Nikeratos does not, as he might imagine, repair his wounded manhood; rather, he becomes a victim of his own undisciplined emotions. He is described as suffering from a somatic and psychic affliction arising from the accumulation of black bile, the physical source of anger (564).[58]

Nikeratos's excessive anger and bouts of madness do not serve simply as foils against which Demeas's admirable self-restraint can be defined. Demeas too is seen as succumbing to anger and black bile when he throws Chrysis out of the house on Moschion's wedding day.[59] In his case, however, the characters who criticize his emotional overreaction do not possess the facts needed to assess whether his response is correctly calibrated to his circumstances. By contrast, the emphasis on Nikeratos's undisciplined emotions is part of comedy's realistic portrayal of a "poor but proud" citizen.[60] Nikeratos is depicted as deeply sensitive to his status. He is initially hesitant when Demeas broaches the topic of the marriage of their children because he does not have the economic status to enter into the alliance as an equal. Similarly, he worries that Demeas is "making a fool" of him when he attributes Plangon's pregnancy to Nikeratos's leaky roof (596), inviting him to share in the face-saving fantasy that it was Zeus rather than Moschion who impregnated his daughter.

Nikeratos's hypersensitivity over his status arises from his poverty. There is a deep-seated correlation between shame and poverty in Athenian society and comedy. This is not the kind of shame that, like Demeas's and Moschion's, matches actions and emotions to social norms.[61] Rather, it is an identity characterized by the perception of being "one-down" and by the "fear of being judged inferior which overrules rational

[57] According to Gomme and Sandbach (1973, 605–6 ad 550), *authekastos* in 550 probably does not have the etymological sense of "the man who calls everything just what it" as used by Aristotle (*E.N.* 1127a23). Rather, by calling Nikeratos an *authekastos* type, Demeas intends something like "a man who goes his own way," or less exactly (according to Gomme and Sandbach) "self-willed." Aristo the Peripatetic regards the *authekastos* as the man who "consults no one over his actions and disregards criticism."

[58] On anger and madness in the *Samia*, see Groton 1987.

[59] Although Demeas thinks he has swallowed his anger and concealed his emotions (*Sam.* 447), other characters view his rejection of Chrysis as a form of madness arising from excessive anger (415, 416, 419).

[60] Keuls 1973, 9.

[61] *Sam.* 23, 27, 47, 48, 67. In Menander's comedy, shame arises from committing or being a victim of a crime against sexual ideology, or from poverty. For sexual behavior bringing shame on the offender, see *Dis Ex.* 16–17, *Epit.* 645; on the victim, see *Dys.* 243ff. On poverty and shame, see esp. *Geōr.* 79ff. The exception is Kharisios in *Epit.* 886–87, whose shame arises from his overstrict interpretation of the civic sexual ideology; see further chapter 8. For a probable Menandrian critique of the association between poverty and shame, see Plut. *Mor.* 128a.

calculation."[62] The intimate link between this feeling of inferiority and poverty suggests that the democratic balancing act between conditions of marked socioeconomic inequality and political equality was not very successful, at least in psychic terms.[63] In comedy, the extreme anger of poor men can be seen as an emotional effort to ward off the shame associated with their social status. For them, expressing anger is a means of not experiencing, and therefore of refusing, shame. A relatively impoverished citizen like Nikeratos must therefore be especially vigorous in his responses to perceived dishonor, as he must ward off the shame always poised to undermine his status as a man and a citizen. In this regard, Nikeratos is exactly like Gorgias in the *Dyskolos*, who warns a suspected sexual predator that poor men make the most dangerous (and angry) enemies because they will do anything and everything to repair their wounded status (*Dys.* 295–98).

The Work of Prostitutes: The Importance of a Gender Stereotype

Demeas performs his manhood by controlling his emotions and he exonerates his son on the basis of Moschion's piety (*eusebeia*), his self-control (*sōphrosunē*), and his much-emphasized *kosmiotēs* (*Sam.* 274–75, 344). Although Demeas thereby seems to invest civic manhood with positive ethical content, his conception acquires its meaning primarily by what it is implicitly defined against: the figure of Chrysis, as he imagines her to be. According to Demeas's logic, if Moschion is innocent of losing sexual control, then Chrysis must be to blame. Thus, the retrieval of Moschion's moral probity hinges on establishing Chrysis's fundamental immorality. To that end, the text evokes several paradigmatic figures of female immorality. Most obviously, the situational parallel with the *Hippolytus* implicitly sets up a comparison between Chrysis and Phaedra, wife of Theseus and quintessential hypersexual stepmother. Just as in the case of the parallel between Demeas and Theseus, however, the tragic allusion remains tacit and operates to provide an implicit contrast: Chrysis's innocence underscores that she is not another Phaedra.

Demeas himself describes Chrysis as "my own Helen" (336–37). By likening Chrysis to the most beautiful and most notorious adulteress in all of Greek literature, he provides his son with an out, an excuse. Ac-

[62] Dover 1974, 237. For shame as an identity in modern societies according to which other people's behavior is defined with reference to the self, see Giddens 1991; Sedgwick 1993.

[63] The belief that a person could alleviate his poverty with energy and industry added to poverty's perceived shamefulness; see further Dover 1974, 239–42.

cording to this reasoning, Moschion is not responsible for fathering the child because Chrysis made him do it; her Helen-like allure, wine, and his youth combined to overcome his reason and his agency. At the same time, the comparison with Helen also helps lessen Demeas's own responsibility for installing a former *hetaira* in his house.[64]

There is in addition another important stereotype underlying Demeas's negative characterization of the "guilty" Chrysis. In his monologues, Demeas figures Chrysis's betrayal in sexual terms, condemning her as his own Helen and a whore.[65] When it comes time to deal with her directly, however, Demeas maintains a stoic silence about her imagined sexual indiscretions for the sake of his son. Instead, he reminds Chrysis of her economic dependence and accuses her of not knowing how to appreciate the luxurious lifestyle he provided (376). He cruelly describes her prospects in the city as a low-end *hetaira* forced to fend off starvation by attending dinner parties at the beck and call of her clients. In this way, he emphasizes Chrysis's enduring status as a *hetaira*.[66] Although she is installed in his home and involved in the kind of exclusive relationship thought to be indicative of concubinage, Chrysis never in fact manages to become a *pallakē* (concubine) in Demeas's eyes.[67]

From the outset, Demeas sees only two categories for Chrysis: wife or *hetaira*.[68] Although Nikeratos implicitly renders her a *pallakē* in his own imagined adultery scenario, Demeas forecloses the possibility.[69] He con-

[64] Demeas is evidently taken by Chrysis's beauty. Even at the moment when he envisages kicking her out of the house, he describes her as "the beautiful Samian" (*Sam.* 352–54).

[65] χαμαιτύπη δ' ἄνθρωπος, ὄλεθρος (*Sam.* 348). On χαμαιτύπη, see Timocles 24 K.-A.; Theopompus *FGrH* F 225, discussed in chapter 7; Licht 1952, 332; Fantham 1986, 47 n. 5; Lamagna 1998, 298 ad 348.

[66] Zagagi (1994, 127) sees Demeas's condemnation of Chrysis as a *hetaira* as a realistic element of the plot, reflecting the traditions of Greek misogyny. While I agree that Demeas draws on the traditions of misogyny, I consider this to be an ideological strategy deployed for dramatic and characterological purposes.

[67] The narrowness of Demeas's conception is significant, because concubines do crop up in the comedies; see 411 K.-A.

[68] Cf. P. G. Brown 1990b, 249, stating that Chrysis's former role as a *hetaira* remains relevant to her status in the play. On the negative stereotype of the female prostitute in Roman comedy, see Crisafulli 1998.

[69] In his own hypothetical adultery scenario, Nikeratos implies that Chrysis is a *pallakē* (*Sam.* 508). Krieter-Spiro (1997, 47–48) understands Nikeratos's assessment to be a legitimate description of Chrysis's actual status, overlooking that the text consistently contrasts the responses of Nikeratos and Demeas. Nikeratos is obviously presented as an unreliable commentator on Demeas's situation, since we know that she is a free woman (*Sam.* 577). Krieter-Spiro (1997, 43–44) does acknowledge, however, that the text equivocates in assigning Chrysis a determinate status. On Chrysis's status, see Jacques 1971, xli–xiv; Fantham 1975, 65–66; P. G. Brown 1990b, 248–49. I agree with Henry (1985, 73), who states that "Chrysis embodies the other characters' views of women as she represents in turn wife, mother, and whore," but I emphasize that the text exploits the ambiguity and malleability of

ceptualizes her in accordance with the official ideology, preserving the democratic division of female social identity into wives and the all the rest precisely to paper over his departure from the standard democratic matrimonial family *form*. When Solon made legitimacy the criteria of family membership, the status of *pallakē* for producing "free" children became obsolete, a relic of aristocratic and predemocratic social structures.[70] By refusing to place Chrysis in the obvious position of *pallakē*, Demeas adheres to the democratic bias against concubinage. At the same time, by preserving or reactivating her status as a *hetaira*, Demeas is able to condemn her as a prostitute, making the standard move found in Attic lawsuits of treating the *hetaira* like the *pornē*—or rather, of denying the difference between the two.[71]

Demeas condemns Chrysis by subtly evoking the "forensic" stereotype of the immoral prostitute as greedy, deceptive, and self-interested. Just as he displays his own properly democratic (gender) disposition by adopting a forensic posture in order to acquit his son, so also the deployment of a forensic stereotype to distance himself from Chrysis further emphasizes his democratic credentials.[72] The figure of the immoral prostitute is a type specifically associated with Attic inheritance cases.[73] The Solonian

---

female social roles for purposes of establishing Demeas's civic credentials and adherence to the official ideology.

[70] According to the Draconian law of justifiable homicide, an Athenian man could kill any man he found with his wife, mother, sister, daughter, or "concubine (*pallakē*) kept for producing free children (*eleutherois paisin*)" (Dem. 23.53). For the attribution of this law to Draco, see Carawan 1998, 78 n. 80. A man's wife and his concubine could both bear socially viable offspring because the primary status distinction that organized social identity in the early polis was the distinction between free persons and slaves (Grace 1973; Humphreys 1991). When legitimacy became the sine qua non of social status, there were no longer any positive benefits to be gained from supporting concubines and fathering children with them; hence the status of *pallakē* became formally obsolete but not practically forbidden. Cf. Vernant 1980, 67 n. 25, on the distinction between the wife, *hetaira*, and concubine. On the *pallakē*, see further Maffi 1989; Patterson 1991b; Mossé 1991; Cox 1998; Lape 2002–03.

[71] It is true that Chrysis is described as a *hetaira* rather than a *pornē* (prostitute). As I discuss in chapter 3, however, democratic civic discourse frequently flattens the distinction between the *hetaira* and the *pornē*, with the *hetaira* losing her claim to special status and prestige (see chapter 3, note 39).

[72] Although the figure of the prostitute in New Comedy and the comic tradition has been frequently discussed (Hauschild 1933; Fantham 1975; W. S. Anderson 1984; Henry 1985; 1986; Konstan 1995, on the *Perikeiromenē*; Wiles 1989; P. G. Brown 1990b, 1993), the contribution of the forensic prostitute to comic depictions has not, to my knowledge, been examined.

[73] On women in the lawsuits, see V. Hunter 1994; Patterson 1994 (on Neaira); Foxhall 1998; Johnstone 1998; Cox 1998; Gagarin 2001. For the negative stereotype of the *hetaira* in comedy, see Henry 1985, esp. 93–102 on *Dis Ex*.

law of testament gave the citizen the right to bequeath his estate; in practice, this meant that the childless man had the right to adopt an heir to inherit his estate and perpetuate his household.[74] In other words, the right to make a will amounted to the right to adopt an heir.[75] There was a catch, however. According to the provisions of the law, any will (and hence any adoption) could be invalidated if it was found to have been made by a citizen whose reason was impaired by lunacy, old age, drugs, disease, or a woman's influence, or by a citizen who was physically coerced in some way.

The proviso that wills and adoptions made under the influence of a woman were to be invalid fits well within the broad program of Solon's family legislation. It is widely agreed that Solon was the first to exclude the bastard from the family and state. The law of testament gave the citizen the right to adopt only the legitimate sons of other men, not any of his own bastard children.[76] Yet the law did not prevent citizens from fathering and rearing bastards. The mother of a man's bastard son would, presumably, have had some interest in her child's welfare and his ability to inherit from his father. By providing a loophole specifically nullifying a will made under female influence, Solon may have been seeking to forestall this female influence or, more generally, to prevent citizens from smuggling their bastard children into the legitimate family.

The establishment of such broad and open-ended conditions under which a will could be contested acted to spur litigation, virtually inviting citizens to challenge wills and adoptions.[77] To do so, a citizen had only to invent a narrative based on the decedent's impaired mental state or the nefarious influence of a woman.[78] In fact, these two factors frequently

[74] Dem. 46.14. Cf. Dem. 44.67, 20.102; Is. 2.13, 3.68, 6.3, 28; Hyp. 3.17–18. The law of testament is widely regarded as genuinely Solonian; see further Wyse 1904, 326; Harrison 1968–71, 1:150.

[75] Gernet 1920, 137ff.; Harrison 1968–71, vol. 1. Contra MacDowell 1978, 100. For testamentary adoption, see Rubinstein 1993, 22–25.

[76] The inability of a man to adopt his bastard son logically follows from the laws that exclude the bastard from inheritance rights. On the basis of the phratry oath as referred to in Is. 7.16, Wolff (1944, 79) and Just (1989, 56 with n. 22) conclude that legitimacy was indispensable for adoption.

[77] Thus, in order to eliminate unnecessary litigation, the Thirty eliminated the Solonian provision allowing wills made under the influence of a woman to be contested ([Arist.] *A.P.* 35.2).

[78] The law of testament can be seen as a "civil" counterpart to the Periclean law of citizenship. The Periclean law incited disputes and provided a public forum for defining and enacting Athenian civic identity with reference to kinship and birth stories (Connor 1994). The Solonian law of testament similarly led to litigation framed within kinship and gender narratives. Johnstone (1999) describes the role of Athenian laws in supplying the narrative frameworks that shaped cultural understandings of disputes and harms but does not discuss their role in constituting "character" types within legal narratives.

crop up together in the lawsuits. Litigants mention an affair with a certain kind of a woman—a *hetaira* or prostitute—as prima facie evidence of the decedent's madness. Accordingly, the very possibility of contesting a will made "under the influence of a woman" encouraged the production of a forensic stock character: the scheming woman, often a prostitute, who could be blamed for everything and anything, from attempting to defraud legitimate heirs to corrupting the reason of previously sensible and sane citizens.

The connection between Solon's law and the construction of this forensic type is made explicit in a lawsuit brought by Callistratus against his wife's brother Olympiodorus in the 340s B.C. Callistratus and his brother-in-law had agreed to divvy up the estate of a citizen who died without leaving a legitimate heir. According to Callistratus, Olympiodorus reneged on the deal and seized the whole estate for himself. Like other litigants, Callistratus pays lip service to the piety that lawsuits between kin are especially shameful and ought not to happen at all.[79] He deflects opprobrium from his own involvement by attributing Olympiodorus's behavior and hence the lawsuit itself to influence of the insolent *hetaira* with whom Olympiodorus lives. His residence with a *hetaira* is adduced as proof of Olympiodorus's madness and affliction with the "black bile" (Dem. 48.54, 56). To substantiate this claim, Callistratus summons the authority of Solon and his law:

> [J]ust as the lawgiver Solon says, he [Olympiodorus] is out of his mind as no man ever was, having come under the influence of a prostitute (*pornē*). And Solon established a law that whatever a man does under the influence of a woman shall be void, and he meant this especially in the case of such a woman [i.e., a prostitute]. (Dem. 48.56)

With deft sleight of hand, the speaker extends the provisions of the Solonian law to stigmatize any action allegedly perpetrated under the influence of a woman. In this way, he masks the innovation in his own use of the figure: he is not claiming that Olympiodorus made a will under the influence of a woman but rather that his alleged disreputable conduct and madness are owed to his relationship with the *hetaira*.

The most developed extant example of this type is Alce, the prostitute accused of corrupting the reason of an old citizen, pillaging his estate, and defrauding the legitimate heirs in Isaeus's speech *On the Estate of Philoctemon*. The speaker in the case is defending the claim of Chaerestratos, the adopted heir of Philoctemon, to inherit the estate of Philoctemon's father, Euctemon, who happened to outlive his son. Another party had come forward claiming that Euctemon had left two legitimate

[79] For this point, see Humphreys 1993; D. Cohen 1995; Christ 1998.

sons by a second wife, an alleged Lemnian woman. The speaker of the case, however, contends that this Lemnian wife is a fiction (one is tempted to see the influence of comedy here) and that the children's real mother is Alce. He blames Alce for convincing Euctemon to reside with her and to pass off her illegitimate children as citizens (Is. 6.17, 21).[80] She is presented as the villain of the piece, even though the speaker admits that Euctemon blackmailed his son into allowing one of the children to be recognized by the phratry (Is. 6.22–23). According to the speaker's logic, Euctemon can be excused and even pitied for blackmailing his heirs and attempting to violate the norms of Athenian citizenship because he was acting under the influence of "drugs or disease"—meaning, in this context, under Alce's influence. The vilification of the female prostitute also serves to distract attention from the elitist implications of those actions. By emphasizing that Euctemon decided to live with a prostitute because of her treacherous influence, rather than because he wanted to and could afford to, the speaker overrides the class associations that would otherwise attend such an arrangement.[81]

Demeas evokes this stereotype for similar purposes in the *Samia*, though he ostensibly uses it to exonerate his son rather than himself. Nevertheless, the two projects are inextricably intertwined. By exculpating his son from the crime of family betrayal, he also exculpates himself from the appearance of civic betrayal implicit in his living arrangements. His decision to reject Chrysis in order to preserve his son not only foregrounds his civic commitments, it also shows that Demeas is not like Euctemon or the other besotted old men of the Attic lawsuits who are perpetually losing their minds and fortunes to calculating prostitutes. By disciplining his desire, or "acting like a man," Demeas demonstrates his autonomy and immunity from Chrysis's influence, allaying the suspicion that either his *oikos* or the polis were ever at risk from the relationship.

Though Demeas draws on and adapts the forensic strategy of blaming the immoral prostitute to redeem both his own and his son's characters, the effects go beyond his intended purposes. In oratory, the jurors never actually see the stock figure of the allegedly avaricious and conniving prostitute; they are forced to depend on the legal narratives of other men and their own culturally conditioned gender assumptions. Comedy, however, dramatizes the stereotype in action, or so Demeas would like his

[80] For the status of these children, see V. Hunter 1994, 114.

[81] He warns the jurors that his opponent is going to digress and speak in a loud voice in an effort to inflame class resentment, contrasting his own poverty with the wealth of speaker's clients (Is. 6.59). The speaker, however, takes the moral high ground by drawing on the democratic ideology of liturgical donation. He promises the jurors that if awarded the estate, his clients will perform even more benefactions for the state, while a victory for his opponents will mean a victory for Alce, who will squander the property and seek other prey (6.60–61).

audience to believe. Demeas figures Chrysis according to the stereotype found in legal narratives, but the comic narrative offers no role for this much-assailed type. There is a stark discrepancy between Demeas's construction of Chrysis's character and the character she discloses in the play in her own words and actions. She is neither self-interested nor greedy nor even particularly sexual. On the contrary, the play depicts her as precisely like the respectable and reproductive woman from whom she was supposed to differ—namely, the female citizen.

Although Demeas's defense of himself and his son depends on portraying Chrysis as sexually and materially avaricious, throughout the play she is appears to have what can only be called a maternal disposition. She is the character most concerned for the welfare of Moschion's child and cannot brook the thought of its being cared for by strangers. She willingly jeopardizes her own position in Demeas's household to nurse the baby. And when in a rage Nikeratos seeks to burn his bastard grandchild, it is Chrysis who protects the infant at the risk of her life. Some critics have questioned Chrysis's motives, but the text itself does not invite such questioning.[82] Her actions are tailored to suit the needs of the plot: she nurses the child so that Demeas can convince himself that she is the mother and hence demonstrate his own attitudes and beliefs in the context of that discovery.

The construction of Chrysis as the play's moral (and maternal) model is animated by the requirements of the plot rather than by an emerging proto-feminist ideology, yet her characterization nevertheless has a kind of feminist effect: the discrepancy between Demeas's depiction of Chrysis as an immoral prostitute and her actual character undermines the stereotype of the immoral prostitute. By deploying the standard negative image of the prostitute to salvage Demeas's character, the play exposes that image as a construction or fiction invented to serve the needs of a masculinist civic ideology. In severing the connection between the female prostitute and immorality, the play unsettles conventional cultural categories of female social identity, opening a space that allows a rethinking of the traditional gender system.

It is worth noting that this dissonance between a male character's negative view of a prostitute and the actual character of the woman in question crops up elsewhere in comedy. In Terence's *Andria*, an Andrian prostitute named Chrysis raises a dislocated female citizen and protects her respectability, playing a maternal role that directly confounds the citizen father's assumptions about the character of the prostitute. On her deathbed, she acts as a stand-in for the girl's *kurios*, "betrothing" her to a

[82] It has sometimes been argued that Chrysis wants to keep the baby permanently, and possibly acquire the status of Demeas's wife by doing so; for a summary of the scholarship on this issue, see Krieter-Spiro 1997, 117–20. There is no evidence in the text for Chrysis's intentions one way or the other.

young Athenian citizen.[83] The depiction of Habrotonon in *Epitrepontes* as a *hetaira*-hero, as the character who solves the comic problem, also thoroughly dismantles the conventional negative stereotype. In seeking to convince his daughter to leave her seemingly philandering husband, Smikrines counsels:

> χαλεπόν, Παμφίλη,
> ἐλευθέρᾳ γυναικὶ πρὸς πόρνην μάχη·
> πλείονα κακουργεῖ, πλεῖον' οἶδ', αἰσχύνεται
> οὐδέν, κολακεύει μᾶλλον. . . .
>
> (*Epit.* 793–96)

> Pamphile, a battle against
> a *pornē* is difficult for a freeborn woman.
> She contrives more, she knows more,
> she is ashamed of nothing and flatters more. . . .

Smikrines warns his daughter that she cannot compete against the crafty and immoral Habrotonon. Yet in the action of the play, Habrotonon works to restore rather than ruin Pamphile's marriage. This seamless coincidence between the needs of the citizen family and the desires of the slave *hetaira* who wants nothing but her freedom exposes Smikrines' negative assessment as a fiction, and an inadequate one at that. At the same time, it shores up the same discrepancy between the traditional ideology and social realities that we find in the *Samia*.

In both the *Samia* and the *Epitrepontes*, the *hetaira*'s maternal disposition not only disrupts the negative forensic stereotype of the female prostitute, it also unsettles the distinction between female citizens and all women deemed nonreproductive for the purposes of the democratic state.[84] The fact that Chrysis bears a son to Demeas, irrespective of the child's fate, effectively erases what is supposed to be the distinguishing feature of wives. Her failed pregnancy—the plot device that enables Demeas to repair and reproduce his democratic masculinity—simultaneously calls into question the difference and distinction between democratic citizens and all the rest, that is, the noncitizen residents of the

[83] Chrysis gave Glycerium to Pamphilus in a modified betrothal ceremony, enjoining him to become her "husband, friend, guardian, and father," giving her property in exchange as the "dowry" (*An.* 292–96). Richardson (1997, 179) remarks that since Chrysis lacked the standing to make a formal will, she gave her property to Pamphilus as a dowry for Glycerium. The "betrothal" formula she uses—*te isti virum do, amicum tutorem patrem* (295)—differs significantly from the Athenian betrothal formula, which focuses on the transaction's material and instrumental purposes. Chrysis's formulation suggests a conception of marriage as a relationship encompassing more than just sexual and procreative ends. The character of Thais in Terence's *Eunuch* also conforms to the pattern I am describing here.

[84] On Chrysis's maternal disposition, see the comments of Keuls 1973, 13, 16; Henry 1985, 73, and 1986, 145. For Chrysis as the ethical exemplar in the play, see also Henry 1985, 70; West 1991, 22–23; Weissenberger 1991, 433–34.

polis. If any woman, not just a female citizen, could bear a man sons, how secure were the boundaries of the citizen body? And on what ultimately did the difference between citizens and noncitizens rest?

The interchangeability between Habrotonon and Pamphile, between *hetaira* and wife in *Epitrepontes* provokes similar questions. There, however, the emphasis is not only on the *hetaira*'s ability to play the maternal role but also on the female citizen's ability to elicit the kind of passion traditionally associated with the *hetaira*.[85] Before the action of the play begins, the protagonist rapes and impregnates his future wife, chancing to find a female citizen in a festival context in which slave women and *hetairai* were also present. Later, when he hires Habrotonon to solace himself after learning that his wife has borne "another man's" bastard child (in reality, his own son), he pays a fortune for her but treats her like a "basket bearer"—that is, like a virgin female citizen, as he should have treated his future wife (438–41).

In these plays, the slippage between *hetaira* and wife, and the interchangeability of these statuses that this slippage suggests, poses an implicit challenge to the exclusionary birth norms of democratic membership by revealing their basis in gender practices. Just as Chrysis's character upsets conventional gender assumptions as well as the exclusionary norms of democratic citizenship, so too her counterpart, the absent female citizen heroine, challenges the reductive vision of female social roles promulgated by the official ideology. While I take up the question of comedy's expansion of conventional female social roles more directly in the next chapter, I conclude here by turning to the fifth act of the *Samia*. Although she is largely absent, the implied presence of the female citizen heroine gestures toward alternative social arrangements in which gender relations acquire a new importance for both men and women in the construction of civic identity.

The Fragility of Manhood

In Menander's comedy, the details of the romantic plot regularly seem to have been wrapped up by the end of the fourth act.[86] The fifth act offers a space for exposing and releasing various tensions left unresolved in the

[85] The tendency for wives and *hetairai* to be conflated in the Athenian imaginary extends back to Old Comedy. Henry (1985) and Zweig (1992) have shown that *hetairai* and wives in Aristophanes' comedy are depicted as similarly lustful and greedy. Menander's comedy draws on the tradition linking *hetairai* and wives but gives it a different emphasis. Both are depicted as objects of male passion rather than as enslaved by their own passions and as similarly reproductive and maternal. See further chapter 8.

[86] On the fourth act, R. L. Hunter states: "Our present evidence suggests that in Menander the central climax often occurred during the fourth act and that by the end of that act a settlement of sorts had been reached" (1985, 40).

romantic plot. For instance, the farcical fifth act of the *Dyskolos* makes literal the violence entailed in the formation of any community. In the fifth act of the *Samia*, Moschion performs a masquerade of military masculinity that simultaneously exposes his own arrested development and suggests the possibility of an expanded role for the female citizen in the Hellenistic polis.[87]

The act opens much as the play began, with a lengthy monologue delivered by Moschion. With this duplication, Moschion has come full circle. Instead of happily celebrating his impending marriage, the event that seemed so out of reach in the prologue, he continues to fret over paternal approval. Suddenly angry that Demeas's unjust accusations have wounded his manhood, he determines to repay Demeas by performing a revenge plot. Although he claims that he wants to prove himself by disappearing from the polis to serve as a mercenary, his promises to Plangon preclude such acts of manliness. Instead, he settles for the next best thing: dressing up like a soldier to perform his manhood before Demeas. He reasons:

εἰ μὲν καλῶς οὖν εἶχε τὰ περὶ τὴν κόρην
καὶ μὴ τοσαῦτ᾽ ἦν ἐμποδών, ὅρκος, πόθος,
χρόνος, συνήθει᾽, οἷς ἐδουλούμην ἐγώ,
οὐκ ἂν παρόντα γ᾽ αὖτις ᾐτιάσατο
αὐτόν με τοιοῦτ᾽ οὐδέν, ἀλλ᾽ ἀποφθαρεὶς
ἐκ τῆς πόλεως ἂν ἐκποδὼν εἰς Βάκτρα ποι
ἢ Καρίαν διέτριβον αἰχμάζων ἐκεῖ·
νῦν δ᾽ οὐ ποήσω διὰ σέ, Πλαγγὼν φιλτάτη,
ἀνδρεῖον οὐθέν· οὐ γὰρ ἔξεστ᾽ οὐδ᾽ ἐᾶι
ὁ τῆς ἐμῆς νῦν κύριος γνώμης Ἔρως.
οὐ μὴν ταπεινῶς οὐδ᾽ ἀγεννῶς παντελῶς
παριδεῖν με δεῖ τοῦτ᾽, ἀλλὰ τῶι λόγωι μόνον,
εἰ μηθὲν ἄλλ᾽, αὐτὸν φοβῆσαι βούλομαι
φάσκων ἀπαίρειν.

(623–36)

If there'd been no problems about the girl and
there weren't so many obstacles in the way—
my oath, desire, time, our relationship, all things
to which I'm enslaved—he'd not have charged me with
an outrage like this to my face, but I'd
have disappeared from the polis, off to Bactria
somewhere, or Caria, living my life
there as a soldier. But now, because of you, Plangon,

[87] See W. S. Anderson 1972; Nicastri 1978; P. G. Brown 1990a.

I will forgo doing anything manly. I can't.
Love, master of my mind now, won't
allow me. Yet I mustn't humbly or
ignobly disregard this altogether, but
just by a trick, if nothing else, I want
to scare him. I'll pretend to go abroad.

Although the way has been paved for the next phase in Moschion's life, he continues to evaluate himself too much in the context of the father–son relationship. In the beginning, Moschion's shame before Demeas prevented him from honoring his promises to Plangon and her mother. According to his slave Parmenon, Moschion's excessive deference to Demeas is literally emasculating, rendering him a "womanly man" (ἀνδρόγυνε, 69). Moschion does, of course, try to face up to his father, preparing for the confrontation like an orator rehearsing for a trial. The narrative displacement of Moschion's story with Demeas's, however, brings with it a concomitant displacement of Moschion's capacity for masculine display and development. Instead, it is Demeas who gets the opportunity "to be a man."

Moschion never lives up to the promise of his manhood. His confrontation with Demeas in the first act is his one and only chance to act like a man; and, of course, it is an opportunity he allows to pass by (63–65). Consequently, all he can do in the fifth act is put on a show of masculinity, and an ineffectual one at that. Moschion pretends to be going off on mercenary service, to punish his father by "disappearing from the polis" (ἀποφθαρεὶς ἐκ τῆς πόλεως, 616–17).[88] He can only playact, he claims, because his obligations to the heroine bind him to the polis.[89] But even dressing up like mercenary fails to work for Moschion, because Demeas immediately sees through his costume. Instead of recognizing his son's need to repair his wounded pride and allowing him a moment of rebellion, Demeas reminds Moschion that he is his son and must adhere to that role irrespective of whatever mistakes his father accidentally makes or has made.

This preempted maturation results in part from the narrative replacement of the son's story by the father's. Moschion never has enough time

[88] Blume (1974, 253) remarks that Moschion's motive for wishing to go off to war inverts the usual comic scenario in which protagonists seek to become mercenaries: i.e., when faced with romantic loss and defeat.

[89] The metadramatic aspects of Moschion's mercenary revenge plot are highly marked. The element of costume is highlighted when he repeatedly demands that Parmenon bring him a cloak and sword (*Sam.* 659–60). In addition, he casts the plot in theatrical terms and swears by Dionysus, to make sure we get the point (667–68). And finally, Moschion worries that Demeas will not play his assigned part, causing the revenge play to be revealed as comedy (682–86).

to step out from behind his father, a move made more difficult by his adopted status. That status enhances the civic significance of Demeas's rejection of Chrysis, because the bonds between adopted relatives were felt to be less strong than those rooted in blood. For Moschion, however, the strength of adoptive kinship is precisely the problem. Because the relationship between Demeas and Moschion is based on a legal rule rather than on biology, and because the Athenians regarded legally created kinship ties as weaker than putatively "natural" ones, Demeas never allows his "son" to assume an identity of his own; rather, he demands Moschion's constant and obedient performance of the son's role.[90]

At the same time, the apparent impossibility for this youth on the verge of adulthood of acting like a man within the polis places his narrative of arrested development in another register. The play offers Moschion two routes to manhood: owning up to his sexual indiscretion or leaving the polis to serve as a mercenary for one of the Hellenistic rulers. What is conspicuous by its absence is the traditional route to democratic manhood, namely serving as a citizen-soldier (see further chapter 7). This absence attests to the citizen-soldier ideal and its attendant military masculinity being eclipsed by the rise of the Hellenistic military kingdoms. Yet the loss of the ideal does not seem to signal the death throes of democratic masculinity. Moschion's military charade farcically enacts his own pretensions to masculinity as well as those of the mercenary. By donning a mercenary costume, Moschion reveals the theatrical and performative—that is, inessential—quality of the mercenary's masculinity. More important than this tacit subversion, however, is the positive route to maturation hinted at by his speech. In claiming to be bound to Plangon by promises as well as by love, Moschion tentatively opens a space for developing civic manhood within the context of gender relations, even if he is not completely ready to act within it. For just as a woman was under the control of her *kurios*, Moschion too claims to be under the control of his own *kurios*, eros. In this way, he suggests that a woman's subordination in the legal and social structure might be offset by a man's emotional and sexual dependence on her. His comments intimate that relations between the sexes might emerge as a new arena for civic manhood. The next chapter takes up this theme in more detail, as it considers the dialectic between female social identity and male socialization in two of Menander's transnational mercenary plays.

[90] On the adoption as coloring the father–son bond, see note 39, above. On the opposition between legal rules and natural affections in democratic Athens, see Humphreys 1993, 6ff.

6

The Mercenary Romance

GENDER AND CIVIC EDUCATION IN THE *PERIKEIROMENĒ* AND *MISOUMENOS*

Socializing the Mercenary Lover

In the fifth act of the *Samia*, Moschion suddenly seeks to become a mercenary to repair his wounded manhood and to repay his father for his unfounded suspicions. Although he ardently desires "to act like a man," as he puts it, his prior romantic commitment forecloses this possibility (630–31). He cannot disappear from the polis to perform his manhood as a mercenary in far-off Bactria or Caria because he is bound to the heroine by his oath, desire, time, and his relationship (623–29). To some extent, by honoring his prior relationship, Moschion is simply making a virtue of necessity. His own behavior—a rape or seduction—generated the commitment to which he claims to be enslaved (625). If the heroine binds him to the polis, making marriage the alternative to mercenary service, it is only after the fact—that is, after Moschion's actions have created the obligation he belatedly and half-heartedly seeks to resist.

Although the ending of the *Samia* suggests that military service and monogamy are mutually exclusive in comedy's generic universe, Menander's *Perikeiromenē* and *Misoumenos* enact the protagonist's transition from martial to marital life. Here, just as in the *Samia*, the heroines are instrumental in the triumph of marriage over the military. While Plangon in the *Samia* serves simply as a binding force, obliging Moschion to remain in the city, the heroines in the *Perikeiromenē* and *Misoumenos* play an active part in protesting the mercenary service of their lovers. In these plays, however, the problem consists not in preventing the heroes from becoming mercenaries but rather in stopping them from acting too much like mercenaries. In each case, the narrative centers on rebuilding or restoring the damaged romantic union, which entails, inter alia, that the mercenary disavow his prior behavior in order to reunite with and marry the heroine.[1] In both plays, the heroine's decisional autonomy, figured

[1] For Menander's mercenary heroes, see MacCary 1972; Wartenberg 1973. On Menander's *Sikyōnioi*, see chapter 7.

negatively in the power to reject, serves as the catalyst for the hero to acquire or display the civic and social competencies that qualify and redeem him as the rightful romantic hero—that is, as a male with the right to enter into the civic matrimonial system.

This chapter examines the multiple ways in which these narratives of conflict and resolution between the sexes are structured by and structuring of large-scale political problems.[2] By recasting the conflict between kingdom and city as a romantic conflict, these plays use the romantic relationship as a site for negotiating the play of power between unequals. At the same time, romantic reunion offers a solution to the "Hellenistic mercenary problem." To be sure, the employment of mercenaries was a fact of Greek warfare long before the Hellenistic epoch and, judging from the complaints of fourth-century Athenian writers, a problem for the law, order, and culture of the polis already in the early and mid–fourth century. But the death of Alexander the Great fundamentally changed their significance. The sudden emergence of numerous competitive military kingdoms requiring large permanent armies for conquest and defense created an unprecedented demand for mercenaries.[3] And, with promises of high pay, figures such as Eumenes of Cardia and Antigonus Monophthalmus were able to attract numerous citizens from the Greek cities into their service.[4] Thus, the sudden rise of large imperial entities whose power was a direct function of the size of their armies posed fundamentally new threats to the population and culture of the polis.

The *Perikeiromenē* and *Misoumenos* both employ romantic reconciliation as a frame in which to negotiate the play of power between unequals and to solve the "mercenary problem." In the *Perikeiromenē*, Polemon learns to subordinate his own power to command violence to the overarching authority of law and legal institutions. In the *Misoumenos*, Thrasonides' redemption hinges on his rejection of a martial ethics based on killing and revenge in favor of a civic ethics valuing consent rather than coercion. In each play, however, the interweaving of romantic and inter-

[2] On the similarities in plot, theme, and formal devices in the *Perikeiromenē* and *Misoumenos*, see MacCary 1972, 282–87; Goldberg 1980, 44–58; Sisti 1986, 12–13; Borgogno 1988, 90; P. G. Brown 1990b, and 1993, 204; Konstan 1995, 195 n. 195.

[3] According to Parke, "the real importance . . . of the mercenary soldier is not made manifest till after the division of the empire into satrapies. For this process meant that each satrap could be his own general, and his political power would become proportionate to the military forces at his disposal. After being for a time suppressed under the dominance of Alexander, individual personalities had an opportunity to assert themselves; and . . . those were the exact circumstances to favour the development of mercenary armies and monarchs whose power was based on them" (1933, 210). See also G. T. Griffith 1935, 33–56, and further below.

[4] See Diod. 18.61.4–5 (on Eumenes); 19. 56.5 (on Antigonus).

national relations cuts two ways, allowing the romantic to energize the political and, conversely, the political to infuse the romantic.[5] Although both plays celebrate the ultimate triumph of civic values over the martial values associated with the Hellenistic kingdoms, they nevertheless employ devices that nearly hijack this generic end. In each case, the story of the mercenary's reform or civic education hinges on the empowerment of a heroine who threatens to undermine the conventional social order even as she secures it. These contradictory narrative impulses are produced by comedy's specific historical situation. As a discourse of the polis, comedy seeks to remodel the signs, symbols, and representatives of the military kingdoms in accordance with polis-based norms. But in working within the context of a romantic relationship, the *Perikeiromenē* and *Misoumenos* cede more authority to their heroines than was culturally available to them, thus upsetting traditional gender categories in the process of containing the threats posed by the military kingdoms.

Power and Punishment: Problems in the *Perikeiromenē*

Although only about 40 to 45 percent of the *Perikeiromenē* has been recovered to date, the broad outline of the plot can be reconstructed as follows.[6] According to the prologue speaker—Agnoia, personified misconception or ignorance—a Corinthian woman found two infants roughly twenty years before the play begins. She kept the female child (the heroine Glykera), treating her as her own daughter, but gave the male (Moschion) to a wealthy neighbor who wanted a son. As the years went by, the incessant campaigning of Alexander's successors to capture Corinth strained affairs in the city, reducing the woman to poverty. Her dire straits seem to have convinced her to give Glykera to Polemon, a mercenary captain. Before she died, however, she revealed to Glykera the secret of her birth in an effort to prevent accidental sibling incest. For she saw that Moschion was young, wealthy, and virtually stalking his unknown sister. One day after her death, when Polemon was away on a campaign, Moschion attempted to seduce Glykera, or at any rate to arrange an assignation.[7] Witnessing the pseudo-seduction, Polemon's slave Sosia dutifully re-

[5] On the mutual structuring of intimate and political relationships in modern societies, see Giddens 1992, 195–96 and passim; Laclau and Mouffe 1985, 149–94.

[6] For the recovery of the play, see Arnott 1979–2000, 2:370. References to the *Perikeiromenē* follow Sandbach. For reconstructions of the play, see Gomme and Sandbach 1973, 465–69; Blanchard 1983; Lloyd-Jones 1990; Lamagna 1994, 20–35.

[7] This scenario seems to present another implicitly negative commentary on Polemon's mercenary service. By going off to campaign, he leaves his mistress vulnerable to the predatory behavior of other men.

ported it to Polemon upon his return. Polemon, overcome by jealousy, immediately sheared off Glykera's hair.[8] In response, Glykera took refuge in the home of Moschion's (foster) mother, Myrrhine.

This is where the dramatic action begins in the play as we have it: with Polemon frantically seeking a way to get Glykera back and Moschion allowing himself to be convinced that Glykera has installed herself in his home to be his own *hetaira* (courtesan). Agnoia claims to have caused these confusions in order to reunite Glykera, Moschion, and their long-lost father, Pataikos. The family reunion takes place just when the romantic reconciliation seems to be ruled out. Unable to speak to Glykera himself, Polemon convinces Pataikos to intercede on his behalf. Far from being won over to reconcile with Polemon, Glykera persuades Pataikos that she is innocent of any wrongdoing and hardens her resolve to make a permanent break with the offending mercenary. When she sends her servant to retrieve her personal belongings from Polemon's house, Pataikos recognizes some of the tokens he left with his infant children whom he had exposed after losing his fortune and his wife. A scene of recognition and reunion ensues that paves the way for the romantic reunion: Glykera pardons Polemon in the end because his monstrous deed became the source of good fortune.[9]

The *Perikeiromenē* seems to tell two stories at once, a tale of family reunion as well as a tale of romantic reconciliation. Arguably, however, the main narrative is about neither of these things. Like all of Menander's extant plays, the *Perikeiromenē* is structured around solving a comic problem, which in this case centers on the initial incident that triggered the breakup: the "haircut." The play problematizes the offense both as the act of a too-jealous man and as a wrongful act of punishment or revenge. In retrospect, Polemon admits as much, describing himself as an incarnation of vengeance and a thoroughly jealous type.

ὡς κατὰ κράτος μ' εἴληφας. ἐ[φιλ
ἀδελφόν, οὐχὶ μοιχόν· ὁ δ' ἀλάστωρ ἐγὼ
καὶ ζηλότυπος ἄνθρωπος α̣[
εὐθὺς ἐπαρῴνουν.

(985–88)

How you've taken me by force: [You kissed]
your brother, not a *moikhos*. But I, as a spirit of vengeance
and a jealous type, [thinking I was wronged],
straightaway took action.

[8] On the lost opening scene, see Gomme and Sandbach 1973, 466–69.

[9] For this point, see Fortenbaugh 1974.

Polemon confesses to "taking action," as he euphemistically puts it, as an *alastōr*—a spirit of vengeance—because he believed that Glykera had kissed a *moikhos* (seducer).[10] In other words, by cutting off Glykera's hair, Polemon was taking vengeance against her for harming him. More precisely, the haircut seems to represent a punishment specifically for "female infidelity," as well as an assault on her status.[11] Polemon may have been seeking to punish Glykera as an adulteress insofar as he wrongly considered her to be his wife. In any event, although the play is probably set in Corinth, it preserves the Athenian legal context that viewed seduction and adultery under the common rubric of *moikheia*—one of the few offenses for which Athenian law allowed self-help.[12] A man who seized a *moikhos* in the act could bind him, and, if he chose, remove the offender's pubic hair.[13] In the classical period, however, no corresponding corporeal punishment could be inflicted on the woman taken with the *moikhos*.[14] Accordingly, by cutting off Glykera's hair, Polemon inflicts on her the symbolic analog of the punishment usually reserved for the man caught in the act.[15]

Polemon's behavior constitutes an offense against Glykera and, perhaps more significantly, against the state itself.[16] Polemon not only "punished" the wrong person (in the eyes of the law), he also did so after the fact, precisely what the law did not allow. If the *moikhos* escaped immediate detection, seduction (*moikheia*) was treated like any other offense.

[10] For *alastōr* as a spirit of vengeance, see Lamagna 1994, 288 ad 408 with references cited.

[11] By cutting off Glykera's hair, Polemon is also effectively marking her as a slave; see further Henry 1985.

[12] Schwartz (1929) and Mossé (1992b) see the use of the Athenian betrothal formula at 1013–14 as evidence that the play featured a mixed union between Glykera, an Athenian, and Polemon, a Corinthian. Since there is no evidence in the text indicating that Glykera is Athenian, and because such a mixed union would have been forbidden by Athenian law and the conventions of comedy, I follow recent commentators in assuming that the play is set in Corinth and involves Corinthian citizens (Gomme and Sandbach 1973, 470 ad 125; Webster 1974, 169; Konstan 1995, 107). The play treats Corinthian law and marriage practices as though they were identical to the Athenian.

[13] See Ar. *Ach.* 849. On self-help in cases of *moikheia*, see D. Cohen 1991a; Schmitz 1997. For the punishments allowed, see further chapter 3, note 46.

[14] A woman who continued to adorn herself and attend the public sacrifices after having been taken in *moikheia* could, however, be publicly stripped and beaten; see Aes. 1.183.

[15] Dover states, "Since women commonly reduced their pubic hair by singeing, the punishment of an adulterer symbolised his transformation into a woman" (1989, 106). In the *Perikeiromenē*, Polemon may be doing the reverse, symbolically stripping Glykera of her femininity.

[16] On the power to punish as constitutive of political authority, see Allen 2000. On the negotiation of personal motives to punish and the rule of law in democratic Athens, see Herman 1993, 1994, 1995; D. Cohen 1995.

While the victim or concerned citizen could prosecute a man as a *moikhos*, it was up to the legal institutions of the state, rather than the victim himself, to determine the alleged offender's guilt or innocence, the punishment to be inflicted, and the damages (if any) that were due. In shearing off Glykera's hair, Polemon usurped the state's punitive power and seized its authority to determine what counts as an injury. Accordingly, the solution to the comic problem ought to entail the repair of Glykera's physical injury and the repair of the state's wounded authority; as we will see, however, the injury to the state takes precedence. In order to regain the heroine, and the reproductive right in the polis that possessing her symbolizes, Polemon must first revise his beliefs to ensure that they conform with civic norms and authority.

The play problematizes Polemon's behavior not only as a transgression of state authority but also as a symptom of a more widespread international political problem. Doris, Glykera's maid, explicitly attributes Polemon's complete lack of civic socialization to the *paranomia* (unlawfulness) characteristic of all mercenaries:[17]

δυστυχής,
ἥτις στρατιώτην ἔλαβεν ἄνδρα. παράνομοι
ἅπαντες, οὐδὲν πιστόν. ὦ κεκτημένη,
ὡς ἄδικα πάσχεις.

(185–88)

Unfortunate woman,
whoever takes a soldier for a partner.
They're all *paranomoi*, not at all trustworthy. How
unjustly you suffer, mistress.

With this assessment, Doris brings together the dual international and interpersonal entailments at issue in the romantic plot. Polemon's violent behavior represents at once a particular act of domestic violence against his partner and the general lawlessness of mercenary soldiers. In retrospectively condemning himself, Polemon also attributes the misdeed to his own deviant character or personality, describing himself as an *alastōr* and a jealous type (ζηλότυπος).[18] This emphasis on jealousy might seem to define the problem as specific to Polemon rather than as a product of his profession.[19] In comedy, however, character is never completely di-

[17] Blanchard (1983, 354) directly links Polemon's unacceptable violent behavior to his profession as a mercenary.

[18] On "ζηλοτυπέω" as a psychological concept in the *Perikeiromenē*, see Fantham 1986, 52.

[19] On jealousy in the *Perikeiromenē* and the traditions of romance and folklore, see Trenkner 1958, 94. Fantham (1986) traces the play's influence on mime and Lucian's *Dialogues of the Courtesans*. Although the term ζηλότυπος occurs twice elsewhere in Menander,

vorced from context. Although Polemon may innately tend to react emotionally, his inability to restrain his emotions is presented as the psychic counterpart to his work as a professional solider. It is hardly an accident that in the end Pataikos explicitly advises Polemon to retire from mercenary service lest he act too rashly or precipitately in the future (1016–17).[20] Thus, the problem with being a mercenary is that it encourages habits of thought and behavior at odds with the psychic and cultural competencies required to live with others in a polis community. At the same time, the interconnections between Polemon's emotional reactions, domestic violence, and his profession as a mercenary allow the conflict between Polemon and Glykera to stand in for the overarching conflicts between the Hellenistic military kingdoms and the increasingly nonmilitarized Greek cities as well as those between mercenaries and Greek citizens.

Because the play employs the heterosexual union as a site for exploring and negotiating contemporary political issues, it also grants new entitlements to the heroine. Glykera's ability to select a partner with the qualities and characteristics she chooses is ultimately what transforms Polemon from a mercenary into a citizen. Accordingly, her understanding of Polemon's behavior and her own injury would seem to be crucial to the meaning and resolution of the comic conflict. In contrast to Doris, she interprets Polemon's action rather than his character. When Pataikos pleads with her to forgive Polemon, she adamantly refuses, declaring: "let him commit hubris [against some other girl] in the future" (722–23).[21] In her next line, which unfortunately is badly damaged, she may have condemned Polemon for treating her like a slave or even worse than a slave.[22] In any case, she clearly condemns Polemon's behavior as an act of hubris, as outrageous and status-harming conduct; if not an exact legal designation, it certainly evokes legal discourse and institutions.

Although Doris's assessment of Polemon seems to be the more damning and damaging, it is correctable. Polemon can and does in the end desist from the profession engendering his *paranomia*. But Glykera's assessment of his action as hubris casts her injury as a harm requiring legal response or correction. While the play never raises the possibility that Glykera might make use of judicial processes to exact compensation for her injury, her very inability to do so informs her behavior. She decides to leave Polemon for good precisely because she believes that he will

in both cases the context is too fragmentary to determine its significance to the play in question (*Mis.* 423 Sandbach = 953 Arnott; *Sik.* fr. 11 Sandbach = fr. 1 Arnott).

[20] See further Blanchard 1983, 361.

[21] For hubris—outrageous or insolent conduct—as a harm to social status, see further chapter 4, note 20.

[22] See van Leeuewen 1919, 85, line 318 (725 Sandbach).

continue to perpetrate acts of hubris with impunity. Thus, though the play empowers Glykera to protest her injury by leaving Polemon, it does not take the additional step of allowing her redress or compensation for having suffered that injury.

Glykera's power arises from the temporary loss of her true social identity. This loss does not give her access to the legal privileges possessed by men, but it does enable her to assist in making law the basis for social relations between men. To that end, the play offers her a momentary reprieve from the constraints of kinship. Pataikos explains to Polemon that he has no right to force Glykera to do anything, because she is her own *kuria*.[23] Pataikos is claiming not that Glykera has the power of a *kurios* (i.e., of a man) but rather that she is not subject to the laws of civic kinship. She has no male *kurios* (husband, father, brother, uncle, or guardian) to make decisions on her behalf.[24] While this device entitles Glykera to reject Polemon, and hence to compel his reform and the rebuilding of sociopolitical relations that it symbolizes, it also produces a countervailing threat to the social organization being secured. For Glykera's emancipation from kinship or male exchange is directly correlated to the threat of incest.[25] Such, at any rate, is the conclusion we are encouraged to draw from Moschion's failed and incestuous seduction plot and from the Corinthian foster mother's covert, if partial, reinscription of Glykera into the web of kinship specifically to prevent sibling incest (139–44). Thus, while the text temporarily releases Glykera from the kinship system and its restraints, it simultaneously subverts this release by depicting the danger that such a liberation brings.

That the play authorizes Glykera to act in advance of her cultural possibilities results in a certain underdetermination on the level of narrative logic. Although Glykera never forgives Polemon for his actions or receives any kind of compensation from him, and even decides to terminate their relationship permanently, she abruptly consents to marry him after being recognized as Pataikos's daughter.[26] To paper over this gap,

[23] Although temporarily liberated from kinship and the reproductive destiny of being a wife, Glykera's choices remain limited by her female body. When she abandons Polemon, Moschion assumes that she will become a *hetaira*. While this assumption is of course the product of Moschion's imagination, it nevertheless points to the paucity of options for an autonomous woman.

[24] See Gomme and Sandbach 1973, 507 ad 497.

[25] Konstan argues (1983, 19) that the marriage imperative in New Comedy dramatizes the obligation to exchange, the positive formulation of the incest taboo.

[26] According to Konstan (1995, 114–19, 9), the absence of any forgiveness is a textual expression of the contradictions in the construction of women's roles in Athens. Menander gives Glykera the autonomy of the courtesan but then subjects her to the constraints of citizen marriage and to the status of the citizen wife. This interpretation of the ideology underlying the plot is surely right, though insufficiently attentive to the particular temporal

the play employs several devices to suggest that Polemon is not entirely unworthy of the marriage he so unexpectedly gains. First, a personification of Agnoia (Ignorance) presides over the action and claims responsibility for Polemon's behavior, implicitly characterizing the haircut as an "involuntary action" in the sense spelled out by Aristotle as an action committed by force or in a state of ignorance (*E.N.* 1109b30–1110a4; cf. *Pk.* 163–66). Although Polemon deliberately cut off Glykera's hair, his "misapprehension about the material circumstances" under which he perpetrated the act might be seen as sufficient to render the action "involuntary," and hence a misfortune (*atukhēma*) or a mistake (*hamartēma*) rather than a wrongful act or a crime (*adikēma*).[27] At any rate, it is likely that Pataikos attempts to convince Glykera to forgive Polemon on precisely these grounds.[28]

This argument, if indeed Pataikos makes it, completely fails to achieve Glykera's pardon. That the haircut may be a misfortune from Polemon's perspective does not cancel out or override Glykera's experience of it as an injury and an insult. Yet though Polemon never receives forgiveness on formal Aristotelian grounds, the quasi-Aristotelian characterization of his action serves the dramatic purpose of allowing him to escape the full, opprobrious connotations of his behavior.[29] It suggests that his behavior was an aberration rather than an expression of a fundamentally corrupt character.[30]

---

setting of this play, which empowers a female character to domesticate a Hellenistic mercenary. Although the text holds her citizen status in abeyance until Polemon's civic education is complete, it does not succeed in masking the discrepancy between her extraordinary role as a reproducer of civic culture and the female citizen's traditional role as a biological reproducer of citizens.

[27] Gomme and Sandbach 1973, 517 ad 723; Arist. *E.N.* 1110b18–19, 1135b11–1136a9, *Rhet.* 1374b4–9; Men. 688 K.-A. For the Aristotelian classification of harms in Menander's comedy, see further Tierney 1936; Webster 1960, 204–5; Barigazzi 1965a, 135–60 (*Pk.*; Fortenbaugh 1974 (*Pk.*); Konstan 1995, 141–52 (*Epit.*); Lamagna 1997 (*Sam.*). Fortenbaugh (1974) shows that the *Perikeiromenē* is not a dramatization of Peripatetic ethics per se because the characterization of Polemon's action as involuntary and a misfortune is not what moves Glykera to pardon him.

[28] He may use the term ἑκούσιον in line 723 (Sudhaus) in pleading on Polemon's behalf. See further Gomme and Sandbach 1973, 517 ad 723.

[29] In the *Perikeiromenē*—and in the *Samia* and *Epitrepontes*—the Aristotelian classification of harms (*E.N.* 1135b11ff., *Rhet.* 1374.4ff.) is used for dramatic and narrative purposes and not, as has sometimes been argued, to make drama into a vehicle for ethical instruction. By drawing on the Aristotelian taxonomy to characterize the often egregious actions of comic protagonists as "mistakes" or "misfortunes" rather than as "unjust" or "criminal acts," comedy enables its protagonists to violate social and sometimes legal norms without completely compromising their characters or standing. On comedy's use of philosophy and philosophical themes, see chapter 4, note 38.

[30] Involuntary actions, according to Aristotle, do not reveal a person's character; they call

To some extent, the conceit that Polemon's action is involuntary covers over Glykera's lack of forgiveness while paving the way for the final reconciliation. At the same time, his status as the rightful romantic hero is also emphasized by his rival Moschion's being so patently the wrong man. Although Polemon is the actual mercenary officer, it is Moschion who acts the part of the stereotypical braggart soldier.[31] Moschion is bold, wealthy, and hard-drinking, and he has an inflated sense of his own attractiveness to women (302–4, 309). And like comic soldiers and mercenaries in general, Moschion exhibits a preference for nonmonogamous and therefore noncivic domestic arrangements. He is interested in having Glykera as a courtesan and expects his own mother to act as his procuress. Polemon cannot help but look good by comparison. Indeed, his preference for monogamy marks him as a citizen husband before the fact.

Learning the Language of Law: The Embedded Drama of Civic Education

Although the *Perikeiromenē* is titled after its injured heroine, the text fails to develop a narrative within which the heroine's story can actually be told. Instead, her injury clears a space for a narrative of male education and socialization. Polemon learns not to use his power in ways that violate the autonomy of others or the authority of the state only after irreparably harming the heroine. The crucial scene occurs in the third act, when Sosia finally convinces Polemon to besiege Myrrhine's house in order to retrieve Glykera. Just before making the assault, however, Pataikos, an old family friend (and, as it happens, Glykera's as yet unrecognized birth father), manages to persuade Polemon to disband his army and to listen to reason.

> ἐρᾶις·
> τοῦτ' οἶδ' ἀκριβῶς· ὥσθ' ὃ μὲν νυνὶ ποεῖς
> ἀπόπληκτόν ἐστιν. ποῖ φέρει γάρ; ἢ τίνα
> ἄξων; ἑαυτῆς ἐστ' ἐκείνη κυρία.
> λοιπὸν τὸ πείθειν τῶι κακῶς διακειμένωι
> ἐρῶντί τ' ἐστίν.
>
> (494–99)

for pity or pardon rather than ethical condemnation or legal redress (*E.N.* 1109b32–33). In the end, Glykera explicitly pardons Polemon, as if in recognition of the Aristotelian framework informing the action (*Pk.* 1021–23). For a discussion of involuntary actions and the grounds for pardon in Aristotle's ethics, see Sauvé 1989.

[31] MacCary 1972, 282; Goldberg 1980, 49–50.

You're in love,
I know this well; so you're acting crazy.
Where are you going? For whom?
She's her own guardian. Only persuasion remains for
the man faring ill in love.

According to Pataikos, love makes Polemon crazy. It gives him a kind of claim of diminished capacity to excuse both his attempt to conduct a military campaign against a private home and his initial attack on Glykera.[32] But at the same time, it makes him receptive to Pataikos's advice. In this way, love operates as a form of power alternative to Polemon's physical force. Indeed, elsewhere in the play (and in the *Misoumenos*), the power of love, figured as the heroine's power over the mercenary, is conceptualized in the same terms as the military power it comes to replace. Love conquers, subdues, and enslaves; and sometimes, it kills, or at least is nearly fatal.[33] Confronted with the prospect of the heroine's rejection, Polemon, like Thrasonides in the *Misoumenos*, threatens suicide.[34]

In this scene, however, Polemon's passion has a more productive effect, convincing him that he should exchange his martial methods of romantic conquest for persuasive speech. Love conquers him through self-interest, since he learns that force and compulsion are powerless to win him the thing he so desperately desires—the heroine's consent. While Polemon's attachment to Glykera generates a new respect for her autonomy, his attitude toward Moschion undergoes no such change. Since he does not want or need anything from Moschion, there does not seem to be anything to prevent him from seeking punishment or retaliation. To justify what he is planning to do, he asks Pataikos, "The man who seduced her while I was away committed a crime against me, didn't he?" (499–500). At this point, we might have expected Pataikos to argue that Moschion's attempt to seduce Glykera cannot be considered an injury to Polemon because Glykera is her own *kuria*—a free agent, as it were. Significantly, however, Pataikos does not present the absence of a legally protected relationship between Polemon and Glykera as the barrier to Polemon's retribution. Rather, he teaches Polemon an additional lesson: that the

[32] For eros as a diminished capacity excuse in cases of New Comic rape, see Scafuro 1997.

[33] For love as enslaving, see *Mis.* fr. 2 (3 Sisti, 4 Arnott) and *Pk.* 985, where Polemon describes Glykera as taking him "by force."

[34] Polemon threatens to suffocate himself (*Pk.* 504–5). At 976 he reiterates the threat, and, if the conjecture ἀπηγχόμην is correct, he threatens to hang himself at 988. Thrasonides in *Misoumenos* also contemplates hanging himself when faced with the heroine's rejection (309–10 Sandbach, Sisti; 710–11 Arnott) and in addition seems to have threatened suicide by sword. On the literary topos of the love suicide, see Trenkner 1958, 61–63.

polis not only has the power to define statuses and social identities but also to determine what counts as injury and redress.

ὥστ' ἐγκαλεῖν
ἀδικεῖ σ' ἐκεῖνος, ἄν ποτ' ἔλθῃς εἰς λόγους.
εἰ δ' ἐκβιάσει, δίκην ὀφλήσεις· οὐκ ἔχει
τιμωρίαν γὰρ τἀδίκημ', ἔγκλημα δέ.

(500–503)

He's wronged you,
so as to entitle you to lodge a complaint, if you can discuss it.
But if you use force, you'll incur the prosecution. This wrong
doesn't call for private vengeance but rather a formal complaint.

Once again, Pataikos counsels Polemon to use language (*logoi*) rather than force to deal with a perceived injury; however, he offers a new reason for turning first to speech in interpersonal relations. When Polemon initially repaid Glykera for her perceived infidelity by committing an act of domestic violence against her, she rejected him. By using force in his romantic relationship, he lost his partner's consent to that relationship. Pataikos teaches him what he should have known all along: the powerlessness of force in romantic negotiations. Pataikos then points out that the stakes will be higher, legally if not personally, if he commits an act of violence.[35] In so doing, he will be transformed from victim into offender, incurring a formal prosecution from a male citizen empowered to tell his own story before the law. The proper response to Moschion's behavior, Pataikos declares, is a legal complaint (ἔγκλημα) rather than an act of personal vengeance (τιμωρίαν).[36]

By converting Polemon's description of the "seducer who wronged me" (499–500) into the judicial vocabulary of complaint and prosecution, Pataikos teaches Polemon to translate his personal injuries into the common evaluative framework of legal discourse. Pataikos thereby seeks not

[35] Some commentators contend that 'εκβιάσει must mean "remove by force," with Glykera being the implied object (Lamagna 1994, 247 ad 252; Trail 2002, 289). Pataikos's language is ambiguous, however, and could mean "use force" (Arnott) generally, or "to lay violent hands" on Moschion, ἐκβιάζω). Even if we assume that Glykera is the object of ἐκβιάσει, it must be Moschion or an entitled male that will prosecute Polemon should he resort to violence. Glykera cannot bring a prosecution on her own and has no *kurios* to protect her interests.

[36] Gomme and Sandbach (1973, 507 ad 499–503) point out that the term τιμωρίαν is ambiguous because it can refer to private retaliation or to state-sanctioned punishment. Pataikos's warning to Polemon in the previous line not to use force indicates that τιμωρία has the sense of private revenge here. It is not clear, however, whether private revenge is being contrasted with a formal or an informal legal complaint. On the meaning of ἔγκλημα, see Konstan 1995, 131; Lamagna 1994, 247 ad 250; Scafuro 1997, 442.

only "to subject" Polemon to the law but also to make Polemon into a particular kind of subject. For the linguistic conversion that subordinates Polemon's power to the law's language of complaint and prosecution, and hence ultimately to the law's authority, also generalizes Polemon's perceived injury and his status as an injured party. The state's legal apparatus specifically standardizes disparate claims, treating one incident of seduction just like any other. While this standardization ensures fairness, promising that like cases will be treated alike, it also standardizes the identities of those who make use of legal institutions. The leveling power of the judicial process is made explicit in Aristotle's discussion of corrective justice, which, as it happens, employs the example of *moikheia* (seduction). In dealing with cases of *moikheia*, according to Aristotle, the law aims at adequation, compensating the victim for his injury: "It makes no difference if a decent person has taken from a base person, or a base person from a decent person, or if a decent or base person has committed *moikheia*. Rather, the law looks only at the nature of the harm, and treats the people involved as equals, if one does injustice while the other suffers it, and one has done the harm while the other has suffered it" (*E.N.* 1132a2–6).[37] Similarly in the *Perikeiromenē*, the state's judicial process has the power to make Polemon and Moschion into equals. The language of prosecution and complaint neutralizes their prior identities, effectively masking Polemon's status as a mercenary and curtailing his power to take revenge.

Gender and International Relations

While Glykera's injury sets the stage for the education of the overviolent mercenary, it also prompts a remaking of the heterosexual union on terms designed to prevent similar harms in the future. For the only means at Polemon's disposal to atone for committing an irreparable act is to promise that such a thing will never happen again. The text, however, constructs a consistent character for Polemon. He is educated by the encounter with Pataikos but not suddenly transformed. Accordingly, still the inarticulate comic mercenary, he begs Pataikos to serve as his surrogate in the negotiations with Glykera. Although we do not know what Polemon himself would have said, in his pleas to Pataikos he expresses a new, if somewhat inchoate, conception of Glykera and their relationship. He beseeches Pataikos to visit Glykera as his ambassador (πρέσβευσον,

[37] Trans. adapted from Irwin 1999.

510) as though she were a polis or independent power, while promising to make his future treatment of her a matter of his own *philotimia*:

> ἐγὼ γὰρ εἴ τι πώποτ' ἠδίκηχ' ὅλως–
> εἰ μὴ διατελῶ πάντα φιλοτιμούμενος–
> τὸν κόσμον αὐτῆς εἰ θεωρήσαις.–
>
> (514–16)

> If I've ever harmed her in any way,
> if I don't continue striving for honor in everything [pertaining to her],
> if you could see her clothes . . .

With these promises and declarations, Polemon is attempting to redefine his relationship with Glykera. In so doing, he is rejecting the homosocial triangle that reduced Glykera to an object to be captured and possessed in a contest between men. This was, of course, the model structuring the rivalry between Moschion and Polemon. Moschion's first thought upon his imagined conquest of Glykera was to mock the vanquished high-ranking mercenary officer, or the chiliarch, as he identifies Polemon (293–94). Glykera's role in defining male status is also made explicit by the rival slaves, who regard the possession of Glykera as a marker of both their masters' and their own masculinity (379–82, 386–96; cf. 527–29). By contrast, after Pataikos's intervention, Polemon seeks to define a relationship with Glykera based on her consent. Yet he struggles to find a language in which to cast such a relationship. In vowing to "continually show a love of honor" in his future dealings with her (εἰ μὴ διατελῶ πάντα φιλοτιμούμενος), he effectively promises to act like a good citizen. By the mid–fourth century, *philotimia*, translated either as a "love of honor" or "zealous ambition," had become a cardinal virtue in democratic Athens.[38] *Philotimia*, however, is associated with performing good service on behalf not of individuals but of the community. In honorific decrees the city most commonly praises liturgists for performing their duties with *philotimia* and exhorts others to do the same.[39] That Polemon invites Pataikos to view Glykera's clothing, evidence of his past generosity and benefactions, immediately after promising to act with *philotimia* suggests that he is drawing on the conventions of public liturgies or, more broadly, on the system of euergetism.[40]

[38] See Whitehead 1986, 242–51; 1983; 1993.

[39] Whitehead 1986, 250–51.

[40] The immediate context in which Polemon seeks to prove his intentions to act with *philotimia* by displaying Glykera's clothing recalls the exchange relationship structuring the liturgical contract. For that reason, it seems likely that his use of φιλοτιμούμενος in 515 relies on the specifically civic conception of *philotimia* and is not semantically neutral, as Gomme and Sandbach suggest (1973, 507 ad 515). For the association of *philotimia* and liturgical donation elsewhere in Menander, see Moschion's "defense" speech (*Sam.* 13–14).

Although Polemon's attempt to reconfigure the romantic relationship along the lines of the liturgical or euergetic bond has an obvious comic edge, it also has an undeniable logic. By evoking the system of liturgies, Polemon is also evoking its characteristic reciprocal structure. Citizens who exerted themselves on the community's behalf could call on the community for *kharis* (a favor) in return.[41] The most common context in which citizens attempted to cash in on their liturgical investments was forensic. In a defendant's speech, the recitation of past public benefactions and the implicit or explicit promise of more in the future operated as a culturally sanctioned bribe: the defendant promised to reward the community for siding with him in the lawsuit.[42] Thus, by implicitly vowing to make Glykera the beneficiary of future expenditures, Polemon is acting like a defendant in a lawsuit, attempting to distract attention from the harm he has committed.[43]

On another level, however, Polemon's attempt to restructure the heterosexual union (a union between unequal partners) on the model of euergetism (a mutually beneficial partnership, also between unequals) may gesture toward contemporary Hellenistic political circumstances. In chapter 2, I discussed the Greek cities' creative adaptation of the traditions of euergetism and public liturgies to negotiate relationships with the Hellenistic rulers and their officials.[44] The earliest evidence for the onset of this process is about 315 B.C., sometime after Antigonus declared freedom and autonomy for the Greeks, virtually inviting them to view him as a benefactor (*euergetēs*). Most commentators tentatively date the *Perikeiromenē* to 313 or thereabouts, on the basis of an alleged allusion to the murder of Alexander, Polyperchon's son.[45] When Moschion proposes to make Daos *prostatēs* of Greek affairs or a *dioikētēs* of the armies in recognition of his service as romantic facilitator, Daos refuses the offer on the grounds that the mercenaries would seize the first opportunity to slit his throat (279–83). Although that is more or less what happened to Alexander after accepting Cassander's deal to become general of the Peloponnesus, it is obviously impossible to determine whether the play is actually alluding to this incident or indeed to rely on it in dating the play.

[41] On litigants' expectation of *kharis* from jurors for their past benefactions, see Ober 1989, 226–33, and chapter 5, note 14.

[42] For the jurors' tendency to acquit men from whom they expected to reap future benefit, see Johnstone 1999, 98, with Lys. 14.43–45.

[43] For this strategy in the *Samia*, see Moschion's liturgical catalogue (13–15), with discussion in chapter 5.

[44] See chapter 2 with note 58.

[45] Although Schwartz's conjecture (1929) that *Pk*. 279–83 is an allusion to the murder of Alexander is often cited, the evidence for that claim is not strong; see Gomme and Sandbach 1973, 482–83 ad 280–81; Lamagna 1994, 195–96 ad 89–91; Arnott 1979–2000, 2:372.

Yet the play does construct a precise historical milieu: it is fairly saturated with references to the Successor Wars. While Moschion catalogues the constellation of offices that the *Diadochoi* used to distribute rule of the Greek world, the slaves conduct a virtual inventory of Hellenistic weaponry and siege tactics.[46] In addition, references to the war, Corinthian troubles, and the "noble crop" of men born for misery in Greece (125, 532–34) situate the play in the context of Cassander's struggle to subdue the Greek cities by force. Corinth no less than Athens suffered his attacks, as well as those of the other successors, throughout the last generation of the fourth century. Accordingly, while the *Perikeiromenē* cannot be dated with precision, it is fair to say that the play alludes to the Successor Wars and their impact on the domestic life of the city. But instead of passively reflecting this state of affairs, the play suggests a solution. By depicting a wealthy mercenary captain's eagerness to step into the role of romantic benefactor, the play places a representative of the Hellenistic kingdoms in a traditional civic role. It thus invites contemporary citizens to see Hellenistic rulers and their assorted officials as civic benefactors while encouraging Hellenistic rulers and officials to accept civically scripted positions.

The Return of the Repressed: Gender and the Constraints of Genre

The comic narrative of conflict and resolution between the sexes—between contestants of unequal power, status, and resources—seems to prefigure or script the transformation of political relations taking place on the international level. If the position of heroine in relation to her mercenary lover provides a symbolic analog to the plight of the Greek cities in relation to the military kingdoms, then the subordinate yet autonomous Hellenistic polis offers an equally suggestive analog to the heroine's position in the gender hierarchy. In other words, by constructing the Hellenistic political contract in terms of a sexual or romantic contract, the text holds forth the promise of remodeling the gender asymmetry of sexual contract along new, more symmetrical lines.

The play as we have it, however, is marked by a profound ambivalence toward traditional gender categories. Although Glykera's initial injury is displaced rather than redressed or forgiven, she retains considerable autonomy after her cultural and political work is complete. The final decision to reconcile with Polemon is clearly her own and not that of her

[46] See *Pk.* 380–82, 388–89, 392–96, with Lamagna 1994, 228 ad 190, and Gomme and Sandbach 1973, 496–97 ad 380–81, on mercenary pay; Lamagna 1994, 232–33 ad 206, and Gomme and Sandbach 1973, 499 ad 396, on the *sarissa*.

newfound father-*kurios*. At the same time, the significance of her consent—her power to select a husband with the traits that meet with her approval—is counterbalanced by the covert recapitulation of the homosocial plot. The construction of an empowered female character is coupled with the deployment of a conventional homosocial narrative pattern in which the exchange of women serves to forge, solidify, and reproduce male bonds and values. For while Polemon never persuades Glykera to forgive him for the initial act of domestic violence per se, he does convince her father. It is Glykera's long-lost father who (with his true identity still hidden) instructs Polemon in the ways of civic competency in the third act, in the ethically if not emotionally climatic scene of the play. He is so impressed with Polemon's sincerity that he tries, albeit without success, to convince Glykera that her too vehement partner should be forgiven. Viewed retrospectively, the scene of ostensibly failed romantic persuasion actually succeeds, but with an audience it apparently had not sought. It enables Polemon to win in advance the forgiveness and indeed approval of the man whose consent will turn out to be necessary (though not sufficient) for his ultimate romantic reconciliation.

The *Perikeiromenē* constructs an empowered heroine without developing a new narrative or plot pattern in which she might act. This portrayal emblematizes the distinctive duality of Menander's comedy: its simultaneous adherence to narratives that reproduce the civic social order and use of conventions that implicitly resist the very social codes they are employed to sustain. In *Perikeiromenē*, however, there is an additional factor at work to dispel and dissipate the intransigence of the gender hierarchy. The emergence of Macedonian-headed military kingdoms seems to have prompted a corresponding emphasis on "Greekness" as a dominant axis of identity, at least in comedy. This newly paramount source of identity surfaces in the *Perikeiromenē* when Pataikos praises Glykera's decision to pardon Polemon:

πάνυ σοῦ φιλῶ τὸ "νῦν διαλλαχθήσομαι"·
ὅτ' εὐτύχηκας, τότε δέχεσθαι τὴν δίκην
τεκμήριον τοῦτ ἐστὶν Ἕλληνος τρόπου.

(1006–8)

I love your "now I'll be reconciled."
Accepting a fair settlement when you've had good fortune:
this is the proof of Greek character.

Pataikos parrots Glykera's actual words, "now I'll be reconciled," but then translates them into "accepting a just settlement."[47] In so doing, he

[47] Although Glykera retains the power to consent to her own romantic affairs, she may

places the romantic reconciliation in a new register—or perhaps more precisely, makes explicit the international register being evoked all along. For "accepting a just settlement" adapts the technical formula of reciprocal contractual or treaty relations between states.[48] In other words, Pataikos rewrites the heterosexual contract as a specific form of political contract, one that creates complete reciprocity between the participants. He thereby constructs Glykera and Polemon as partners of equal standing in the relationship. This reconstruction of gender along more symmetrical lines is made possible by the prioritizing of Glykera's Greek character, a source of identity capable of suppressing the traditional social significance of her gender identity. In the act of forgiving Polemon, Glykera enacts a Greek identity based (in Pataikos's estimation) on a common code of ethics and values that, at least temporarily, subordinates the significance of her gender identity.[49] With this emphasis, the play offers a new understanding of gender relations without seeming to contest the reigning gender hierarchy.

Negotiations of Martial and Marital Values in the *Misoumenos*

The changing shape of international political landscapes brought new aspects and conceptions of personal identity to the fore, making available new understandings of gender (in comedy, at any rate). In the *Perikeiromenē*, the project of articulating a common Greek identity operates,

---

lose the ability to express that consent in the final act of the play. In lines 1021–22 someone states: "Your monstrous act has now become for us the start of good [experience]; the same character adds in 1023a, "That's why you are forgiven." Because a second hand in the manuscript assigns these lines to Glykera, and because it makes sense for her to explain her reason for pardoning Polemon, several editors give these lines to Glykera (Arnott 1995, 29–30, and 1996; Lamagna 1994; G. M. Brown 1974). Sandbach assigns the lines to Pataikos. Gomme and Sandbach (1973, 529–30 ad 1006ff.) lay out the arguments for this attribution; see also Frost 1989, 99–100. They point out that a speaking part for Glykera would have meant a breach in the three actor rule. My own feeling is that these lines should be assigned to Glykera precisely because the attribution does constitute a violation of generic decorum. The contravention of the three actor rule in the close of the play reproduces on the dramaturgic level the tension between Glykera's empowered character and her limited social and narrative possibilities.

[48] Capps states, "The expression διδόναι καὶ δέξεσθαι τὰ δίκαια (Thuc. 1.37.5, cf. 5.59.5) is a formula of complete reciprocity in contractual or treaty relations" (1910, 217 ad 888).

[49] Webster remarks that Menander "nationalizes" the characteristics of forgiveness and discrimination referred to as "equity" (*epieikeia*) in philosophical discourse (1960, 205 with n. 5). Lamagna (1994, 295 ad 430) also notes that Greek identity in Menander is rooted in ethical considerations involving equanimity.

in part, to diminish the social significance of gender difference. Similar transformations of traditional identity categories take place in the *Misoumenos*, another (now fragmentary) play about a mercenary who alienates his mistress by enacting his professional identity in his private life. Just as in the *Perikeiromenē*, the romantic conflict reproduces in miniature the large-scale problems of international relations. The *Misoumenos*, however, more directly attacks the entire project of Hellenistic warfare. Indeed, the play launches a historically specific critique of Hellenistic warfare by drawing on and adapting the epic and tragic traditions of martial manhood.

Any analysis of the *Misoumenos* must, of course, be prefaced with an admission that it is based on a very fragmentary text.[50] We have only about 160 complete lines of the play, and several fragments and discussions of Thrasonides, the mercenary protagonist, whose remarkable self-restraint particularly attracted the attention of later Stoic writers.[51] That said, it is possible to reconstruct the main outline of the romantic plot as follows.[52] Shortly before the opening of the play, Thrasonides bought the significantly named heroine—Krateia—as a prisoner of war. Although he gives her freedom and treats her as his wife, she remains his "spear prize" (αἰχμάλωτος), as she is described in the play.[53] While the relationship seems to have begun well enough, when they returned to Athens from Cyprus, where Thrasonides was apparently campaigning on behalf of one of the Cypriot kings, Krateia inexplicably turned against him, baffling both Thrasonides and his slave Getas.[54]

Thrasonides seems to have made the mistake of boasting about a certain sword in his possession, probably claiming to have won it in battle.[55]

[50] Since Arnott renumbers the *Misoumenos*, I give line references to the texts of Sandbach, Sisti, and Arnott. Unless otherwise noted, the Greek text cited throughout is Sandbach.

[51] See Arnott 1979–2000, 2:252. On Thrasonides, see 2 Sandbach (3 Sisti, 4 Arnott); test. 1 Sandbach (test. 1 Sisti, test. 1 Arnott); test. 2 Sisti, test. 2 Arnott; Barigazzi 1985, 125.

[52] For reconstructions of the plot of the *Misoumenos*, see Webster 1973; Turner 1977, 1984; Gomme and Sandbach 1973, 437–44; Sisti 1986, 7–13; Arnott 1979–2000, vol. 2, and 1996c.

[53] On Krateia as spear prize, see *Mis*. A 37–40, appendix (Sisti, 37 Arnott) and 235–36 (Sisti, 636–37 Arnott), where Getas explains to her father: αἰχμάλωτος γενομένη / αὕτη πρὸς ἡμᾶς ἦλθε τοῦτον τὸν τρόπον. On Krateia's status, see Borgogno 1988, 95–97.

[54] Fr. 5 (4 Sisti, 5 Arnott). On the date of the *Misoumenos* as between 320 and 310, see Turner 1984, 249–50. On the setting of the play as Athens, see Gomme and Sandbach 1973, 439; Turner 1984; Sisti 1986, 84; Borgogno 1988; contra Webster 1973, 290.

[55] Although there is no evidence in the text as it stands that Thrasonides acted like a stereotypical braggart soldier, it seems certain that he did in some lost portion of the play, since late commentators associate him especially with boasting (*alazoneia*). Choricius of Gaza states that it was Thrasonides' boastfulness that drove the heroine away; fr. 1 (test. 1 Sisti, test. 1 Arnott). In addition, a connection between the sword and boasting seems to

Unfortunately for him, Krateia recognizes the sword as having belonged to her brother and concludes that Thrasonides has in fact killed him.[56] The play opens just after this occurs, with Thrasonides despondently pacing in front of his house as he tries to understand Krateia's sudden and unfathomable hatred toward him. The problem becomes more complex in the third act when Krateia's father arrives, demanding to ransom her. Rather than restoring her to her father, Thrasonides seeks to marry her. When Demeas and Krateia adamantly refuse his pleas, he is faced with a dilemma: whether to keep his "concubine" for himself or to restore her to her father and thus go against his own desperate desire. This decision, in fact, forms the ethical center of the play. Although the norms of reciprocity seem to dictate that he ransom the heroine, both Krateia and Demeas fail to uphold the proprieties of social reciprocity in their dealings with Thrasonides. Accordingly, the play puts him in the position of having to chose between self-interest and social norms while his obligations to uphold those social norms are weakened. That he returns Krateia, against self-interest and after having been mistreated, redeems him as the romantic protagonist. It seems that Krateia's brother arrived immediately after she was released, exonerating Thrasonides from his imagined crime and enabling him to marry the heroine.

In contrast to Polemon, Thrasonides is characterized as possessing the socialized and self-controlled disposition necessary for living in a civic community. Moreover, he is actually innocent of committing the deed that leads to the romantic estrangement. He did not in fact kill Krateia's brother. But because he was willing to claim responsibility for doing so, and assumed that such an act would be to his credit, he is implicated in the values and ideology that the text protests against. In other words, although Thrasonides' name came to be synonymous with the braggart soldier type in antiquity, the comic problem here, as in the *Perikeiromenē*, is more serious than the mercenary's inappropriate speech habits.[57] More precisely, the problem centers on the killing Thrasonides either claims to have committed or allows to be attributed to him. Ordinarily, the realities of what mercenaries actually did (fight and kill) had no place within comedy's conventional narrative patterns. Such material, we learn in the *Aspis*, falls within the generic purview of tragedy rather than comedy. Like the *Misoumenos*, the *Aspis* deploys the mistaken death motif to sidestep this generic taboo. The presumed death of the mercenary Kleostra-

have been drawn in the linguistic register by the use of the word σπάθη to refer to the sword in question and the metaphoric use of the verb σπαθᾶν to mean "to boast" in place of the usual comic term for boasting (ἀλαζονεύεσθαι).

[56] For the sword's dramatic function, see Turner 1984.

[57] See fr. 1 (test. 1 Sisti, test. 1 Arnott).

tos enables that play to explore the effects of Hellenistic warfare undertaken for plunder and booty on affective relations within the family and city. In the *Misoumenos*, however, the mistaken death makes possible a consideration of the killing itself, and what Hellenistic warfare means for citizens and their families.[58]

Ultimately, Thrasonides' innocence is not enough to redeem him as the rightful romantic protagonist, since the problem really involves his beliefs rather than his actions. Why, after all, did he think that playing the soldier's part would be to his credit? The play allows him to restore his wounded credibility, not (as in Polemon's case) with an embedded drama of civic education but rather by letting him display his true character. The mistaken death serves both as the source of the comic problem and, in a crucial way, its solution. For it creates two situations that call attention to Thrasonides' status as a successful soldier while giving him leeway to make choices that disclose his true identity as a Greek citizen, with all ethical competencies entailed by such citizenship. The play casts Thrasonides as a Homeric warrior returning with a concubine—a spear prize—only to allow him to refuse to the play the part in which he has been cast. With this emphasis, the play evokes and revises the values of military manhood encapsulated in the Homeric and, to a lesser extant, the tragic traditions. The point of this revision, however, is not to contest pillars of the Greek cultural tradition but rather to offer a historically specific critique of contemporary conditions in which warfare had lost its ethical grounding in conceptions of civic duty and defense.

Paradoxically, the text achieves this historical specificity by a certain suppression of history. Although Krateia is referred to as Thrasonides' "spear prize," he actually bought her as a slave captive. If the play was set in Athens, or if Thrasonides was an Athenian by birth, as seems likely, the buying and selling of Krateia would have been prohibited by law. On Lycurgus's initiative, sometime between 338 and 324, the Athenians passed a law forbidding any citizen or inhabitant of Athens to buy a free person captured in war ([Plut.] *Vit. X Orat.* 842a). One of the founding principles of democratic citizenship established by Solon in the early sixth century expressly forbid debt slavery or the sale of the citizen's person. Later, the unprecedented traffic in prisoners brought about by the conquests of Philip and Alexander directly challenged the democratic

[58] We might suspect that Thrasonides' position as a mercenary was not thoroughly problematized insofar as he was fighting against Ptolemy I on behalf of the Cypriot kings. But this is no way lessens his implication in the values and practices the text critiques, since by fighting in a war involving the successors he seems to have put himself in a position of claiming credit for killing an Athenian citizen—especially egregious, because he probably was an Athenian citizen himself. For Hellenistic warfare as mixing up the traditional signs of civic and social identities, see further chapter 7 with note 86.

state's ability to ensure the bodily freedom of its citizens.[59] Accordingly, the Lycurgan law is, to some extent, a reiteration of the long-standing Solonian principle giving citizens legal protection against falling into slavery. At the same time, however, the law represents an extension of the norms of democratic citizenship since it seeks to grant legal protection from slavery to all free persons rather than only to Athenians. Significantly, there is no trace of this law in the *Misoumenos*. In fact, in the relatively well-preserved portion of the play dealing directly with the question of restoring Krateia to her father, the emphasis falls explicitly on normative rather than legal considerations. By suppressing or eliding the Lycurgan law in this way, the play constructs Thrasonides' decision to restore Krateia to her family as an ethically significant choice instead of a matter of legal necessity.

The Conquering Captive: Genre and Gender Inversion

As the *Misoumenos* enacts a revision of the story of the conquering soldier, it also performs a similar revision of the captive's story. The theme of the warrior returning with his spear prize concubine is common on the tragic stage. Tragedy often uses the strife between the concubine and the wife already installed in the warrior's home as a way of indirectly commenting on civic problems in the domestic space.[60] Unlike her tragic foremothers—Iole, Cassandra, and Andromache—Krateia is not forced to contend with a wife already in Thrasonides' household. Rather, Thrasonides treats her as his wife, signaling both his presumption to make a marriage without the performance of the state's authorizing speech act and his preference for monogamy that proleptically characterizes him as the rightful romantic protagonist.

Krateia's situation as spear captive is perhaps most strongly evocative of Tecmessa's position in Sophocles' *Ajax*. Tecmessa, like Krateia, has become the wifelike concubine to the very man responsible for killing her natal family (*Ajax* 490–91). This situational similarity highlights the contrasting behavior of the two captive women. Where Tecmessa completely identifies with her captor, Krateia retains her loyalty to her birth family, honoring the kinship bond even in death. Although she initially consents to a sexual relationship with Thrasonides, she terminates it when she comes to believe that he is responsible for the death of her

[59] On the law as a reaction to Philip's practice of enslaving former citizens, see Rosivach 1999, 141 n. 57; Schlaifer 1936, 188. There is no evidence that the Lycurgan law was repealed in the early Hellenistic period. On the use of prisoners as a merchantable commodity in Menander's time, see De Souza 1999.

[60] Foley 2001, 87–105; Ogden 1996, 194–211.

brother. Unlike all her tragic forebears, whose only power consists in a strategic consent to their captors, and sometimes not even that, Krateia rejects Thrasonides and, more significantly, gets away with it.[61]

The radical revision of the captive's story is announced in the opening scene, which features the distraught Thrasonides pacing in front of his home, lamenting his ill-fated love to the night. Unlike Polemon, he has no need of siege tactics to reclaim his beloved nor worries about her independent legal status. Although Krateia is available to him in his own house and his desire for her is extreme, he paradoxically refrains, exercising heroic self-restraint (as commentators frequently aver). He explains to Getas, his slave here playing the role of the "tragic" attendant to the lovesick, "I am being pitifully outraged (ἐλεῖν' ὑβρίζομαι) . . . by my spear captive" (*Mis.* A 36–37, appendix [Sisti, 36–37 Arnott]). With this claim, he completely inverts the expected relationship between soldier and concubine. Whereas usually it is the woman—the captive—who suffers hubris, a status reduction entailed by the very fact of her captivity, here it is the captive who commits the status injury to the captor. In Thrasonides' case, the victor has become the vanquished, a reversal that probably accounts for his initial shame even to admit to the rift with Krateia (A 41 [Sisti, 41 Arnott]).

The unprecedented situation of a spear prize refusing her captor is emphasized not only by these verbal cues but also and more explicitly by the generic intertext structuring the scene. Instead of acting like a soldier with complete power over his slave concubine, Thrasonides plays the part of the excluded lover performing a *paraclausithuron*: an address or serenade delivered before the beloved's door as a means of gaining entrance.[62] This embedded genre calls immediate attention to the striking reversal of roles taking place. Instead of raping his captive or coercing her consent, this conquering soldier confesses to complete subjugation at the hands of his seemingly powerless prisoner of war, and to his exclusion from his own home.[63] As Thrasonides himself puts it:

> παιδισκάριόν με καταδεδούλωκ' εὐτελές,
> ὃν οὐδὲ εἷς τῶν πολεμίων <οὐ>πώποτε.
>
> (fr. 2 [3 Sisti, 4 Arnott])

[61] Scodel (1998) argues that female captives in Euripidean tragedy possess the limited freedom of being able to negotiate their sexual value.

[62] Cf. Turner 1984, 245; Goldberg 1980, 52. On the *exclusus amator* and *paraclausithuron*, see Copley 1956 (writing before the rediscovery of the *Misoumenos*).

[63] *Mis.* 10–12 A appendix (Sisti, 10–12 Arnott). Henry remarks, "Thrasonides loves Krateia and therefore will not rape her, his self control shows an unprecedented respect for the person" (1985, 106). Significantly, Thrasonides uses the verb ἀγαπᾶν' (307, 308 [Sisti, 708, 709 Arnott]) when professing his feelings to Krateia, a verb that denotes love and affection without reference to sexual desire; Gomme and Sandbach 1973, 458 ad 307.

A cheap little slave girl has enslaved me,
I, who've never been enslaved by an enemy before.

Civic Reciprocity and the Revision of Epic Manhood

Krateia's power paradoxically derives from a traditional woman's virtue: silence. While this may seem to be a curiously backhanded form of power, if a form of power at all, it underscores the heroine's autonomy and linguistic agency. The play presumes that she has the capacity to engage in deliberation and to make her own decisions. Krateia's resistance to persuasion and her refusal of speech effectively wounds Thrasonides more than any physical injury could. Although, as might be expected, Krateia is disparaged for wielding a power so far in excess of her gender and social position, she is not criticized for transgressing normative gender protocols. Rather, she is specifically censured by Getas (and possibly Thrasonides) for departing from the norms of Greekness and humanity.[64] In the putative final breakup scene, Getas draws a stark contrast between Thrasonides' effusive sentimentality and Krateia's silent savagery:

ἀλλ' οὐχὶ τοῦτο δεινόν, ἀλλ' αὕτη πάλιν
ἀ[φορ]ᾶι λ̣έγο̣ντος "ἀντιβολῶ, Κράτεια, σέ,
μή μ' ἐγκαταλίπῃς· παρθένον σ' εἴληφ' ἐγώ,
ἀνὴρ ἐκλήθην πρῶτος, ἠγάπησά σε,
ἀγ]απῶ, φιλῶ, Κράτεια φιλτάτη· τί σοι
λυπηρόν ἐστι τῶν παρ' ἐμοί; τεθνηκότα
πεύσει μ' ἐὰν μ' ἐγκαταλίπῃς." οὐδ' ἀπόκρισις.
  βάρβαρος, λέαινά τις
ἄν̣[θρωπος].[65]

(304–10, 312–13 [Sisti, 705–11, 712–13 Arnott])

This wasn't so bad, though, but the girl then looked
away when he said, "I beg you, don't
leave me, Krateia. I took you as
a virgin. I was first called your husband. I loved you,
love and cherish you, darling Krateia. What's

[64] Henry states (1985, 107) that Getas does not denigrate Krateia as a treacherous *hetaira* but rather for failing to live up to Greek ethical norms. This is an important point; however, we should remember that Krateia is not characterized as a *hetaira* in the play.

[65] The text in 313 is Arnott. At *Mis.* 284–85 (Sisti, 685–86 Arnott) Getas describes Demeas and Krateia as savage and inhuman. If the supplements for 42 Arnott are correct, Thrasonides also called Krateia a serpent and a lioness.

so painful for you in your life with me? You'll hear
I'm dead, if you abandon me." No answer!
  The girl's a barbarian, a lioness.

Although Greek thought conventionally equates women and barbarians, this is not the tradition that Getas is drawing on. In Menander's extant works, the designation "barbarian" most commonly has an ethical meaning, referring to a person's deviation from Hellenic ethical and cultural mores.[66] The term is used to discipline Greeks perceived to have departed from the norms of reciprocity, often with respect to pity or empathy. Accordingly, the very criticism of Krateia for behaving like a barbarian is a sign of her elevated status insofar as it presumes that she, no less than a man, has the capacity to abide by Greek ethical norms. While Getas's criticism points to a diminishing significance of gender in the construction of social identity, his immediate purpose is to contrast Krateia's barbarian inhumanity with what appears to him to be Thrasonides' incomprehensible generosity. He condemns Thrasonides for restoring Krateia to her father, for showing reciprocity to those who failed to show it to him.

ἐγὼ μὲν [αὐτήν], μὰ τὸν Ἀπόλλω τουτονί,
οὐκ ἂν ἀπέλυσ'. Ἑλληνικὸν καὶ πανταχ[οῦ
γινόμενον ἴσμεν. ἀλλ' ἐλεεῖν ὀρθῶς ἔχει
τὸν ἀντελεοῦνθ'. ὅταν δὲ μηδ' ὑμεῖς ἐμέ,
οὐδὲ λόγον ὑμῶν οὐδ' ἐπιστροφὴν ἔχω.

(314–18 [Sisti, 715–19 Arnott])

Now I would never have released [her], by
Apollo here. We know it's a Greek custom,
and goes on everywhere. But pity's only right
if it's reciprocated. When you two take no account of me,
I have no concern or regard for you.

Ironically, Getas—a barbarian and a slave—postures as the ethical spokesmen of the play, the character who knows "standard" Greek cultural mores better than the Greeks whom he serves. He offers a rigid and uncompromising interpretation of the Hesiodic injunction "Give to one

[66] For Greeks described as barbarian for their ethical lapses, see *Epit.* 898–99, 924; *Sam.* 519. For morality as the mark of Greek character, see *Pk.* 1006–8. For the ethical sense of *barbaros* in New Comedy, see Long 1986, 151–56. In some cases, the term "barbarian" designates non-Greeks (*Asp.* 25, 42, 74, 103, 140). At *Geōr.* 56ff., the barbarian servants are distinguished from the Greek farmworker on the basis of an ethics of care and reciprocity; see further Dworacki 1993. On reciprocity as a Greek ethical norm, see M. W. Blundell 1985; von Reden 1995.

who gives, but do not give to one who does not give" (Hes. *Erg.* 345). By his estimation, the failure of either Krateia or her father to abide by a basic norm of social reciprocity—communicative exchange—has freed Thrasonides from the obligation to release her. However, altruism (generalized reciprocity) is also a Greek ethical value. By releasing Krateia when not technically obliged to do so by the social code (at least as it is set forth in the text), Thrasonides performs an altruistic act that validates his claim to "Greekness," or what amounts to civic and ethical competency.

More important, Thrasonides refuses to play the role in which he has been cast. As he is forced to decide between self-interest and a father's demands to ransom his daughter, Thrasonides' situation recalls the primal conflict of the *Iliad*.[67] Like Agamemnon, Thrasonides frantically seeks to keep his "spear prize" in the face of paternal protest. Yet the situation differs in important details. The Greeks at Troy urge Agamemnon to return his concubine to her father, a priest of Apollo; Thrasonides' cohort, a lone slave, urges him to do precisely the opposite. In both cases, however, the advisors exhort the hero-soldier to obey the dictates of social reciprocity. In contrast to Agamemnon, who initially refuses to give up a concubine he values more than his wife, Thrasonides not only gives up Krateia despite his own desire, but he also does so after having been offended by her and her father. Thus, although the primal scene of the *Iliad* is evoked here, that scene has been significantly rewritten. Thrasonides is placed in a situation in which a decision like Agamemnon's might have been justified, but by refusing to take revenge he demonstrates his rejection of the martial values he had initially laid claim to. In the course of doing so, Thrasonides also offers a radical revision of traditional gender roles.

In the epic and tragic traditions, a warrior's possession of a concubine captive enhances his honor and status, effectively marking him as a victor. Similarly, Thrasonides considers his relationship with Krateia to have bearing on his honor and reputation. But crucially, what counts for him is how he treats Krateia rather than simply "having" her.

ὄν[ε]ιδος αὐτῆι τοῦτο καταλιπεῖν σε δεῖ
ἀθάνατον. εὖ παθοῦσ' ἐτιμωρήσατο
τὸν τἀγάθ' αὐτῆι δόντα.

(804–6 Arnott)[68]

You must leave this as an eternal
reproach for her: "Having been well treated, she took
vengeance against the one who assisted her."

[67] By portraying Thrasonides as having bought rather than captured Krateia, the play softens the opprobrious connotations of the Iliadic intertext and of Thrasonides' role as a soldier more generally.

[68] The text cited for these lines is Arnott.

With this claim, Thrasonides assumes that Krateia has decisional autonomy, that she is an agent whose actions are subject to moral evaluation (praise and blame) rather than an object whose purpose is to augment masculine honor. He thus presumes that ethics rather than gender provides the foundation for social relations and, by implication, social identities. While Thrasonides' statement undermines the gender hierarchy, it does not similarly undercut or suppress the political order. By describing himself as Krateia's benefactor (τὸν τἀγάθ' αὐτῆι δόντα), Thrasonides refigures the romantic relation as a liturgical bond, casting himself as the elite or royal liturgical donor and Krateia as the civic recipient of his largesse. His use of the verb τιμωρεῖν (to avenge or take vengeance) to describe Krateia's response inverts the customary protocol. Instead of recompensing Thrasonides' generosity with goodwill, Krateia takes vengeance against him—as if she had been harmed rather than helped. Her inversion of euergetic etiquette leads to a second change in the system. In the hortative clause of honorary decrees for liturgical donors, the Greek cities claim to remember their benefactors.[69] Here, however, Thrasonides warns that it is Krateia who will win a deathless reproach.

This application of euergetic language and ideas to the romantic bond is the same move that Polemon attempts in *Perikeiromenē*. That the impetus for this political structuring comes from the mercenary in both plays attests to the mercenary's willingness to be socialized and inscribed into the world of the polis in spite of his real or apparent violation of civic mores. Indeed, the comic mercenary's modeling of the romantic bond on the system of public benefactions may have influenced or reinforced the changes in international relations, as the Greek cities drew on the system of public liturgies and the traditions of euergetism to fashion their relationships with the more powerful Hellenistic rulers and to socialize their emissaries.[70] In comedy, however, the effect of this socialization of the mercenary is double-sided: the price of championing polis structures in the context of the romantic relationship is a lessening of the traditional asymmetry structuring relations between men and women.[71]

While Polemon never actually succeeds in winning Glykera back on his own, Thrasonides' behavior clearly does absolve and exonerate him. Once the confusions and illusions of the plot have been dispelled, he

[69] For examples of the hortative condition in honorary decrees for citizens, see IG II^2 448 lines 47ff.; IG II^2 657 lines 51ff.; Shear 1978, lines 84ff. See further Gauthier 1985, 9–10; Ma 1999, 183–85.

[70] See further Gauthier 1985; Billows 1995; Ma 1999. For the specifically socializing role of the cities' euergetic discourse, see Ma 1999, 206–11.

[71] The modeling of the romantic bond on euergetism diminished but did not eliminate gender asymmetry; and in practice, euergetism did not result in egalitarian relations between the rulers and cities.

wins an immediate and unqualified romantic victory. When Demeas asks Krateia if she wants to marry Thrasonides, she responds with an unequivocal yes. Just as in the *Perikeiromenē*, the significance of female consent might seem to be blunted because the heroine is ventriloquized by a male in the text. There, Pataikos approvingly parrots Glykera's line "Now I'll be reconciled" (*Pk.* 1006). And here, the slave Getas reports Krateia's response to the anxious Thrasonides (*Mis.* 438–39 [Sisti, 968–69 Arnott]). In this case, however, the secondhand report emphasizes the importance of Krateia's consent precisely because Thrasonides is so desperate to hear it, demanding that Getas deliver the exact words (436–37 [Sisti, 966–67 Arnott]).

Ethics and Comedy's Construction of Transnational or Hellenic Citizenship

The *Perikeiromenē* and *Misoumenos* figure romantic reconciliation by drawing on the political language of euergetism and international relations. In each case, this construction is part of a larger reconfiguration as ethics rather than gender comes to operate as the dominant axis of social identity, for women as well as men. Although neither play is a protofeminist tract, both can be so read. Liberatory possibilities arise in each play because of the transnational cultural work the romantic narrative performs. In the more narrowly focused nationalist or Athenocentric plays, the making of a marriage often operates to cancel the stratifying effects of economic difference. The protagonist's desire for the heroine trumps economic considerations and makes possible a marriage across class lines. The heroines do not generally play a significant role in the refashioning of the social order in plays of this type because the homosocial contexts take precedence over the heterosexual relationship. That is to say, the action focuses on how the protagonist wins the consent not of the heroine herself but of other men. In transnational plays featuring a flawed but redeemable mercenary protagonist, however, the emphasis on repairing a romantic union provides an opening to negotiate relations of domination and dependence and to forge acceptable civic resolutions to the contest between polis culture and the emergent Hellenistic kingdoms. To achieve these ends, the *Perikeiromenē* and *Misoumenos* cede extraordinary cultural and moral authority to their heroines. In so doing, they set social precedents, making space in the cultural imaginary for female agency and entitlement.

By way of conclusion, it seems useful to examine in more detail the particular historical circumstances that underlie comedy's unsettling of conventional gender categories. Initially, Polemon and Thrasonides each display behavior at variance with civic norms, whether their disregard be for law, personal autonomy, or citizen lives. In so doing, they recall the stereotype of the mercenary as the antithesis of the citizen, as a figure unable to abide by laws or civic moral norms, found in fourth-century Athenian civic discourse. For example, Demosthenes calls mercenary commanders "the common enemies of mankind (*koinoi ekhthroi*), and of all men who wish to dwell in law and freedom" (23.138–39). Isocrates uses the same phrase, "common enemies" (*koinoi ekhthroi*), when describing contemporary mercenaries and the threat they pose to civic life (8.46–47). Comedy, however, complicates what seems to be a standard critique of the mercenary by driving a wedge between the mercenary role and the character who occupies it.[72]

The *Misoumenos*, by contrast, problematizes war rather than the mercenary or mercenary service. Demeas underscores this emphasis:

> καὶ δῆλον ὡς ἔσπαρκε τῶν οἴκοι τινὰς
> ὁ κοινὸς ἐχθρὸς πόλεμος ἄλλον ἀλλαχῇ.
>
> (233–34 [Sisti, 634–35 Arnott])

> It's clear that war is the common enemy, it's scattered
> asunder the members of my household.

While Demosthenes and Isocrates target the mercenary as the common enemy of mankind, Demeas adapts the formula to condemn war as the enemy, coming perilously close to offering overt criticism of the Hellenistic kingdoms. Demeas's comment is only the most explicit statement of the general antipathy felt by citizens in comedy toward the wars and affairs of the successors. For instance, in Terence's *Andria* the loss of the heroine's true identity and near loss of her reproductive future is attributed to the war in Athens (934–36). In Menander's *Heauton Timoroumenos*, a father initially tries to put an end to his son's love affair by sending him to win fame and fortune in the mercenary service of the king. He soon regrets his decision, coming to privilege familial ties over wars in faraway places.[73]

Comedy discredits war rather than the mercenary because the conditions of warfare had fundamentally changed in the Hellenistic period. Except for brief periods in which the aims of the successors and those of the cities coalesced, such as during the Four Years' War in Athens, warfare in the Hellenistic period lost its ethical foundation in civic duty and defense. Wars were now fought for the sake of the imperial aims of Alex-

[72] In Polemon's case, his life as a mercenary fosters his existing tendencies toward violence and overreaction. Nevertheless, the play makes clear that his behavioral problems are the product of his profession rather than of his innate disposition.

[73] The *Aspis* is also critical of contemporary practices of warfare; see chapter 7.

ander's successors and for booty and plunder; and they were fought constantly. The Hellenistic kingdoms were military powers relying almost entirely on mercenary armies. Even when they were not engaged in warfare, they did not disband their armies at the end of the campaigning season, as had been the case in the classical period before the rise of Philip. Consequently, with little opportunity to resume a civilian life, the Hellenistic mercenary progressively lost his connections to the polis.[74]

For a number of reasons, the Greek cities could not afford to ignore this situation. With their constant need for mercenaries, the Hellenistic rulers aggressively recruited Greek citizens and, when necessary, resorted to conscription.[75] According to Diodorus, Eumenes of Cardia was particularly successful in strategically soliciting mercenaries with promises of high pay, attracting many to serve as mercenaries "of their own free will even from the cities of Greece" (18.61.4).[76] He also reports that when Agathocles promised to distribute enemy land to his soldiers, "a good many Athenians and no small number of other Greeks were quick to join in the undertaking, for they hoped to portion out the most fertile part of Libya for colonization" (20.40.6).

The rise of mercenary service in the Hellenistic period threatened the demographic base of the polis both because mercenaries were constantly needed and because camp life emerged as a viable alternative to the polis formation.[77] Accordingly, the Greek cities needed to retain connections with their mercenaries rather than condemning all mercenaries as barbarian outcasts in the manner of fourth-century civic discourse.[78] Athens seems to have been successful in this project; for instance, sources from the third century attest that Athenian citizens serving as mercenary officers intervened on the city's behalf with the Hellenistic rulers.[79]

Although the Greek cities survived the transition to the Hellenistic age, in the time in which Menander wrote their survival was far from a fait accompli. With the narrative of the mercenary's romance, comedy did its part to facilitate the process—to ensure that citizens did not "disappear from the polis," the scenario that Moschion envisages in the *Samia*

[74] Parke 1933, 207–8.

[75] Diod. 18.50.3–4. The use of conscription is attested in Antigonus's letter to Skepsis where he states: "you and your allies are burdened by military service and expenses" (*RC* 1.44). The Hellenic league refounded by the Antigonids in 302 also required compulsory military service of some kind.

[76] This problem also animates Menander's *Aspis*. See further chapter 7. In a more novel tactic, Ophellas, a seasoned veteran of Alexander's wars, leveraged a marriage alliance with the Athenian Euthydike to recruit mercenaries from Athens (Diod. 20.40.1–42.5)

[77] On the mercenary army as an alternative social formation to the polis, see Dalby 1992; Trundle 1999.

[78] Isoc. 4.115, 117, 167–68, 8.44; *Letter to Archidamus* 9.10; Dem. 23.139.

[79] E.g., see Shear 1978 on Kallias of Sphettos and his brother.

(627–29). By constructing the mercenary as a flawed but sympathetic character, comedy gets to have it both ways, acknowledging that citizens might serve as mercenaries while simultaneously asserting the superiority of polis culture. Where fourth-century discourse emphasizes the depravity and barbarity of mercenaries, effectively constructing the mercenary and citizen as mutually exclusive categories, comedy creates a common ground between them. It carves out this space in the ethical and moral terrain. Like the citizen, the mercenary is able to enact or acquire specifically Greek ethical competencies. With this emphasis comedy bridges the gap between mercenaries and citizens, allowing the mercenary to reenter his civic life. The price of this accommodation, however, is an unsettling of traditional gender categories.

By transforming the mercenary into a husband, Menander's mercenary romances helped preserve and adapt polis institutions before the fact; at the same time, they supplied the cultural models that facilitated that adaptation. Thus the sympathetic mercenary character is a product of a precise historical moment: the transition to the Hellenistic age. Its historical specificity explains why this particular type disappears in Roman adaptations of Greek New Comedy. In the context of Rome, with its citizen army, there was no longer a compelling need to forge a common link between citizens and mercenaries. Yet even as Menander's mercenary romances adapt the challenges of the Hellenistic period to ensure the reproduction of polis culture, they simultaneously hold forth the promise of transforming that culture. The strategies that undo forms of domination and subordination based on military power spill over into the gender system, dismantling the traditional subordination of women to men. The construction of a pragmatic domain of "Greek ethics" available to mercenaries and citizens offered a conception of social relations also capable of reconstructing the conventional gender hierarchy along more egalitarian lines.

7

Trials of Masculinity in Democratic Discourse and Menander's *Sikyōnioi*

The Loss of the Citizen-Soldier Ideal

Menander's *Perikeiromenē* and *Misoumenos* enclose and solve the conflict between the Greek cities and the Hellenistic kingdoms in stories of romantic reconciliation. Specifically, by transforming the transient mercenary into a settled and civilized inhabitant of the polis (that is, into a husband), these plays offer a civic solution to the demographic and cultural challenges of Hellenistic mercenary service. But the rapid rise in the number of mercenaries was only one side of the military problem that the Hellenistic kingdoms presented to the Greek cities. It was accompanied by a corresponding decrease in opportunities for citizens to serve as soldiers on behalf of their own cities. In the Hellenistic period, the mercenary virtually replaced the citizen-soldier. The impact of this change can hardly be overestimated, since the ability to serve as a citizen-soldier was traditionally what defined the citizen as a citizen in Athens (no less than in Sparta and Thebes).

Warfare (actual or symbolic) was the traditional route to maturation in Greek culture.[1] It was also a central component of citizenship in Athens.[2] Every citizen in Athens between the ages of 18 and 60 could be called on for military service during the summer months.[3] In the funeral oration, Thucydides' Pericles describes the democratic citizen as a natural soldier in need of no specialized military training (Thuc. 2.39). The seamless identification of the Athenian citizen with the soldier was consolidated during the Persian Wars of the fifth century B.C.; Athenian propaganda of the period equates military domination with images of aggressive masculinity, and in some cases with sexual domination.[4] The masculinist ideology underlying the citizen-soldier ideal served to legitimate Athenian

[1] See Vernant 1980; Vidal-Naquet 1986; Winkler 1990b.

[2] On the equation of citizen and soldier, see Ridley 1979; Loraux 1986. For the general sociopolitical significance of hoplite fighting, see Hanson 1989, 1996.

[3] On citizens being liable for military service between the ages of 18 and 60, see [Arist.] *A.P.* 53.4; Andrewes 1981.

[4] For the allegorical coding of military domination as sexual domination, see E. Hall 1993; Cartledge 1998; Humphreys 1999.

imperialism and, equally important, to produce and sustain the egalitarian norms of democratic citizenship. The building of the navy in the fifth century enabled all citizens—even those who could not afford to serve as hoplites—to fully participate militarily, sharing the dangers of war and so justifying their share in the political realm. In the final analysis, every citizen could be counted as an equal insofar as he possessed a masculine military body and was willing to use it in the service of the state.

The rise of Macedon and the Hellenistic military kingdoms posed a challenge to the citizen's military masculinity. In 322, with the destruction of the Athenian navy and the city's loss of domestic and foreign autonomy, the ideal of the citizen-soldier was all but destroyed.[5] Although the Athenians did fight for the city again, they usually did so with the assistance of foreign rulers rather than as members of an independent citizen army fighting on behalf of their own polis.[6] For this reason, the eclipse of Athenian military power has often been associated with a supposed decline in democratic politics.[7] As we have already seen, however, the recurrent democratic rebellions of the late fourth and early third centuries attest to the Athenians' abiding dedication to and indeed identification with democracy. What changed with the decline of Athenian military power and the corresponding collapse of the citizen-soldier ideal was the ideological and practical footing on which this identification rested. In the Hellenistic period, the military masculinity of the citizen-soldier was no longer available.

Athens's emerging position as a dependent polis called for a new understanding of what it meant to be a democratic citizen and a man. It

[5] According to Morrison, the Athenian defeat in the Lamian/Hellenic War "marks the end of Athens as a sea-power in antiquity" (1987, 97). Although the defeat in 322 marks a real change in Athens's status as a military power, the decline of the citizen-soldier ideal actually began much earlier, perhaps even in the fifth century. Isocrates and Demosthenes castigate the Athenians for their unwillingness to serve as soldiers (see, e.g., Isoc. 8.44). Hunt (1998, 11–13) argues that the increased use of slaves had diminished the prestige of military service already in the fifth century. But such weakening of the citizen-soldier ideal before the Macedonians had effectively eliminated it should not lead us to underestimate the impact of that elimination. There is a vast difference between the citizens' deciding to employ mercenaries rather than serve themselves and having that decision imposed from the outside. The citizen-soldier ideal could survive and do its ideological work as long as the Athenians could choose to activate it.

[6] The Athenians killed in the Four Years' War against Cassander received a traditional state burial in 303; see Paus. 1.29.7. On the other hand, the dependence of citizen-soldiers on outside assistance is acknowledged by a dedication of elite soldiers (*epilektoi*) to Demetrius Poliorcetes in that same year (*ISE* 7). For the persistence of military values, see also the honorary decree for the ephebes fighting in the Chremonidean War (M. M. Austin 1981 #117).

[7] See Cawkwell 1996.

required a "remasculinization" or reformulation of democratic manhood.[8] The reorganization of the *ephebeia* that took place in 335/4 is perhaps the most obvious example of a strategic remasculinizing project.[9] It was only after being defeated by Philip at Chaeronea that the Athenians implemented a formal program of military training for citizens. Thereafter, at the time of registration as a citizen at age 18, every Athenian, irrespective of economic status, was required to participate in a two-year hoplite training program.[10] This attempt to legislate the citizen-soldier ideal seems to be a form of denial, an effort to ward off the realization that the citizen's military masculinity had really changed. Certain aspects of the institution, however, suggest that there was a moral component to ephebic education. Although the content of the ephebes' moral and civic education is not specified in Aristotle's description of the institution, the names used for the supervisors of ephebes—*sōphronistai* and *kosmētēs*—imply that one of their duties was to teach or inculcate *sōphrosunē* and discipline in young citizens.[11] Similarly, praise of the ephebes themselves for "orderliness and discipline" in public inscriptions attests to the moral component of this ostensibly military reform.[12]

This chapter considers the uneven process whereby the ideological footing of democratic masculinity shifted from the military to the moral domain in response to Athens's weakening military power.[13] This negotiation obviously constitutes only one portion of the much longer history of citizen identity in Athens. My aim here is not to tell that story in its entirety but rather to demonstrate comedy's participation in the processes of ideological change. My basic claim is that a conception and practice of moral manliness emerged to compensate for the decline of

[8] I borrow the term "remasculinization" from Susan Jeffords (1989), who uses to it to describe the reformulation of American masculinity after the defeat in Vietnam. For projects of remasculinization in fourth-century Athens, see Humphreys 1993, xvii.

[9] The revamping of the military associated with Lycurgus's reforms can also be seen as part of the remasculinizing project; in his posthumous grant of *sitēsis* in 307, Lycurgus is praised for stockpiling weapons on the acropolis and maintaining a fleet of 400 operational triremes (Plut. *Vit. X Orat.* 852c). For this decree, see further chapter 2.

[10] [Arist.] *A.P.* 42. On the inclusion of thetes in the reform, see Sekunda 1992; de Marcellus 1994.

[11] See Ober 2001, 203–4. Ober links the moral component of ephebic education to critical-philosophical ideas. Although I agree that the ephebic reform represents an amalgam of philosophical and civic ideas, I see this cross-fertilization as catalyzed by a generalized crisis of identity and masculinity following the Athenian defeat at Chaeronea.

[12] See, e.g., the honorary decree for the ephebes fighting in the Chremonidean War (M. M. Austin 1981, 117). The ephebic inscriptions are collected in Reinmuth (1971).

[13] There is at present no diachronic study of democratic manhood. In formulating my approach, I have consulted Winkler (1990a), Halperin (1990), R. Osborne (1997), Humphreys (1999), and Fisher (1998b). I have also drawn on S. Rose's critique (1999) of synchronic approaches to morals discourse.

the once-dominant military masculinity of democratic citizenship. "Moral manliness," as used here, refers to the roles of gender and morality in defining the manhood specific to the democratic citizen. In some cases, however, moral manliness is tethered to genealogical and racial considerations as well. For instance, democratic speakers assume that a citizen's birth credentials or inherited legacy of service to the democratic state will manifest in the citizen's adherence to shared moral norms.[14]

The reformulation of democratic manhood began in the mid–fourth century, if not earlier, when Philip II brought the previously backwater kingdom of Macedon to new prominence and power. His spectacular military successes threatened not only Athens's place in the Greek world but also threatened its self-image as the guarantor of Greek freedom. While Philip's activities prompted concern and alarm, there was no general consensus about what they meant for Athens or what Athens's response ought to be. The notorious feud between Aeschines and Demosthenes, now encapsulated in two sets of paired speeches (Aes. 2 and Dem. 19, Aes. 3 and Dem. 18), centers precisely on this Macedonian question.[15] These speeches provide an important window on domestic ideologies, on the shifts in Athenian self-definition prompted by large-scale international changes. Demosthenes and Aeschines each offer advice about how to deal with Philip by telling the Athenians who they are and how they should behave. Demosthenes consistently urges the Athenians to meet Philip with an aggressive military response. He justifies this advice—advice that was apparently unwelcome to many—by appealing to Athens's ancestral identity as a collective of citizen-soldiers and champions of Greek freedom. By contrast, Aeschines bases his arguments for peace with Philip on a conception of citizen identity rooted in the citizen's relation to himself (on his moral manliness), rather than to his ancestors. With this emphasis, Aeschines is able to explain Athens's failed military initiatives by turning Athenian attention to the enemies within, to the immoral and fraudulent citizens working against the state. At the same time, by rooting citizen identity in internal considerations (moral manliness and common blood), Aeschines offers the Athenians a face-saving way of coming to terms with Philip's hegemony in Greece.

For present purposes, Aeschines' speeches are important for the conceptions and ideas they make available in public discourse. While it is true enough that Aeschines lost out in the contest with Demosthenes, the

[14] For example, Aeschines attributes Demosthenes' *ponēria*—wickedness or immorality—to his Scythian blood (3.172). See also chapter 1, notes 45, 46.

[15] For the policy issues at stake, see Cawkwell 1969; Montgomery 1983; Sealey 1993; Harris 1994, 1995; Sawada 1996; Buckler 2000. In addition, nine of Demosthenes' deliberative speeches explicitly address the issue of how Athens ought to deal with Philip (Dem. 1–6, 8, 10, 13).

Athenians lost the war with the Macedonians. The Athenian defeat at Chaeronea and later defeat in the Lamian War made Aeschines' promotion of moral manliness newly relevant in fashioning democratic masculinity. It is precisely this agenda that surfaces in Menander's *Sikyōnioi*. After briefly reviewing the shifting terrain of democratic masculinity in the speeches of Aeschines and Demosthenes, I turn to the play, considering how comedy, at least in this case, assisted in the process of transforming democratic masculinity in the wake of the attenuation of the citizen-soldier ideal. The *Sikyōnioi* features a romantic contest between a manly and moral democratic man and an effeminate and slightly sleazy oligarchic rival. Yet it does not depict a world in which citizen-soldiers have been transmogrified into moral men. The play enacts the triumph of the moral democratic man without doing away with the military ideal. The morally upright hero is a mercenary soldier who seems to embody both the old and the new ideal, suggesting that comedy here wants to have it both ways: to retain an antiquated military masculinity within an emergent moral paradigm of democratic citizen identity.

The Macedonian Question and Athenian Civic Identity

The rise of Macedon forever changed the balance of power in the Greek world, as well as Athens's privileged place in that world. Philip's successes in frustrating Athenian policy initiatives—especially where Amphipolis was concerned—made his dominance impossible to ignore. It is precisely because Philip's activities posed a threat not only to Athenian interests but also to Athenian identity that Demosthenes devotes so much of his policy advice to reminding the Athenians of who they are and, equally important, of who Philip is. Although Demosthenes concedes that Philip is a dangerous enemy willing to endure any loss or deprivation to achieve his aim of world domination, he also reveals Philip's vulnerabilities and weaknesses. For instance, he satirizes Philip as a buffoon and braggart deluded about his own power and possibilities by his retinue of flatterers and comic poets (Dem. 2.17–20).[16] While the New Comic braggart soldier figure has its origins in Old Comedy, Demosthenes' portrait of Philip may well presage the specific comic strategy of deflating the Macedonian kingdoms by ridiculing their emissaries, that is, braggart soldiers.[17]

[16] For Demosthenes' strategic use of satire in the *First Philippic*, see Rowe 1968. According to Rowe, Demosthenes lampoons the Athenian approach to Philip, rather than Philip himself, in order to shock the Athenians into recognizing the reality of the Macedonian threat. On the question of what Philip's actual intentions toward Athens may have been, see Ellis 1976; on Philip's dealings with the Greek cities more generally, see Mitchell 1997.

[17] Demosthenes uses a similar comic strategy against Aeschines, characterizing him as an *alazōn*, a braggart figure familiar from comedy; see Harding 1994, 216; Rowe 1966.

Most significant, Demosthenes insists that Philip is a nobody, a barbarian from Macedon with no ancestral legacy (Dem. 9.16, 30–31; cf. 18.68). Demosthenes castigates the Athenians for their inconsistency, for allowing Philip to seize power when they would not allow "some slave or suppositious child" to do so (9.30–31). While Philip and the Macedonians are beneath slaves in Demosthenes' human hierarchy, the Athenians are at the very top. Demosthenes is, of course, all too aware that the Athenians of his day were not living up to their privileged pedigree or their role as defenders against the forces of barbarian oppression. He explains the discrepancy as a kind of practical lapse, a failure of the Athenians to identify with the past, rather than as reflecting degeneration or decline. Consequently, to remedy the abdication of their ancestral mandate and to reproduce Athenian military supremacy, Demosthenes puts forth a model of pragmatic political reproduction.[18] He urges the citizens to gaze at and imitate their illustrious forebears living on in tombs and trophies throughout the city (15.35).

Demosthenes, in continually exhorting the Athenians to find themselves in monuments of death, in ancestral tombs and trophies, seems to attest to the passing of the very identity he so vigorously tries to revive; certainly the Athenians were not quick to act on his advice. Moreover, Demosthenes' ultraconservative model of Athenian identity was not the only paradigm available. In 346 the Athenians accepted a peace agreement with Philip of Macedon that controversially excluded their Phocian allies. Although certain orators, notably Aeschines, seem to have reported that Philip promised to settle the war between Phocis and Thebes in a way that would suit Athens's best interests, he in fact disbanded the Phocian cities. Accordingly, Demosthenes and his associate Timarchus announced their intention to prosecute Aeschines for his allegedly treacherous and treasonous support of the peace. Aeschines successfully removed Timarchus on what amounts to a morals charge (see further below), but in 343 Demosthenes finally brought him to trial.

By 343 it was clearly no longer possible to maintain the pretense that Philip was going to act in Athens's best interests in any matter whatsoever. He was rapidly gaining control of the entire Greek world, and the Athenians were doing little to stop him. Nevertheless, Aeschines continued to proclaim the wisdom of his peace policy, apparently without a thought for the military ideals of democratic citizenship or the ideals of Greek freedom. This approach gave Demosthenes a way to soften his own harsh rhetoric in his Assembly speeches. Instead of castigating a

[18] See Dem. 9.21, 74–75; 10.73–74; 13.26–27. For the male appropriation of the processes of social reproduction in democratic Athens, see Foxhall 1998. Demosthenes subordinates the concept of biological reproduction to a form of male reproduction based on the citizen's mimetic power.

recalcitrant demos for failing to look on and become one with their martial ancestors, he blames Aeschines for advising the citizens to forget the military past and to forbid talk of ancient battles and trophies (Dem. 19.16, 307, 311). Aeschines, of course, denies making such recommendations. Whatever the truth of the matter, the important point is that for Demosthenes, Aeschines was in effect forfeiting Athens's ancestral legacy simply by promoting and defending peace with an adversary like Philip.[19]

According to Demosthenes, the only possible explanations for Aeschines' behavior were that he had been bribed or that he had made a mistake in trusting Philip in the first place. Aeschines concedes neither of these points. Remarkably, in his own defense in 343 he continues to support peace with the increasingly powerful Macedonians. This was an ideologically difficult position to maintain in a context in which democratic citizens were defined not only as soldiers but also as champions of Greek freedom. Aeschines had to ward off the perception that his toleration for Macedonian rule was inspired by cowardice, a failure of manhood, or bribery. He therefore defends his own peace policy with a twofold strategy involving an attack on Demosthenes' manhood and the promotion of a new moral manliness as the bedrock of citizen identity.[20] Ironically, Demosthenes the hawk rather than Aeschines the dove turns out to be the coward, or "womanly man."

Aeschines undermines Demosthenes' perceived ability to offer military advice by questioning his status as a man. According to Aeschines, there is virtually no transgression of manhood protocols that he fails to commit: Demosthenes is a cross-dresser, a bloodless coward, infertile, and, worst of all, a *kinaidos* (Aes. 1.131; 2.139; 3.209, 247, 160). He demands:

> πότερα γὰρ ἂν προσδοκᾷς αὐτοὺς εὔξασθαι μυρίους ὁπλίτας ὁμοίους Φίλωνι γενέσθαι, καὶ τὰ σώματα οὕτω διακειμένους καὶ τὴν ψυχὴν οὕτω σώφρονας, ἢ τρισμυρίους κιναίδους οἵους περ σύ; (2.151)

[19] The question of "imitating the ancestors" looms large in Aeschines' defense speech. At 2.63, he denies Demosthenes' charge that he persuaded the Athenians to vote for the peace by telling them to pay no attention to those speakers who spoke about the battles and trophies of the ancestors, or about helping the Greeks. At 2.74–75, he concedes that other speakers exhorted the Athenians to gaze at the propylaea, and to remember the battle of Salamis and the tombs and trophies of their forebears. Aeschines defends his own policy by reminding the Athenians not of the *successful* Persian Wars but rather of the ruinous Peloponnesian War, exhorting them to imitate the wisdom rather than the mistakes of the ancestors. Aeschines discredits war and its advocates by linking the desire for war to foreigners and fraudulent citizens, i.e., those without citizen blood (2.74–76; see also 172–77).

[20] Aeschines stresses the genealogical and racial components of good and bad citizenship in his defense speech, while in his first and third speeches he more directly moralizes the construct of democratic citizen identity.

> Which do you think they [the Athenians] would pray for—ten thousand hoplites like Philon, with bodies as well-made as his and souls so disciplined, or thirty thousand *kinaidoi* exactly like you?

This passage forms the centerpiece of J. Winkler's seminal study of democratic manhood. According to Winkler, the hoplite and the *kinaidos* personify the protocols of democratic manhood;[21] in a study of comedy, we might say they are the stock characters in the script of democratic masculinity. The hoplite *is* the citizen-soldier ideal. What exactly a *kinaidos* "is," however, is much less clear. Associated with love between men, the *kinaidos* was considered deviant, lewd, and lecherous. Rather than seeking a one-word equivalent, Winkler suggests that *kinaidos* is best understood as a relational term: "The heft and weight of a problematic term like *kinaidos* cannot be estimated in isolation; it has to be measured within the system of cultural images used in public discussions about the proper behavior of citizen soldiers."[22]

According to this analysis, the *kinaidos* inhabits one pole of a structural opposition, the negative against which the norm—the manly and self-controlled hoplite—was defined. Yet despite its apparent importance in constituting democratic manhood, the hoplite–*kinaidos* polarity remains a vividly expressed but infrequently deployed collocation in the extant sources, as Winkler acknowledges. In fact, the passage cited above is the sole example in which the *kinaidos* appears as the antitype of the citizen-soldier. Winkler explains this silence by likening the norms of democratic manhood to training wheels on a bicycle—that is, to props felt only when a man begins to lose his balance.[23]

If the poles of democratic manhood had the status of shared cultural knowledge, conceptions so deeply ingrained that they could go without saying, then their sudden appearance in Aeschines' defense speech is all the more remarkable. That the only time the word *kinaidos* surfaces in extant Attic oratory is in his abuse of Demosthenes seems to have some historical significance. Although one might have expected Aeschines to apply it to Timarchus—the target of his first speech, who is characterized as a dissolute sex addict—he in fact reserves this special term of abuse for Demosthenes (Aes. 1.131, 181; 2.88, 99, 151). I would argue that Aeschines takes the unusual step of making explicit the usually implicit norms of democratic manhood precisely because he does not want to be perceived as departing from them in his own actions and advice.

[21] Winkler 1990a, 45.

[22] Winkler 1990a, 47. The *kinaidos* is at the center of modern debates concerning the history of sexuality; see Richlin 1993; Sissa 1999; Winkler 1990a; Gleason 1990; Halperin 1990, 2002.

[23] Winkler 1990a, 46.

He covers over the novelty of his political position, which looked perilously like acquiescence to Macedonian rule, by systematically impugning the manhood of his warmongering opponent. In this way, he neutralizes the perception that either his policies or Philip's power have "unmanned" the Athenians by directing the jurors' attention to the womanly and cowardly political leader in their midst. Thus the passage that most strongly supports Winkler's synchronic structuralist study also points to diachronic change in the traditional understanding.

By summoning the conventional norms of democratic manhood to undermine Demosthenes and his too conventional advice, Aeschines clears a space in which to remodel the materials of democratic manhood to accommodate his own political policies as well as Athens's waning military power. This reformulation can be detected even in Aeschines' ostensibly traditional construction of the hoplite. Aeschines' model hoplite is well conditioned in body and, equally important, continent and controlled (*sōphrōn*) in soul. While the idea of hoplite self-control may have been long-standing, the vocabulary in which Aeschines couches it is not. In contrast to other democratic speakers, Aeschines valorizes the soldier's state of soul (2.151). In so doing, he offers a conception of civic manhood not dependent on mastering others on the battlefield. For Aeschines, internal mastery of the self is as important as mastering others (see also 1.41–42, 189).

Aeschines also buttresses his own masculinity by militarizing and athleticizing his role as a democratic speaker.[24] He describes himself and similarly minded policy advisors as co-competitors in the struggle for peace (2.183). With this strategy, he distracts attention from the nonmilitary nature of his own policy advice. At the same time, his speeches contain a reformulation of democratic masculinity along moral lines. Before turning to his most explicit moralization of democratic manhood and citizen identity, I want to clarify what I mean by "moralization" and the idea of moral manliness. A moral component was long associated with hoplite ethics, since the success of the phalanx depended on the self-

[24] There has been some debate on the political salience of Aeschines' use of athletic metaphors. Ober states, "Aeschines reinforces his pretensions to aristocratic culture by frequently employing athletic metaphors in his speeches. Apparently he hoped to be perceived as the sort of man who spent a good deal of time in the gymnasia and so naturally used athletic turns of phrase" (1989, 283). Lane Fox, however, claims that "athletic metaphors are not unduly prominent in Aeschines . . . , nor always applied to the orator himself" (1994, 138–39). Finally, Golden (2000, 170) refutes Lane Fox, showing that Aeschines does in fact use athletic metaphors with particular frequency. I see this strategy as tied to Aeschines' need to ward off the perception that his peace policy in any way stemmed from a failure of manhood. On the question of whether the gymnasium was in fact "aristocratic" or had been democratized by the fourth century, see Fisher 1998a (democratized and a source of social mobility), and Golden 2000, 171–72 (skeptical).

discipline of every individual soldier. But in Aeschines' constructions of democratic manhood, the locus of relevant moral concern is shifted into the terrain of sex and gender—exactly as it is in Menander's *Sikyōnioi*.

In Aeschines' speeches, a conception of individual self-mastery assumes a new priority as a defining axis of democratic manhood. Although my treatment of this rerouting of the coordinates of democratic masculinity is indebted to Foucauldian techniques of cultural analysis, my focus and conclusions differ from those offered in *The Use of Pleasure*, volume 2 of *The History of Sexuality*. For Foucault, the moral problem of Athenian sex arose because of a presumed isomorphism between political and sexual relations, and because sexual relations were, in his view, constructed along a binary axis in which one participant was exclusively active and the other exclusively passive. An elaborate etiquette of sexual morality was therefore supposedly developed to keep young citizens who played the receptive role in male same-sex couplings from being stigmatized as "passive" and hence unfit for their political role. This view, however, too narrowly restricts Athenian morals discourse to the active–passive polarity.[25] In addition, Foucault defines the freedom of the Athenian citizen in terms of internal self-regulation and self-mastery with respect to the pleasures. Yet he bases this definition not on civic discourse but on the philosophical and prescriptive texts offered by writers who were in some way responding to and critiquing democratic mores, not dispassionately describing or reporting them.[26] By treating the philosophical texts as paradigmatic, Foucault not only elides the productive encounter between philosophical and civic discourses, but he also covers over the diachronic process by which a morals discourse entered into the construction of democratic civic identity.

Aeschines grounds democratic manhood in the citizen's ability to mas-

[25] Foucault (1985, 85), relying on Dover's seminal study of Greek homosexuality, states that "for the Greeks, the opposition between activity and passivity was essential, pervading the domain of sexual behaviors and that of moral attitudes as well." For criticisms and refinements of this specific aspect of Foucault's view, see Poster 1986; Halperin 1990; Winkler 1990a; D. Cohen 1991a, 171–73; Golden 1991; Thorton 1991; Davidson 1997; Sissa 1999. Cf. Foxhall 1998, on Foucault's neglect of gender dynamics; Hubbard 1998, on the symmetry of modern and ancient constructions of sexuality as an identity; and Wohl 1999, for a combined Foucauldian and psychoanalytic approach to the "eros" of Alcibiades.

[26] Foucault 1985, 78–98. J. Winkler (1990a, 50) also concludes that an ethics of self-mastery was a staple of democratic and popular morality because characters in the Platonic dialogues claim that expressions like "being stronger than oneself" (*kreittōn heautou*) and "weaker than oneself" (*hēttōn heautou*) were part of the ordinary language (Pl. *Prot.* 353a, c, 357e; *Rep.* 430e; but cf. *Gorgias* 491d). Yet there is a difference between everyday expressions describing being overcome by pleasure and the political freight attached to such conditions. For the responses of philosophical and critical writers to democratic culture, see Ober 1998; Johnstone 1994 (on Xenophon). On Xenophon's project of justifying elite superiority on the basis of individual self-mastery, see also Hunt 1998, 144–53.

ter his desires and maintain masculine gender norms, which include such seemingly simple things as dressing like a man rather than a woman. In his speech against Timarchus, Timarchus is branded as the antitype of the democratic citizen because of his enslavement to "all the things that ought not master a wellborn and free man" (Aes. 1.42; cf. 34, 190–91, 194). This speech, dating to 345, marks the entry of the vocabulary of elite moral psychology into the discourse of democratic identity (as least as far as the extant orations are concerned). Aeschines is the only orator to render *akrasia* a danger to the democratic polis, arguing that Timarchus's anticivic behavior arises from this psychological condition.[27] His appeal to *akrasia*, which can be defined as "incontinence" or in some cases as "weakness of will," to account for a citizen's deviance is unparalleled in extant Athenian oratory. Prior to the *Timarchus* speech, the only use of the term in a democratic oratorical context occurs in Demosthenes' second Olynthiac speech, where he attributes an incontinent life (*akrasian tou biou*) to Philip of Macedon, a "barbarian" (2.18). It was the philosophers, rather than the orators, who theorized the concept of *akrasia* to account for a person's susceptibility to being overcome by pleasure in spite of himself (or herself).

While Aeschines stigmatizes Timarchus as an incontinent pleasure addict, he positions Demosthenes even lower on the ladder of depravity, branding him a legacy hunter rather than a lover (1.171–72).[28] In other words, Demosthenes' *akrasia* manifests in the form of insatiable money loving rather than in the endless pursuit of pleasure. It is beyond the scope of this study to offer a comprehensive investigation of Aeschines' moralization of democratic manhood or the strategic purposes and historical complex animating this moral turn. Here, I consider only Aeschines' most explicit statement of the moral manliness of the democratic citizen because it prefigures the ideological contest enacted in Menander's *Sikyōnioi*.

The Moral Manliness of the Democratic Man

In contrast to other defendants seeking to avoid a conviction, Aeschines does not enumerate his liturgical donations or acts of civic generosity to

[27] For *akrasia*, see Aes. 1.95, 141–42, 160. More commonly, however, Aeschines cloaks philosophical concepts in democratic language. Rather than harping on the problem of *akrasia*, and thus perhaps attracting attention to the source of his ideas, Aeschines remodels the democratic concept of hubris as an outrage or status harm perpetrated by others. In Aeschines' first speech, hubris designates a self-inflicted status injury arising from the citizen's inability to master his desires, i.e., from *akrasia* (see Aes. 1.29, 55, 108, 116, 185). On Aeschines' unusual use of the term hubris, see Dover 1989, 36–39; cf. Fisher 1992, 109–10.

[28] See Dover 1989, 46–47.

the jurors-judges. This is not to say that he allows the opportunity to invoke the jurors' *kharis* to pass by. Rather, he reminds the jurors that by winning a conviction against Timarchus, he provided the youth of the city with an exhortation to *sōphrosunē* (2.180–81). Whether or not the jurors were convinced by his posturing as a purveyor of moral guidance, they did acquit Aeschines in the trial of 343. His next recorded foray into democratic politics does not take place until 336, when he decided to prosecute Ctesiphon, the proposer of the honorary crown for Demosthenes in recognition of his efforts to defend the state after Chaeronea. Aeschines argued that it was an outrage that the coward whose policies led to the disaster should be rewarded. When the case finally came to trial in 330, he used the occasion to attack Demosthenes' entire political career. As one might expect, he persists in his tack of undermining Demosthenes' manhood and foreign descent. After all, the strategy worked in his own defense in 343. For instance, in the aftermath of Philip's assassination in 336 Demosthenes allegedly predicted that his son Alexander would not dare to venture out of Macedon. By 330 Alexander had already proven himself by, inter alia, conquering the Persian Empire. Aeschines explains this prediction as Demosthenes' projection of his own "bloodless" cowardice onto Alexander (3.160–61).

Yet in 330 it was also clear that Demosthenes' warnings about Philip's grandiose ambitions were well-founded. Moreover, Alexander's brutal destruction of Thebes in 335 had dispelled any illusions the Athenians might have harbored about regaining their freedom upon Philip's death. Aeschines thus faced the delicate task of demonstrating the ultimate folly of Demosthenes' pro-war policies—policies that in hindsight appeared startlingly prescient—while at the same time salvaging a conception of democratic manhood. This latter point was crucial because Demosthenes planned to discredit him as an oligarch for his pro-Macedonian leanings (3.207).

In order to counter Demosthenes' allegations, Aeschines contrasts his own seemingly authoritative definition of the *dēmotikos*, or democratic man, with that of the *oligarkhikos*—oligarchic man (3.168–75). In so doing, he implicitly denies Demosthenes' attempt to correlate internal political divisions between oligarchs and democrats with pro- and anti-Macedonian attitudes, respectively. Instead, he links democratic political identity to the citizen's moral psychology and bloodline. In this way, he reorients the conventional contrast between oligarchs and democrats along the lines of genealogy and race (Athenian blood and ancestry), gender (adherence to manhood protocols), and morality (adherence to sexual and ethical norms, etc.). According to Aeschines, the democratic man must have five principal attributes. First, he must be of free birth from a native Athenian man and woman (3.169). Like other Attic orators, Aeschines assumes that democratic sentiment and loyalty are hereditary

(3.171–72).[29] Second, Aeschines also emphasizes the genealogical component of democratic identity. The democratic citizen must have a proper ancestral legacy—forebears who either served the democracy well or, at any rate, did not harm it.[30]

Third, Aeschines insists that the democratic citizen must be *metrios* and *sōphrōn*. In many ways, this emphasis is traditional. The good citizen was long idealized as a *metrios* (middling man), "defined through his everyday actions—providing well for his family and community, having a strong sense of shame, and above all keeping his appetites under control."[31] But only in Aeschines' speeches is the term *metrios* specifically employed to mean "keeping one's appetites under control." Finally, the fourth and fifth attributes of the democratic man, according to Aeschines, are good judgment, which includes an ability to speak, and a manly soul (3.170). Needless to say, he finds none of these practical or inherited traits in the "oligarchic" Demosthenes, who is painted as licentious, cowardly, foreign, disloyal, and of course antidemocratic (3.172–74). By contrast, according to Aeschines, the true democratic man (*dēmotikos*) is by definition *sōphrōn* (3.168). He renders democratic political identity a *bios*, a way of life whose expression is not limited to political institutions and contexts. What is conspicuous by its absence from Aeschines' account is "economic class," the axis along which democrats and oligarchs were conventionally defined. While gender, genealogy, and morality may have long been elements of citizen identity, in Aeschines' speeches they become the linchpins of democratic ideology, presaging the distinctions between oligarchs and democrats that we find in Menander's *Sikyōnioi*.

Although Aeschines privileges an interiorized source of democratic identity, he does not do away with the military masculinity of citizenship. The good citizen must have a brave or manly soul (*andreion . . . tēn psukhēn*), to ensure that he not desert the demos in a time of danger (3.170). By emphasizing the importance of manhood in the soul, Aeschines can defend his own peace policy without seeming to depart from the military masculinity that traditionally underpinned democratic citizenship. At the same time, he reinforces his own civic masculinity by depicting Demosthenes as afflicted with an innate cowardice (3.175–76). The strategy of placing blame on an individual, rather than on his policy advice or on the actions of the demos, enables Aeschines to fend off any questioning of his own advice or of Athenian military setbacks. In the immediate circumstances, the rhetorical ploy did not solve Aeschines'

[29] Cf. Aes. 2.78, 93, 172–77; And. 4.22–23; chapter 1 above.

[30] For democratic genealogy, see Aes. 3.169; see also Plut. *Mor.* 852a on Lycurgus.

[31] Morris 1996, 22; cf. Foucault 1985, 63–77; Winkler 1990a, 48–50.

problem: he failed to get even one-fifth of the votes and was thus forced to retire from democratic politics. Nevertheless, the vision of democratic identity he offers anticipates and perhaps provides a template for the ideological restructuring urgently needed after Athens's catastrophic defeat in the Lamian War and the city's loss of domestic as well as foreign autonomy.

Menander's *Sikyōnioi*: The Male Recognition Plot

The debate between Aeschines and Demosthenes is part of the ideological negotiations through which the Athenians came to terms with the eclipse of their military power and the attendant decline of the citizen-soldier ideal while maintaining a strong and seemingly traditional conception of citizen identity. Ultimately, that Aeschines lost out in the contest with Demosthenes is immaterial; what is important is what he was able to say, the arguments and conceptualizations he was able to make available in public discourse. His attempt to promulgate a new domestic civic ideology based on a morals discourse must be taken together with his foreign policy advice, his discrediting of war and imperialism, and his acquiescence to Philip's power in Greece. By the time of Menander's extant plays and fragments, many of the changes the orators were responding to (and provoking) were more or less complete. That is, the passing of the citizen-soldier ideal, and the new conception of civic identity it propelled, seems to have already occurred. Although the loss of the citizen-soldier ideal may be registered in the tale of Moschion's arrested maturation in the *Samia* and in Chaereas's activities as an ephebe rapist in the *Eunuch*, it is imperceptible on the narrative level. Comic characters never lament or even acknowledge that they have lost the opportunity to become men by fighting on behalf of the polis.[32] Instead, comic protagonists enjoy an easy transition to manhood by making their marriages, as if this were always the norm rather than a new necessity brought about by the rise of Macedonian military kingdoms.

Menander's *Sikyōnioi*, however, constitutes a remarkable exception to this general rule. The fourth act contains a contest between the protagonist, Stratophanes, and his rival, Moschion, to win the heroine, Philoumene. This structure produces especially strong ideological effects because it counterpoises the qualities and characteristics of the hero that lead to romantic victory with those of the romantic loser.[33] In this case, the play contrasts the marriage-minded hero with a rival bent on possess-

[32] For the forms of masculinity displayed by New Comic characters, see Pierce 1998.

[33] For the importance of the *Sikyōnioi* in attesting the political dimension of Menander's comedy, see Garzya 1969; Blanchard 1983, 366 with n. 147.

ing a freeborn girl as a slave and a mistress. One of the unusual features of this romantic contest is how directly it correlates the political behavior of the romantic contestants with their sexual dispositions. Stratophanes is characterized as democratic and inclined toward monogamy, while Moschion is implicitly characterized as oligarchic and interested in *moikheia*—nonmarital sexual activity with a female citizen. With this emphasis, the play translates the hoplite–*kinaidos* polarity into comedy's romantic script, recasting the hoplite as a manly and monogamous soldier and the *kinaidos* as an effeminate seducer (*moikhos*); or, we might say that it fits Aeschines' democratic and oligarchic character types into a comic narrative frame. But there is an important catch and complication. Although the hero is a soldier, he is not a citizen-soldier; rather, he is a Sikyonian mercenary. Leaving aside the problem posed by Stratophanes' presumed Sikyonian identity for a moment, his being a democratically oriented mercenary might be taken to represent an adaptation of Hellenistic mercenary service to compensate for the lost field of civic military masculinity. The significance of the hero's status as a mercenary has more to do, however, with the story of democratic return that unfolds in tandem with the romantic plot.

The story of the return of a manly democratic soldier and his romantic triumph over an oligarchic rival symbolizes comedy's adaptation of the political plot of democratic restoration after a period of exile, as I discuss in more detail below. Not only does the soldier turn out to be a lost citizen, but he is also discovered to be the brother of his oligarchic rival. In this way, comedy uses kinship to mend internal political wounds, the division between democrats and oligarchs encouraged and intensified by the Macedonian interventions. Although the original performance date of the *Sikyōnioi* is unknown, it has sometimes been linked to a period of democratic restoration, either 318 or 307 and following.[34] An argument for the earlier date might be the favorable depiction of the "Sikyonian" mercenary captain in this play. In 318 the democracy restored an honorary decree granting citizenship and other honors to Euphron of Sikyon that had been revoked by the oligarchs sometime during the first Macedonian oligarchy.[35] Euphron was honored for his efforts in the Lamian War and, in particular, for making Sikyon the first Athenian ally in the Peloponnese. That the relief sculpture adorning the inscription is exceptionally ornate and dramatic—it depicts Euphron arriving in haste, pre-

[34] For 318 as the date, see Guida 1974, 225. Webster remarks that the "emphasis on the political activity of the poor citizen would suit very well the atmosphere of the restored democracy when Demetrius the Besieger had expelled the tyrant Demetrius of Phaleron in 307" (1973, 291).

[35] IG II^2 448. On Sikyonian–Athenian relations and the date of the play, see Belardinelli 1994, 69–71, with references cited.

sumably to fight on behalf of Greek freedom—seems to indicate the high value the Athenians placed on the Sikyonian alliance and Euphron's efforts.[36]

But the narrative of the play itself is more evocative of the democratic fervor following the expulsion of Demetrius of Phaleron, for the hero is not the only lost citizen in this comedy. The premise of the play is that the heroine, Philoumene, was abducted from Attica as a child and has returned ten years later upon reaching a marriageable age. The coincidence between the return of democracy in 307, after its ten-year "exile," and the return of the lost citizen virgin after roughly the same length of time seems to offer an allegory linking democratic restoration to renewed fertility, or at any rate to legitimate civic reproduction. If the play is offering a romantic allegory of the political plot of democratic exile and return, it is an allegory promulgated by the democracy itself. The Athenians likened the return of democracy after a period of repression to the myth of Demeter and Kore and their Mysteries at Eleusis. While serving as *agōnothetēs* in 284/3 the comic poet Philippides, who had attacked Stratocles for enabling Demetrius Poliorcetes' irregular initiation into the Mysteries, established a new contest for Demeter and Kore as a memorial of democratic freedom.[37] Thus, it seems no accident that the climax of the romantic plot in the *Sikyōnioi* takes place before Demeter's temple at Eleusis and culminates with the Kore-heroine being entrusted to the priestess (see further below).

While the play evokes a democratic return, it also depicts the effeminizing effects that oligarchy was perceived to have on the city and its citizens. Unquestionably a historical tradition links Demetrius of Phaleron with a deficit of manliness and with policies leading to the unmanning of the city (see chapter 2). Given the dearth of evidence, the dating of the *Sikyōnioi* to a period of democratic restoration must remain uncertain, and it is not my aim in this chapter to provide an argument for the play's original performance date. Rather, I focus on the comedy's narrative and themes as creating a specific context of democratic return and political reconciliation—internal to the play—that evokes actual democratic restorations periodically occurring from 403 through the mid–third century.

Judging from the preserved portions of the prologue, and substantial parts of the fourth and fifth acts, the *Sikyōnioi* was one of Menander's

[36] On the relief and its unusual anecdotal nature, see Lawton 1995, 108.

[37] IG II^2 657 lines 42–45; *eleutherias* in line 45 is a restoration. Demetrius Poliorcetes' interest in the Mysteries and Demeter may also be related to his perceived role as a democratic liberator. See further the ithyphallic hymn the Athenians composed for the Eleusinian Mysteries honoring Demetrius and asking for his assistance, Athen. 253d–f; Duris *FGrH* 76 F 13, with Habicht 1956, 232–33; Mikalson 1998, 94–98.

more melodramatic comedies.[38] The adventures of Philoumene might be seen as a Hellenistic equivalent to the *Perils of Pauline* as she and her servant struggle to preserve her chastity from no fewer than three suitors (Stratophanes, Moschion, and a Boeotian creditor).[39] Her adventures begin at the age of four, when she and her faithful servant Dromon are kidnapped by pirates and sold in a slave market in Caria. A Sikyonian identified as a noble and wealthy captain, either Stratophanes himself or his foster father, purchases them (13–15). From a fragment of the play that probably derives from the prologue, we learn that Stratophanes took pains to raise Philoumene in way befitting a freeborn girl (fr. 1 Sandbach).[40]

The action begins about ten years later, when Philoumene has reached a marriageable age. For reasons that are unclear in the text as we have it, she and Dromon ran away from Stratophanes' home, evidently while he was away on a mercenary campaign, and sought refuge at the temple of Demeter in Eleusis. She seems to have been afraid that her guardian (*kurios*) intended to do her some harm.[41] The question is whether this guardian was Stratophanes himself or the Boeotian creditor, seeking to claim his property to recover a debt incurred by his presumed Sikyonian father.[42] Since Stratophanes is the hero, it is unlikely that he was actually going to do anything that would disqualify him from his narrative position. Philoumene's decision to flee, if based on a fear of Stratophanes rather than the creditor, may simply reflect her recognition that to remain in his household upon reaching sexual maturity would permanently compromise her perceived respectability and civic standing.

Although Stratophanes is in love with Philoumene, once she declares herself to the Eleusinian populace to be an Athenian citizen he cannot bring her back to his household to live as his ward, his slave, or his mistress. The only way he can have access to her is to marry her; however, he needs Athenian citizen status to do so. Accordingly, the comic

[38] Arnott (1979–2000, 3:198) notes that only about 180 lines out of an estimated 1,000 have been recovered. For reconstructions of the plot, see Kassel 1965; Lloyd-Jones 1990; Gomme and Sandbach 1973, 634–36; Belardinelli 1994, 50–53; Arnott 1997a, b, c; and Jacques 2000.

[39] It is clear that there are multiple men seeking Philoumene from Stratophanes' request to the Assembly to protect the girl from his rivals (*Sik.* 255).

[40] Based on this fragment, commentators speculate that Stratophanes originally bought Philoumene as a maid for his mistress Malthake but then fell in love with Philoumene (or at any rate decided to respect her status) and raised her appropriately. See Gomme and Sandbach 1973, 671; Henry 1985, 89; Belardinelli 1994, 234–37.

[41] The line containing Dromon's explanation to the Eleusinian Assembly as to why Philoumene is seeking refuge is damaged: ὁ κύριος κακὸν ποήσηι κ[. . . . . . . (*Sik.* 194).

[42] Gomme and Sandbach (1973, 653 ad 193–95) suppose that the identity of the guardian is Stratophanes himself because at 241, after making the Eleusinian Assembly Philoumene's collective guardian, Stratophanes declares that she has nothing to fear from him.

problem in this play centers on removing the status barrier to the "right" marriage. The narrative tells the story of how Stratophanes, a presumed Sikyonian mercenary captain, becomes an Athenian citizen—or more precisely, it tells the story of how he is finally recognized for being who he has been all along. This status transformation is made possible when, at the end of the third act, Stratophanes receives a letter and tokens sent by his "mother" just before her death. The letter reveals to Stratophanes that he was not really her child, and indeed not Sikyonian at all but Athenian. She disclosed this information in order to release him from his father's obligation to the menacing Boeotian creditor. Armed with this new information, he and his entourage, including the parasite Theron, rush to the temple at Eleusis where an assembly has convened to hear Philoumene's claims.

At this juncture, we should note that the *Sikyōnioi* contains a second romantic plot involving the parasite Theron; its details are uncertain in the play's current state of preservation. Like other comic parasites, Theron plots and schemes to further the romantic interests of his patron. Significantly, however, his efforts on Stratophanes' behalf are motivated not by a desire for food (the mark of the lower nature of the comic parasite) but rather by a desire for marriage (the mark of the citizen subject in comedy). Theron is in love with Malthake, the *hetaira* attached to Stratophanes' household who may have been his former mistress. For reasons that remain obscure, Theron's ability to marry Malthake depends on Stratophanes' recognition as an Athenian citizen and his marriage to Philoumene (144–45). The play concludes with Theron trying to win Malthake's consent to the marriage and probably succeeding (411–20).[43] That this marriage was an anomaly or stage curiosity is attested by Pollux's report that Theron had to don a white costume for his marriage in place of the usual black or gray garb that marks the parasite character.[44] Yet, although the parasite's romance represents a relaxation of the comic convention limiting matrimonial and romantic success to citizens, it actually has a conservative rather than liberatory effect: the marriage of Theron and Malthake would have been akin to a metic marriage, not the union of citizens. The double romance plot in the *Sikyōnioi* thus reproduces the democratic citizen body as well as a body of status-deficient insiders against whom the citizen body could be defined. This reconstitution and perpetuation of the internal boundaries between citizens and noncitizens is part of the deeply conservative ethos of this intensely nationalistic play that, I will argue in conclusion, links democratic return to a reinstallation of traditional ideologies of gender and status.

[43] For a reconstruction of this scene, see Arnott 1997a, 100–101; Quincey 1966.

[44] Fr. 9 Sandbach; see also Henry 1985, 90–91.

Ideology and Intertextuality

The continuous narrative of the play begins in the fourth act with a messenger speech that reports the political romantic contest between Stratophanes and Moschion to win Philoumene. The speech is introduced immediately following a hostile exchange between an oligarchic man, probably named Smikrines, and an unidentified democratic man.[45] The preserved portion of the scene begins with Smikrines' comment:

ὄχλος εἶ φλυάρου μεστός, ὦ πόνηρε σύ,
δίκαια τὸν κλάοντα προσδοκῶν λέγειν
καὶ τὸν δεόμενον· τοῦ δὲ μηδὲ ἓν ποεῖν
ὑγιὲς σχεδὸν ταῦτ' ἔστι νῦν τεκμήριον·
οὐ κρίνεθ' ἀλήθεια τοῦτον τὸν τρόπον,
ἀλλ' ἐν ὀλίγωι πολλῶι γε μᾶ[λλον συνεδρίωι.

(150–55)[46]

You're really one of the mob, really full of it, wretch,
if you expect a man who weeps to speak
with justice or honesty. Now, these things are a sign that
someone is not being honest.
You won't judge the truth in this way;
rather it's much better to use a small [committee.]

The speaker responds "You're a wicked oligarch, Smikrines" (ὀλιγαρχικός γ' εἶ καὶ πονηρός, Σμ[ικρίνη, 156), angrily turning Smikrines' ethical condemnation back on Smikrines himself. What is at stake between Smikrines and the speaker is not only the meaning of "wickedness" (*ponēria*), but also and more centrally the ethical valence of democratic speech practices. Smikrines insists that mass audiences are persuaded by a speaker's emotional pleas and other theatrics rather than by the truth content of their words. Just as Smikrines is about to leave the stage, grumbling about shutting up his democratic interlocutor like a metic (and thus again revealing his unabashed elitism), an eyewitness to an assembly at Eleusis arrives—as it happens, another ardent democrat (167–68, 169). Identifying himself as Eleusinios, named after Demeter's deme,

[45] Barigazzi (1965b, 18) argues that the *dēmotēs* and the messenger are one and the same person because each character expresses strong democratic allegiances; cf. Webster 1974, 185. Kassel's argument (1965) that Smikrines' interlocutor exits the stage at 167 and is replaced by the messenger, Eleusinios, is now widely accepted. For the messenger's name, see Arnott 1997c, 29 ad 187–188; Kassel 1965, 9. On the name Smikrines, see Belardinelli 1994, 150–51 ad 156.

[46] Trans. adapted from Arnott.

the messenger can be seen as an embodiment of the deme itself (187–88).

The most commented-on feature of the ensuing scene is its strong recollections (both citational and situational) of the trial scene in Euripides' *Orestes*, also reported in a messenger speech.[47] In each case, a messenger describes a "trial" held to determine the fate of a man and a woman. In the *Orestes*, the Assembly votes to condemn the sibling matricides, Orestes and Electra; in the *Sikyōnioi*, the Assembly grants refuge to Philoumene and allows Stratophanes to secure his status in order to arrange his marriage with her. Thus, the recollections of the *Orestes* operate, in part, to underscore that comedy is the place where things work out. In the *Sikyōnioi*, just as in the *Samia*, tragic evocations serve as foils or false leads that illuminate the true meaning of the comic situation.[48]

The *Orestes* was produced in Athens in 408, during a time of internal conflict between democrats and oligarchs that was exacerbated by the ongoing war with Sparta. In this respect, the historical context of the tragedy recalls the internal sociopolitical context that the *Sikyōnioi* creates. As the conflict between Smikrines and the unidentified democratic man shows, the play portrays an internal political schism between oligarchs and democrats. In each play, the speakers in the embedded trial represent divergent political constituencies. In the *Orestes*, a manly farmer (literally, *autourgos*) is praised as a hardworking and moral member of the class that saves the state but is seldom seen in town; he is contrasted with a shameless and corrupt demagogue. Although the farmer argues in good democratic jurisprudential fashion that Orestes should be acquitted because by murdering the adulterous Clytemnestra he set a precedent that would discourage other women from similar transgressions, the unruly demagogue wins out.[49] In Euripidean tragedy, the farmer often stands for the middle class: his economic status, self-sufficient but not wealthy, aligns him with democrats while his general avoidance of politics and litigation appeals to the oligarchic program.[50]

In the *Sikyōnioi*, Eleusinios identifies himself with this Euripidean character by parroting his description. Where the farmer is introduced as

[47] *Sik*. 176–77, cf. *Or*. 866–67; *Sik*. 182, cf. *Or*. 920; *Sik*. 188, cf. *Or*. 871. On the *Orestes* intertext, see Katsouris 1975, 29–54; Arnott 1986, 1–10; Goldberg 1993, 328–39; Belardinelli 1994, 54–56. On comedy's use of tragedy generally, see chapter 5, note 52.

[48] Goldberg (1993) also argues that the importance of the intertext is contrastive, concluding that the inability of Euripides' human characters to solve the problem of matricide without divine intervention emphasizes the success of Menander's ordinary comic characters in dealing with questions of citizen status in the Assembly.

[49] Connor 1992, 189 and n. 79.

[50] For the character of the *autourgos* in Euripides' *Suppliant Women*, *Electra*, and *Orestes*, see Carter 1986, 88–92.

an "*autourgos*, a member of the only class who saves the state" (αὐτο-υργός, οἵπερ καὶ μόνοι σῴζουσι γῆν, *Or*. 920), Eleusinios calls himself a "democrat, a member of the only class who saves the state" (δημο]τικός, οἵπερ καὶ μόνοι σῴζουσι γῆν, *Sik*. 182).[51] This revision of the tragic script calls attention to Eleusinios's unadulterated democratic disposition and his general difference from the Euripidean *autourgos*. Although the recollection of the tragic *autourgos* may have initially lulled the oligarchic Smikrines, Eleusinios quickly shows that unlike the *autourgos*, he is an oligarch's worst nightmare, always involved in politics and other people's troubles.

Moschion's Revealing Complexion

Perhaps the most significant difference between Eleusinios and his tragic predecessor is his narrative position. Rather than being cast as a manly but ultimately impotent political speaker, Eleusinios is the messenger. The democratic character's control of the narrative both sets the stage for the *demotic* control of public speech in the Assembly and emphasizes that the democratic perspective is ultimately the only one that the play allows. In his version of the story, Eleusinios directly links Philoumene's appearance at the temple with the spontaneous eruption of democratic politics: the demos was called into being (190–91). This depiction of democratic process as unconstrained and irrepressible evokes the "transgressive" political energy associated with the renewal of democracy after a period of repression. At any rate, the democratic restorations after the oligarchies of the late fifth century, and after Antipater's oligarchy in 318, are characterized by similar expansions of political space outside the traditionally marked institutional boundaries.[52]

Eleusionios begins the narrative by relating what Philoumene's servant Dromon explained to the *demos*. Although the beginning of the account is missing, when the text resumes he mentions a menacing guardian (*kurios*) and declares himself a suppliant before the Assembly along with the girl. The *demos* immediately accepts their claims and responds in perfect unison with the shout, "the girl is a citizen (*politis*)" (197). After the initial uproar and confusion following the announcement of Philoumene's citizen status dies down, a young man, Moschion, approaches

[51] For the supplement in 182, see Gomme and Sandbach 1973, 651 ad 182. On Eleusinios's democratic disposition, see especially Garzya 1969, 481–84.

[52] See Thuc. 8.93; Lys. 13.32; Plut. *Phoc*. 23.2. For democracy's general tendency to overflow institutional parameters, see Wolin 1996.

Dromon to see about getting the girl without recourse to the political process. Eleusinios reports the incident as follows:

σιωπῆς γενομένης προσίσταται
μειράκιον ἐγγὺς τῶι θεράποντι λευκόχρων
ὑπόλειον ἀγένειόν τι καὶ μικρὸν λαλεῖν
ἐβούλετ᾽· οὐκ εἰάσαμεν. "μεῖζον λέγε"
εὐθύς τις ἀνεβόησε καὶ "τί βούλεται;
τίς ἐστι; τί λέγεις;"

(199–204)

When things quieted down,
a young man, white-skinned, smooth, and beardless,
went up to the servant and tried to say something in secret;
but we didn't allow it. "Speak up,"
someone shouted at once, and another "What does he want?
Who is he? What are you saying"?

Rather than speaking to the Assembly about the girl, Moschion simply tries to take her for himself, subverting the Assembly's authority and the sexual ideology of Athenian citizenship. Since Moschion is Smikrines' son, as we later learn, his disdain for democratic speech and political institutions is not so surprising. Yet, though he commits an offense against the protocols of democratic politics, Eleusinios emphasizes instead his transgression of the gender norms of democratic manhood; in fact, he deploys a strategy to discredit the rival lover remarkably similar to Aeschines' tactic against his political rivals. He describes Moschion as "white-skinned," "smooth," and "beardless" (200–201; cf. 264), signs of political and gender deviancy. In Athenian drama, and in Greek thought generally, one of the key markers of gender difference is skin color: women are white-skinned or pale, while men are supposed to have a ruddy or suntanned complexion.[53] Thus we learn later in the play that one of the features that makes Philoumene so attractive is precisely her white skin (399).

The gender semiotics of skin color is encoded in the system of New Comic masks. The second-century A.D. lexicographer Pollux describes ten masks worn by young men in New Comedy. In nine of the ten cases, the color of the mask is explicitly identified as red or suntanned. The exception is the mask of the "delicate" (*haplos*) youth, mask number 13. According to Pollux, the delicate youth is the "youngest of all, white—

[53] Thus, the cross-dressing women of Aristophanes' *Ecclesiazusai* must get a tan in order to pose as men. In the *Dyskolos*, one of things that convinces Knemon of Sostratos's moral probity is his sunburned and ruddy complexion.

leukos—reared in the shade, suggesting softness."[54] Characters who wear the *haplos* mask are often cast as the rival lover, their physical characteristics predicting their romantic failure.[55] In the *Sikyōnioi*, Moschion's white skin and delicate mask designates him as the loser in advance. In addition, the emphasis on the color of his skin hints at a problem of sexual continence. In the Hellenistic physiognomy attributed to Aristotle, white skin—λευκόχρων—is said to be a sign of lust (λάγνου σημεῖα).[56]

Commentators have long recognized the connection between the system of New Comic masks and physiognomy, a school of thought that judges the body, particularly the face, and the general bodily habitus as signs of a person's true nature.[57] The contemporary debate on the relationship between physiognomy and the system of New Comic masks hinges on the meaning that the masks had for the audience. While some commentators argue that the masks add crucial information to the plays, others claim that the masks did no more than designate the general social position of their bearers.[58] The *Sikyōnioi* sheds light on this controversy by providing a commentary on the social meaning of physiognomy and the mask of the *haplos* youth. Because Eleusinios must report what transpired at the Assembly to another character in the text, he is forced to make explicit physical information that might not have otherwise required verbal expression.

The messenger does not, of course, say that the Assembly did not trust Moschion because he was white-skinned. Like a good rhetorician, he allows his audience to make the connection. The Assembly refuses to listen to or to believe Moschion's attempt to cover up his behavior, because the language of his body contradicts his words. Eleusinios explains the Assembly's reaction by translating Moschion's physiognomic profile into its sociosexual meaning.

[54] For Moschion as Pollux's *haplos* youth (*Onomastikon* 4.147), see Kassel 1965, 10; Handley 1965b, 48. For the Moschion character, see further Wiles 1991, 176–77; chapter 5, note 23.

[55] Moschion in the *Samia* is probably the exception because he seems to have seduced rather than raped the heroine; see chapter 5.

[56] "Pale-skinned" (λευκόχρων) occurs only twice in Menander, both times in reference to Moschion (*Sik.* 200, 258). Kassel (1965, 10) adduces the pseudo-Aristotelian *Physiognomica* (1.31, 808b4) to elucidate its usage there; cf. Gomme and Sandbach 1973, 654. For the importance of the *Physiognomica* to the system of masking in New Comedy, see especially Wiles 1991, 85ff.

[57] On the contrast between Moschion and Stratophanes in *Sikyōnioi*, see Wiles 1991, 88–89; cf. P. G. Brown 1987; MacCary 1970, 1972. On the tradition of physiognomy more generally, see Gleason 1990; Winkler 1990a; Blondell 2002, 70–74.

[58] Arguing against MacCary, P. G. Brown states: "A character's external appearance told the audience his age, sex, status and profession: and certain stock characters were thus instantly recognizable" (1987, 182). Wiles argues that a dialectic between verbal and visual codes produces dramatic meaning (1991, 85–99, esp. 97).

καὶ κόκκινος γενόμενος ὑπανεδύετο
κοὐ] παντελῶς ἦν βδελυρός, οὐ σφόδρ' ἤρεσεν
ἡ]μῖν δέ, μοιχώδης δὲ μᾶλλον κατεφάνη.

(208–10)

And turning beet red, he withdrew a little;
he wasn't completely disgusting, but we didn't
like him much—he looked like a seducer.

Moschion is branded a *moikhos* (seducer) on the basis of his too smooth and too white skin. The very idea that it was possible to detect a *moikhos* or any type of sexual deviant on the basis of his physical characteristics was popularized by the physiognomers and rhetoricians. Because the *moikhos*'s secret activities were such a threat to the individual and the community, it became imperative to correlate what went on behind closed doors with some visible sign.[59] Thus, one handbook assures anxious readers that the *moikhos* can be identified simply by his too handsome appearance or by his wandering about at night ([Arist.] *S.E.* 167b9). Because seduction and adultery were traditionally associated with the house, with the indoors, the *moikhos* was also associated with paleness; his body was thought to take on a feminine pallor from consorting too much with women. Thus, in Plautus's *Truculentus*, another "Stratophanes," a braggart soldier in this play, denounces a dandified city rival as a pale and soft seducer (*Truc.* 609–10).

A man's pale skin does more than index a gender and sexual aberration; in some cases it also signals a "deviant" political identity. This deviance could be figured in either oligarchic or democratic terms. Elite writers describe urban democrats—the "shoemakers" in Aristophanes' *Ecclesiazusai* (383–87) and the artisans in Xenophon's *Oeconomicus* (4.3)—as pale, physically deformed, and effectively unmanned from working indoors, out of the sun.[60] The Macedonian takeovers of the late fourth century, however, affected internal divisions within the polis as well as the ideological stakes underlying those divisions. With Macedonian help, elite citizens who had been pushed out of politics or forced to subordinate themselves to the dominant democratic ideology found themselves very much in the center of things again. For many this must have been a hollow victory, if a victory at all, since the price was the city's subordination to various autocratic powers. But there is another cultural tradition linking the physiognomic profiles of the oligarch and the seducer. Like the seducer made pale by his indoor activities, the oligarch too, in some circles, was characterized by his pale skin and unmanly

[59] For this point, see Davidson 1997, 164.
[60] See also Whibley 1896, 40–43.

bodily appearance. The explanation of the causes of the constitutional devolution from oligarchy into democracy in the *Republic* elucidates this conception. Describing the corrupt form of oligarchy, Socrates relates the scorn and disdain felt by the sinewy and sunburned poor man at the sight of a wealthy, "reared in the shade" oligarch (Pl. *Rep.* 556b). Whether because they were self-indulgent and extravagant or because they had no place in the democratic polis, wealthy and oligarchically inclined citizens became associated with the house and consequently with "womanly" white skin. Oligarchs and seducers thus could be correlated by their physiognomic profiles as well as their economic status (cf. Arist. *Rhet.* 1372a23, 1391a19). This is the tradition that we find in the *Sikyōnioi*: the play evokes a physiognomic strategy figuring oligarchic identity in terms of feminine gender characteristics in order to stigmatize Athenians who embraced or acquiesced to the Macedonian-sponsored oligarchies.

An emphasis on Moschion's politically inflected gender markers surfaces again at the end of the scene when he makes a second attempt to intervene in the proceedings. The messenger refers to him as the white-skinned one (258). After Moschion protests the Assembly's decision about the girl, individual Assembly members silence him with the following abuse:

"ἆρ' οὐκ ἀποκτενεῖς τὸν ἐξυρημένον;"
"μὰ Δί', ἀλλά σ', ὅστις—" "οὐ γάρ; οὐκ ἐκ τοῦ μέσου,
λάσταυρε;"

(264–66)

"Won't somebody kill the shaven one?"
"No, rather you, whoever you are—" "Won't you get of here,
lastaure?"

In this passage, Moschion is branded as a *lastauros* rather than a *moikhos*. *Lastauros* is a rare word; the lexicographers define it as a virtual synonym for *katapugōn*, a lecherous or lewd man, the fifth-century equivalent for *kinaidos*—the term that, as I noted above, Aeschines deploys to damage Demosthenes' manhood and hence political competence.[61] Since both of these terms have been linked with male homosexuality, it may appear that the Assembly members are disparaging Moschion for two different forms of sexual deviancy: being a seducer in heterosexual en-

[61] LSJ glosses *lastauros* as an epithet for *kinaidos*. There are only two classical attestations of *lastauros*: Theopompus (*FGrH* 115 F 224; see below) and Menander's *Sikyōnioi*. According to Phrynichos, *lastauros* is a synonym for *katapugōn*; his definition is quoted in Gomme and Sandbach 1973, 658 ad 266. In Mel. *A.P.* 12, 41 *lastauros* is used to describe participants in male same-sex relations. For *kinaidos* and *katapugōn* as synonyms, see Davidson 1997, 167–83.

counters and being a *kinaidos*, a figure too attached to same-sex love. To take this discrepancy as indicating that comedy (perhaps comically) is confusing the categories of sexual degeneracy would be a mistake; sexual object choice does not seem to have been a key factor in determining Athenian identity categories.[62] What, then, made the *moikhos* and *kinaidos/lastauros* so similar that they could be used as virtual synonyms? The most probable explanation is that both comic types were associated with desires judged to be excessive and immoderate.[63] According to this view, the "heterosexual" seducer and the "homosexual" lover known as the *kinaidos* were both considered sex addicts, male versions of the modern "nymphomaniac."[64]

The *Lastauros*: An Anti-Macedonian Tradition?

While it is not so surprising that Moschion is labeled a *moikhos* and a *lastauros*, given Athenian sexual and moral proprieties, comedy's conventions of linguistic propriety make his branding as a *lastauros* remarkable. Menander's comedy is not altogether free from the obscene and "low" language associated more with Old Comedy, but in every other case such language is attributed to slaves and directed against other slaves, cooks, waiters, or women.[65] Here, exceptionally, a citizen uses an "obscenity" to demean and silence another citizen. Accordingly, there may be a historically specific reason for comedy's condemnation of Moschion as a *lastauros*.[66] Moschion is characterized as wealthy and effeminate and oligarchically inclined—that is, as someone who would have been a citizen under the Macedonian-sponsored oligarchies. It seems no accident that the only other classical attestation of the word *lastauros* comes from Theopompus's notorious description of Philip's scandalous companion court. It is worth quoting the relevant passages since they attest the association of Macedonian leadership with immorality, with gender atrocities such as shaving, and with nonreproductive sexuality—in other words, with the very sorts of transgressions that Moschion, the Athenian (pro-Macedonian?) oligarch, seems to commit.[67]

Theopompus describes Philip's companions:

[62] Winkler 1990a, 70; Foucault 1985, 85; Halperin 1990; Davidson 1997. Contra, Hubbard 1998.

[63] For this point, see Davidson 1997, 167–82, esp. 179; Sissa 1999, 152.

[64] Davidson 1997, 173–74.

[65] On linguistic characterization in Menander, see Sandbach 1970. On obscene language in Old Comedy, see Henderson 1991.

[66] *Lastauros* and *bdeluria* occur only here in Menander's extant fragments and plays.

[67] On shaving as a sign of effeminacy see, e.g., Ar. *Thesm.* 191.

> His companions had come together from many places. Some came from Macedon itself, others from Thessaly, and others from the rest of Greece. They were not chosen by merit, but if there was someone amongst the Greeks or barbarians who was lecherous (*lastauros*), disgusting (*bdeluros*), or brazen in character, nearly all of these were gathered together in Macedon and were called the companions of Philip. (Theopompus *FGrH* 115 F 224 lines 23–29 [= Athen. 166f–167c])[68]

After crediting Philip with making his companions competitors in lewdness (*bdeluria*), he continues:

> Did not some of them, although they were men, continue to be close-shaven and smooth-skinned? Did not others dare to mount each other, even though they had beards? And they would lead around two or three male prostitutes, and they provided to others an equal use of themselves. For that reason one might justly have supposed them to be not companions (*hetairoi*) but courtesans (*hetairai*) and might not have called them soldiers (*stratiōtai*) but whores (*khamaitupai*). (Theopompus *FGrH* 115 F 225a lines 32–41 = F 225b lines 32–41)[69]

By rendering Moschion a *lastauros* and ridiculing his effeminate smooth-shaven appearance, the *Sikyōnioi* seems to be adapting an anti-Macedonian tradition linking the Macedonian leadership with immorality in order to discredit Athenians perceived to be Macedonian sympathizers.[70] Certainly, the orators (save Aeschines) employ a moral discourse to differentiate Athenians and Macedonians.[71] The difference is that while Theopompus emphasizes that Philip's companions engage in an effeminizing form of homosexual practice, the *Sikyōnioi* links Moschion's masculine deficiency primarily to (attempted) nonmarital womanizing—although he is also labeled a *lastauros*. In both cases, however, the force of the critique may arise more from the results of the sex acts in question than from the acts themselves or the form of desire compelling them. In each example, Macedonians and Macedonian sympathizers are

[68] Trans. Flower 1994, 218. Theopompus *FGrH* 115 F 224 and F 225 (= 166f–167c and 260d–261a) probably originally formed one continuous passage, see Flower (1994, 105–6).

[69] See also Plb. 8.11.5–13, Athen. 260d–261a. Trans. adapted from Flower 1994, 218–19.

[70] The tradition that the "effeminizing" practice of shaving spread under Alexander may belong to this context; see Athen. 565a = Chrysippus 3.198 von Arnim 1964; see also Alexis 394 K = Athen. 565b. On Alexander's shaving, A. D. Smith states, "It was a strikingly new manner of self-presentation that contrasted both with that of his father and that of the Greeks of the city-states. . . . To be clean shaven quickly became the new mode among Alexander's officers and soldiers" (1991, 21). On the politics of Alexander's image, see also Stewart 1993.

[71] Demosthenes in particular emphasizes Philip's supposed licentiousness; see Harding 1994, 217; Shrimpton 1991, 157–80.

associated not only with practices deemed "immoral" and leading to the contravention of gender norms, but also with nonreproductive sexualities, whether homosexual or nonconjugal.[72] In other words, the most potent criticism against an enemy may been the imputation of his sterility and hence his time-limited existence, a kind of sexual counterpart to the mutability of fortune theme of Hellenistic historiography. In this context it is worth emphasizing that comedy's valorization of citizen monogamy takes on a new significance as a means of political self-fashioning when viewed against the polygamous and "woman-collecting" practices of the Macedonians.

The text problematizes Moschion's nonreproductive and immoral (from the polis's point of view) sexual behavior by drawing attention to the features of his body that signal his similarity and difference from upstanding democratic citizens and, likewise, reveal his adherence to and deviation from their communal mores and expectations. The most important precedent for this physiognomic strategy is found in democratic discourse. The corporeal construction of Moschion as a romantic loser and internal outsider echoes Aeschines' physiognomic assault on the anti-Macedonian politician Timarchus for alleged acts of serial prostitution and general profligacy.[73] Both texts racialize the sexual body, correlating deviance from communal sociosexual and political mores with putatively visible corporeal deformations. Both texts use sexual behavior as the basis on which to construct an embodied identity that marks its bearer as moral or immoral, and thus as an insider or outsider. And, in each case, the sexual serves the political. That is to say, democratic ideology is the reference point from which alleged sexual deviance is calibrated and constructed.

In his prosecution speech, Aeschines sought to prove that Timarchus was guilty of the grossest sexual improprieties and was therefore ineligible to speak and act within democratic political institutions. In making his case, he faced the difficulty familiar to rhetoricians and concerned citizens wishing to identify potential *moikhoi*: he had to link unseen sexual acts to some visible sign. In the absence of direct evidence, Aeschines

[72] An anti-Macedonian tradition linking Philip's court with promiscuous and destructive (and obviously nonreproductive) male homosexuality is probably also reflected in the story of Philip's death at the hands of his former lover Pausanias. According to Diodorus's account, Attalus, an influential member of Philip's court, got Pausanias drunk and arranged to have him sexually assaulted. When Philip failed to punish Attalus for the outrage, Pausanias reportedly conceived a deep resentment, leading him to murder Philip (Diod. 16.93–94).

[73] There was no Athenian law against prostitution per se; Aeschines uses the scrutiny of public speakers to prosecute Timarchus. According to its provisions, any man who mistreated his parents, was derelict in his military duties for the state, wasted an inheritance, or prostituted himself was forbidden from advising the people and from all forms of political participation. On the provisions of law, see Aes. 1.27–31.

summons Timarchus's guilty body as a witness, arguing, like a physiognomer, that a man's habits and moral behavior leave indelible marks on his body. To prove his point to the jurors, he draws an analogy with the case of the athlete:

> Which of you is unfamiliar with the disgusting conduct (*bdeluria*) of Timarchus? In the case of people who exercise, even if we don't attend the *gymnasia*, we can recognize them from a glance at their fit condition (*euhexias*). In the same way we recognize men who have worked as prostitutes from their shameless and impudent manner and from their general behavior even if we're not present at their activities. For the man who has shown contempt for the laws and *sōphrosunē* on the most important issues comes to be in a state of soul (*hexis tēs psukhēs*) which is plainly revealed by the disorder of his character. (1.189)[74]

The *Sikyōnioi* employs a similar maneuver to characterize Moschion as the romantic rival and loser, but its use of physiognomic profiling differs in several respects from the forensic text. While Aeschines condemns Timarchus's sexual depravity with men (and in fewer instances with women), the comic marriage plot pattern translates the moralizing strategy into its own heterosexual narrative terms. But in addition, since Aeschines is seeking a conviction, he insists that Timarchus is completely disgusting (*bdeluros*) and wholly lacking in shame.[75] Because the signs of Timarchus's depravity may have been somewhat difficult to perceive, if indeed not invisible, Aeschines makes a virtue of necessity by emphasizing the invisibility, and therefore the absence, of a crucial bodily marker of moral regularity. According to Aeschines, Timarchus's inability to blush at his misdeeds testifies to his lack of shame (1.105). In the *Sikyōnioi*, by contrast, the messenger is careful to soften his criticism of Moschion by mentioning that he is not completely "loathsome" (*bdeluros*). Although he has the pale complexion of a seducer, he is not irredeemable. Again, his body testifies for him: Moschion turns beet red when the Assembly members detect him trying to acquire Philoumene by circumventing the political process. His involuntary corporeal response to the Assembly's censure marks Moschion's acceptance of the community's values and norms. Even though he is seeking to subvert democratic sexual mores by making a freeborn girl his servant/mistress, Moschion's body displays his adherence to the very political and moral regularities he would resist.[76] Thus, as elsewhere, shame enables comedy to have it both

[74] Trans. adapted from Fisher 2001.

[75] LSJ lists "disgusting, loathsome, and blackguardly" for the adjective *bdeluros*. The term is strongly associated with the lack of shame; e.g., Aes. 1.26, 30, 46, 70, 105, 189; Theophr. *Char.* 11.2. For the use of *bdeluros* in Aes. 1, see Sissa 1999, 159–62.

[76] For the inability to blush as a sign of shamelessness, see Men. 751 K.-A. On blushing as a sign of moral conformity, see also Ter. *Ad.* 643, *An.* 873; Men. 262 K.-A. In the *Epitre-*

ways, allowing characters to violate or nearly violate civic sexual norms while ultimately reaffirming those very norms (see chapter 5).

It is vitally important that Moschion not be completely rejected as a loathsome outsider—as Timarchus ultimately is—on the basis of his physiognomic profile or improper sexual intentions. As often happens in comedy, the *Sikyōnioi* concludes with a romantic triumph and a family reunion. In this case, the oligarchic Smikrines turns out to be Stratophanes' long-lost father, while Moschion, his rival, is discovered to be his brother (280–311). In this way, a tale of family reunion serves to reconcile the oligarchic and democratic segments of society.

Stratophanes' Embodied Biography

In the messenger's report of the Assembly's actions, the depiction of Moschion's improperly gendered body and antidemocratic sexual and political behavior serves as a foil against which the body and the civic and moral competencies of the second speaker, the hero Stratophanes, are defined. The messenger does not describe the physical condition of his body or appearance except to say that he is "especially manly" (ὄ]ψει τις ἀνδρικὸς πάνυ, 215). In this way, he subtly draws a physical contrast between the effeminate Moschion and masculine Stratophanes. Rather than merely drawing the contrast in physical terms, the messenger describes Stratophanes' rhetorical performance and reports the content of his speech. In so doing, he establishes a connection between Stratophanes' masculine appearance and his political and moral disposition. Stratophanes seems to have begun by performing his emotions rather than speaking, bursting into tears at the sight of the girl and ripping at his hair.[77] This passionate emotional response authenticates his claims in advance, guaranteeing his words and inciting a desire for them. Moved by his physical distress, the Assembly members invite him to speak (223). Their request and the performance of emotion that elicits it are crucial, because as a foreigner Stratophanes could not speak except by direct invi-

---

pontes, however, Kharisios's blushing is not a sign of his conformance with the official state ideology; see further chapter 8.

[77] ὡς δ' ἐνέβλεψ' ἐγγύθεν
τὴν πα]ῖδ', ἐξαπίνης ποταμόν τινα
δακρύων ἀφίησ' ο]ὗτος, ἐμπαθῶς τε τῶν
τριχῶν ἑαυτοῦ λαμ]βάνεται βρυχώμενος.

(*Sik.* 218–21)

When he looked [at the girl]
up close, he suddenly [let flow] a river
[of tears], and clutching [his hair],
burst out passionately.

tation of the demos.[78] Unfortunately, the first eight lines of Stratophanes' speech are badly damaged, although it is clear that he claims credit for raising Philoumene (226, 237). When the text resumes, he has finished narrating the history of his involvement with the heroine and is making his recommendations to the Assembly.

πα]τρὸς
αὐτῆς, ἐμὸν δ' ὄντ' ἀποδίδωμι τῆι κόρηι·
τροφεῖ' ἀφίημ', οὐδὲν ἀξιῶ λαβεῖν.
εὑρισκέτω τὸν πατέρα καὶ τοὺς συγγενεῖς·
οὐκ ἀντιτάττομ' οὐθέν." "εὖ γ'." "ἀκούσατε
καὶ τἀμὰ δ', ἄνδρες. ὄντες αὐτοὶ κύριου
ταύτης—ἀφεῖται τοῦ φόβου γὰρ ὑπό γ' ἐμοῦ—
πρὸς τὴν ἱέρειαν θέσθε καὶ τηρησάτω
ὑμῖν ἐκείνη τὴν κόρην."

(235–43)

[This servant] belonged to her father
and is now mine, but I give him to the girl,
I renounce any return for my expense in rearing her, I make no claims of any kind.
Let her look for her father and her family,
I'll place no obstacles in her way.
"Good man!" we said.
"Then listen to my suggestion, gentlemen," he said. "You are now her
guardian; she has nothing to fear, at least from me.
Take her to the priestess and let her look
after the maiden for you."

Stratophanes first gives the servant Dromon to Philoumene and announces that he will not seek any recompense for rearing her. After establishing his generosity and goodwill in this way, he shows respect for the authority of the Assembly. He declares that the Assembly members are now Philoumene's collective guardian (*kurios*). In this way, he draws an implicit correlation between the authority (or *kuria*) of the Assembly and the authority of Athenian men over women: one implies the other. That is, sexual control seems to be symbolic of political control. By becoming the collective guardian of the girl, the deme Assembly asserts its own political authority while at the same time neutralizing the oligarchic threat posed in sexual terms by the *moikhos* in their midst.

Stratophanes' respect for the political and sexual jurisdiction of the demos meets with immediate and unanimous approval—respect that apparently wins him the right to tell his own story. Whereas the Assembly

[78] See Hansen 1991.

members promptly silenced Moschion, they spontaneously praise Stratophanes and invite him to speak.

ἀνέκραγον
"ὀρθῶς γε" πάντες, εἶτα "λέγε" πάντες πάλιν.
"Σικυώνιος τὸ πρότερον εἶναι προσεδόκων
κἀγώ· πάρεστι δ' οὑτοσί μοι νῦν φέρων
μητρὸς διαθήκας καὶ γένους γνωρίσματα·
οἶμαι δὲ καὐτός, εἴ τι τοῖς γεγραμμένοις
τούτοις τεκμαίρεσθαί με πιστεῦσαί τε δεῖ,
εἶναι πολίτης ὑμέτερος. τὴν ἐλπίδα
μήπω μ' ἀφέλησθ', ἀλλ' ἂν φανῶ τῆς παρθένου
κἀγὼ πολίτης, ἣν ἔσωισα τῶι πατρί,
ἐάσατ' αἰτῆσαί με τοῦτον καὶ λαβεῖν·
τῶν ἀντιπραττόντων δ' ἐμοὶ τῆς παρθένου
μηθεὶς γενέσθω κύριος πρὶν ἂν φανῆι
ἐκεῖνος." "ὀρθῶς καὶ δίκαι', ὀρθῶς", "ἄγε
πρὸς τὴν ἱέρειαν, ἄγε λαβών."

(244–58)

"Very proper,"
everyone shouted, "tell us more."
And he said, "I used to think I was a Sikyonian.
But this servant here has just brought me my
mother's will, and tokens of my birth.
If I can trust the evidence of these documents,
I think that I, like you, am an Athenian citizen.
Don't rob me of this hope yet.
If I can prove that I am a fellow citizen of the girl
whom I've protected for her father,
let me ask him for her hand in marriage, and make her my wife.
And don't let any of my rivals gain control of the girl
before her father appears."
"Quite right," "That's reasonable," "Certainly" came the cries.
"Come then, take her to the priestess."

Certainly this must count as one of the most unromantic marriage proposals in all of literature. At this point, Philoumene knows nothing of Stratophanes' newfound Athenian identity. In fact, she never gets the opportunity to consent to her own marriage: the men surrounding her do it for her, first the Assembly members and then her father. This is all the more striking because, as we have seen, in other plays featuring a mercenary hero, the heroine does have a say in her own matrimonial fate (see chapter 6). She exercises some volition even when her prior sexual activity with the hero makes her marriage a virtual necessity. By contrast, Philoumene is a virgin and thus not obliged to marry Stratophanes for the sake of her civic sexual respectability. Nevertheless, she is cast as a mute suppliant maiden whose romantic and reproductive fate must be determined first by democratic political process and next by her father and future husband.

Perhaps more remarkable than this strong assertion of gender difference is the characterization and fate of Stratophanes himself. The Assembly members unanimously agree to place a female citizen in safekeeping for a man who to all appearances is a foreign mercenary soldier. The apparent anomaly, the discrepancy between Stratophanes' surface identity and behavior of the Assembly, points precisely to the ideological thrust of this male recognition plot. In the female recognition plot pattern, the device acts to reinforce the norms of civic membership by emphasizing the natural recognizability of female citizens. It thereby redraws the boundary between citizens and noncitizens that the young citizen's desire initially seems to challenge.[79] This emphasis is also present in the *Sikyōnioi*: Stratophanes' manly body signals his true Athenian identity in advance, while simultaneously exposing the external signs of his identity as unreliable and arbitrary. Yet the Assembly members approve his request not only because of the manly appearance of his body, but also because of the history it attests. By emphasizing that Stratophanes' physical appearance reveals his habits and moral disposition, the play develops Aeschines' conceit that the body is a window to the state of the citizen's soul. At the same time, Stratophanes' success with the Assembly also hinges on his ability to act like a citizen in the setting of democratic politics. By stressing the natural and recognizable democratic talent and moral disposition of a man raised in a foreign city and serving as a mercenary, the male recognition play essentializes not only the exclusive membership norms of the democratic polis but also the practices and principles of democratic citizenship.

Metadrama and the Illusion of Identity

That Stratophanes' performance is part of a play, itself "re-performed" by another character, might seem to undermine the idea of a natural political performance by tacitly aligning performance with theater and pretense. In fact, by dramatizing the performative basis of democratic politics, the play may upset both the idea of natural democratic political

[79] For the ideological effects of the recognition motif, see Konstan 1983, 30–31; McCarthy 2000, 124–25 and passim.

norms and the idea of a natural difference between citizens and noncitizens. If to be recognized as a democratic citizen one only has to act like one, then on what does the difference between citizens and noncitizens ultimately rest? The male recognition motif, as it naturalizes democratic political norms and values, thus seems also to raise a subversive question.

The text ingeniously counteracts the sense that Stratophanes' performance is a theatrical or feigned performance by adopting a kind of reverse metadramatic strategy. When the Assembly members approve Stratophanes' request, Moschion immediately objects:

ὁ λευκόχρως
ἐκεῖνος ἐξαίφνης τε παραπηδᾶι πάλιν
καί φησι "ταυτὶ συμπέποιθ', ὡς οὑτοσὶ
νῦν ἐξαπίνης εἴληφε διαθήκας ποθὲν
ἐστί τε πολίτης ὑμέτερος, τραγωιδίαι
κενῆι τ' ἀγόμενος τὴν κόρην ἀφήσετ[αι."

(258–63)

That white-skinned youth
suddenly jumped up and said,
"Are you asking me to believe that this man
has suddenly got hold of a will from somewhere,
and that he's a citizen, and that when he gets the girl
by means of this empty tragedy, he'll let her go?"

Moschion is, of course, correct to highlight the theatrical and performative nature of Stratophanes' behavior. He even purports to identify the genre in which the mercenary acts: tragic melodrama.[80] But the device he points to as defining the genre, the recognition token (in this case a will), is equally at home in comedy. It hardly matters whether Moschion gets the genre right or not, since his very act of speaking discredits his words in advance. Because a compromised character (the pale *moikhos/lastauros*) utters it, the metadramatic disclosure operates to reinforce comedy's naturalistic political illusion. This same strategy probably informs Smikrines' charge that democratic emotional displays are no more than feigned performances. The impugning of emotional exhibitions in politics by a discredited oligarchic character serves to emphasize rather than to challenge the authenticity of Stratophanes' subsequent impassioned political performance.

The *Sikyōnioi* uses metatheater to produce and strengthen the notion

[80] On the expression τραγωιδία κενή ("empty drama" or "melodrama"), see Lanowski 1965, 245–53; Gomme and Sandbach 1973, 657; Hurst 1990, 110–11; Hunter 1985, 119, Belardinelli 1994, 183–84 ad 262–63.

that citizens are naturally recognizable.[81] Not surprisingly, the fifth act provides a farcical commentary on this very theme that drives home the point. In the fourth act, Stratophanes makes the Assembly members the heroine's collective guardian (*kurios*) and persuades them to protect the girl until he can establish his own Athenian civic identity and so marry her. At the end of the act, Stratophanes is recognized as a citizen and reunited with his long-lost family, discovering Smikrines to be his father and Moschion his brother. At this juncture, however, the question of the heroine's identity remains unanswered. Although the Assembly immediately accepts Dromon's claim that Philoumene is a citizen, this in itself is insufficient to enable her to enter into a legitimate marriage. She needs a male family member, a *kurios*, to perform the *enguē* ceremony certifying her eligibility to bear to legitimate children in the matrimonial context. In the fifth act, Theron, Stratophanes' Athenian parasite, attempts to manufacture just such a citizen.

Theron seeks to solve Stratophanes' matrimonial problems by suborning perjury to establish Philoumene's Athenian citizen status.[82] Dromon apparently described Philoumene's father as short and snub-nosed (352–53). The fifth act opens with Theron attempting to coach a short and snub-nosed man to play the part of Philoumene's father in a law court scheme.[83] In the process of leading his recalcitrant and slightly hostile stand-in, Theron inadvertently prompts the old man to disclose missing parts of the story. When he refuses Theron's bribe, he identifies himself as Kichesias of the deme Scambonides, using the demotic although he had not been supplied with the line. Theron is delighted with Kichesias's realistic improvisation. As they continue to play out what Theron thinks is no more than an act, Kichesias becomes more and more distraught, bursting into tears at the mere mention of the long-lost daughter. Of course, Kichesias is not acting at all: he really is Philoumene's father.

In this scene, the actors collaborate in staging a law court plot. By having Kichesias rehearse his own role in the play, Theron exposes the performative and staged nature of both law court and comic dramas. Yet Kichesias is not acting in this seeming play within the play: his tears turn

[81] The fact that one speaker utters the proverb "An evil face, a cowardly heart within" attests to the emphasis on physiognomy in the play (κακὴ μὲν ὄψις ἐν δὲ δείλαιαι φρένες, fr. 5 Sandbach).

[82] Scafuro (1994, 180–81) adduces the false witnessing plots in the *Sikyōnioi* and in Plautus's *Poenulus* (1099–173), and the related citizenship plots in Terence's *Andria* and *Phormio*, to support the view that Athenian judicial practice relied on witnessing techniques to establish citizen status.

[83] For metatheatrical elements in Menander's illusionistic comedy, see Gutzwiller 2000 (who does not discuss this scene) and chapter 4 above; on the play-within-the-play topos, see Blänsdorf 1982.

out to be a genuine expression of emotion. As the pretenses of theater are used to reveal Kichesias's true identity, the metatheatrical impulse produces rather than dismantles illusion and ideology in this naturalistic comedy. The effect is reinforced by an additional alteration of comic convention. Unlike his counterparts in other comic plays (e.g., Phormio in Terence's play of that name), the parasite Theron fails in his attempt to manipulate legal practice in the interests of obtaining the heroine for his patron. By dramatizing the parasite's inability to perform his typical generic role—an unexpected inability to subvert democratic practice—the play emphasizes the naturalness of its own illusion, which in this case happens to be the naturalness and indeed transparency of democratic culture itself.

Remasculinizing and Reproducing the Democratic State

The importance of questions of identity and recognition in the *Sikyōnioi* is rooted in the endemic social stress and demographic change of the Hellenistic polis.[84] The play's construction of the body as the baseline of identity answers in part to the particular anxieties linked by comedy to conditions of Hellenistic mercenary service.[85] In comedy, mercenary service is depicted as threatening to dissolve identity, as well the demographic and cultural foundations of the polis. In the classical period, warfare was regularized and ritualized, fought at agreed-on times according to agreed-on rules by citizens whose equipment announced their place in the civic and social hierarchies.[86] In the Hellenistic period, the classical order broke down, with wars increasingly fought in exotic locals, sometimes under chaotic circumstances, and with ethnically mixed armies under the aegis of non-polis-based imperial powers. Comedy resisters the uncertainties of these conditions by making the mercenary's weapons and armor into tokens of misrecognition—for example, the sword in the *Misoumenos* and the shield in the *Aspis*.[87] For instance, in the *Aspis* when Kleostratos's slave sees his shield beside a bloated corpse, he wrongly

[84] The Alexander scholar W. W. Tarn famously criticized New Comedy for its fantastic and outlandish plots (1952, 273). Piracy, kidnappings, and infant exposures were not, he insisted, the stuff of everyday life in the Hellenistic polis. While this may be true, comedy's evident preoccupation with such motifs attests to a general anxiety centering on questions of dislocation and identity. For piracy in the Hellenistic period and the common practice of taking of human captives, see de Souza 1999, 65.

[85] Konstan 1983, 24.

[86] See Connor 1988; Hanson 1989.

[87] This uncoupling of weapons and citizen bodies is the male equivalent of the dissolution of the kinship system (the incest threat) that sometimes surfaces in plays of female recognition. See Plautus's *Curculio* and *Epidicus*, and Menander's *Perikeiromenē*.

assumes that his master has died.[88] In reality, in the rush to defend against the natives on Kleostratos's mercenary campaign, another soldier had borrowed his shield. That the body of the dead soldier, the thing that should have secured his identity, is disfigured beyond recognition concretely renders comic anxieties concerning the displacement and dissolution of identity in Hellenistic warfare.

The *Sikyōnioi* constructs the body as a surety against such misrecognition and dissolution, and additional historically specific considerations animate the text's emphasis on Stratophanes' manly body and the play's conceit that democrats and oligarchs can be identified by somatic signs. I conclude by discussing the historical and cultural pattern that unfolds in tandem with the play's romance narrative. In the *Sikyōnioi*, the story of the recovery of a lost citizen's true identity is also the story of a displaced democratic soldier's return.[89] The return of the masculine Stratophanes and his triumph over an effeminate oligarchic rival can be viewed as a romantic allegory for the remasculinization of the state after a period of oligarchy. The play's *nostos* theme echoes actual historical narratives of the return of manly democratic men after periods of oligarchy. At the close of the Peloponnesian War, Athens experienced two short-lived but traumatic oligarchic coups. In each case, the democracy reestablished itself outside the oligarchic city while oligarchs in the city were accused, inter alia, of sexually outraging the wives of the exiled democrats.[90] In 404/3, the exiled and disfranchised democrats seized a stronghold in the Attic deme of Phyle. Eventually, they captured the Piraeus and forced the oligarchs to retreat to Eleusis (perhaps not coincidentally the setting of the *Sikyōnioi*).

In the Attic lawsuits following the restoration and amnesty, the question of whether a man remained in the city under the oligarchy or joined the democracy in exile became the touchstone of democratic identity.[91] In

[88] For the recovery of the bodies in classical warfare, see Hanson 1989.

[89] This *nostos* motif also encompasses the heroine, who, significantly, takes refuge at Demeter's temple and whose return to the city coincides with her sexual maturity. The identity of the prologue speaker may have added a symbolic emphasis to this element of the plot. Lloyd-Jones (1990, 74–75) suggests that either Demeter or one of the minor divinities of the Eleusinian cult (perhaps Kalligeneia) spoke the prologue; see also Guida 1974, 233–34. Arnott (1997b, 3) suggests that Persephone, herself the victim of abduction, is an especially likely candidate, given the circumstances of the play. For the symbolic importance of the prologue speaker's identity to the meaning of a comedy, see R. L. Hunter 1987.

[90] Thuc. 8.74, 86; Xen. *Hell.* 2.4.17; Isoc. *Paneg.* 113; Lys. 13.68, with reference to the slave Agoratus, a henchman of the Thirty. On the association of oligarchs with sexual outrage, see Fisher 1992.

[91] For instance, the speaker in Lys. 25 must explain why he remained in the city when ardent democrats fled to Phyle. On the speaker's antidemocratic sentiments, see Christ 1998, 98–100.

his prosecution of Ctesiphon, Aeschines emphasizes his own inherited democratic manhood by telling the jurors that both his mother and his father shared the democracy's exile. He stresses that during the oligarchy his father enacted his manhood outside the city by serving as a mercenary in Asia (Aes. 2.147). He repeatedly juxtaposes the manliness and bravery of the men from Phyle with the cowardice of Demosthenes, a man whose supreme military achievement was to fortify the walls, as if in testament to his own cowardice.

The drama of the democratic mercenary's return in the *Sikyōnioi* seems to recall the story of the men from Phyle, men whom later writers credited with redemocratizing and remasculinizing the city after a period of oligarchic repression; it translates the oligarchic political threat into a sexual threat against a native virgin. Sexual coding of this sort has a long history in allegories of political domination in the ancient world. In Athens, however, where male sexual control of freeborn native women was used to produce the democratic political community as well as to protect its boundaries and integrity, such a narrative was more than allegorical. In this play, the return of the heroine to democratic male supervision coincides with the (re)constitution of democratic politics. At the same time, the question of her romantic and reproductive fate is cast as the very stuff of political debate. That emphasis exposes the usually tacit politics of the marriage plot pattern.

The correlation between political authority and sexual control probably accounts for this play's unprecedented focus on the heroine's virginity. The first question Philoumene's father asks after learning that his long-lost daughter is alive is whether she has been saved well, or just saved (371–72). In case anyone does not understand what he is asking, the servant answers, "She's a virgin, with no experience of a man" (372–73). This is the only case in Menander's extant comedy in which a father or any male family member reunited with a lost female relative asks such a question.[92] Normally, plays of female recognition stress the reunion of the family rather than the sexual status of the heroine. At any rate, in most cases the lost female citizen is no longer a virgin but has been living as the de facto wife of the hero. In the *Sikyōnioi*, by contrast, what seems to convince Kichesias to give his newfound daughter in marriage to the hero is precisely that Stratophanes has preserved her virginity (379).

The attention paid to the heroine's sexual integrity stems in part from her status as an embodiment of the democratic city. Her virginal—intact and untouched—return to the city after an absence of ten years evokes

[92] The question of a lost female citizen's virginity does arise in Terence's *Eunuch*. There, however, a courtesan seeks to protect a female's citizen's virginity in order to increase the value of her own good deed (748, 867–70).

the historical refoundation of democracy after a period of repression. At the same time, the emphasis on her virginity is redolent of the Athenian paternalist ideology of warfare that arose in response to Macedonian imperialism. The Macedonian conquests of the second half of the fourth century changed Athenian understandings of war and its basis. In part, this was a result of Athens being put on the defensive, a posture that may have propelled a certain anxiety for, and tacit identification with, the weak—that is, the women and children. Philip's military practices furthered these concerns. Rather than following the traditional Greek practice of killing the men of captured cities and enslaving the women and children, Philip enslaved both the men and women of the cities he captured.[93] The vulnerability of free men to such reversals of fortune may account for the Athenian concern for the Olynthian women's plight after the destruction of their city.[94]

During the fifth and most of the fourth centuries, the Athenians did not rouse military support by appealing to the need to protect the women and children.[95] But in Hyperides' funeral oration for those who died in the Lamian War, the necessity of defending freeborn women, virgins, and children against Macedonian insolence (i.e., sexual violence) takes center stage as a justification for war (Hyp. 6.20 [col. 8]). In fact, the heroic general Leosthenes and the others who died in the war are explic-

[93] For this point, see Rosivach 1999.

[94] In civic discourse, there is a distinct anxiety that Athenian citizens are complicit in these outrages, with Philip's bribes inducing them to betray their city and its foundational principle concerning the respect for the bodily integrity of free persons. Demosthenes accuses the ambassador Philocrates of bringing formerly free Olynthian women to Athens for hubris, which may mean sexual violence or prostitution (19.309). Similarly, he accuses Aeschines of taking part in the physical abuse and near rape of an Olynthian captive at a dinner party, which ominously took place at the home of a descendant of one of the Thirty (19.196–98). The report in Dinarchus that the Athenians put a certain Euthymachus to death for putting an Olynthian girl in a brothel also belongs to this context (Din. 1.23). Finally, Dinarchus links Demosthenes' acceptance of bribes to the sexual outrage of the Theban women after the destruction of Thebes in 335 (1.24). Cf. Plut. *Alex.* 12.

[95] Schaps states, "It was commonplace to urge soldiers to fight to protect their wives and to arouse hatred for the enemy by accusing him of planning to abuse women" (1982, 196–97, citing Thuc. 7.69.2, 7.68.2, 8.74.3 to attest the practice in Athens). But such conceptualizations are notably absent from the official discourse in which the Athenians defined themselves as citizen-soldiers (save for Hyp. 6). According to Loraux, "at the solemn hour of the collective funeral, the funeral oration offers the citizen no other family but the city" (1986, 105). She further notes, "A single exception, Lysias 2.35, 36, and 39, is of course mentioned by Lacey (*The Family in Classical Greece*, p. 78), who, insensitive to the exceptionally realistic character of the account of Salamis in Lysias, sees the defense of the family and patrimony as one of the central themes of the funeral oration" (1986, 386 n. 124; cf. n. 123). In Hyperides, the stress on protecting women and children operates to figure the Macedonians as barbarous and unjust, and conversely, to emphasize the justice and nobility of the Greek cause in championing the weak against the strong.

itly praised for preserving the system of lawful marriage (6.27 [col. 9]). Hyperides claims that the cause against the Macedonians trumps the Trojan War: the Greeks at Troy fought to avenge a single woman, while the Athenians were leading a struggle to save all Greek women from impending sexual outrage (6.36 [col. 12]).[96]

The unique concern for the heroine's virginity in the *Sikyōnioi* is inflected with this new paternalist ideology. That emphasis, together with the general atmosphere of democratic nationalism pervading the play, also accounts for its unusual construction of gender. In other works featuring a mercenary hero, the transnational *Perikeiromenē* and *Misoumenos*, the heroines acquire a power in excess of their conventional cultural and narrative position. Those plays counterpoise the culture of the polis with an imagined Hellenistic other figured by the Hellenistic mercenary soldier. Because the romantic narratives in the *Perikeiromenē* and *Misoumenos* fortify the polis against this external threat, internal gender boundaries (at least among freeborn citizens) appear less constitutively important. The difference between citizens and Hellenistic outsiders, rather than the difference between the sexes, becomes paramount in the construction of civic identity. By contrast, the exuberant democratic return in the *Sikyōnioi* brings with it a corresponding restoration of democratic gender ideology in its most oppressive and officializing form. Rather than gaining a power in advance of her cultural possibilities, this heroine is virginal and silent, the compliant reproductive being that that democratic ideology required her to be.[97]

While the heroine's safe return (re)institutes democratic politics and promises the legitimate reproduction of the state, the return of the manly democratic hero, whose masculinity was preserved outside the oligarchic city, remasculinizes the state. With this emphasis, the Eleusinian romance of democratic fertility looks both backward and forward. The return and romantic triumph of Stratophanes, an embodiment of military manliness, optimistically harkens back to the ideal of the citizen-soldier. Yet Stratophanes' status as a mercenary suggests at least a tacit recognition of the loss of the old ideal. It is surely significant that he wins consent to marry the heroine, first from a democratic Assembly and later from her father, by displaying his respect for democratic moral norms

[96] See also, however, the tradition that Alexander restrained himself and his troops from raping the women of captured cities (at least in some cases); Cole 1984, 112–13, with Plut. *Alex*. 12, *Mor*. 259e–260d.

[97] It is possible, of course, that heroine spoke in the nonpreserved portions of the play. But even if she did, she is silent precisely at the moment when other heroines in mercenary plays are not—that is, in the matter of arranging her own marriage. By contrast, Malthake the *hetaira* with whom the parasite Theron is in love may have the power to consent to her own marriage (see *Sik*. 419).

rather than his martial prowess. In other words, the point of casting the romantic hero as a soldier in this play may be precisely to show that the true Athenian citizen is not a soldier in this world. Viewed from this perspective, the play provides a kind of testament to the enduring ethos of democratic citizenship and the mutable masculinity that sustained it.

8

Conclusion

INEVITABLE REPRODUCTION?

Throughout this book I have argued that comedy's romantic narratives contributed to democratic continuity as well as to the cultural survival of the Greek polis during the transition to the Hellenistic age. The marriage plot supplied a flexible and fertile narrative pattern in which democratic principles and practices could be affirmed and sustained in the context of social relations. At the same time, comedy developed conventions in accordance with a civic conceptual system that contained and refashioned the problems posed by the rise of Hellenistic autocracies and their unprecedented use of mercenaries. In so doing, comedy performed the reproduction of democratic national culture and Greek transnational polis culture before it had actually occurred.

As comedy offered cultural scripts that enabled the citizens of other Greek states to come to terms with the changes of the Hellenistic period while maintaining the priority of the Athenians' own long-standing traditions and identities, it also created a space in which traditional civic scripts could be revised to include new characters or subject positions. Although comic plots invariably reiterate the exclusionary norms of democratic citizenship, comedy's themes, conventions, and plot devices often work against the civic status quo they are employed to secure. This polyvalent poetics—comedy's tendency both to reproduce and to rebel against existing Athenian political and cultural arrangements—owes much to the genre's historical position straddling two epochs, the classical age of the polis and the cosmopolitan world of the Hellenistic kingdoms. In this transitional period, the need to keep intact the conceptual, cultural, and physical barriers between the city and what was "outside" acquired new urgency. The sudden necessity of defining local citizens against the various external threats represented by the kingdoms allowed for a corresponding lessening in the constituting work that internal status boundaries between citizens and resident noncitizens were required to do.

Because a citizen's place in the polis hierarchy was suddenly less important than the integrity of the polis as a civic community, comedy was able to get away with temporarily blurring internal status boundaries (albeit in the context of stories that ultimately reaffirmed them). Yet comedy's very ability to reproduce the norms of citizen status in scandalous fashion—that is, by blurring them and exposing their arbitrary and conventional basis—tells us something about the norms and ideology of the democratic citizenship system itself. It is no accident that displaced female citizens in comedy are able to serve as surrogates for slaves, foreigners, and *hetairai* of varying statuses, or that *hetairai* can operate as stand-ins for female citizens. This poetics of interchangeable female bodies was made possible precisely by the contradictions in female social identity that lay at the base of Athenian democratic culture.

Before the Periclean citizenship law was enacted, the prevailing conception of female identity seems to have been rooted in gender.[1] According to the conventional "race of women" ideology, women were neither Athenians nor citizens but rather simply and only "women."[2] In other words, for women gender constituted a form of racial identity. The implementation of the Periclean law complicated and challenged this traditional conception by requiring that the citizen have a native wife, thereby fostering a belief that women transmitted Athenianness to their children just as Athenian men did.[3] Although the tacit recognition of maternal inheritance necessarily included women in the Athenian racial pool (as the numerous attacks on citizens' supposed foreign blood in the maternal line well demonstrate), it did not do away with the older conception of women as belonging to their own gender-race.[4] Civic discourse continues to differentiate female citizens from noncitizens primarily on the basis of gender rather than in terms of their Athenianness or lack thereof. The persistence of the older ideology is well attested by the rhetorical strategies employed by Apollodorus in his efforts to persuade a democratic jury to convict Neaira for impersonating a female citizen wife. His argument hinges on the notion that the infiltration of a Corinthian *hetaira* into the citizen body of legitimate wives constitutes the gravest of threats to the state. Yet even though Neaira was a Corinthian native, Apollo-

[1] In the elite tradition, however, women were defined in terms of class and status; the practice of aristocratic marriage exchange presupposes as much (Vernant 1980; Herman 1987). According to Morris (1996, 36), elitist ideology blurs "distinctions between male and female, present and past, mortal and divine, Greek and Lydian, to reinforce a distinction between aristocrat and commoner," while middling or democratic ideology hardens these distinctions in the service of effacing the aristocratic—commoner divide. Thus, the emphasis on gender difference exhibited in cultural productions like Aeschylus's *Oresteia* can be seen as a democratic response to the elite tendency toward gender symmetry.

[2] For the race of women, see Loraux 1993; Zeitlin 1996; King 1998.

[3] For a belief in maternal inheritance (in sources dating from after the implementation of the Periclean citizenship law), see chapter 1, note 22, and chapter 3, note 5.

[4] See, e.g., the polemics against Prometheus for fabricating the "hateful" and promiscuous race of women in Men. 508 K.-A. For the conflict between the race of women ideology and the operation of the Periclean law, see further chapter 3, note 5.

dorus never claims that either she or the bastards she was allegedly foisting on the state were contaminating the Athenian bloodline. He instead presents the harm of her supposed offense as an overturning of the city's gender and moral norms rather than as an affront to the city's racial purity. He warns the jurors that a failure to render a proper verdict will have catastrophic consequences for the state:

> So it would be far better that this trial had not taken place at all than that you should acquit now that it has. This is because there will be freedom for prostitutes (*pornai*) to marry whomever they wish and declare that the father of their children is any man who happens to be around. The laws will be invalidated while the ways of *hetairai* will gain authority to do as they please. . . .
>
> However, if the law is held in contempt by you, with her acquittal, and becomes invalid, definitely the work of prostitutes will reach the daughters of female citizens, the ones unable to be betrothed because of poverty, while the privilege of free women will pass to the *hetairai*, if they are given permission to be able to have children in any manner they wish and take part in the honors and sacrifices of the city. (Dem. 59.112, 114)

According to Apollodorus, an acquittal for Neaira will send the dangerous message to all *hetairai* that they too can get away with impersonating a female citizen and bearing legitimate children. In other words, Apollodorus is claiming that an acquittal will create a de facto right of citizenship for female prostitutes. By predicting that prostitutes will be able "to bear children as they please," Apollodorus exposes the thinness of the difference between the female citizen and the prostitute. Similarly, his fear that legitimate female citizens will be forced to become prostitutes in order to compete in the matrimonial market against wealthy prostitute rivals reveals that the sexuality of citizen women made them like the women from whom they were supposed to differ. If all women could serve as sexual and reproductive objects, what exactly was the difference between female citizens and noncitizens?

Thus, although female citizens came to be valued as carriers of Athenianness, extant civic discourse never officially recognizes them as such. Rather, female citizens and noncitizens continued to be differentiated on the basis of gender—specifically, on the primary salience of their bodies for Athenian men as either reproductive or sexual.[5] The apparent refusal to grant women an official "racial" identity demonstrates the tenacity of Athenian gender categories. Yet the price of keeping women in their conventional position was a weakening of the exclusionary norms of Athenian citizenship and the racial purity that those norms constituted and conserved. The official ideology endeavored to harden the gender-based

[5] See especially Is. 3 and [Dem.] 59.

distinctions that secured the boundaries of the state, but in reality everyone knew that all women, not only Athenian women, had the capacity to be both sexual and reproductive beings for Athenian men.[6] Thus, the fact that any woman, wife or not, Athenian or not, could give a man sexual satisfaction as well as children made tenuous the distinctions that the female body was supposed to secure: the distinctions between insider and outsider, Athenian and non-Athenian, legitimate citizen and bastard, and free person and slave. By depicting the practical interchangeability of slave courtesan and wife, or female citizen and foreigner, comedy exposes the contradictions in the logic of citizenship and the practical underdetermination of the status boundaries supposed to separate Athenian citizen men from all the rest. In other words, comedy's simultaneously conservative and subversive plots were to some extent made possible because the citizenship system was based on gender practices rather than on immutable essentialist distinctions.

The citizenship system was vulnerable not only because noncitizen women could bear the children of citizens but also because citizen women, in various circumstances, could bear *nothoi* as well. Comedy routinely capitalizes on these vulnerabilities, or on the underdetermination of female identity at the level of cultural practice, in its citizen-making plots. By way of conclusion, it will be useful to examine Menander's *Epitrepontes*, a work that both exploits the immanent tensions in the logic of citizenship and insistently raises the possibility of modifying the citizenship system and the ideologies on which it was based. Although the play employs a variant of the rape plot pattern, it does not, as Menandrian rape plots generally do, attenuate the lines of social stratification in the polis by bringing together a man and a woman representing disparate segments of society (the wealthy and the less wealthy, or the city and the country). In the *Epitrepontes*, Pamphile, the rape victim, is wealthy. What is more, she has already unknowingly married Kharisios, her rapist; in other words, the rape is technically extraneous to the formation of the marriage required by comedy's generic conventions. Yet though the play eschews the dismantling of economic distinctions characteristic of Menander's nationalistically oriented rape plays, it nevertheless challenges the internal status barriers separating and stratifying members of the polis. Rather than focusing on the rape per se, the play is most deeply concerned with its consequences: the birth of a presumed *nothos* and the imagined violation of the norms of legitimate sexual and political repro-

[6] The treatment of wives and *hetairai* as similarly lustful in Aristophanes' comedy (Henry 1985; Zweig 1992) suggests that there was a fairly pronounced gap between the official ideology and cultural attitudes. For the dissonance between Athenian gender ideology and practice, see also Winkler 1990a; Roy 1997.

duction represented by that birth.[7] The ethical climax of the play comes in a reversal and recognition speech in which the male hero forgives his wife for giving birth to a bastard child.[8] With this emphasis, the play sanctions a departure from the state's rules of legitimate sexual reproduction and thus implicitly a weakening of the internal status boundaries produced and maintained by those rules.

The premise of the play is that Kharisios has raped and impregnated his wife Pamphile at a nocturnal festival prior to their marriage, a fact that neither of them realizes when they marry. While Kharisios is away on business, Pamphile gives birth to the child issuing from the rape and exposes it. When Kharisios returns and learns from his slave Onesimos that Pamphile has exposed a child that he assumes cannot be his own, he moves in with a neighbor and hires a high-priced *hetaira* (Habrotonon) to console himself. In the meantime, Onesimos, Kharisios's slave, happens to recognize one of the tokens Pamphile exposed with the baby (who has of course been rescued) as a ring that Kharisios lost at the previous year's Tauropolia. Onesimos correctly surmises that Kharisios raped a woman at the festival who seized his ring and left it with the child to identify its father (450–53). Instead of confronting Kharisios with his suspicion, Onesimos agrees to a plan devised by Habrotonon. The *hetaira* had been was present at the same festival and happened to see a beautiful and rich young girl crying after having been raped (483–90). Rather than trying to find the victim (Pamphile herself), Habrotonon decides to make absolutely certain that Kharisios is the baby's father by pretending to be the very girl whom he assaulted.[9]

Habrotonon's success in convincing Kharisios that he raped her, when in fact Pamphile was his victim, vividly underscores the practical interchangeability of the *hetaira* and female citizen that is a virtual principle of comedy's poetics of female bodies.[10] And because Habrotonon is a slave, the blurring of the boundary between *hetaira* and female citizen here also upsets the distinction between free persons and slaves. But on the level of the narrative, the equivalence that the plot posits between Pamphile and Habrotonon serves to produce another, less typical, alignment of characters. By impersonating Pamphile, Habrotonon convinces Kharisios that

[7] For this point, see Konstan 1995.

[8] For the tragic elements of Kharisios's speech (*Epit.* 894ff., 908ff.), see Gomme and Sandbach 1973, 363 ad 910; on 922, see 353 ad 691. For Kharisios's psychological reversal (*peripeteia*) and recognition (*anagnōrisis*), see Goldberg 1980, 69.

[9] Habrotonon effectively conducts an internal drama of the larger plot that, as Gutzwiller (2000, 120–21) shows, likens her to the playwright and prologue speaker. On the metadramatic aspects of Habrotonon's role, see Stockert 1997, 8–9.

[10] For Habrotonon's ability to pose as Pamphile, see *Epit.* 513–19, 526–32. For the interchangeability of *hetairai* and female citizens in Menander's comedy, see further chapter 5.

he is responsible for the birth of an illegitimate child.[11] Immediately after being confronted with this new knowledge about himself, Kharisios overhears Pamphile defending her marriage and refusing her father's demand that she divorce him because of his apparent profligacy. Instead of showing concern for Habrotonon and their supposed child, as Onesimos and Habrotonon had expected him to do, Kharisios can think only about Pamphile. At this juncture, he emerges on stage, in what was probably his first appearance, to make his crucial speech of self-recognition and reversal:[12]

ἐγώ τις ἀναμάρτητος, εἰς δόξαν βλέπων
καὶ τὸ καλὸν ὅ τι πότ' ἐστι καὶ ταἰσχρὸν σκοπῶν,
ἀκέραιος, ἀνεπίπληκτος αὐτὸς τῶι βίωι—
εὖ μοι κέχρηται καὶ προσηκόντως πάνυ
τὸ δαιμόνιον—ἐνταῦθ' ἔδειξ' ἄνθρωπος ὤν.
"ὦ τρισκακόδαιμον, μεγάλα φυσᾶις καὶ λαλεῖς,
ἀκούσιον γυναικὸς ἀτύχημ' οὐ φέρεις,
αὐτὸν δὲ δείξω σ' εἰς ὅμοι' ἐπταικότα,
καὶ χρήσετ' αὐτή σοι τότ' ἠπίως, σὺ δὲ
ταύτην ἀτιμάζεις· ἐπιδειχθήσει θ' ἅμα
ἀτυχὴς γεγονὼς καὶ σκαιὸς ἀγνώμων τ' ἀνήρ."
ὅμοιά γ' εἶπεν οἷς σὺ διενόου τότε
πρὸς τὸν πατέρα, κοινωνὸς ἥκειν τοῦ βίου
κ]οὐ δεῖν τἀτύχημ' αὐτὴν φύγεῖν
τὸ συμβεβηκός. σὺ δέ τις ὑψηλὸς σφόδρα
[text breaks off]

(908–22)

A faultless man, I watched my reputation,
I pondered the noble and the shameful,
untouched by vice, and beyond reproach—
But now some power has well
and quite correctly treated me
as I deserved—I've shown at last
that I am human. "Unlucky man, you
give yourself airs and talk so big, you won't tolerate
a woman's forced misfortune. I'll
show that you have stumbled just the same yourself.

[11] Konstan (1995) demonstrates that Kharisios sees himself as suffering a misfortune analogous to Pamphile's not because he has committed a rape while she has suffered one, as many previous commentators have maintained (see references cited 204–5, nn. 7, 8, 13, 14, 18), but specifically because he has produced a bastard child just as he believes she has.

[12] For Kharisios's speech as the ethical climax of the play, see Del Corno 1966, 179; Konstan 1995.

Then she will treat you tenderly, while you
dishonor her. You'll be shown as a man who
was at once unfortunate and
a heartless brute." Did she
say to her father then the sorts of things you would have said?
"I'm here," [she said,] "to share his life. Mishaps
occur. I mustn't run away."
But you're so high and mighty . . .[13]

Although Kharisios's comparison of his situation in producing a *nothos* to Pamphile's may seem like bad faith, insofar as his part in the child's conception involved the exercise of agency, the text does not interrogate or evaluate his behavior on this level.[14] Rather, what is crucial is Kharisios's apparently newfound awareness that one can produce a child by accident. He repeatedly refers to Pamphile's production of a *nothos* as a "misfortune" (*atukhēma*, 898, 914), and views his own circumstances in fathering a *nothos* in similar terms (*ētukhēka*, 891; cf. 918).[15] This is significant because in Aristotelian ethics, an *atukhēma* was understood to be an involuntary action, and therefore not amenable to ethical evaluation; it was an act thought to call for pity and forgiveness rather than judgment.[16] By emphasizing that Pamphile has suffered an *atukhēma*, Kharisios is

[13] Trans. adapted from Arnott and Balme 2001.

[14] According to Aristotle, a sex act is a voluntary action, irrespective of its passionate motivation, and so can be subjected to moral evaluation; see *M.M.* 1188a3–4 and *E.N.* 1113b16–9, where a man's begetting of children is used as a paradigmatic example of a voluntary action involving moral choice. Thus, although *Epitrepontes* employs an Aristotelian language of harms, it does not follow or endorse Aristotelian philosophy; for this point see further chapter 6, note 27.

[15] The critical passage in which Kharisios compares his situation to Pamphile's occurs in the part of his speech that is reported by Onesimos:

"ἐγὼ" γὰρ "ἀλιτήριος" πυκνὸν πάνυ
ἔλεγεν "τοιοῦτον ἔργον ἐξειργασμένος
αὐτὸς γεγονώς τε παιδίου νόθου πατὴρ
οὐκ ἔσχον οὐδ' ἔδωκα συγγνώμης μέρος
οὐθὲν ἀτυχούσηι ταὔτ' ἐκείνηι, βάρβαρος
ἀνηλεής τε."

(894–99)

Konstan (1995, 146–47) shows that *atukhein* and *atukhēma* in the *Epitrepontes* refer to the circumstances of producing a bastard child. For previous interpretations, see Gomme and Sandbach 1973, 361 ad 891, 362 ad 898; Capps 1910, 111; Blanchard 1983, 333–34. Yet Kharisios does seem to acknowledge an asymmetry between his own reproductive behavior and Pamphile's. Although he describes his part in producing a *nothos* in terms of "committing a crime/act" (ἔργον ἐξειργασμένος, 895), he does not impute a similar agency to Pamphile, at least in the extant portions of the text. At the same time, by repeatedly likening his situation in having fathered a bastard child to Pamphile's situation in having given birth to one, he ignores the discrepancy between their respective autonomies (895–98; cf. 891, 914).

[16] See further chapter 6 with note 27.

thus tacitly acknowledging his own mistake in condemning her for an action that she did not have the decisional autonomy to choose or control. Kharisios might have therefore come to the conclusion that women ought to be granted agency or choice in the realm of sexual relations so that they might gain some control over their fertility, making the production of children a legitimate sphere for moral evaluation, at least by the standards of democratic Athens. But instead of taking this tack, which would grant Pamphile moral agency, Kharisios rejects the overstrict reproductive ideals embodied in law as a legitimate basis on which to render ethical judgment.

According to Kharisios, he held Pamphile to an impossible double standard because he literally did not know himself. He was living in a fantasy of his own moral perfection (which in this context specifically means abiding by the state's reproductive norms), until a higher power shattered his illusion by revealing that he, like Pamphile, had produced an illegitimate child. Given this assessment, we might say that Kharisios had rejected Pamphile because he was projecting onto her the behavior he was unable to recognize in himself. In repudiating his illusory self-righteousness, Kharisios is also rejecting the ideology of Athenian citizenship, at least in the strong form expressed in comedy's generic rule system. For by leaving a wife known to have given birth to a *nothos*, Kharisios was doing no more than what was necessary to maintain the social and political codes that sustained the legitimacy and hence exclusivity of the citizen body.[17] Because he learns from firsthand experience the difficulty of preventing the production of bastards, given the unquestioned cultural sanctioning of sex outside marriage for men, Kharisios comes to consider departures from the state's norms of sexual reproduction as only "human," as misfortunes that might befall either men or women.[18]

Kharisios's new capacity to empathize with Pamphile stems in part from the affinities he perceives between her situation and his own, as well as from the notable discrepancies he detects in their behavior toward one other. He contrasts his "pitiless" and "barbaric" (βάβαρος ἀνηλεής, 898–

[17] From the standpoint of ideology, it hardly matters that Pamphile had exposed the child and hence did not directly put the integrity of the citizen body at risk. The very fact that she was known to have borne a *nothos* called into question her perceived ability to bear legitimate children and heirs.

[18] The emanicipatory implications of this conclusion extend beyond the position of female citizens, since it is only a small conceptual step from Kharisios's recognition that reproductive accidents are only "human" to the further recognition that the issue of those accidents, i.e., the children, are beings worthy of rearing rather than exposing. Similarly, the acknowledgment and toleration of fallibility in the reproductive sphere tacitly challenge the distinction that made some forms of reproduction legitimate while stigmatizing others, i.e., the distinction between citizens and noncitizens.

89) treatment of Pamphile in her misfortune with her ability to forgive and defend him in spite of his desertion and the hiring of Habrotonon (894–99, 916–17). With this emphasis, the text ethnicizes the moral code; that is, it articulates the contrast between Pamphile and Kharisios by invoking the Greek–barbarian polarity.[19] By emphasizing Pamphile's adherence to a common "Greek," or at any rate nonbarbarian, structure of feeling and code of conduct, the play allows Pamphile to emerge as a moral exemplar for her errant husband in a way that seems not to contest prevailing gender categories. It is as if placing a woman on top was such a subversive step that comedy had to conceal it by presenting Pamphile as a pillar of Greek morality rather than as a woman per se. Nevertheless, despite this attempted camouflage, the *Epitrepontes* seems to go further than other reconciliation plays in delegating cultural and moral authority to its heroine. Like the heroines of the *Perikeiromenē* and *Misoumenos*, Pamphile has the ability to consent to her own matrimonial (if not sexual) relationship; she refuses her father's demands that she divorce, and thus implicitly contests the economic values underlying his demands. But in addition, Pamphile is cast as the morally superior character insofar as her behavior sets the positive example for the men in the play to follow.

We might, of course, question the liberatory significance of a dramatic representation that empowers a woman only to defend a dysfunctional marriage and a husband who has mistreated her. Are there emancipatory implications in a text that enlists its heroine to champion the very structures that secure female oppression? The answer, I think, must be yes. For on the level of the narrative it is Pamphile's very dedication to her marriage that, paradoxically, wins her a release from the official ideology of marriage and sexual control. That is to say, Kharisios forgives Pamphile for producing a *nothos* at least in part because she defends her marriage in the face of her father's insistence that she divorce. By granting Pamphile this kind of backhanded decisional autonomy, the *Epitrepontes* works within existing gender assumptions even as it challenges them. Moreover, though the discovery that Pamphile is the mother of Kharisios's child enables the play to preserve the genre's ban on bastardy and hence the state's rules of sexual reproduction, the recuperation of the exclusionary norms of citizenship required by the generic rule system does not seamlessly recuperate the complex of cultural attitudes. Indeed, Kharisios's maturation and psychological development hinges precisely on his rejection of the belief system required to maintain and reproduce those norms over time. Finally, and perhaps most significantly, the resto-

[19] For this strategy in the *Perikeiromenē* and *Misoumenos*, see chapter 6. For the ethical meaning of *barbaros* in New Comedy, see Long 1986, 151–56.

ration of Pamphile's civic chastity does not detract from the play's effective installation of an empowered female in the cultural imaginary.

Cultural productions such as the *Epitrepontes* and other Menandrian plays simultaneously create space for renegotiating relations between the sexes and insistently raise the possibility of remodeling democratic culture along more inclusionary and egalitarian lines. Yet neither of these promises was actually fulfilled during the transition to the Hellenistic age. Although women made gains in social status in the Hellenistic polis, in Athens the traditional gender hierarchy seems to have remained intact.[20] Similarly, the exclusion of slaves and foreigners from Athenian citizenship remained entrenched. Moreover, on the political level, the history of democratic resistance to Macedonian power comes to a close with the Athenian defeat in the Chremonidean War, at least according to the extant sources. If comedy assisted not only in reproducing democratic culture but also in further "democratizing" it by extending new consideration to traditionally subordinate members of the polis, women, slaves, and foreigners, then how can we account for this twofold "failure"? The answer, I suggest, has less to do with the performative inefficacy of comedy than with the very reproducibility of democratic culture itself.

Although comedy often deploys devices and conventions that pressure the norms of Athenian citizenship, the narrative outcome of the plays inevitably reaffirms its foundational principles of nativity and legitimacy. Comedy could not in the end think past a citizenship system that doubled as a kinship system, but neither could democratic culture itself. At various pivotal moments in Athenian history the question of redrawing the boundaries of the citizen body along more inclusionary lines enters into political discourse. After the successful expulsion of the Thirty and restoration of the democracy in 403/2, a measure was proposed to enfranchise the slaves who fought in the democratic cause.[21] Their having fought together seems to have created some perceived common ground between the citizen and slave, challenging the exclusion of the slave soldier from civic membership.[22] Though the decree was successfully prosecuted as unconstitutional, its having been made at all attests to the possibility of escaping the reigning ideology of citizenship.

[20] According to Pomeroy, women in the Hellenistic polis, especially women from the upper classes, made gains in political, legal, and economic status; however, she concludes that "In Athens, in contrast to some other parts of the Greek world, there was little, if any, economic or legal emancipation of citizen women" (1975: 130–31). For women in the Hellenistic polis, see also van Bremen 1996; Shipley 2000, 102–6.

[21] On the decree of Thrasybulus, see [Arist.] *A.P.* 40.2; Ostwald 1986, 503–4.

[22] For the use of slaves in war during the fifth and fourth centuries, see Ridley 1979, 510, and Hunt 1998, who argues that the use of slaves in the Athenian military was far more common in the fifth century than has generally been thought.

An even more dramatic reappraisal of the norms of citizenship took place after the battle of Chaeronea. As mentioned in chapter 1, to defend against an expected Macedonian invasion, the orator Hyperides proposed a decree to free the slaves and to enfranchise metics and those who had been disfranchised in the scrutiny of 346 (Lycur. 1.36, 41; [Plut.] *Vit. X Orat*. 848f–849a). This was an extremely radical and innovative measure because it proposed to grant citizenship to the large body of foreigners residing within the territory and to grant freedom to every slave (Hyp. fr. 18.3 Burtt)—perhaps to as many as 150,000 persons. We will never know how this would have affected the balance of power between Athens and Macedon, because by showing leniency, Philip once again lulled the Athenians into complacency. When the Macedonian invasion failed to materialize, Hyperides, like Thrasybulus before him, was brought to trial for proposing an illegal measure. In defending his action, Hyperides argued that the need to defend against Macedonian military power trumped existing laws and that the battle of Chaeronea itself authored the decree (fr. 18.1 Burtt; [Plut.] *Vit. X Orat*. 849a).

For Hyperides, dramatic changes in the international landscape called for an equally dramatic response on the domestic front, indeed for a rethinking of Athenian identity. The necessity of defending against an external enemy raised the explicit possibility of creating a new national solidarity. That the Athenians were in the end stubbornly resistant to rethinking their identity and values, however, attests to the deep-seated ideology of citizenship produced by Athens's overlapping norms of familial and political membership. I began this book by discussing Lycurgus's rhetorical strategy of undoing the defeat at Chaeronea by emphasizing instead the defeat of Hyperides' proposal, and hence the preservation of the cherished purity of the Athenian bloodline (Lycur. 1.41). We can hardly fault comedy's inability to think past the kinship norms of Athenian citizenship when the Athenians themselves, faced with ongoing and urgent military threats, could only take consolation in a racial purity made possible by the rules of sexual reproduction.

Although the survival of Athenian democracy between 338 and 260 might seem to be just another chapter in the history of democratic resiliency, the fact remains that the story comes to a close: the democracy fails to renew itself after 260. Rather than chiding the democratic polis for its inability to resist the Macedonian kingdoms or to reach a workable accommodation with them, we should pay attention to its failure to do so, for it offers a valuable object lesson in the history of identities and identity formation. It suggests that a political identity purchased with narratives of blood and belonging, nativity and legitimacy, begets not resiliency but rather a tragic reproducibility, an inability to adapt to environmental challenges as true resiliency can.

Bibliography

Allen, D. 2000. *The World of Prometheus: The Politics of Punishing in Democratic Athens*. Princeton.

Althusser, L. A. 1971. "Ideology and Ideological State Apparatuses." In *Lenin and Philosophy and Other Essays*, 127–86. Trans. B. Brewster. New York.

Anderson, M. 1970. "Knemon's *Hamartia*." *G&R* 17: 199–217.

Anderson, W. S. 1972. "The Ending of the *Samia* and Other Menandrian Comedies." In *Studi classici in onore di Quintino Cataudella*, 2:155–79. Catania.

———. 1984. "Love Plots in Menander and His Roman Adapters." *Ramus* 13: 124–34.

Andrewes, A. 1981. "The Hoplite Katalogos." In G. S. Shrimpton and D. L. McCargar, eds., *Classical Contributions: Studies in Honour of Malcolm Francis McGregor*, 1–3. Locust Valley, N.Y.

Arnott, W. G. 1964. "The Confrontation of Sostratos and Gorgias." *Phoenix* 18: 110–23.

———. 1970. "Menander: Discoveries since the *Dyskolos*." *Arethusa* 3: 49–70.

———, ed. and trans. 1979–2000. *Menander*. 3 vols. Cambridge, Mass.

———. 1981. "Moral Values in Menander." *Philol.* 125: 215–27.

———. 1986. "Menander and Earlier Greek Drama." In *Studies in Honor of T. B. L. Webster*, 1–9. Bristol.

———. 1995. "Further Notes on Menander's Perikeiromene." *ZPE* 109: 11–30.

———. 1996a. *Alexis: The Fragments: A Commentary*. Cambridge.

———. 1996b. "Menander." In S. Hornblower and A. Spawforth, eds., *Oxford Classical Dictionary*, 956–57. 3rd ed. Oxford.

———. 1996c. "Notes on Menander's Misoumenos." *ZPE* 110: 27–40.

———. 1997a. "Final Notes on Menander's *Sikyonioi* (vv. 343–423 with Frs. 1, 2 and 7)." *ZPE* 118: 95–103.

———. 1997b. "First Notes on Menander's *Sikyonioi*." *ZPE* 116: 1–10.

———. 1997c. "Further Notes on Menander's *Sikyonioi* (vv. 110–322)." *ZPE* 117: 21–43.

———. 1998a. "First Notes on Menander's *Samia*." *ZPE* 121: 35–44.

———. 1998b. "Second Notes on Menander's *Samia* (Acts II–V)." *ZPE* 122: 7–20.

———. 2000a. "Notes on Some New Papyri of Menander's *Epitrepontes*." In E. Stärk and G. Vogt-Spira, eds., *Dramatische Wäldchen: Festschrift für Eckard Lefèvre zum 65*, 153–63. Zurich.

———. 2000b. "Stage Business in Menander's *Samia*." In S. Gödde and T. Heinze, eds., *Skenika: Beiträge zum antiken Theater und seiner Rezeption*, 113–24. Darmstadt.

Ashton, N. G. 1984. "The Lamian War—*stat magni nominis umbra*." *JHS* 104: 152–57.

Auger, D. 1979. "Le théâtre d'Aristophane: Le mythe, l'utopie et les femmes." *Les Cahiers de Fontenay* [*Aristophane, les femmes et la cité*] 17: 71–97.

Austin, C., ed. 1970. *Aspis et Samia*, by Menander. Vol. 2, *Subsidia interpretationis*. Berlin.

Austin, J. L. 1962. *How to Do Things with Words*. Cambridge.

Austin, M. M. 1981. *The Hellenistic World from Alexander to the Roman Conquest*. Cambridge.

Avery, H. C. 1991. "Was Eratosthenes the Oligarch Eratosthenes the Adulterer?" *Hermes* 119: 380–84.

Bain, D. 1977. *Actors and Audience: A Study of Asides and Related Conventions in Greek Drama*. Oxford.

———, ed. 1983. *Samia*, by Menander. Warminster.

———. 1984. "Female Speech in Menander." *Antichthon* 18: 24–42.

Balibar, E. 1995. "Culture and Identity (Working Notes)." In J. Rajchman, ed., *The Identity in Question*, 173–98. New York.

———. 1991. "The Nation Form." Trans. C. Turner. In E. Balibar and I. Wallerstein. *Race, Nation, Class: Ambiguous Identities*, 86–106. London.

Balme, M. 2001. *Menander: The Plays and Fragments*. Oxford.

Barigazzi, A. 1965a. *La formazione spirituale di Menandro*. Turin.

———. 1965b. "Sul *Sicionio* di Menandro." *SIFC* 37: 7–84.

———. 1985. "Menandro: L'inizio del Misumenos." *Prom.* 11: 97–126.

Barsby, J. 1993. "Problems of Adaptation in the *Eunuchus* of Terence." In N. W. Slater and B. Zimmermann, eds., *Intertextualität in der griechisch-römischen Komödie*, 160–79. Stuttgart.

———, ed. and comm. 1999. *Eunuchus*, by Terence. Cambridge.

Barton, C. A. 1999. "The Roman Blush: The Delicate Matter of Self-Control." In J. I. Porter, ed., *Constructions of the Body in Classical Antiquity*, 212–34. Ann Arbor.

Bassi, K. 1998. *Acting Like Men: Gender, Drama, and Nostalgia in Ancient Greece*. Ann Arbor.

Bauböck, R. 1994. *Transnational Citizenship: Membership and Rights in International Migration*. Brookfield, Vt.

Bayer, E. 1969. *Demetrios Phalereus, der Athener*. Stuttgart.

Beard, M. 1993. "Looking (harder) for Roman Myth: Dumézil, Declamation, and the Problems of Definition." In F. Graf, ed., *Colloquium Rauricum*, 3: 44–64. Stuttgart.

Belardinelli, A. M. 1994. *Menandro Sicioni*. Bari.

Belsey, C. 1985. "Disrupting Sexual Difference: Meaning and Gender in the Comedies." In J. Drakakis, ed., *Alternative Shakespeares*, 166–90. London.

———. 1994. *Desire: Love Stories in Western Culture*. Oxford.

Billows, R.A. 1990. *Antigonos the One-Eyed and the Creation of the Hellenistic State*. Berkeley.

———. 1995. *Kings and Colonists: Aspects of Macedonian Imperialism*. Leiden.

Blanchard, A. 1983. *Essai sur la composition des comédies de Ménandre*. Paris.

Blänsdorf, J. 1982. "Die Komödienintrige als Spiel im Spiel." *A&A* 28: 131–54.

Blondell, R. 2002. *The Play of Character in Plato's Dialogues*. Cambridge.

Blume, H.-D. 1974. *Menanders "Samia": Eine Interpretation*. Darmstadt.

———. 1998. *Menander*. Darmstadt.

Blundell, J. 1980. *Menander and the Monologue*. Göttingen.

Blundell, M. W. 1985. *Helping Friends and Harming Enemies*. Cambridge.

Boegehold, A. L. 1994. "Perikles' Citizenship Law of 451/0 B.C." In A. L. Boegehold and A. C. Scafuro, eds., *Athenian Identity and Civic Ideology*, 57–66. Baltimore.

Borgogno, A. 1988. "Sul nuovissimo *Misumenos* di Menandro." *QUCC* 30: 87–97.

Bosworth, A. B. 1988. *Conquest and Empire: The Reign of Alexander the Great*. Cambridge.

Bourdieu, P. 1977. *Outline of a Theory of Practice*. Trans. R. Nice. Cambridge.

———. 1991. *Language and Symbolic Power*. Ed. J. B. Thompson. Trans. G. Raymond and M. Adamson. Cambridge.

Bourriot, F. 1995. *Kalos kagathos, kalokagathia: D'un terme de propagande de sophistes à une notion sociale et philosophique: étude d'histoire athénienne*. Hildescheim.

Brock, R. 1994. "The Labour of Women in Classical Athens." *CQ* 44: 336–46.

Brown, G. M. 1974. "The End of Menander's Perikeiromene." *BICS* 21: 43–54.

Brown, P. G. McC. 1983. "Menander's Dramatic Technique and the Law of Athens." *CQ* 33: 412–20.

———. 1987. "Masks, Names, and Characters in New Comedy." *Hermes* 115: 181–202.

———. 1990a. "The Bodmer Codex of Menander and the Endings of Terence's *Eunuchus* and Other Roman Comedies." In E. W. Handley and A. Hurst, eds., *Relire Ménandre*, 37–61. Recherches et rencontres 2. Geneva.

———. 1990b. "Plots and Prostitutes in Greek New Comedy." *Papers of the Leeds Latin Seminar* 6: 241–66.

———. 1991. "Athenian Attitudes to Rape and Seduction: The Evidence of Menander, *Dyskolos* 289–93." *CQ* 41: 533–34.

———. 1992a. "The Construction of Menander's *Dyskolos*, Acts 1–4." *ZPE* 94: 8–20.

———. 1992b. "Menander, Fragments 745 and 746 K.T, Menander's *Kolax*, and Parasites and Flatterers in Greek Comedy." *ZPE* 92: 91–107.

———. 1993. "Love and Marriage in Greek New Comedy." *CQ* 43: 184–205.

Brown, W. 1995. *States of Injury: Power and Freedom in Late Modernity*. Princeton.

Buckler, J. 2000. "Demosthenes and Aeschines." In I. Worthington, ed., *Demosthenes: Orator and Statesman*, 90–114. London.

Burstein, S. 1980. "Menander and Politics: The Fragments of the Halieis." In S. M. Burstein and L. A. Okin, eds., *Panhellenica: Essays in Ancient History and Historiography in Honor of Truesdell S. Brown*, 69–76. Lawrence, Kan.

Burtt, J. O., trans. 1954. *Minor Attic Orators*. vol. 2. Cambridge, Mass.

Butler, J. 1993. *Bodies That Matter: On the Discursive Limits of Sex*. New York.

———. 1997. *Excitable Speech: A Politics of the Performative*. New York.

Cairns, D. L. 1996. "*Hybris*, Dishonour, and Thinking Big." *JHS* 116: 1–32.

Calame, C. 1999. *The Poetics of Eros in Ancient Greece*. Trans. J. Lloyd. Princeton.

Cantarella, E. 1991. "*Moicheia*: Reconsidering a Problem." In M. Gagarin, ed., *Symposium 1990: Vorträge zur griechischen und hellenistischen Rechtsgeschichte*, 289–96. Cologne.

Capps, E., ed. 1910. *Four Plays of Menander*. Boston.

Carawan, E. 1998. *The Rhetoric and Law of Draco*. Oxford.

Carey, C., ed. 1992. *Apollodoros against Neaira: (Demosthenes) 59*. Warminster.

———. 1993. "The Return of the Radish or Just When You Thought It Was Safe to Go Back into the Kitchen." *LCM* 18: 53–55.

———. 1994. "Comic Ridicule and Democracy." In R. Osborne and S. Hornblower, eds., *Ritual, Finance, Politics: Athenian Democratic Accounts Presented to David Lewis*, 68–83. Oxford.

———. 1995. "Rape and Adultery in Athenian Law." *CQ* 45: 407–17.

———. 1998. "The Shape of Athenian Laws." *CQ* 48: 93–109.

Carrière, J. C. 1979. *Le carnival et la politique: Une introduction à la comédie grecque—suivre d'un choix de fragments*. Paris.

Carter, L. B. 1986. *The Quiet Athenian*. Oxford.

Cartledge, P. 1998. "The *machismo* of the Athenian Empire—or the Reign of the Phaulus?" In L. Foxhall and J. Salmon, eds., *When Men Were Men*, 54–67. London.

Casson, L. 1976. "The Athenian Upper Class and New Comedy." *TAPA* 106: 29–59.

Cawkwell, G. 1969. "The Crowning of Demosthenes." *CQ* 19: 163–80.

———. 1996. "The End of Greek Liberty." In R. W. Wallace and E. M. Harris, eds., *Transitions to Empire*, 98–121. London.

Chantraine, P. 1968–80. *Dictionnaire étymologique de la langue grecque: Histoire des mots*. 4 vols. Paris.

Christ, M. R. 1990. "Liturgy Avoidance and *Antidosis* in Classical Athens." *TAPA* 120: 147–70.

———. 1998. *The Litigious Athenian*. Baltimore.

Cohen, B. 2001. "Ethnic Identity in Democratic Athens and the Visual Vocabulary of Male Costume." In I. Malkin, ed., *Ancient Perceptions of Greek Ethnicity*, 235–74. Washington, D.C.

Cohen, D. 1990. "The Social Context of Adultery at Athens." In P. Cartledge, P. Millett, and S. Todd, eds., *Nomos: Essays in Athenian Law, Politics, and Society*, 147–165. Cambridge.

———. 1991a. *Law, Sexuality, and Society*. Cambridge.

———. 1991b. "Sexuality Violence and the Athenian Law of Hubris." *G&R* 38: 171–88.

———. 1995. *Law, Violence, and Community in Classical Athens*. Cambridge.

Cohen, E. E. 2000. *The Athenian Nation*. Princeton.

Cohn-Haft, L. 1995. "Divorce in Classical Athens." *JHS* 115: 1–14.

Cole, S. 1984. "Greek Sanctions against Sexual Assault." *CP* 79: 97–113.

Connell, R. W. 1987. *Gender and Power: Society, the Person, and Sexual Politics*. Stanford.

Connor, W. R. 1987. "Tribes, Festivals, and Processions: Civic Ceremonial and Political Manipulation in Ancient Greece." *JHS* 107: 40–50.

———. 1988. "Early Greek Land Warfare as Symbolic Expression." *P&P*, no. 119: 3–27.

———. 1989. "City Dionysia and Athenian Democracy." *C&M* 40: 7–32.

———. 1992 [1971]. *The New Politicians of Fifth-Century Athens*. Indianapolis.

———. 1994. "The Problem of Athenian Civic Identity." In A. Boegehold and A. Scafuro, eds., *Athenian Identity and Civic Ideology*, 34–44. Baltimore.

Conte, G. B. 1994. *Genres and Readers*. Trans. G. Most. Baltimore.

Copley, F. O. 1942. "On the Origin of Certain Features of the Paraclausithyron." *TAPA* 73: 96–107.
———. 1956. *Exclusus Amator*. APA Monographs 17. Madison, Wis..
Cott, N. 1995. "Giving Character to Our Whole Civil Polity: Marriage and the Public Order in the Late Nineteenth Century." In L. Kerber et al., eds., *U.S. History as Women's History*, 107–21. Chapel Hill, N.C.
Cox, C. 1998. *Household Interests: Property, Marriage Strategies, and Family Dynamics in Ancient Athens*. Princeton.
———. 2002a. "Crossing Boundaries through Marriage in Menander's Dyskolos." *CQ* 52: 391–94.
———. 2002b. "Is Sostratus' Family Urban in Menander's Dyskolos?" *CJ* 97: 351–58.
Crisafulli, T. 1998. "Representations of the Feminine: The Prostitute in Roman Comedy." In T. W. Hillard, R. A. Kearsley, C. E. V. Nixon, and A. M. Nobbs, eds., *Ancient History in a Modern University*, 223–29. Grand Rapids, Mich.
Csapo, E. 2000. "From Aristophanes to Menander? Genre Transformation in Greek Comedy." In M. Depew and D. Obbink, eds., *Matrices of Genre: Authors, Canons, and Society*, 115–34. Cambridge, Mass.
Csapo, E., and W. Slater. 1994. *The Context of Ancient Drama*. Ann Arbor.
Dahl, R. 1989. *Democracy and Its Critics*. New Haven.
Dalby, A. 1992. "Greeks Abroad: Social Organization and Food among the Ten Thousand." *JHS* 112: 16–30.
Davidson, J. 1997. *Courtesans and Fishcakes: The Consuming Passions of the Greeks*. London.
Davies, J. K. 1977/78. "Athenian Citizenship: The Descent Group and the Alternatives." *CJ* 73: 105–21.
———. 1981. *Wealth and the Power of Wealth in Classical Athens*. New York.
Dedoussi, C. 1988a. "The Borrowing Play in *Dyskolos* 891–930." *BICS* 35: 79–83.
———. 1988b. "The Future of Plangon's Child in Menander's *Samia*." *LCM* 13: 39–42.
Del Corno, D., ed. and trans. 1966. *Le commedie*, by Menander. Vol. 1. Milan.
———. 1970. "Prologhi menandrei." *ACME* 33: 99–108.
De Souza, P. 1999. *Piracy in the Graeco-Roman World*. Cambridge.
Diller, A. 1937. *Race Mixture among the Greeks before Alexander*. Urbana, Ill.
Dilts, M. R., ed. 1992. *Scholia in Aeschinem*. Stuttgart.
Doblhofer, G. 1994. *Vergewaltigung in der Antike*. Stuttgart.
Dolar, M. 1993. "Beyond Interpellation." *Qui Parle* 6.2: 75–94.
Dougherty, C. 1996. "Democratic Contradictions and the Synoptic Illusion of Euripides' *Ion*." In J. Ober and C. Hedrick, eds., *Demokratia*, 249–70. Princeton.
Dover, K. J. 1974. *Greek Popular Morality in the Time of Plato and Aristotle*. Oxford.
———. 1989. *Greek Homosexuality*. Updated ed. Cambridge, Mass.
———. 1996. "Timocles." In S. Hornblower and A. Spawforth, eds., *The Oxford Classical Dictionary*, 1528. 3rd ed. Oxford.
Dow, S., and A. H. Travis. 1943. "Demetrios of Phaleron and His Lawgiving." *Hesp*. 12: 144–65.
duBois, P. 1988. *Sowing the Body: Psychoanalysis and Ancient Representations of Women*. Chicago.

Dworacki, S. 1973. "The Prologues in the Comedies of Menander." *Eos* 61: 33–47.
———. 1993. "Die Barbaren in den Komödien des Menander." In S. Jäkel, ed., *Power and Spirit*, 99–110. Turku, [Finland].
Easterling, P. E. 1995. "Menander—Loss and Survival." In A. Griffiths, ed., *Stage Directions: Essays in Honour of E. W. Handley*, 153–60. London.
Edmonds, J. M. 1961. *The Fragments of Attic Comedy after Meinecke, Bergk, and Kock*. Vol. 3A. Leiden.
Edwards, A. 1993. "Historicizing the Popular Grotesque: Bakhtin's *Rabelais* and Attic Old Comedy." In R. Scodel, ed., *Theater and Society in the Classical World*, 89–118. Ann Arbor.
Elderkin, G. W. 1934. "The Curculio of Plautus." *AJA* 39: 29–36.
Ellis, J. R. 1976. *Philip II and Macedonian Imperialism*. London.
Faubion, J. D. 1996. "Kinship Is Dead. Long Live Kinship." *Comparative Studies in Society and History* 38: 67–91.
Fantham, E. 1971. "*Heauton Timorumenos* and *Adelphoe*: A Study of Fatherhood in Terence and Menander. " *Latomus* 30: 970–98.
———. 1975. "Sex, Status, and Survival in Hellenistic Athens: A Study of Women in New Comedy." *Phoenix* 29: 44–74.
———. 1986. "ΖΗΛΟΤΥΠΙΑ: A Brief Excursion into Sex, Violence, and Literary History." *Phoenix* 40: 45–58.
Faraguna, M. 1992. *Atene nell' età di Alessandro*. Rome.
Felman, S. 1983. *The Literary Speech Act: Don Juan with J. L. Austin, or Seduction in Two Languages*. Trans. C. Porter. Ithaca.
Ferguson, W. S. 1911a. *Hellenistic Athens*. London.
———. 1911b. "The Laws of Demetrius of Phalerum and their Guardians." *Klio* 11: 265–76.
Finley, M. I. 1952. *Studies in Land and Credit in Ancient Athens, 500–200* B.C.: The Horos Inscriptions. New Brunswick, N.J.
Fisher, N. R. E. 1990. "The Law of Hubris in Athens." In P. Cartledge, P. Millett, and S. Todd, eds., *Nomos: Essays in Athenian Law, Politics, and Society*, 123–38. Cambridge.
———. 1992. *Hybris*. Warminster.
———. 1998a. "Gymnasia and Democratic Values of Leisure." In P. Cartledge, P. Millet, and S. von Reden, eds., *Kosmos: Essays in Order, Conflict, and Community in Classical Athens*, 84–104. Cambridge.
———. 1998b. "Violence, Masculinity, and the Law in Classical Athens." In L. Foxhall and J. Salmon, eds., *When Men Were Men: Masculinity, Power, and Identity in Classical Antiquity*, 68–97. New York.
———, trans. 2001. *Against Timarchos*, by Aeschines. Oxford.
Flower, M. A. 1994. *Theopompus of Chios: History and Rhetoric in the Fourth Century*. Oxford.
Flury, P. 1968. *Liebe und Liebessprache bei Menander, Plautus, Terenz*. Heidelberg.
Foley, H. 2001. *Female Acts in Greek Tragedy*. Princeton.
Fortenbaugh, W. W. 1974. "Menander's *Perikeiromene*: Misfortune, Vehemence, and Polemon." *Phoenix* 28: 430–43.
Fortenbaugh, W. W., and E. Schütrumpf, eds. 2000. *Demetrius of Phaleron: Text, Translation, and Discussion*. New Brunswick, N.J.

Foucault, M. 1985. *The Use of Pleasure*. Vol. 2 of *The History of Sexuality*. Trans. R. Hurley. New York.

Foxhall, L. 1989. "Household, Gender, Property in Classical Athens." *CQ* 39: 22–44.

———. 1991. "Response to Eva Cantarella." In M. Gagarin, ed., *Symposium 1990: Vorträge zur griechischen und hellenistischen Rechtsgeschichte*, 297–303. Cologne.

———. 1996. "The Law and the Lady: Women and Legal Proceedings in Classical Athens." In L. Foxhall and A. D. E. Lewis, eds., *Greek Law in Its Political Setting: Justifications Not Justice*, 133–52. Oxford.

———. 1998. "Pandora Unbound: A Feminist Critique of Foucault's History of Sexuality." In D. H. J. Larmour, P. A. Miller, and C. Platter, eds., *Rethinking Sexuality: Foucault and Classical Antiquity*, 122–37. Princeton.

Fraenkel, E. 1960. *Elementi Plautini in Plauto*. Florence.

Fredershausen, O. 1912. "Weitere Studien über das Recht bei Plautus und Terenz." *Hermes* 47: 199–249.

Fredrickson, G. M. 2002. *Racism. A Short History*. Princeton.

Frost, K. B. 1988. *Entrances and Exits in Menander*. Oxford.

Frye, N. 1957. *Anatomy of Criticism*. Princeton.

Gabbert, J. 1986. "Pragmatic Democracy in Hellenistic Athens." *AncW* 13: 29–33.

Gabrielsen, V. 1986. "φανερά and ἀφανὴς οὐσία in Classical Athens." *C&M* 37: 99–114.

———. 1987. "The Antidosis Procedure in Classical Athens." *C&M* 38: 7–38.

Gagarin, M. 2000. "The Legislation of Demetrius of Phaleron and the Transformation of Athenian Law." In W. W. Fortenbaugh and E. Schütrumpf, eds., *Demetrius of Phaleron: Text, Translation, and Discussion*, 347–65. New Brunswick, N.J.

———. 2001. "Women's Voices in Attic Oratory." In A. Lardinois and L. McClure, eds., *Making Silence Speak: Women's Voices in Greek Literature and Society*, 161–76. Princeton.

Gaiser, K. 1967. "Menander und der Peripatos." *A&A* 13: 8–40.

Gallant, T. W. 1991. *Risk and Survival in Ancient Greece*. Stanford.

Garland, B. J. 1981. "Gynaikonomoi: An Investigation of Greek Censors of Women." Ph.d. diss., Johns Hopkins University.

Garzya, A. 1969. "Il *Sicionio* di Menandro e la realta' politica del tempo." *Dion.* 43: 481–84.

Gauthier, P. 1985. *Les cités grecques et leurs bienfaiteurs (IVe–Ier siècle avant J.C.)*. Paris.

———. 1993. "Les Cités hellénistiques." In M. Hansen, ed., *The Ancient Greek City State*, 211–31. Copenhagen.

Gehrke, H. J. 1976. *Phokion: Studien zur Erfassung seiner historischen Gestalt*. Munich.

———. 1978. "Das Verhältnis von Politik und Philosophie im Wirken des Demetrios von Phaleron." *Chiron* 8: 149–193.

Gernet, L. 1920. "La création du testament." *REG* 33: 123–68, 249–90.

———. 1921. "Sur l'Epiclerat." *REG* 34: 337–79.

———. 1981. *The Anthropology of Ancient Greece*. Trans. J. Hamilton and B. Nagy. Baltimore.

Ghiron-Bistagne, P. 1976. *Recherches sur les acteurs dans la Grèce antique*. Paris.

Giddens, A. 1979. *Central Problems in Social Theory: Action, Structure, and Contradiction in Social Analysis*. Berkeley.

———. 1991. *Modernity and Self-Identity: Self and Society in the Late Modern Age*. Stanford.

———. 1992. *The Transformation of Intimacy: Sexuality, Love, and Eroticism in Modern Societies*. Stanford.

Giglioni, G. B. 1982. "Communità e solitudine: Tensioni sociali nei rapporti fra città ecampagna nell'Atene del quinto e del quarto secolo A.C." *SCO* 32: 59–95.

———. 1984. *Menandro e la politica della convivenza: La storia attraverso i testi letterari*. Como.

Gilula, D. 1987. "Menander's Comedies: Best with Dessert and Wine." *Athenaeum* 65: 511–16.

Giovannini, A. 1993. "Greek Cities and Greek Commonwealth." In A. W. Bulloch, E. S. Gruen, A. A. Long, and A. Stewart, eds., *Images and Ideologies: Self-Definition in the Hellenistic World*, 265–86. Berkeley.

Gleason, M. W. 1990. "The Semiotics of Gender: Physiognomy and Self-Fashioning in the Second Century C.E." In D. Halperin, J. J. Winkler, and F. I. Zeitlin, eds., *Before Sexuality: The Construction of Erotic Experience in the Ancient World*, 389–416. Princeton.

Goldberg, S. 1980. *The Making of Menander's Comedy*. London.

———. 1993. "Models and Memory in the Comedy of Menander." *Comparative Drama* 27: 328–40.

Golden, M. 1990. *Children and Childhood in Classical Athens*. Baltimore.

———. 1991. "Thirteen Years of Homosexuality." *EMC* 35: 327–40.

———. 2000. "Demosthenes and the Social Historian." In I. Worthington, ed., *Demosthenes: Statesmen and Orator*, 159–80. London.

Goldhill, S. 1990. "The Great Dionysia and Civic Ideology." In J. J. Winkler and F. I. Zeitlin, eds., *Nothing to Do With Dionysos? Athenian Drama in Its Social Context*, 97–129. Princeton.

———. 1998. "The Seductions of the Gaze: Socrates and His Girlfriends." In P. Cartledge, P. Millet, and S. von Reden, eds., *Kosmos: Essays in Order, Conflict, and Community in Classical Athens*, 105–24. Cambridge.

———. 2000. "Civic Ideology and the Problem of Difference: The Politics of Aeschylean Tragedy, Once Again." *JHS* 120: 34–56.

Gomme, A. W. 1937. *Essays in Greek History and Literature*. Oxford.

Gomme, A. W., and F. H. Sandbach, eds. 1973. *Menander: A Commentary*. Oxford.

Gow, A. S. F. , ed. 1965. *The Fragments*, by Machon. Cambridge.

Grace, E. 1973. "Status Distinctions in the Draconian Law." *Eirene* 11: 5–30.

Grant, J. N. 1986. "The Father–Son Relationship and the Ending of Menander's *Samia*." *Phoenix* 40: 172–84.

Green, P. 1990. *Alexander to Actium: The Historic Evolution of the Hellenistic Age*. Berkeley.

Greenblatt, S. 1988. *Shakespearean Negotiations: The Circulation of Social Energy in Renaissance England*. Berkeley.

Griffith, G. T. 1935. *Mercenaries of the Hellenistic World*. Cambridge.

Griffith, M. 1995. "Brilliant Dynasts: Power and Politics in the *Oresteia*." *CA* 2: 37–65.

Groton, A. 1987. "Anger in Menander's *Samia*." *AJP* 108: 437–43.

Gruen, E. 1993. "The Polis in the Hellenistic World." In R. M. Rosen and J. Farrell, eds., *Nomodeiktes: Greek Studies in Honor of Martin Ostwald*, 339–54. Ann Arbor.

Guida, A. 1974. "Note sul *Sicionio* di Menandro." *SIFC* 46: 211–34.

Guillaumin, C. 1995. *Racism, Sexism, Power, and Ideology*. London.

Gulick, C. B., trans. 1927–41. *The Deipnosophists*, by Athenaeus. 7 vols. Cambridge, Mass.

Gutzwiller, K. 2000. "The Tragic Mask of Comedy: Metatheatricality in Menander." *CA* 19: 102–37.

Habicht, C. 1956. *Gottmenschentum und griechische Städte*. Munich.

———. 1993. "The Comic Poet Archedikos." *Hesp*. 63: 253–56.

———. 1997. *Athens from Alexander to Antony*. Cambridge.

Hackl, U. 1987. "Die Aufhebung der attischen Demokratie nach dem Lamischen Krieg 322 v. Chr." *Klio* 69: 58–71.

Hall, E. 1989. *Inventing the Barbarian: Greek Self-Definition through Tragedy*. Oxford.

———. 1993. "Asia Unmanned." In *War and Society in the Greek World*, 108–33. London.

———. 1995. "Lawcourt Dramas: The Power of Performance in Greek Forensic Oratory." *BICS* 40: 39–58.

———. 1997. "The Sociology of Athenian Tragedy." In P. E. Easterling, ed., *The Cambridge Companion to Greek Tragedy*, 93–126. Cambridge.

Hall, J. 1997. *Ethnic Identity in Greek Antiquity*. Cambridge.

———. 2002. *Hellenicity: Between Ethnicity and Culture*. Chicago.

Halliwell, S. 1991a. "Comic Satire and Freedom of Speech in Classical Athens." *JHS* 111: 48–70.

———. 1991b. "The Uses of Laughter in Greek Culture." *CQ* 41: 297–96.

Halperin, D. 1990. *One Hundred Years of Homosexuality and Other Essays on Greek Love*. New York.

———. 2002. "Forgetting Foucault: Acts, Identities, and the History of Sexuality." In M. C. Nussbaum and J. Sihvola, eds., *The Sleep of Reason: Erotic Experience and Sexual Ethics in Ancient Greece and Rome*, 21–54. Chicago.

Handley, E. W., ed. and comm. 1965a. *Dyskolos*, by Menander. Cambridge.

———. 1965b. "Notes on the Sikyonios of Menander." *BICS* 12: 38–62.

———. 1979. "Recent Papyrus Finds: Menander." *BICS* 26: 81–87.

———. 1989. "Comedy." In P. E. Easterling and B. M. W. Knox, eds., *The Cambridge History of Classical Literature*, 103–73. Cambridge.

———. 1997. "Some Thoughts on New Comedy and Its Public." *Pallas* 47: 185–200.

Hansen, M. H. 1986. *Demography and Democracy: The Number of Athenian Citizens in the Fourth Century*. Herning, Denmark.

———. 1991. *The Athenian Democracy in the Age of Demosthenes*. Oxford.

Hanson, V. D. 1989. *The Western Way of War*. New York.

———. 1996. "Hoplites into Democrats: The Changing Ideology of the Athenian Infantry." In J. Ober and C. Hedrick, eds., *Dêmokratia: A Conversation on Democracies, Ancient and Modern*, 289–312. Princeton.

Harding, P. 1987. "Rhetoric and Politics in Fourth-Century Athens." *Phoenix* 41: 25–39.

———. 1994. "Comedy and Rhetoric." In I. Worthington, ed., *Persuasion: Greek Rhetoric in Action*, 196–221. London.

Harris, E. M. 1990. "Did the Athenians Regard Seduction as a Worse Crime than Rape?" *CQ* 40: 370–77.

———. 1994. "Law and Oratory." In I. Worthington, ed., *Persuasion: Greek Rhetoric in Action*, 130–50. London.

———. 1995. *Aeschines and Athenian Politics*. New York.

———, trans. 2001. Lycurgus. *Against Leocrates*, by Lycurgus. In I. Worthington, C. R. Cooper, and E. M. Harris, trans., *Dinarchus, Hyperides, and Lycurgus*, 159–203. Austin, Tex.

Harrison, A. R. W. 1968–71. *The Law of Athens*. 2 vols. Oxford.

Hartmann, E. 2000. "'Bastards' in Classical Athens." In K. Pollman, ed., *Double Standards in the Ancient and Medieval World*, 43–54. Göttingen.

Hauschild, H. 1933. *Die gestalt der Hetäre in der griechischen Komödie*. Leipzig.

Heckel, W. 1992. *The Marshals of Alexander's Empire*. London.

———. 1999. "The Politics of Antipatros: 324–319 B.C." In *Ancient Macedonia VI*, 1: 489–98. Thessaloníki.

Hedrick, C. 2000. "Epigraphic Writing and the Democratic Restoration of 307." In P. Flensted-Jensen, T. H. Nielsen, and L. Rubinstein, eds., *Polis and Politics: Studies in Ancient Greek History*, 327–36. Copenhagen.

Heisserer, A. J. 1980. *Alexander the Great and the Greeks: The Epigraphic Evidence*. Norman, Okla.

Henderson, J. 1990. "The Demos and Comic Competition." In J. J. Winkler and F. I. Zeitlin, eds., *Nothing to Do with Dionysos? Athenian Drama in Its Social Context*, 271–314. Princeton.

———. 1991. *The Maculate Muse: Obscene Language in Attic Comedy*. 2nd ed. Oxford.

Henrichs, A. 1993. "Response." In A. W. Bulloch, E. S. Gruen, A. A. Long, and A. Stewart, eds., *Images and Ideologies: Self-Definition in the Hellenistic World*, 171–95. Berkeley.

Henry, M. 1985. *Menander's Courtesans and the Greek Comic Tradition*. Frankfurt.

———. 1986. "Ethos, Mythos, Praxis: Women in Menander's Comedy." *Helios* 13.2: 141–50.

———. 1992. "The Edible Woman: Athenaeus's Concept of the Pornographic." In A. Richlin, ed., *Pornography and Representation in Greece and Rome*, 250–68. Oxford.

Herman, G. 1987. *Ritualised Friendship in the Greek City*. Cambridge.

———. 1993. "Tribal and Civic Codes of Behavior in Lysias I." *CQ* 43: 406–19.

———. 1994. "How Violent Was Athenian Society?" In R. Osborne and S.

Hornblower, eds., *Ritual, Finance, Politics: Athenian Democratic Accounts Presented to David Lewis*, 99–117. Oxford.

———. 1995. "Honour, Revenge, and the State in Fourth-Century Athens." In W. Eder, ed., *Die athenische Demokratie im 4. Jahrhundert v. Chr.: Vollendung oder Verfall einer Verfassungsform?*, 43–60. Stuttgart.

Hignett, C. 1952. *A History of the Athenian Constitution to the End of the Fifth Century* B.C. Oxford.

Hoffmann, G. 1986. "L'espace théâtral et social du *Dyscolos* de Menandre." *Metis* 1: 269–90.

———. 1998. "La richesse et les riches dans les comédies de Ménandre." *Pallas* 48: 135–44.

Hofmeister, T. 1997. "αἱ πᾶσαι πόλεις: Polis and Oikoumenê in Menander." In G. W. Dobrov, ed., *The City as Comedy*, 289–342. Chapel Hill, N.C.

Holzberg, N. 1974. *Menander: Untersuchungen zur dramatischen Technik*. Nuremberg.

Howard, J. E. 1994. *The Stage and Social Struggle in Early Modern England*. London.

Hubbard, T. 1998. "Popular Perceptions of Elite Homosexuality in Classical Athens." *Arion* 6.1: 48–78.

Humphreys, S. C. 1974. "The Nothoi of Kynosarges." *JHS* 94: 88–95.

———. 1985a. "Lycurgus of Butadae: An Athenian Aristocrat." In J. W. Eadie and J. Ober, eds., *The Craft of the Ancient Historian: Essays in Honor of Chester G. Starr*, 199–252. Lanham, Md.

———. 1985b. "Social Relations on Stage: Witnesses in Classical Athens." *History and Anthropology* 1: 313–69.

———. 1991. "A Historical Approach to Drakon's Law on Homicide." In M. Gagarin, ed., *Symposion 1990: Vorträge zur griechischen und hellenistischen Rechtsgeschichte*, 17–45. Cologne.

———. 1993. *The Family, Women, and Death*. Ann Arbor.

———. 1999. "From a Grin to Death: The Body in the Greek Discovery of Politics." In J. Porter, ed., *Constructions of the Classical Body*, 126–46. Ann Arbor.

Hunt, P. 1998. *Slaves, Warfare, and Ideology in the Greek Historians*. Cambridge.

Hunter, R. L., ed. 1983. *The Fragments*, by Eubulus. Cambridge.

———. 1985. *The New Comedy of Greece and Rome*. Cambridge.

———. 1987. "Middle Comedy and the *Amphitruo* of Plautus." *Dion.* 57: 281–98.

———. 2000. "The Politics of Plutarch's Comparison of Aristophanes and Menander." In S. Gödde and T. Heinze, eds., *Skenika: Beiträge zum antiken Theater und seiner Rezeption*, 267–76. Darmstadt.

Hunter, V. 1990. "Gossip and Politics in Classical Athens." *Phoenix* 44: 299–325.

———. 1994. *Policing Athens: Social Control in the Attic Lawsuits, 420–320* B.C. Princeton.

Hurst, A. 1990. "Ménandre et la tragédie." In E. W. Handley and A. Hurst, eds., *Relire Ménandre*, 93–122. Geneva.

Ireland, S. 1983. "Menander and the Comedy of Disappointment." *LCM* 8.3: 45–47.

Irwin, T., trans. 1999. *Nicomachean Ethics*, by Aristotle. 2nd ed. Indianapolis.

Isager, S. 1980/81. "The Marriage Pattern in Classical Athens: Men and Women in Isaios." *C&M* 33: 81–96.

Jacoby, F. 1923–58. *Die Fragmente der griechischen Historiker*. Berlin.

Jacques, J. M., ed. 1971. *La Samienne*, by Menander. Paris.

———, ed. 1976. *Le Dyskolos*, by Menander. Paris.

———. 2000. "Bemerkungen über den Sikyonier des Menander." In S. Gödde and T. Heinze, eds., *Skenika: Beiträge zum antiken Theater und seiner Rezeption*, 125–33. Darmstadt.

Jameson, F. 1981. *The Political Unconscious: Narrative as a Socially Symbolic Act*. Ithaca.

Jameson, M. H. 1997. "Women and Democracy in Fourth Century Athens." In P. Brulé and J. Oulhen, eds., *Esclavage, guerre, économie en Grèce ancienne*, 95–107. Rennes.

Jeffords, S. 1989. *The Remasculinization of America: Gender and the Vietnam War*. Bloomington, Ind.

Johnstone, S. 1994. "Virtuous Toil, Vicious Work, Xenophon on Aristocratic Style." *CP* 89: 219–40.

———. 1998. "Cracking the Code of Silence: Athenian Legal Oratory and the History of Slaves and Women." In S. Joshel and S. Murnaghan, eds., *Women and Slaves in Greco Roman Culture: Differential Equations*, 221–35. London.

———. 1999. *Disputes and Democracy: The Consequences of Litigation in Ancient Athens*. Austin, Tex.

Just, R. 1989. *Women in Athenian Law and Life*. London.

Kapparis, K. A. 1993. "Is Eratosthenes in Lys. 1 the Same Person as Eratosthenes in Lys. 12?" *Hermes* 121: 364–65.

———. 1995. "When Were the Athenian Adultery Laws Introduced?" *RIDA* 42: 97–122.

———. 1996. "Humiliating the Adulterer: The Law and the Practice in Classical Athens." *RIDA* 43: 63–77.

———, ed. 1999. *Against Neaira: [D. 59]*, by Apollodoros. Berlin.

Karabelias, E. 1970. "Une nouvelle source pour l'étude du droit attique: Le '*Bouclier*' de Ménandre." *RD* 48: 357–89.

Karnezis, J. E. 1977. "Law in the *Aspis*." *Platon* 29: 152–55.

Kassel, R. 1965. "Menanders *Sikyonier*." *Eranos* 63: 1–21.

Kassel, R., and C. Austin, eds. 1983–. *Poetae Comici Graeci*. Berlin.

Katsouris, A. G. 1975. *Tragic Patterns in Menander*. Athens.

———. 1995. *Menander Bibliography*. Thessaloníki.

Katz, M. A. 1995. "Ideology and 'the Status of Women' in Ancient Greece." In R. Hawley and B. Levick, eds., *Women in Antiquity: New Assessments*, 21–43. London.

———. 1999. "Women and Democracy in Ancient Greece." In T. M. Falkner, N. Felson, and D. Konstan, eds., *Contextualizing Classics: Ideology, Performance, Dialogue: Essays in Honor of John J. Peradotto*, 41–68. Lanham, Md.

Kebric, R. B. 1977. *In the Shadow of Macedon: Duris of Samos*. Wiesbaden.

Keuls, E. 1969. "Mystery Elements in Menander's *Dyskolos*." *TAPA* 100: 209–20.

———. 1973. "The *Samia* of Menander: An Interpretation of Its Plot and Theme." *ZPE* 10: 1–12.

Keyes, C. W. 1940. "Half-Sister Marriage in New Comedy and the Epidicus." *TAPA* 71: 217–29.

King, H. 1998. *Hippocrates' Woman: Reading the Female Body in Ancient Greece*. London and New York.

Kock, T. 1880–88. *Comicorum Atticorum fragmenta*. 3 vols. Leipzig.

Konstan, D. 1983. *Roman Comedy*. Ithaca.

———. 1995. *Greek Comedy and Ideology*. Oxford.

———. 1997. *Friendship in the Classical World*. Cambridge.

Kopytoff, I. 1986. "The Cultural Biography of Things: Commoditization as Process." In A. Appadurai, ed., *The Social Life of Things: Commodities in Cultural Perspective*, 64–91. Cambridge.

Körte, A., and A. Thierfelder, eds. 1957. *Menandri quae supersunt*. 2 vols. Leipzig.

Kralli, I. 2000. "Athens and the Hellenistic Kings (338–261 B.C.): The Language of the Decrees." *CQ* 50: 113–32.

Krentz, P. 1982. *The Thirty at Athens*. Ithaca.

Krieter-Spiro, M. 1997. *Sklaven, Köche und Hetären: das Dienstpersonal bei Menander: Stellung, Rolle, Komik, und Sprache*. Stuttgart.

Kurke, L. 1991. *The Traffic in Praise: Pindar and the Poetics of Social Economy*. Ithaca.

———. 1992. "The Politics of *Habrosynê* in Archaic Greece." *CA* 11: 90–120.

———. 1999. *Coins, Bodies, Games, and Gold: The Politics of Meaning in Archaic Greece*. Princeton.

———. 2002. "Gender, Politics, and Subversion in the *Chreiai* of Machon." *PCPS* 48: 20–65.

Laclau, E., and C. Mouffe. 1985. *Hegemony and Socialist Strategy: Towards a Radical Democratic Politics*. Trans. W. Moore and P. Cammack. London.

Lamagna, M. 1994. *La Faniculla Tosata*. Naples.

———. 1997–98. "Per *La Samia* di Menandro: Presupposti etico attuazione scenica." *RAAN* 67: 129–45.

———, ed. 1998. *La donna di Samo*. Naples.

Lane Fox, R. 1994. "Aeschines and Athenian Democracy." In R. Osborne and S. Hornblower, eds., *Ritual, Finance, Politics: Athenian Democratic Accounts Presented to David Lewis*, 135–55. Oxford.

Lanowski, J. 1965. "ΚΕΝΗ ΤΡΑΓΩΙΔΙΑ." *Eos* 55: 245–53.

Lape, S. 2000. "Law as Civic Destiny: Making Citizens in Menander's New Comedy." *ESJ* 17: 41–62.

———. 2001. "Democratic Ideology and the Poetics of Rape in Menander's Comedy." *CA* 20: 79–120.

———. 2002–03. "Solon and the Institution of the Democratic Family Form." *CJ* 98: 117–39.

———. Forthcoming. "Racializing Democracy: The Politics of Sexual Reproduction in Democratic Athens." *Parallax*, special volume.

Larmour, D. H. J., P. A. Miller, and C. Platter, eds. 1998. "Introduction. Situating *The History of Sexuality*." *Rethinking Sexuality: Foucault and Classical Antiquity*, 3–41. Princeton.

Lawton, C. 1995. *Attic Document Reliefs: Art and Politics in Ancient Athens*. Oxford.

Leader, R. E. 1997. "In Death Not Divided: Gender, Family, and State on Classical Athenian Grave Stelae." *AJA* 101: 683–99.

Leduc, C. 1992. “Marriage in Ancient Greece.” In P. S. Pantel, ed., *A History of Women in the West*.Vol. 1, *From Ancient Goddesses to Christian Saints*, 235–95. Cambridge.

LeGuen, B. 1995. “Théâtre et cités à l'époque hellénistique.” *REG* 108: 59–90.

Lehmann, G. A. 1988. “Der ‘Lamische Kreig’ und die ‘Freiheit der Hellenen’. Überlegungen zur heironymianischen Tradition.” *ZPE* 73: 121–49.

———. 1997. *Oligarchische Herrschaft im klassischen Athen: zu den Krisen und Katastrophen der attischen Demokratie im 5. und 4. Jahrhundert v. Chr.* Düsseldorf.

Lévy, E. 1985. “Astos and politès d'Homère à Hérodote.” *Ktéma* 10: 53–66.

Licht, H. [pseud.]. 1952 [1932]. *Sexual Life in Ancient Greece*. Trans. J. Freese. Ed. L. H. Dawson. New York.

Liddell, H. G., R. Scott, and H. S. Jones, eds. 1968. *Greek-English Lexicon*. 9th ed., with suppl. Oxford.

Lloyd-Jones, H. 1990 [1972]. “Notes on the Sikyonios of Menander.” In *Greek Comedy, Hellenistic Literature, and Miscellanea: The Academic Papers of Sir Hugh Lloyd-Jones*, 77–86. Oxford.

Long, T. 1986. *Barbarians in Greek Comedy*. Carbondale, Ill.

Loraux, N. 1986. *The Invention of Athens: The Funeral Oration in Classical Athens*. Trans. A. Sheridan. Cambridge.

———. 1993. *The Children of Athena: Athenian Ideas about Citizenship and the Division between the Sexes*. Trans. C. Levine. Princeton.

Lord, C. 1977. “Aristotle, Menander, and the *Adelphoe* of Terence.” *TAPA* 107: 183–202.

———, trans. 1984. *The Politics*, by Aristotle. Chicago.

Lotze, D. 1981. “Zwischen Politen und Metöken: Passivbürger im klassichen Athen?” *Klio* 63: 159–178.

Lowe, J. C. B. 1983. “The *Eunuchus*: Terence and Menander.” *CQ* 33: 428–44.

Lowe, N. J. 1987. “Tragic Space and Comic Timing in Menander's *Dyskolos*.” *BICS* 34: 126–38.

———. 2000. *The Classical Plot and the Invention of Western Narrative*. Cambridge.

Ludwig, W. 1968. “The Originality of Terence and His Greek Models.” *GRBS* 9: 169–82.

———. 1973. “Von Terenz zu Menander.” In E. Lefèvre, ed., *Die römische Komödie: Plautus und Terenz*, 354–408. Darmstadt.

Ma, J. 1999. *Antiochos III and the Cities of Western Asia Minor*. Oxford.

MacCary, W. T. 1969. “Menander's Slaves: Their Names, Roles, and Masks.” *TAPA* 100: 277–94.

———. 1970. “Menander's Characters: Their Names, Roles, and Masks.” *TAPA* 101: 277–90.

———. 1972. “Menander's Soldiers: Their Names, Roles, and Masks.” *AJP* 93: 279–98.

MacDowell, D. M. 1976. “Bastards as Athenian Citizens.” *CQ* 26: 88–91.

———. 1978. *The Law in Classical Athens*. Ithaca.

———. 1982. “Love versus the Law: An Essay on Menander's *Aspis*.” *G&R* 29: 42–52.

MacIntyre, A. 1984. *After Virtue: A Study in Moral Theory*. 2nd ed. Notre Dame, Ind.

MacKinnon, C. 1989. *Toward a Feminist Theory of the State*. Cambridge, Mass.

Maffi, A. 1989. "Matrimonio, concubinato e filiazione illegitima nell'Atene degli oratori." In G. Thür, ed., *Symposion 1985: Vortrage zur griechischen und hellenistischen Rechtsgeschichte*, 177–214. Cologne.

Maitland, J. 1992. "Dynasty and Family in the Athenian City: A View from Attic Tragedy." *CQ* 42: 26–40.

Major, W. 1997. "Menander in a Macedonian World." *GRBS* 38: 41–74.

Manville, P. B. 1990. *The Origins of Citizenship in Ancient Athens*. Princeton.

Marasco, G., ed. 1984. *Demochare di Leuconoe: Politica e cultura a Athene fra iv e .iii sec*. Florence.

Marcellus, H de. 1994. "The Origins and Nature of the Attic Ephebeia to 200 B.C." D.Phil. thesis, Oxford University.

———. 1996. "IG XIV 1184 and the Ephebic Service of Menander." *ZPE* 110: 69–76.

Martin, R. P. 1984. "Hesiod, Odysseus, and the Instruction of Princes." *TAPA* 114: 29–48.

Masaracchia, A. 1981. "La tematica amorosa in Menandro." In *Letterature comparate: Problemi e Metodo: Studi in onore di E. Paratare*, 213–38. Bologna.

Masaracchia, E. 1978–79. "Il quinto atto della Samia menandrea." *Helikon* 18–19: 258–75.

McCarthy, K. 2000. *Slaves, Masters, and the Art of Authority in Plautine Comedy*. Princeton.

McClure, L. 1999. *Spoken Like a Woman. Speech and Gender in Athenian Drama*. Princeton.

McGlew, J. F. 1993. *Tyranny and Political Culture in Ancient Greece*. Ithaca.

Mette, H. J. 1969. "Moschion ὁ κόσμιος." *Hermes* 97: 432–39.

Mikalson, J. 1998. *Religion in Hellenistic Athens*. Berkeley.

Miller, H. F. 1984. "The Practical and Economic Background to the Greek Mercenary Explosion. *G&R* 31: 153–59.

Mitchel, F. 1970. *Lykourgan Athens, 338–322*. Cincinnati.

Mitchell, L. G. 1997. *Greeks Bearing Gifts: The Public Use of Private Relationships in the Greek World, 435–323 B.C.* Cambridge.

Modrzejewski, J. M. 1981. "La structure juridique du mariage grec." In E. Bresciani et al., eds., *Scritti in onore di Orsolina Montevecchi*, 231–68. Bologna.

Moglen, H. 2001. *The Trauma of Gender: A Feminist Theory of the English Novel*. Berkeley.

Montanari, E. 1981. *Il mito dell' autoctonia: linee di una dinamica mitico-politica ateniese*. Rome.

Montgomery, H. 1983. *The Way to Chaeronea: Foreign Policy, Decision-Making, and Political Influence in Demosthenes' Speeches*. Bergen.

Montrose, L. A. 1989. "Professing the Renaissance: The Poetics and Politics of Culture." In H. A. Veeser, ed., *The New Historicism*, 15–36. New York.

Moretti, L., ed. 1967–75. *Inscrizioni storiche ellenistiche*. 2 vols. Florence.

Morris, I. 1996. "The Strong Principle of Equality and the Archaic Origins of Greek Democracy." In J. Ober and C. Hedrick, *Dêmokratia: A Conversation on Democracies, Ancient and Modern*, 19–48. Princeton.

———. 2000. *Archaeology as Cultural History*. Oxford.

Morrison, J. S. 1987. "Athenian Sea-Power in 323/2 BC: Dream and Reality." *JHS* 107: 88–97.

Mossé, C. 1982. "Lycurgus l'Athénien, homme du passé ou précurseur de l'avenir?" *QS* 30: 25–36.

———. 1989. "Quelques remarques sur la famille à Athènes à la fin du IVème Siècle: Le témoignage du théâtre de Ménandre." In F. J. F. Nieto, ed., *Symposion 1982: Vorträge zur griechischen und hellenistischen Rechtsgeschichte*, 129–34. Cologne.

———. 1991. "La place de la *pallaké* dans la famille athénienne." In M. Gagarin, ed., *Symposium 1990: Vorträge zur griechischen und hellenistischen Rechtsgeschichte*, 273–79. Cologne.

———. 1992a. "Démétrios de Phalère, un philosophe au pouvoi." In C. Jacob and F. de Polignac, eds., *Alexandrie IIIème siècle av. J.-C.*, 83–92. Paris.

———. 1992b. "L'*étranger* dans le theatre de menandre." In R. Lonis, ed., *L'Etranger dans le monde grec II: Actes du deuxième Colloque sur l'étranger*, 271–77. Nancy.

———. 1995. *Politique et société en Grèce ancienne: Le "modèle" athénien*. Paris.

Mouffe, C. 1992. "Feminism, Citizenship, and Radical Democratic Politics." In J. Butler and J. W. Scott, eds., *Feminists Theorize the Political*, 369–84. New York.

Murnaghan, S. 1988. "How Can a Woman Be More Like a Man: The Dialogue between Ischomachus and His Wife in Xenophon's *Oeconomicus*." *Helios* 15: 9–22.

Murray, G. 1943. "Ritual Elements in the New Comedy." *CQ* 37: 46–54.

Murray, O. 1990. "The Affair of the Mysteries: Democracy and the Drinking Group." In O. Murray, ed., *Sympotica: A Symposium on the Symposion*, 149–61. Oxford.

Nesselrath, H-G. 1990. *Die attische Mittlere Komödie: Ihre Stellung in der antiken Literaturkritik und Literaturgeschichte*. Berlin.

Newton, J. L. 1989. "History as Usual? Feminism and the 'New Historicism.'" In H. A. Veeser, ed., *The New Historicism*, 152–67. New York.

Nicastri, L. 1978. "Sul problema del V atto in Menandro." *Vichiana* 7: 168–78.

Oakley, J., and R. Sinos. 1993. *The Wedding in Ancient Athens*. Madison, Wis.

Ober, J. 1989. *Mass and Elite in Democratic Athens: Rhetoric, Ideology, and the Power of the People*. Princeton.

———. 1996. *The Athenian Revolution: Essays on Ancient Greek Democracy and Political Theory*. Princeton.

———. 1998. *Political Dissent in Democratic Athens: Intellectual Critics of Popular Rule*. Princeton.

———. 2000. "Quasi-Rights: Participatory Citizenship and Negative Liberties in Democratic Athens." *Social Philosophy and Policy* 17: 27–61.

———. 2001. "The Debate over Civic Education in Classical Athens." In Y. L. Too, ed., *Education in Greek and Roman Antiquity*, 178–207. Leiden.

Ober, J., and B. Strauss 1990. "Drama, Political Rhetoric, and the Discourse of Athenian Democracy." In J. J. Winkler and F. I. Zeitlin, eds., *Nothing to Do with Dionysos? Athenian Drama in Its Social Context*, 237–70. Princeton.

Ogden, D. 1996. *Greek Bastardy in the Classical and Hellenistic Periods*. Oxford.

———. 1997. *The Crooked Kings of Ancient Greece*. London.

Omitowoju, R. 2002. *Rape and the Politics of Consent in Classical Athens*. Cambridge.

Ormand, K. 1999. *Exchange and the Maiden: Marriage in Sophoclean Tragedy*. Austin, Tex.

Osborne, M. J. 1979. "Kallias, Phaidros, and the Revolt of Athens in 287 B.C." *ZPE* 35: 181–94.

———. 1981. "Lykourgos Again." *ZPE* 42: 172–74.

———. 1981–83. *Naturalization in Athens*. 4 vols. Brussels.

———. 1982. "Entertainment in the Prytaneion at Athens." *ZPE* 41: 153–70.

Osborne, R. 1985. *Demos: The Discovery of Classical Attika*. Cambridge.

———. 1990. "The Demos and Its Divisions in Classical Athens." In O. Murray and S. R. F. Price, eds., *The Greek City from Homer to Aristotle*, 265–93. Oxford.

———. 1997. "Law and the Representation of Women in Athens." *P&P*, no. 155: 3–33.

Ostwald, M. 1986. *From Popular Sovereignty to the Sovereignty of Law: Law, Society, and Politics in Fifth-Century Athens*. Berkeley.

———. 2000a. *Oligarchia: The Development of a Constitutional Form in Ancient Greece*. Stuttgart.

———. 2000b. "Oligarchy and Oligarchs in Ancient Greece." In P. Flensted-Jensen, T. H. Nielsen, and L. Rubinstein, eds., *Polis and Politics: Studies in Ancient Greek History*, 385–96. Copenhagen.

O'Sullivan, L. 2001. "Philochorus, Pollux, and the *Nomophulakes* of Demetrius of Phaleron." *JHS* 121: 51–62.

Paoli, U. E. 1961. "Note giurdiche sul *Dyskolos* di Menandro." *MH* 18: 53–62.

———. 1962. *Comici latini e diritto attico*. Milan.

———. 1976. *Altri studi di diritto Greco e Romano*. Milan.

Parke, H. W. 1933. *Greek Mercenary Soldiers from the Earliest Times to the Battle of Ipsos*. Oxford.

Parker, R. 1996. *Athenian Religion: A History*. Oxford.

Pateman, C. 1988. *The Sexual Contract*. Stanford.

Patterson, C. 1981. *Pericles' Citizenship Law of 451–50 B.C.* New York.

———. 1990. "Those Athenian Bastards." *CA* 9: 39–73.

———. 1991a. "Marriage and Married Women in Athenian Law." In S. Pomeroy, ed., *Women's History and Ancient History*, 48–72. Chapel Hill, N.C.

———. 1991b. "Response to Claude Mossé." In M. Gagarin, ed., *Symposium 1990: Vorträge zur griechischen und hellenistischen Rechtsgeschichte*, 281–87. Cologne.

———. 1994. "The Case against Neaira and the Public Ideology of the Athenian Family." In A. Scafuro and A. L. Boegehold, eds., *Athenian Identity and Civic Ideology*, 199–216. Baltimore.

———. 1998. *The Family in Greek History*. Cambridge.

Perotti, P. A. 1989–90. "La I orazione di Lisia fu mai pronunciata?" *Sandalion* 12–13: 43–48.

Petrey, S. 1988. *Realism and Revolution: Balzac, Stendhal, Zola, and the Performances of History*. Ithaca.

Philipp, G. B. 1973. "Philippides, ein politischer Komiker in hellenistischer Zeit." *Gymnasium* 80: 493–509.

Pickard-Cambridge, A. 1988. *The Dramatic Festivals of Athens.* 2nd ed. Rev. J. Gould and D. M. Lewis. Oxford.

Pierce, K. 1997. "The Portrayal of Rape in New Comedy." In S. Deacy and K. Pierce, eds., *Rape in Antiquity*, 163–84. London.

———. 1998. "Ideals of Masculinity in New Comedy." In L. Foxhall and J. Salmon, eds., *Thinking Men: Masculinity and Its Self-Representation in the Classical Tradition*, 130–47. London.

Pomeroy, S. 1975. *Goddesses, Whores, Wives, and Slaves: Women in Classical Antiquity*. New York.

———. 1997. *Families in Classical and Hellenistic Greece: Representations and Realities*. Oxford.

Porter, J. R. 1997. "Adultery by the Book: Lysias I (On the Murder of Eratosthenes) and Comic Diegesis." *EMC* 40: 421–53.

———. 2000. "Euripides and Menander: Epitrepontes, act. IV." In M. Cropp, K. Lee, and D. Sansone, eds., *Euripides and Tragic Theatre in the Late Fifth Century*, 157–73. Champaign, Ill.

Poster, M. 1986. "Foucault and the Tyranny of Greece." In D. C. Hoy, ed., *Foucault: A Critical Reader*, 205–20. Oxford.

Potter, D. 1987. "Telesphoros, Cousin of Demetrius: A Note on the Trial of Menander." *Historia* 36: 491–95.

Pouilloux, J. 1954–58. *Recherches sur l'histoire et les cultes de Thasos*. 2 vols. Paris.

Préaux, C. 1957. "Ménandre et la société athénienne." *CE* 32: 84–100.

———. 1960. "Les fonctions du droit dans la comedie nouvelle." *CE* 25: 222–39.

Price, S. R. F. 1984. *Rituals and Power: The Roman Imperial Cult in Asia Minor*. Cambridge.

Quincey, J. H. 1966. "The End of Menander's Sikyonian." *Phoenix* 20: 116–19.

Raaflaub, K. 1996. "Equalities and Inequalities in Athenian Democracy." In J. Ober and C. Hedrick, eds., *Dêmokratia: A Conversation on Democracies, Ancient and Modern*, 139–74. Princeton.

Rabinowitz, N. S. 1993. *Anxiety Veiled: Euripides and the Traffic in Women*. Ithaca.

Ramage, E. 1966. "City and Country in Menander's *Dyskolos*." *Philol.* 119: 194–211.

Reckford, K. J. 1987. *Aristophanes' Old-and-New Comedy*. Chapel Hill, N.C.

Reinmuth, O. W. 1971. *The Ephebic Inscriptions of the Fourth Century* B.C. Leiden.

Rhodes, P. J. 1978. "Bastards as Athenian Citizens." *CQ* 28: 89–92.

———. 1981. *A Commentary on the Aristotelian Athenaion Politeia*. Oxford.

Rhodes, P. J., and D. M. Lewis. 1997. *The Decrees of the Greek States*. Oxford.

Richardson, L., Jr. 1997. "The Moral Problems of Terence's *Andria* and Reconstruction of Menander's *Andria* and *Perinthia*." *GRBS* 38: 173–86.

Richlin, A. 1993. "Not before Homosexuality: The Materiality of the *Cinaedus* and the Roman Law against Love between Men." *Journal of the History of Sexuality* 3: 523–73.

Ridley, R. 1979. "The Hoplite as Citizen: Athenian Military Institutions in Their Social Context." *AC* 48: 508–48.

Rocco, C. 1997. *Tragedy and Enlightenment: Athenian Political Thought and the Dilemmas of Modernity*. Berkeley.

Rose, P. W. 1992. *Sons of the Gods, Children of Earth: Ideology and Literary Form in Ancient Greece*. Ithaca.

Rose, S. 1999. "Cultural Analysis and Moral Discourses: Episodes, Continuities, and Transformations." In V. Bonnell and L. Hunt, eds., *Beyond the Cultural Turn: New Directions in the Study of Society and Culture*, 217–38. Berkeley.
Rosivach, V. 1987. "Autochthony and the Athenians." *CQ* 37: 294–306.
———. 1998. *When a Young Man Falls in Love: The Sexual Exploitation of Women in New Comedy*. London.
———. 1999. "Enslaving Barbaroi and the Athenian Ideology of Slavery." *Historia* 48.2: 129–57.
———. 2000. "The Audiences of New Comedy." *G&R* 47: 169–71.
———. 2001. "Class Matters in the *Dyskolos* of Menander." *CQ* 51: 127–34.
Rowe, G. O. 1966. "The Portrait of Aeschines in the Oration *On the Crown*." *TAPA* 97: 397–406.
———. 1968. "Demosthenes First Philippic: The Satiric Mode." *TAPA* 99: 361–74.
Roy, J. 1997. "An Alternative Sexual Morality for Classical Athens." *G&R* 44: 11–22.
———. 1999. "Polis and Oikos in Classical Athens." *G&R* 46:1–18.
Rubinstein, L. 1993. *Adoption in IV. Century Athens*. Copenhagen.
Rudd, N. 1981. "Romantic Love in Classical Times?" *Ramus* 10: 140–58.
Rudhardt, J. 1962. "Le reconnaissance de la paternité: Sa nature et portée dans la société athénienne." *MH* 19: 39–64.
Sahlins, M. 1985. *Islands of History*. Chicago.
Salmenkivi, E. 1997. "Family Life in the Comedies of Menander." In J. Frössén, ed., *Early Hellenistic Athens. Symptoms of Change*. Helsinki.
Sandbach, F. H. 1970. "Menander's Manipulation of Language for Dramatic Purposes." In E. G. Turner, ed., *Ménandre: Entretiens sur l'antiquité classique*, 111–36. Geneva.
———. 1986. "Two Notes on Menander (*Epitrepontes* and *Samia*)." *LCM* 11.9: 156–60.
———, ed. 1990. *Menandri reliquiae selectae*. Rev. ed. Oxford.
Sauvé, S. 1989. "Why Involuntary Actions Are Painful." *Southern Journal of Philosophy*, suppl. 27: 127–58.
Sawada, N. 1996. "Athenian Politics in the Age of Alexander the Great: A Reconsideration of the Trial of Ctesiphon." *Chiron* 26: 57–84.
Saxonhouse, A. 1986. "Myths and the Origins of Cities: Reflections on the Autochthony Theme in Euripides' *Ion*." In P. Euben, ed., *Greek Tragedy and Political Theory*, 252–73. Berkeley.
Scafuro, A. 1994. "Witnessing and False Witnessing: Proving Citizenship and Kin Identity in Fourth Century Athens." In A. Scafuro and A. L. Boegehold, eds., *Athenian Identity and Civic Ideology*, 156–98. Baltimore.
———. 1997. *The Forensic Stage: Settling Disputes in Graeco-Roman New Comedy*. Cambridge.
Schäfer, A. 1965. *Menanders Dyskolos: Untersuchungen zur dramatischen Technik*. Meisenheim am Glan.
Schaps, D. M. 1977. "The Woman Least Mentioned: Etiquette and Women's Names." *CQ* 27: 323–31.
———. 1979. *Economic Rights of Women in Ancient Greece*. Edinburgh.
———. 1982. "The Women of Greece in Wartime." *CP* 77: 193–213.

———. 1998. "What Was Free about a Free Athenian Woman?" *TAPA* 128: 161–88.

Schlaifer, R. 1936. "Greek Theories of Slavery from Homer to Aristotle." *HSCP* 47: 165–204.

Schmitt, O. 1992. *Der Lamische Krieg*. Diss. Bonn.

Schmitz, W. 1997. "Der nomos moicheias—Das athenische Gesetz über den Ehebruch." *ZRG* 114: 45–140.

Schwartz, E. 1929. "Zu Menanders Perikeiromene." *Hermes* 64: 1–16.

Schwenk, C. J. 1985. *Athens in the Age of Alexander: The Dated Laws and Decrees of "the Lycurgan Era," 338–322 B.C.* Chicago.

Scodel, R. 1993. "Tragic Sacrifice and Menandrian Cooking." In R. Scodel, ed., *Theater and Society in the Classical World*, 161–76. Ann Arbor.

———. 1998. "The Captive's Dilemma: Sexual Acquiescence in Euripides' *Hecuba* and *Troades*." *HSCP* 98: 137–54.

Scott, J. W. 1988. *Gender and the Politics of History*. New York.

Sealey, R. 1984. "On Lawful Concubinage in Athens." *CA* 3: 111–33.

———. 1993. *Demosthenes and His Time*. Oxford.

Sedgwick, E. K. 1985. *Between Men: English Literature and Male Homosocial Desire*. New York.

———. 1993. "Queer Performativity: Henry James's *The Art of the Novel*." *GLQ* 1: 1–16.

Sekunda, N. V. 1992. "Athenian Demography and Military Strength, 338–322." *ABSA* 87: 311–55.

Shapiro, H. A. 1998. "Autochthony and the Visual Arts in Fifth-Century Athens." In D. Boedeker and K. Raaflaub, eds., *Democracy, Empire, and the Arts in Fifth-Century Athens*, 127–51. Cambridge.

Shear, T. L., Jr. 1978. *Kallias of Sphettos and the Revolt of Athens in 286 B.C.* Hesperia Supplement 17. Princeton.

Shipley, G. 2000. *The Greek World after Alexander*. London.

Shrimpton, G. 1991. *Theopompus the Historian*. Montreal.

Simpson, R. H. 1959. "Antigonus the One-Eyed and the Greeks." *Historia* 8: 385–409.

Sissa, G. 1999. "Sexual Bodybuilding: Aeschines against Timarchus." In J. Porter, ed., *Constructions of the Classical Body*, 147–68. Ann Arbor.

Sisti, F., ed and trans. 1974. *Samia*, by Menander. Rome.

———, ed. and trans. 1986. *Misumenos*, by Menander. Genoa.

———. 1987. "Menandro." In *Dizionario degli Scrittori Greci e Latini*, 2: 1335–57. Milan.

Smith, A. D. 1991. *National Identity*. Reno, Nev.

Smith, P. 1988. *Discerning the Subject*. Minneapolis.

Smith, R. R. R. 1991. *Hellenistic Sculpture: A Handbook*. London.

Sokolowski, F. 1955. *Lois sacrées de l'Asie Mineure*. Paris.

Sommerstein, A. 1998. "Rape and Young Manhood in Athenian Comedy." In L. Foxhall and J. Salmon, eds., *Thinking Men: Masculinity and Its Self-Representation in the Classical Tradition*, 100–114. London.

Squires, J. 1999. *Gender in Political Theory*. Cambridge.

Stears, K. 1995. "Dead Women's Society: Constructing Female Gender in Classical Athenian Funerary Sculpture." In N. Spencer, ed., *Time, Tradition, and Society in Greek Archaeology: Bridging the "Great Divide,"* 109–31. London.

Steidle, W. 1973. "Menander bei Terenz." *RH* 116: 303–47.

Stevens, J. 1999. *Reproducing the State*. Princeton.

Stewart, A. 1993. *Faces of Power: Alexander's Image in Hellenistic Politics*. Berkeley.

Stockert, W. 1997. "Metatheatrikalisches in Menander's 'Epitrepontes.'" *WS* 110: 5–8.

Stoessl, F. 1973. "Unkenntnis und Mißverstehen als Prinzip und Quelle der Komik in Menanders Samia." *RhM* 116: 21–45.

Strauss, B. 1994. *Fathers and Sons in Athens: Ideology and Society in the Era of the Peloponnesian War*. Princeton.

———. 1996. "The Athenian Trireme, School of Democracy." In J. Ober and C. Hedrick, eds., *Demokratia: A Conversation on Democracies, Ancient and Modern*, 313–26. Princeton.

Tarn, W. W. 1952. *Hellenistic Civilization*. London.

Thompson, W. E. 1967. "The Marriage of First Cousins in Athenian Society." *Phoenix* 21: 273–82.

———. 1981. "Athenian Attitudes toward Wills." *Prudentia* 13.1: 13–23.

Thorton, B. S. 1991. "Constructionism and Ancient Greek Sex." *Helios* 18.2: 181–93.

———. 1997. *Eros: The Myth of Ancient Greek Sexuality*. Boulder, Colo.

Tierney, M. 1936. "Aristotle and Menander." *Proceedings of the Royal Irish Academy* 43: 241–54.

Todd, S. 1990. "Lady Chatterley's Lover and the Attic Orators: The Social Composition of the Athenian Jury." *JHS* 110: 146–73.

———. 1993. *The Shape of Athenian Law*. Oxford.

———, trans. 2000. *Lysias*. Austin, Tex.

Todorov, T. 1990. *Genres in Discourse*. Trans. C. Porter. Cambridge.

Tracy, S. V. 1995. *Athenian Democracy in Transition: Attic Letter Cutters of 340–290 B.C.* Berkeley.

———. 2000. "Demetrius of Phaleron: Who Was He and Who Was He Not?" In W. W. Fortenbaugh and E. Schütrumpf, eds., *Demetrius of Phaleron: Text, Translation, and Discussion*, 331–45. New Brunswick, N.J.

Traill, A. 2001. "*Perikeiomene* 486–510: The Legality of Polemon's Self-Help Remedy." *Mouseion* 1: 279–94.

Trenkner, S. 1958. *The Greek Novella in the Classical Period*. Cambridge.

Treu, K. 1981. "Menanders Menschen als Polisbürger." *Philol.* 125: 211–14.

Trundle, M. 1999. "Identity and Community among Greek Mercenaries." *AHB* 13.1: 28–38.

Turner, E. G. 1977. *The Lost Beginning of Menander, Misoumenos*. Proceedings of the British Academy 63. London.

———. 1984. "Menander and the New Society." *Proceedings of the Seventh Congress of the International Federation of the Societies of Classical Studies*, 1: 243–59. Budapest. Originally published in *CE* 54 (1979): 106–26.

Tzifopoulos, Y. Z. 1995. "Proverbs in Menander's *Dyskolos*: The Rhetoric of Popular Wisdom." *Mnem.* 18: 169–77.

van Bremen, R. 1996. *The Limits of Participation: Women and Civic Life in the Greek East in the Hellenistic and Roman Periods.* Amsterdam.

van Leeuwen, J. 1919. *Menandri fabularum reliquiae in exemplarium vetustorum foliis laceris servatae.* Leiden.

Vatin, C. 1970. *Recherches sur le mariage et la condition de la femme mariée à l'époque hellénistique.* Paris.

Vérilhac, A.-M., and C. Vial. 1998. *Le mariage grec du vi^e siècle av. J.-C. à l'époque d'Auguste.* Paris.

Vernant, J. P. 1980. *Myth and Society in Ancient Greece.* Trans. J. Lloyd. Sussex.

Vidal-Naquet, P. 1986. *The Black Hunter.* Baltimore.

Vogt-Spira, G. 1992. *Dramaturgie des Zufalls.* Munich.

von Arnim, H., ed. 1964. *Stoicorum veterum fragmenta.* Stuttgart.

von Reden, S. 1995. *Exchange in Ancient Greece.* London.

———. 1998. "The Commodification of Symbols: Reciprocity and Its Perversions in Menander." In C. Gill, N. Postlethwaite, and R. Seaford, eds., *Reciprocity in Ancient Greece*, 255–78. Oxford.

Walcot, P. 1987. "Romantic Love and True Love: Greek Attitudes to Marriage." *AncSoc* 18: 5–33.

Wallace, R.W. 1989. *The Areopagos Council, to 307 B.C.* Baltimore.

———. 1995. "On Not Legislating Sexual Conduct in Fourth-Century Athens." In G. Thür, ed., *Symposion 1995: Vorträge zur griechischen und hellenistischen Rechtsgeschichte*, 57–95. Cologne.

———. 1996. "Law, Freedom, and the Concept of Citizen's Rights in Democratic Athens." In J. Ober and C. Hedrick, eds., *Demokratia: A Conversation on Democracies, Ancient and Modern*, 105–20. Princeton.

Walsh, G. B. 1978. "The Rhetoric of Birthright and Race in Euripides' *Ion*." *Hermes* 106: 301–15.

Walters, K. R. 1983. "Perikles' Citizenship Law." *CA* 2: 314–36.

Walzer, M. 1983. *Spheres of Justice.* New York.

Wartenberg, G. 1973. "Der Soldat in der griechisch-hellenistischen Komödie und in den römischen Komikerfragmenten." In W. Hofmann and G. Wartenberg, *Der Bramarbas in der antiken Komödie*, 9–84. Berlin.

Webster, T. B. L. 1960. *Studies in Menander.* Manchester.

———. 1970. *Studies in Later Greek Comedy.* 2nd ed. Manchester.

———. 1973. "Woman Hates Soldier: A Structural Approach to New Comedy." *GRBS* 14: 287–97.

———. 1974. *An Introduction to Menander.* Oxford.

Wehrli, F. 1936. *Motivstudien zur griechisben Komödie.* Zurich.

———, ed. 1968. *Die Schule des Aristoteles.* Vol. 4, *Demetrios von Phaleron.* Basel.

Weissenberger, M. 1991. "Vater-Sohn-Beziehhung und Komödienhandlung in Menanders 'Samia.'" *Hermes* 119: 415–34.

Welles, C. B. 1934. *Royal Correspondence in the Hellenistic Period.* London.

West, S. 1991. "Notes on the Samia." *ZPE* 88: 11–23.

Whibley, L. 1896. *Greek Oligarchies: Their Character and Organization.* London.

White, S. 1992. *Sovereign Virtue: Aristotle on the Relation between Happiness and Prosperity*. Stanford.

Whitehead, D. 1977. *The Ideology of the Athenian Metic*. Proceedings of the Cambridge Philosophical Society, supplementary vol. 4. Cambridge.

———. 1983. "Competitive Outlay and Community Profit: *Philotimia* in Democratic Athens." *C&M* 34: 55–74.

———. 1986. *The Demes of Attica, 508/7–ca. 250 B.C.* Princeton.

———. 1991. "Norms of Citizenship in Ancient Greece." In A. Molho, K. Raaflaub, and J. Emlen, eds., *City-States in Classical Antiquity and Medieval Italy: Athens and Rome, Florence and Venice*, 135–54. Stuttgart.

———. 1993. "Cardinal Virtues: The Language of Public Approbation in Democratic Athens." *C&M* 44: 37–95.

———, ed. and trans. 2001. *Hypereides: The Forensic Speeches*. Oxford.

Wiles, D. 1984. "Menander's *Dyskolos* and Demetrius of Phaleron's Dilemma: A Study of the Play in Its Historical Context—The Trial of Phokion, the Ideals of a Moderate Oligarch, and the Rancor of the Disfranchised." *G&R* 31: 170–80.

———. 1991. *The Masks of Menander: Sign and Meaning in Greek and Roman Performance*. Cambridge.

———. 2001 [1989]. "Marriage and Prostitution in Classical New Comedy." In E. Segal, ed., *Oxford Readings in Menander, Plautus, and Terence*, 42–52. Oxford.

Wilkins, J. 2000. *The Boastful Chef: The Discourse of Food in Ancient Greek Comedy*. Oxford.

Will, W. 1983. *Athen und Alexander: Undersuchungen zur Geschichte der Stadt von 338 bis 322 v. Chr*. Munich.

Williams, B. 1993. *Shame and Necessity*. Berkeley.

Williams, J. 1987. "The Peripatetic School and Demetrius of Phalerum's Reforms in Athens." *AncW* 15: 87–98.

———. 1997. "Ideology and the Constitution of Demetrius of Phalerum." In C. D. Hamilton and P. Krentz, eds., *Polis and Polemos: Essays on Politics, War, and History in Honor of Donald Kagan*, 327–46. Claremont, Calif.

Wilson, P. J. 1996. "Tragic Rhetoric: The Use of Tragedy and the Tragic in the Fourth Century." In M. S. Silk, ed. *Tragedy and the Tragic: Greek Theater and Beyond*, 310–31. Oxford.

———. 1997. "Leading the Tragic *Khoros*: Tragic Prestige in the Democratic City." In C. Pelling, ed., *Greek Tragedy and the Historian*, 81–108. Oxford.

———. 2000. *The Athenian Institution of the Khoregia: The Chorus, the City, and the Stage*. Cambridge.

Winkler, J. J. 1990a. *The Constraints of Desire: The Anthropology of Sex and Gender in Ancient Greece*. New York.

———. 1990b. "The Ephebe's Song: Tragoidia and Polis." In J. J. Winkler and F. I. Zeitlin, eds., *Nothing to Do With Dionysos? Athenian Drama in Its Social Context*, 20–62. Princeton.

Wohl, V. 1998. *Intimate Commerce: Exchange, Gender, and Subjectivity in Greek Tragedy*. Austin, Tex..

———. 1999. "The Eros of Alcibiades." *CA* 18: 349–85.

Wolff, H. J. 1944. "Marriage Law and Family Organization in Ancient Athens: A Study of the Interrelation of Public and Private Law in the Greek City." *Traditio* 2: 43–95.

Wolin, S. 1996. "Transgression, Equality, and Voice." In J. Ober and C. Hedrick, eds., *Dêmokratia: A Conversation on Democracies, Ancient and Modern*, 63–90. Princeton.

Wolpert, A. 2001. "Lysias 1 and the Politics of the Oikos." *CJ* 96: 415–24.

Wood, E. M., and N. Wood. 1978. *Class Ideology and Ancient Political Theory. Socrates, Plato, & Aristotle in Social Context*. Oxford.

Worthington, I., C. R. Cooper, and E. M. Harris, trans. 2001. *Dinarchus, Hyperides, and Lycurgus*. Austin, Tex.

Wyse, W. 1904. *The Speeches of Isaeus*. Cambridge.

Yunis, H. 2000. "Politics as Literature: Demosthenes and the Burden of the Athenian Past." *Arion* 8: 97–118.

Zagagi, N. 1979. "Sostratos as a Comic, Over-active, and Impatient Lover." *ZPE* 36: 39–49.

———. 1994. *The Comedy of Menander: Convention, Variation, and Originality*. London.

Zeitlin, F. I. 1996. *Playing the Other: Gender and Society in Classical Greek Literature*. Chicago.

———. 1999. "Aristophanes and the Performance of Utopia in the *Ecclesiazousae*." In P. E. Easterling and S. Goldhill, eds., *Performance Culture and Athenian Democracy*, 167–97. Cambridge.

Zizek, S. 1994. "The Spectre of Ideology." In S. Zizek, ed., *Mapping Ideology*, 1–33. London.

Zucker, F. 1950. "Freundschaftsbewährung in der Neuen Attischen Komödie: ein Kapitel Hellenistischer Ethik und Humanität." In *Berichte über die Verhandlungen der sächsischen Akademie der Wissenschaften*, 98:3–38. Berlin.

Zweig, B. 1992. "The Mute Nude Female Characters in Aristophanes' Plays." In A. Richlin, ed., *Pornography and Representation in Greece and Rome*, 73–89. Oxford.

Acknowledgments

I would like to thank the teachers and colleagues who have helped me in writing this book. My dissertation advisors, Richard Martin and Josh Ober, were inestimable; Richard Hunter also generously read and commented on the dissertation. My colleagues at the University of Washington provided congeniality and an intellectual community. I owe a debt of gratitude to Stephen Hinds for his guidance. At the University of Texas, I had the opportunity to discuss many of the legal and philosophical issues addressed in this project with Michael Gagarin and Steven White. Anonymous readers for Cambridge University Press and Princeton University Press offered many helpful criticisms. Jeanie Grant Moore and Josh Ober kindly read and commented on the completed manuscript. I am most grateful to F. Devett for his support and generosity.

An earlier version of chapter 3 was delivered at the Simpson Center for the Humanities at the University of Washington in the spring of 2000. Chapter 6 was delivered at the American Philological Association's annual meeting in 1999. Earlier versions of chapter 7 were delivered in the classics departments at the University of Southern California (2000), the University of Texas (2000), and the University of Wisconsin (2002), and in the Theater Department at the University of Wisconsin (2001). I am grateful to the audiences at each of these events for their thoughtful comments.

At the dissertation stage, this project was funded by a Whiting Dissertation Fellowship and a fellowship from the Center for Human Values. I received a teaching release in the spring quarter of 2000, while a member of the Society of Scholars in the Walter Chapin Simpson Center for the Humanities at the University of Washington. In 2001/02, I held a Solmsen Fellowship from the Institute for Research in the Humanities, University of Wisconsin, as well as an American Council of Learned Societies Fellowship.

Earlier versions of chapters 3 and 4 appeared in the *European Studies Journal* vols. xvii and xviii (Fall 2000/Spring 2001), and *Helios* 28 (2002). Portions of chapter 1 appeared in *Classical Antiquity*, 20 (2001). I would like to thank the University of Iowa Press, Texas Tech University Press, and the University of California Press for permission to reprint these materials here.

The mosaic on the cover illustrates a scene from Menander's *Samia* in which the *hetaira* Chrysis is protecting a citizen's baby. I would like to thank *Antike Kunst* for permission to reprint this photo from S. Charitonidis et al., *Les mosaïques de la Maison du Ménandre à Mytilène*, *Antike Kunst* Beiheft 6 (1970) color plate 4,1 (phot. E. Serafis).

Index Locorum

General Index